Why Do You Need This New Edition?

If you're wondering why you should buy this new edition of *What Matters in America*, here are four good reasons!

1. Two new chapters present multiple perspectives on the **economy** and what it really means to go **"green."**

2. Almost half of the book's selections are new, including timely new perspectives on the **erosion of personal privacy**; new issues facing **immigration; the social impact of the Internet**; the **changing face of the workforce**; the i**nfluence of advertising**, and much more—most written since the last edition.

3. This new edition features a **cross-section of blogs** demonstrating the breadth and depth of information available and how people are sharing information and viewpoints online. Students are encouraged to post their own response to the blog discussion.

4. The Introduction now includes discussion of **critical reading of visuals**—explaining how visuals work to balance our discussion on critical reading and writing. Included here are detailed analyses of a current print ad and a recent editorial cartoon.

PEARSON

What Matters in America

Reading and Writing About Contemporary Culture

Third Edition

Gary Goshgarian
Northeastern University

with

Kathryn Goodfellow
Northeastern University

PEARSON

Boston Columbus Indianapolis New York San Francisco Upper Saddle River
Amsterdam Cape Town Dubai London Madrid Milan Munich Paris Montreal Toronto
Delhi Mexico City São Paulo Sydney Hong Kong Seoul Singapore Taipei Tokyo

Executive Editor: Suzanne Phelps Chambers
Development Editor: Anne Leung
Senior Marketing Manager: Sandra McGuire
Production Manager: S.S. Kulig
Project Coordination, Text Design, and
  Electronic Page Makeup: PreMediaGlobal
Cover Designer/Manager: Wendy Ann
  Fredericks
Cover Art: © Jim West/PhotoEdit
Senior Manufacturing Buyer: Roy Pickering
Printer/Binder: R.R. Donnelley and Sons
Cover Printer: R.R. Donnelley and Sons

Credits and acknowledgments borrowed from other sources and reproduced, with permission,
in this textbook appear on the appropriate page within text [or on pages 397-401].

Library of Congress Cataloging-in-Publication Data
Goshgarian, Gary.
What matters in America / Gary Goshgarian. -- 3rd ed.
   p. cm.
   ISBN 978-0-205-23074-7
   1. Readers—Popular culture. 2. English language—Rhetoric—Problems,
exercises, etc. 3. Report writing—Problems, exercises, etc. 4. Critical thinking—
Problems, exercises, etc. 5. Popular culture—Problems, exercises, etc. I. Title.
   PE1127.P6G67 2011
   808'.0427—dc23

                                                              2011038773

10 9 8 7 6 5 —V056— 14 13

www.pearsonhighered.com

ISBN 10: 0-205-23074-1
ISBN 13: 978-0-205-23074-7

Contents

4 Do the Media Promote a Culture of Fear and Violence? 148

Extreme Reality: How Media Coverage Exaggerates Risks and Dangers 150
John Stossel

"If you watch television news regularly, you can't help but think that the world is a very scary place."

The Female Fear Factor 154
Myrna Blyth

"When it comes to selling fear, television and women's magazines live by one rule—there's no such thing as overkill, no pun intended."

Blog Matters: Growing Up in a Culture of Fear: From Columbine to Banning of MySpace 162
danah boyd

Violent Media Numbs Viewers to Pain of Others 165
Diane Swanbrow

Over 300 college students played either a violent video game or a nonviolent one for 20 mintues, and then overheard a staged fight in which the victim sustained an injury and groaned in pain. The result? Students who had played the violent game took almost *four* times longer to offer any help to the victim.

Hate Violence? Turn It Off! 167
Tim Goodman

"Just because you've given little Jimmy his own TV set upstairs and now you can't stop him from watching *Jackass* on MTV or *Oz* on HBO, don't cry foul and ruin it for the rest of us."

VISUAL CONNECTIONS 172

It's a Scary World 172

In Search of Notorious Ph.D.s 173
Lindsay Johns

Black musicians who indulge in representations of hypermasculinity are simply conceding much-sought-after gains in racial equality. Icons such as 50 Cent and Snoop Dogg persist in trading racial dignity for a quick buck, and are conforming to the oldest racial stereotype of all: that black is wholly physical, and white is cerebral.

Violent Media Is Good for Kids   181

Renowned comic-book author Gerard Jones argues that bloody video games, gun-glorifying gangsta rap, and other forms of "creative violence" help far more children than they hurt, by giving kids a tool to master their rage. Is he insightful, or insane?

5 What Does Freedom of Speech Really Mean?   188

Free Inquiry? Not on Campus   190

"[The champions of censorship] are thickest on the ground in our colleges and universities. Since the late 1980s, what should be the most open, debate-driven, and tolerant sector of society has been in thrall to the diversity and political correctness that now form the aggressive secular religion of America's elites."

Hate Cannot Be Tolerated   198

"Hate speech is rarely an invitation to a conversation. More like a slap in the face, it reviles and silences."

Academic Bill of Rights   201

The author presents eight principles that call for an academic environment where decisions are made irrespective of one's personal political or religious beliefs. But are these principles unbiased?

Blog Matters: Sixth Circuit Orders Federal District Court to Rule on Student Blogger's Free Speech and Due Process Claims   210

6   What's the Big Deal About Immigration?   224

"The handle on your recliner does not qualify as an exercise machine."

10 What Does It Mean to Be "Green"? 366

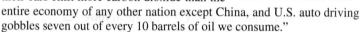

Rhetorical Contents

Persuasion and Argument: Appealing to Reason and Emotion

Illustration: Explaining with Examples and Statistics

Preface

Like its predecessor, *What Matters in America,* third edition, is designed to stimulate critical thinking skills in introductory writing students through a variety of contemporary subjects connected to popular culture, media, and society. Toward that end, this book provides a collection of well-written, thought-provoking, thematically organized readings that students can relate to—readings that stimulate classroom discussion, critical thinking, and writing.

Likewise, the book's study apparatus aims at eliciting thoughtful response, while providing students with the tools they need to approach each reading as informed, critical thinkers.

Preceding each reading is an author headnote and a short paragraph, *Connecting to the Topic*, that orients students to the subject matter. *Words in Context* provides students with the vocabulary support they may need to understand the material.

Directly following each reading are four areas of inquiry designed to help students think about the reading and the issue within a broader framework. *Considering the Issues* questions encourage students to think about issues raised by the reading in a thematic context. *Craft and Content* questions ask students to consider rhetorical issues connected to the reading itself. *Critical Thinking* and *Writing About the Issues* questions promote analytical approaches to the reading and support thoughtful writing projects.

Visuals are interspersed throughout the text, and many include *Visual Connections* exercises designed to help students think about the ways images, photographs, and cartoons present ideas graphically. Also, each chapter in *What Matters in America* contains an editorial cartoon on the title page, followed by critical thinking questions designed to elicit thoughtful consideration of each image. Instructions on how to view editorial cartoons is included in the book's introductory material as explained below.

Each chapter closes with a *Topical Considerations* section that encourages students to make broad thematic associations related to the chapter's overarching subject matter. The tools in this section include group projects, research topics, and web exercises.

New To This Edition

- **Expanded Introduction with new section, "Critically Reading a Visual World."** In response to reviewers' requests, the Introduction now includes a comprehensive discussion of how visuals work to balance our discussion on critical reading and writing. As critical readers of written arguments, we do not accept what's said simply at face value. We consider the author's intent, audience, style, tone, and supporting evidence. Likewise, to understanding the persuasive power of "visual language," we need to take a close look at the premise, claims, details, supporting evidence, and stylistic touches embedded in any visual piece. As with written arguments, we should ask ourselves: Who is the target *audience*? What are the *claims* made in the images? What shared history or cultural *assumptions*—or warrants—does the visual make? What is the supporting *evidence*? In this discussion, we analyze in some detail a current print ad and a recent editorial cartoon to illustrate how we can gain an edge in approaching the visual world. In the chapters that follow, students will find a variety of visual presentations and questions that ask them to consider the ways visuals employ shape, texture, depth, layout, and point of view to sway our opinion or tell us a story. Also, students will see how symbolism, brand recognition, stereotyping, and cultural expectations contribute to the ways illustrations communicate their ideas and influence our reactions.

- **Timely new topics.** Based on reviewer feedback, we kept the best readings from the previous edition and replaced others. Almost half of the selections here are new, most written since the last edition was published. This revision also features two new chapters: "Will Our Economy Ever Bounce Back?" and "What Does It Mean to Be 'Green?'" The new chapters on the hoped-for economic recovery contains essays that will help students think about broader financial issues as well as what they'll face in the job market. Given today's economy, today's graduates will be facing a different consumer atmosphere from what their parents and grandparents faced. And one key reason is that today's generation is different from previous generations by being less driven to spend than to save. As noted in some of the essays here, today's graduates are thinking *thrift*. And thrift is green. Thrift is about the future. Thrift is good. The second new contains essays that ask what individual citizens do or can do to help the natural and human environment. Authors examine people's eating habits, recycling efforts, and life styles that are authentically "green," including some urban dwellers who have given up driving cars.

- **Updated topics.** Each of the other eight chapters has been updated to reflect current events, such as the eroding of personal privacy (Chapter 2), the influence on us by recent ads (Chapter 3), and the latest issues on immigration (Chapter 6).

- **Expanded visuals.** We have also expanded the visuals for each chapter, including new graphics in "Visual Connections" as well as more charts and graphs.

- **Expanded and updated Blog Matters.** The "Blog Matters" of each chapter have all been updated. As students well know, blogs are becoming increasingly influential for sharing ideas, conveying information, and spreading opinions. Millions of blogs fill the Internet, and hundreds are added each day. In fact, most reputable journals, such as *Scientific American*, *The New Republic*, and *Slate Magazine* feature regular blogs run by journalists and topic experts. Blogs can link to other blogs, news articles, essays of interest, and government sites providing data. They can also simply serve as online diaries. This third edition of *What Matters in America* features a cross-section of blogs, demonstrating the breadth and depth of information available and how people are sharing such information and viewpoints online.

Chapter Topics

Most of the book's material comes from essays and articles written within the last five years, and over half were written in the last two years. With over 60 short essays and visuals, from over 35 periodicals, journals, newspapers, and recently released books, the text's readings are organized into 10 thematic areas, framed as questions.

1. Is the Internet Changing Our Social Lives?
2. Does Personal Privacy Have Limits?
3. How Does Advertising Influence Us?
4. Do the Media Promote a Culture of Fear and Violence?
5. What Does Freedom of Speech Really Mean?
6. What's the Big Deal About Immigration?
7. Why Do We Work?
8. Is Fast Food Responsible for a Crisis in Public Health?
9. Will Our Economy Ever Bounce Back?
10. What Does It Mean to Be "Green?"

These themes were chosen to reflect a wide spectrum of issues that affect all of us. Most importantly, they capture some of the conflicts and paradoxes that make our culture unique. For ours is a culture caught in conflicts; from fashion and advertising, to television and privacy, we are a people that crave the modern, yet long for the past. We are as much a society steeped in traditional values and identities as we a culture that redefines itself in response to trends and new ideas.

Variety of Readings

Expository communication comes in all shapes and models. This book includes newspaper stories, editorials, political cartoons, advertisements, academic essays, magazine articles, television interviews, Internet articles from "e-zines," student essays, humor columns, and a lot more. Students will read personal narratives, objective essays, position papers, political arguments, and research reports. Readings come from a wide variety of sources expressing many different points of view including *Mother Jones*, the *Nation, Science and Spirit*, the *Wall Street Journal*, the *New York Times*, the *National Review*, the *Boston Globe*, the *Atlantic, City Journal, New Black Magazine, Newsweek*, and *TIME*. We have also included readings from student newspapers and campus magazines, as well as online articles from *Slate* and *Salon*. And of course, blog entries provide a diversity of voice as well as opinion.

Instructor's Manual

The *Instructor's Manual* includes suggested responses to the Rhetorical Considerations and Critical Thinking questions in the text as well as ideas for directing class discussion and eliciting student response.

Acknowledgments

Many people behind the scenes deserve gratitude for bringing this third edition of *What Matters in America* to publication. It would be impossible to thank all of them, but I am particularly grateful to those instructors who provided their input and advice by answering lengthy questionnaires on the effectiveness of the essays in the prototype chapters of the text. Their helpful comments and suggestions have been incorporated into this finished volume.

Annamaria Deidesheimer, Morrisville State College
Sara Kaplan, Del Mar College
Tina Ramsey, Yuba College
William Clay Kinchen Smith, Santa Fe College
Judith L. Snyder, Northern Virginia Community College

Special thanks goes to Kathryn Goodfellow for her assistance in developing the content, locating articles, and writing the study apparatus. This book would not have been possible without her thoughtful contributions, enthusiasm, and unwavering work ethic. I also thank Amy Trumbull for her help in securing permissions for the readings featured in this volume and Kristine Perlmutter for her valuable assistance formulating some of the study questions for this edition. I also extend my to those students who allowed us to reprint their essays in this text.

Finally, my thanks to the people of Longman Publishers, especially executive editor Suzanne Phelps-Chambers and her assistant Laney Whitt, and developmental editor Anne Leung, who helped conceptualize this new edition.

Introduction
Critical Thinking, Reading, and Writing

What Is Critical Thinking?

Whenever you question the message or implications of what you see and read, you are exercising critical thinking. You look beneath the surface of words and images and debate their meaning and significance. You ask for definitions, weigh claims, evaluate information, look for proof, question assumptions, and make judgments.

Critical Thinking and Reading Critically

When you read critically, you think critically. Instead of passively accepting what's written, you actively decide for yourself what is or is not important or logical or correct. And you do so because you bring to your reading your own perspective, experience, education, and personal values, as well as your powers of comprehension and analysis. Such skills apply to every facet of your life.

Critical Reading Is a Process of Discovery

Critical reading initiates a dialogue between you and an author. You discover an author's view on a subject; you discover the strengths and weaknesses of the author's thesis or argument, and you decide if you agree or disagree with the author's views. At the same time, critical reading encourages you to question accepted norms, views, and beliefs. You will find yourself asking tough questions about your own experiences and views—and by so doing, you develop the skills you need to be an active participant in today's global society.

Critical Reading Is the Key to Good Writing

Critical reading also helps you become a better writer, because critical reading is the first step to good writing. Good readers look at another

1

author's writing the way an architect looks at a house: They study the fine details and how those details connect and create the whole. Likewise, good readers consider the particular slants and strategies of appeal. Good writers always have a clear sense of their audience—their readers' racial makeup, gender, and educational background; their political and/or religious persuasions; their values, prejudices, and assumptions about life; and so forth.

Critical reading helps you evaluate your own writing. The more you analyze and react to another's written work, the better you will analyze and react to your own. You will learn to ask yourself: Is my argument logical? Do my points come across clearly? Are my examples solid enough? Is this the best wording? Is my conclusion persuasive? Do I have a clear sense of my audience? What appeal strategy did I take—to logic, emotions, or ethics?

How to Read Critically

To help you read critically, use these six basic steps:

- Keep a journal about what you read.
- Annotate what you read.
- Outline what you read.
- Summarize what you read.
- Question what you read.
- Analyze what you read.

Keep a Journal About What You Read

Unlike writing an essay or a paper, keeping a journal is a personal exploration in which you develop your own ideas without set rules. It is an opportunity to write without restrictions and without judgment.

What do you include in your journal? Although it may serve as a means to understand an essay you're assigned, you are not required to write only about the essay itself. Perhaps the piece reminds you of something in your personal experience. Maybe it triggers an opinion you didn't know you had. Or perhaps you wish to explore a particular phrase or idea presented by the author. Date your entries and include the titles of the articles to which you are responding. Eventually, you should have a substantial number of pages to review so you can see how your ideas and writing style are developing over time.

Annotate What You Read

It's a good idea to underline (or highlight) key passages and to make marginal notes when reading an essay. In annotating a piece of writing, you are engaging in a dialogue with the author. As in any meaningful dialogue, you may hear things you may not have known, things that may be interesting and exciting to you, things that you may agree or disagree with, or things that give you cause to ponder. The other side of the dialogue, of course, is your response. In annotating a piece of writing, that response takes the form of underlining (or highlighting) key passages and jotting down comments in the margin. Such comments can take the form of brief sentences like the following:

- That's not true.
- You're contradicting yourself.
- I see your point, but I don't agree.
- That's not a good choice of words.
- You're jumping to conclusions.
- Good point. I never thought of that.
- That was nicely stated.
- This is an extreme view.

Annotating can also help you become a stronger reader. Underline or circle unfamiliar words and references, and look them up. Highlight or underline the main thesis statement or claim and jot down "Claim" or "Thesis" in the margin.

Here is an excerpt from "Hate Violence? Turn It Off!" by Tim Goodman. (You can read the entire essay beginning on page 167.)

1   Perhaps it's a sign of progress that Americans are becoming just as concerned about violence on television as they are about sex. For years, a barely concealed nipple or a tame bed scene was deemed worse than hundreds of people being brutally shot down on cop shows and the like.   Sarcastic tone

2   Now you can't pick up the paper without some watchdog group denouncing Hollywood for ruining their   What watchdog group? children's lives with a plethora of violent images nightly. Some kid goes postal at his high school and "Starsky and   Look up reference Hutch" is the root cause.

3   We're getting our priorities right and wrong simultaneously. If sexuality is now not the enemy, great. But to continue to demonize Hollywood for its portrayals of violence   Main point is to put our heads in the sand about the world we live in.

4   Worse, it's just plain wrong, reeks of censorship and, in the context of parents worried about their children, it's looking for a scapegoat when lax parenting skills are   Look up "scapegoat" more to blame.

5   For example, parents have put pressure on their elected officials to "do something" about violence, and the result has been a ratings system that surveys suggest most } *Check out rating system* parents never use. And then there's the vaunted "V-chip," } *Research how V-chip works* which effectively shifted parental responsibility to the government and doesn't consider the simplest way for everyone to solve this problem: <u>Vote with your remote.</u> } *Catchy slogan*

6   <u>Some of us like violence. Some of us like shows that have a gritty realism to them, rather than the glossy pap offered up by most networks.</u> } *What kind or degree of violence is he thinking about?* And think of all the people without children who, as grown-ups, choose to watch programming clearly geared to adults. Just because you've given little Jimmy his own TV set upstairs and now you } *Should parents bear sole responsibility?* can't stop him from watching "Jackass" on MTV or "Oz" on HBO, don't cry foul and ruin it for the rest of us.

7   This is an old and now increasingly tired defense of art, anti-censorship and the need for parents to take more responsibility for what their children are watching. Don't like it? Don't watch it. There are enough elements in place now—blocking devices, ratings, V-chips, etc.—that to whine about how Hollywood should tone it down (as you allow the blood-and-guts nightly news to waft over dinner) completely misses the point about whose kid it is.

8   Then again, many adults also dislike violence. Fine. <u>Vote with the remote.</u> Go to PBS, the History } *Slogan again* Channel, Disney—whatever—just stop <u>writing letters to politicians who have already had a chilling effect</u> } *Give example* <u>(thus a watering- and dumbing-down of content) on what we already see.</u>

9   Most recently, there has been a backlash against "The Sopranos," with many people thinking there's been an amping up of the violence and at least two very disturbing episodes filled with violence toward women.

Outline What You Read

Briefly outlining an essay is a good way to see how writers structure their ideas. When you diagram the thesis statement, claims, and the supporting evidence, you can better assess the quality of the writing and decide how convincing it is. You may already be familiar with detailed, formal essay outlines where structure is broken down into main ideas and subsections. However, for our purposes here, I suggest simply jotting down a one-sentence summary of each paragraph to create a concise outline of an essay's components.

Summarize What You Read

Summarizing is perhaps the most important technique to develop for understanding and evaluating what you read. For a summary, write a brief (about 100 words) synopsis of the reading in your own words. Note the claim or thesis of the discussion (or argument) and the chief supporting points. It is important to write these points down, rather than highlight them with a pen or pencil, because the act of jotting down a summary helps you absorb the argument. At times, it may be impossible to avoid using the author's own words in a summary. But if you do, remember to use quotation marks.

Question What You Read

The separate steps of critical reading naturally overlap as you read. While reading an essay, you will simultaneously summarize and evaluate the writer's points in your head, perhaps adding your own ideas and arguments. If something strikes you as particularly interesting or insightful, make a mental note. Likewise, if something rubs you the wrong way, argue back. For beginning writers, a good strategy is to convert that automatic mental response into actual note taking.

In your journal or in the margins of the text, question and challenge the writer. Questions to ask include:

- What did you mean by that?
- Can you back up that statement?
- How do you define that term?
- How did you draw that conclusion?
- Do all the experts agree?
- Is this evidence dated?
- So what? Why does it matter?
- What is your point?
- Why do we need to know this?

Even if you do not feel personally qualified to pass judgment on an author's views, get into the habit of thinking of other views on the issue. If you've read or heard of experiences different from the author's or arguments based on opposing views, jot them down.

Analyze What You Read

To analyze something means breaking it down into its components, examining those components closely to evaluate their significance, and determining how they relate as a whole. You do this when you outline an essay. But analyzing what you read also requires interpreting and evaluating the points of a discussion or argument as well as its language and structure.

Analyzing an essay after establishing its main idea will help you understand what may not be evident at first. A closer examination of the author's words takes you beneath the surface and sharpens your understanding of the issue.

Although there is no set procedure for analyzing a piece of prose, here are some specific questions you should raise when reading an essay, especially one that is trying to influence or change your opinion:

- Who is the audience the author is addressing?
- What are the author's assumptions?
- What are the author's purposes and intentions?
- How well does the author accomplish those purposes?
- How convincing is the evidence presented? Is it sufficient and specific? Relevant? Reliable and not dated? Slanted?
- How good are the sources of the evidence used? Were they based on personal experience, scientific data, or outside authorities?
- Did the author address opposing views on the issue?
- Is the author's perspective persuasive?

What Is Critical Writing?

Critical writing is a systematic process. Experienced writers do not plan, write, edit, and proofread all at the same time. Rather, critical writing occurs one thoughtful step at a time.

Some writing assignments may require more steps than others. An in-class freewriting exercise may take only one or two steps—light planning and writing. An essay question on a midterm examination may permit enough time for only three steps—planning, writing, and proofreading. A simple plan for such an assignment needs to answer only two questions: "What am I going to say?" and "How am I going to develop my idea convincingly?"

Developing Ideas

Even the most experienced writers sometimes have trouble getting started. Common problems you may encounter include focusing your ideas, knowing where to begin, having too much or too little to say, and determining your position on an issue. But there are strategies that can help promote the free expression of your ideas and make you more comfortable with writing. Two of the most common are brainstorming and freewriting.

Brainstorming

The goal of brainstorming is to generate and focus ideas. Brainstorming can be a personal exercise or a group project. You begin with a blank sheet of paper (or a blackboard) and, without paying attention to spelling, order, or grammar, simply list ideas about the topic as they come to you. You should spend at least 10 minutes brainstorming, building on the ideas you write down. There are no "dumb" ideas in brainstorming—the smallest detail may turn into a great essay.

Let us assume, for example, that you decide to write a paper supporting Tim Goodman's assertion in "Hate Violence? Turn It Off!" Brainstorming for a few minutes may provide something like this:

> Goodman's main idea is captured in the title, but the essay's tone is very sarcastic. Is essay more or less persuasive? Will reader find tone condescending? Insulting? Does this weaken his argument?

> What watchdog groups denounce Hollywood for violent images? Find examples online. Are the claims of these groups reasonable or not?

> Who is to blame for children watching violent TV or movies? Is it Hollywood or lax parents?

> Check out how the "V-chip" works.

> List occasions when I've seen young kids watching inappropriately violent films or TV shows. Who's responsible for this? What could be done to change it?

> The phrase "Vote with your remote" is catchy and seems sensible. But is it a realistic solution?

> It's easy to control what young kids watch, but what about tweens? Is it solely the responsibility of parents to control their viewing? Is it possible for parents to control what tweens view?

> Is censorship the only way to protect young teens from viewing violence? Is censorship too high a price to pay?

> Interview parents of young children to get their views on this issue. Interview parents of teenagers. Interview teenagers. How do their opinions compare?

> Research the movie rating system. Does it seem to have an impact on what young children watch? On what teens watch?

You may notice that this brainstorming example is more like a list with little structure, no apparent order, and even spelling errors. Its purpose is to elicit all the ideas you have about a subject so you can read your ideas and identify an interesting topic to develop.

Freewriting

As you can see from the above, brainstorming is the listing or bulleting of ideas, reactions, writing strategies, and research possibilities as they occur to you. The next step is freewriting, which is a more focused preliminary step to the actual formal writing process. In freewriting, you write down your free flow of ideas on the topic without regard to spelling, grammar, or punctuation. To help keep your focus, note your topic at the top of your paper, then spend 10 or 15 minutes writing down the free flow of ideas on the topic as they occur to you. And above all, don't stop writing—even if you feel that what you are writing is silly or irrelevant or digressing. Any one, or a combination, of the ideas expressed in a freewrite can be developed into a thoughtful essay.

Here is an example of a freewriting exercise:

> At first, I was put off by Goodman's piece. I found the tone angry and condescending—especially with remarks like "Now you can't pick up a paper without some watchdog group denouncing Hollywood for ruining their children's lives with a plethora of violent images nightly." (I didn't even know what "plethora" meant.) Goodman seemed to think that violence on television is a boring, unimportant concern. But as I read on, Goodman got me interested in the topic. Especially when he talked about Hollywood as a scapegoat for lazy parents. That made me wonder who really is responsible for what children and young people watch. Should Hollywood be blamed if kids watch films made for adults? Goodman mentioned several options available to protect young viewers from violent shows and movies—"V-chips," rating systems, and the simple act of changing the channel. For young children, these can work. But then I got to thinking about tweens and adolescents. All children over 10 can get around their parents' efforts to control what they watch. With so many channels on cable TV and lots of unsupervised time, they can view almost anything they want including pornography and explicit violence. But does it make sense to resort to censorship? And with a V-chip? Goodman feels this shifts parental responsibility to the government. Do we want a society where the government restricts what people watch? Is Hollywood a scapegoat for lax parenting as Goodman claims? I am a little confused. Perhaps I'll write a paper focusing specifically on young adolescents and violence in television. If channel blocking and ratings systems fail, what alternatives exist? Maybe I could interview some teenagers to see what they think. Do they really watch a lot of violence on TV? Or do they use common sense? If they do watch violence, does it influence their behavior? Do they really change the channel? Maybe I could write a paper about these ideas and come up with suggestions as to how to help teens make good choices.

Narrowing Your Topic and Developing Your Thesis

Although brainstorming and freewriting help generate ideas, you still need to narrow down one idea to something more manageable. But this can be quite a challenge since you might like more than one idea, or you may be afraid of limiting yourself to only one concept. Choose an idea that will interest you and your audience. Remember that if you do not like the way one idea begins to develop, you can always go back to your brainstorming list and choose another to develop instead. Once you identify your topic, you are ready to develop the thesis statement for your essay.

Based on the freewriting exercise described earlier, we will follow a student who has decided to write his paper on the idea that educating adolescents on the potentially harmful effects of television violence might be a better solution than government regulation. The idea stems from a response to Goodman's essay, but it will develop into a thesis that uniquely belongs to the student.

Developing a Thesis

The **thesis** is a form of contract between the writer and reader. It makes a claim or declaration—telling your audience exactly what you are going to discuss. It should be stated in the opening paragraph, with the rest of the essay developing and supporting it.

Your thesis should guide the development of your essay. Don't be constrained by your first thesis. If your paper is changing as you write, your thesis may evolve as well. Remember to go back and revise the thesis so that it matches the points made in your essay.

Although the thesis represents the last step in developing the topic for your essay, it is only the beginning of the actual writing process. For his paper, our student worked out the following opening paragraph to help develop his thesis:

> It is widely assumed that violence, whether in film or on television, negatively affects teenagers and that regulations are necessary to protect them. These regulations include V-chips, ratings systems, and even artistic censorship. However, it is clear that these regulations are ineffective. We are better off as a society if teenagers are educated in visual literacy, learn early on to "vote with the remote," and make independent decisions about their viewing choices [thesis statement].

Identifying Your Audience

Knowing what your audience needs and expects from your essay will help you compose a convincing, effective paper. The following questions can help you identify the expectations of your audience:

- Who is my audience?
- What do they already know about my topic?

- What question do they have about my topic?
- What do they need to know to understand my point?
- What is the best order to present the information they need to know?
- How do they feel about this topic?
- Why would they want to read my essay?

Based on these questions, our student determined that his audience would be his teacher and expository writing classmates. All of them would be familiar with Goodman's article and would have discussed it to some extent in class. They might have different opinions on the issue, so supporting evidence (from both Goodman's article and some outside research) would be necessary to effectively make his point. Because the essay would be about an issue directly concerning teachers, parents, and students, it should generate some level of personal interest and, thus, engage his readers.

Organizing and Drafting Your Essay

There are many ways to organize your paper. Some students prefer to use the standard outline technique, complete with roman numerals and indented subpoints. Other students prefer more flexible flowcharts. The key to organizing is to define your focus and plan how to support your thesis statement from point to point in a logical order.

When writing your essay, think of your draft as a work in progress. Your objective should be to present your ideas in a logical order. You can address spelling, grammar, and sentence structure later. If you get stuck writing one paragraph or section, move on to another. You may choose to write your draft sequentially, or you may choose to move from your thesis to your body paragraphs, leaving your introduction and conclusion for last. Feel free to leave gaps or write notes to yourself in brackets to indicate areas to develop later when revising. Do not make the mistake of thinking that your first draft has to be your final draft. Remember that writing is a process of revision—you can always go back and fix things later.

Developing Paragraphs and Making Transitions

A paragraph is a group of sentences that supports and develops a central idea. The central idea serves as the core point of the paragraph, and the surrounding sentences support it.

Three primary types of sentences compose a paragraph: the topic sentence, supporting sentences, and transitional sentences.

The core point, or the **topic sentence**, is usually the first or second sentence in the paragraph. It is the controlling idea of the paragraph. Placing the topic sentence first lets the reader immediately know what the paragraph is about. However, sometimes a transition sentence or some supporting material needs to precede the topic sentence, in which case the topic sentence may appear as the second or third sentence in the paragraph. The topic sentence should connect logically to the topic sentences in the paragraphs before and after it.

Supporting sentences do just that; they support the topic sentence. This support may be from outside sources in the form of quotations or paraphrased material, or it may be from your own ideas. Think of the support sentences as "proving" the validity of your topic sentence.

Transitional sentences link paragraphs together, making the essay cohesive and readable. Transitional sentences are usually the first and last sentences of the paragraph. When they appear at the end of the paragraph, they foreshadow the topic to come. Words such as *in addition, yet, moreover, furthermore, meanwhile, likewise, also, since, before, hence, on the other hand, as well,* and *thus* are often used in transitional sentences. These words can also be used within the body of the paragraph to clarify and smooth the progression from idea to idea. For example, the last sentence in our student's introductory paragraph sets up the reader's expectations that the paragraphs that follow will explain why V-chips and other viewing regulations are ineffective and why society would be better off if teenagers learned to make educated decisions about what they view.

Paragraphs have no required length. Remember, however, that an essay comprising long, detailed paragraphs might prove tiresome and confusing to the reader. Likewise, short, choppy paragraphs may sacrifice clarity and leave the reader with unanswered questions. Remember that a paragraph presents a single unified idea. It should be just long enough to effectively support its subject. Begin a new paragraph when your subject changes.

Use this list to help keep your paragraphs organized and coherent:

- Organize material logically—present your core idea early in the paragraph.
- Include a topic sentence that expresses the core point of the paragraph.
- Support and explain the core point.
- Use transitional sentences to indicate where you are going and where you have been.

Let us see how our student applies these ideas to the second paragraph of his essay.

In his piece, "Hate Violence? Turn It Off!" Goodman discounts the value of currently available measures designed to control violence on TV or in film. To understand his position, we should first be familiar with these measures and understand how a teenager views them [*topic sentence*]. The first is the V-chip, a technology that lets parents block television programming they don't want their children to watch [*supporting sentence*]. Television shows are rated according to a system created by the broadcasting industry, and a parent can program the V-chip to block shows with particular ratings [*supporting sentence*]. The problem is that any clever teen can easily deprogram and reprogram this chip, and Mom and Dad are none the wiser [*supporting sentence*]. A second measure is the familiar film-rating system of the Motion Picture Association of America: G, PG, PG-13, N-17 ratings [*supporting sentence*]. But even if an N-17 rating prohibits young teens from seeing a film in a theater, they can always see it when it's available on DVD. The third attempt is artistic censorship [*supporting sentence*]. As Goodman says, censoring a show like the wildly successful and artistically acclaimed HBO series *The Sopranos* poses more risks than benefits for society [*supporting sentence*]. Do we really want our teens living in a world where a panel of parents, special interest groups, or a religious institution makes decisions as to what an artist can or cannot create [*transitional sentence*]? No, and that's why visual literacy may be the best strategy to protect teens from excessive violence in film and on television.

Editing and Revising

Once you have drafted a paper and, if possible, spent some time away from it, you should begin editing and revising it. To edit your paper, read it closely, marking the words, phrases, and sections you want to change. Have a grammar handbook nearby to quickly reference any grammatical questions that may arise. Look for things that seem out of place or sound awkward, passages that lack adequate support and detail, and sentences that seem wordy or unclear. Many students find that reading the essay aloud helps them to recognize awkward sentences and ambiguous wording.

As you read, you should always ask if what you have written refers back to your thesis:

- Does this paragraph support my thesis?
- What does my reader need to know?
- Do my paragraphs flow in a logical order?
- Have I deviated from my point?

As you revise your paper, think about the voice and style you are using to present your material. Is your style smooth and confident? How much of yourself is in the essay, and is this level appropriate for the type of paper you are writing? Some writers, for example, overuse the pronoun *I*. If you find that this is the case, try to rework your sentences to decrease the use of this pronoun.

Proofreading Effectively

To proofread correctly, you must read slowly and critically. Look for and mark errors in spelling and usage, sentence fragments and comma splices, inconsistencies in number between nouns and pronouns and between subjects and verbs, faulty parallelism, other grammatical errors, unintentional repetitions, and omissions.

After you have identified the errors, go back and correct them. When you have finished, proofread the paper again to make sure you have caught everything. As you proofread for grammar and style, ask yourself the questions listed above and make corrections on your paper. Be prepared to re-read your essay multiple times. Having only one or two small grammatical corrections is a good indication that you are done revising.

If your schedule permits, you might want to show your paper to a friend or instructor for review. Obtaining feedback from your audience is another way you can test the effectiveness of your paper. An outside reviewer will probably think of questions you have not thought of, and if you revise to answer those questions, you will make your paper stronger.

Critically Reading a Visual World

As critical readers of written arguments, we do not take the author simply at face value. We consider the author's purpose and intent, audience, style, tone, and supporting evidence. We must apply these same analytical tools to "read" visual arguments effectively. As with written language, understanding the persuasive power of "visual language" requires a close examination and interpretation of the premise, claims, details, supporting evidence, and stylistic touches embedded in any visual piece. We should ask ourselves the following four questions when examining visual arguments:

- Who is the target *audience?*
- What are the *claims* made in the images?
- What shared history or cultural *assumptions*—or warrants—does the image make?
- What is the supporting *evidence?*

Whether a photograph, work of art, print ad, or editorial cartoon, every visual employs color, shape, texture, depth, and point of view to create its effect. Some want to sell us something, others want to sway our opinion or tell a story. It is easy to allow our gut reaction to serve as our guide in a

visual world, but critically approaching this world gives us an edge. Therefore, to understand how visuals work and to analyze the way they influence us, here are some questions to ask about print images, such as those in
newspapers and magazine ads:

- What element within the frame catches your attention immediately?
- What is the central image? What is the background image? Fore-
  ground image? What are the surrounding images? What is significant
  in the placement of these images? Their relationship to one another?
- What verbal information is included? How is it made prominent?
  How is it related to the other graphics or images?
- What specific details (people, objects, locale) are emphasized? Which
  are exaggerated or idealized?
- What is the effect of color and lighting?
- What emotional effect is created by the images—pleasure? longing?
  anxiety? nostalgia?
- Do the graphics and images make you want to know more about the
  subject or product?
- What special significance might objects in the image have?
- Is there any symbolism imbedded in the images?

Considering these questions helps us to survey a visual argument critically and enables us to formulate reasoned assessments of its message
and intent. In the following pages, we will analyze in greater detail some
visual arguments presented in a current print ad and an editorial cartoon.
In the following chapters, we have included a variety of visual presentations and questions that ask you to consider the ways symbolism, brand
recognition, stereotyping, and cultural expectations contribute to how such
illustrations communicate their ideas and influence our reactions.

Advertisements

Any form of visual expression serves to open the mind of the observer to
new discoveries and ideas. And advertising is no different as it, too, selects
and crafts visual images toward an end of expanding awareness. However,
advertising has a different objective. Its goal is not to expand and enlighten
thought but to direct the viewer to a single basic response: Buy this product!

Images have clout, and none are so obvious or so craftily designed as
those from the world of advertising. Advertising images are everywhere—
television, newspapers, the Internet, magazines, the sides of buses, and on
highway billboards. Each year, companies collectively spend more than
$150 billion on print ads and television commercials (more than the gross
national product of many countries). Advertisements comprise at least a

quarter of each television hour and form the bulk of many newspapers and magazines. Tapping into our most basic emotions, their appeal goes right to the quick of our fantasies: happiness, material wealth, eternal youth, social acceptance, sexual fulfillment, and power.

Yet, most of us are so accustomed to the onslaught of such images that we see them without looking and hear them without listening. But if we stopped to examine how the images work, we might be amazed at their powerful and complex psychological force. And we might be surprised at how much effort goes into the crafting of such images—an effort solely intended to make us spend our money.

Like a written argument, every print ad or commercial has an *audience, claims, assumptions,* and *evidence.* Sometimes these elements are obvious; sometimes they are understated; sometimes they are implied. They may boast testimonials by average folk or celebrities or cite hard scientific evidence. And sometimes they simply manipulate our desire to be happy or socially accepted. But common to every ad and commercial, no matter what the medium, is the *claim* that you should buy this product.

Print ads are potentially complex mixtures of images, graphics, and text. So in analyzing an ad, you should be aware of the use of photography, the placement of those images, and the use of text, company logos, and other graphics such as illustrations, drawings, sidebar boxes, and so on. You should also keep in mind that every aspect of the image has been considered and carefully designed. Let's take a look at how a recent magazine ad for Fresh Step cat litter uses some of these elements, including social appeal, the use of color, light, and setting to convince us to buy this product.

Fresh Step Ad

When analyzing a print ad, we should try to determine what first captures our attention. In the Fresh Step ad, it is the huge and arresting image of the cat. In particular, the cat's worried facial expression, its paws tucked between its legs, and the curved tail. This order seems logical considering the purpose of the ad. The cat's posture clearly and comically suggests that it is in serious need of kitty litter. We then we notice the room's décor, the furniture and decorations. At the bottom, the Fresh Step logo jumps out at us, directing our eyes to the fine print: "Cats everywhere are having a hard time smelling their litter boxes."

Who Is the Audience?

The ad could appeal to anyone who has a cat. It could be argued that based on the details of the interior the audience might be older individuals, people with expensive, traditional taste—perhaps an elderly couple who loves cats. On the other hand, the ad is comically appealing to anyone who purchases

Cats everywhere are having a hard time smelling their litter boxes.

cat litter. The humor of the ad—the visual joke of a cat's urgent need to locate its litter box—draws in a wide audience.

What Is the Claim?

Because advertisers are vying for our attention, they must project their claim as efficiently as possible in order to discourage us from turning the page. The stated or implied claim of all advertising is that the product will make life better for us. Of course, most ads aren't so bold in their claims, but the promise is there by inference. The claim of this ad is that if you own a cat and want to have an odor-free home, buy Fresh Step. Furthermore, by purchasing this brand of cat litter, you become part of a community of tasteful, savvy cat owners.

What Is the Evidence?

The evidence for the desirability of Fresh Step is in the visuals and the text. The visuals suggest that people with taste buy Fresh Step. Likewise, the cat's need for a litter box is made all the more urgent by the orderly, dainty, old-fashioned, and neatly appointed room the cat is placed in. The furniture, walls, and decorative touches suggest an occupant who is most likely elderly, very particular, traditional, and fussy. The furniture is of another era. The combination of French provincial table and chair, colonial wainscoting, stenciled wallpaper, a Currier and Ives–type painting, Victorian lighting, and neatly arranged Russian dolls all suggest an occupant whom the cat could easily offend. And the text tells us why: because Fresh Step is so good at eliminating odors, that even cats—noted for their keen sense of smell—"have a hard time smelling their litter boxes."

What Are the Assumptions?

The creators of this ad made three assumptions about us, the audience: (1) that many cat owners need litter boxes for their pets; (2) that most people value odor-free rooms; and (3) that people associate an expensive decor with people of discriminating preferences. Thus, most people will be satisfied purchasing Fresh Step cat litter.

Editorial or Political Cartoons

Editorial cartoons have been a part of American life almost as long as has advertising. They are a mainstay feature on the editorial pages in most newspapers—those pages reserved for columnists, contributing editors, and illustrators to present their views in words and pen and ink.

A stand-alone editorial cartoon—as opposed to a strip of multiple frames—is a powerful and terse form of communication that combines pen-and-ink drawings with dialogue balloons and captions. They're not just visual jokes, but visual humor that comments on social/political issues while drawing on viewers' experience and knowledge. As such, they are stories of a moment in the flow of familiar current events. And the key words here are *moment* and *familiar*. Although a cartoon captures a split instant in time, it also infers what came before and, perhaps, what may happen next—either in the next moment or in some indefinite future.

For a cartoon to be effective, it must make the issue clear at a glance, and it must establish where it stands in the argument. To do so, cartoonists resort to images that are instantly recognizable, that we don't have to work hard to grasp. Locales are determined by giveaway props: An airplane out the window suggests an airport; a cactus and cattle skull, a desert; an overstuffed armchair and TV, the standard living room. Likewise, human emotions are instantly conveyed: pleasure is a huge toothy grin; fury is steam blowing out of a figure's ears; love is two figures making goo-goo eyes with floating hearts overhead. People themselves may have exaggerated features to emphasize a point or emotion.

Editorial cartoons rely on such visual clichés to convey their messages instantly. That is, they employ stock figures for their representation—images instantly recognizable from cultural stereotypes like the fat-cat tycoon, the mobster thug, and the sexy female movie star. And these come to us in familiar outfits and props that give away their identities and profession. The cartoon judge has a black robe and gavel; the prisoner wears striped overalls and a ball and chain; the physician dons a smock and holds a stethoscope; the doomsayer is a scrawny long-haired guy carrying a sign saying, "The end is near." These are visual clichés known by the culture at large, and we instantly recognize them.

The visual cliché may be what catches our eye in the editorial cartoon, but the message lies in what the cartoonist does with it—that is twisting the cliché or turning it around.

Mike Luckovich's "Let's Be Responsible" Cartoon

Consider Mike Luckovich's cartoon (from the *Atlanta Journal-Constitution*) that addresses the issue of texting while driving. The visual cliché is a group of friends gathering in a very ordinary bar. We know that from the familiar props: the bar sign, the single dangling light fixture, bottles of alcohol, draft pulls, and the broad back of the bartender. Even the patrons are familiar figures—four casually dressed individuals who look neither prosperous nor polished. Note the dark-haired young man wears T-shirt with a cartoon figure on it; another male sports unconventionally messy hair and the suggestion of beads around his neck. The woman has overstyled blond hair, and the bald man wears a plain white shirt. The twist, of course, is that instead of clasping a martini or a beer, the patrons of this bar are all regarding their cell phones. Not a drink appears on the table (though we can assume that they have had or will be having considerable alcohol since they are concerned about who will be driving). Maybe not.

The issue, of course, is the debate about driving while texting. The cartoon addresses the increasing number of deadly accidents caused by drivers who were texting rather than paying attention to the road. A public debate still rages about outlawing texting while driving. According to a recent *New York Times*/CBS News poll (NYTimes.com/polls), nearly all Americans say sending a text message while driving should be illegal; and half of all Americans say texting behind the wheel should be punished at least as harshly as drunk driving. The concern is reflected in some legislation: It is now illegal in at least 15 states to text while driving, and the federal government is exerting pressure to ban it in all states.

The cartoon's joke is in the twist—the gap between the familiar and the unexpected. The familiar is the bar scene; the unexpected is the fact that the patrons are not holding alcoholic drinks but texting devices. What

is important is a sober texter not a sober driver. Thus, the caption: "Let's be responsible. On the drive back, who's the designated texter?"

What Is the Cartoon's Claim?

The claim here is that driving while texting is as dangerous and possibly more dangerous than driving while drinking. This claim is implicit in the satirical image of the bar patrons holding their cell phones and concentrating on texting. And it is implicit in the comment, "Let's be responsible. On the drive back, who's the designated texter?"

What Are the Cartoon's Assumptions?

This cartoon makes the assumption that people are preoccupied with texting and that they recognize that texting while driving is irresponsible and dangerous. It also presumes that readers are aware of the spate of serious accidents caused by "texters" and that they equate such behavior with drunk driving. Furthermore, the cartoon assumes familiarity with the campaign to designate a sober driver if other passengers are drinking. Part of the humor of the cartoon is based on the substitution of texting devices for alcohol.

What Is the Cartoon's Evidence?

The cartoon presents the ironic and humorous notion that its bar patrons are not even thinking about drinks. None are present. Instead, they are preoccupied with text messaging. This is the vice they go to the bar to indulge. They are so consumed with texting that they want to be certain they can continue on the drive home. The implication is that they will not be able to restrain themselves and must appoint a "designated texter" so texting will not be interrupted.

You will notice that the title page of each unit in this book features an editorial cartoon addressing the thematic focus of the unit. As you view each, consider the visual clichés the cartoonist uses. What information is important for the viewer to know? What assumptions does the cartoonist make? What issue is the cartoonist holding up for public scrutiny, and why?

Discussing What You Read, in Class and Online

We all have the yearning to express ourselves freely and clearly—to contribute to open discussion and debate, to be an active participant in the group. Ideally, the classroom is the perfect venue for students to practice communication skills—to exchange ideas and explore differences of opinions. With the guidance of an instructor and with the mutual support and respect of classmates, an environment can exist where each student feels comfortable exercising his or her discussion skills and feedback is encouraged. The result is a class that's fun, engaging, and informative—a class that enjoys a group spirit of mutual respect and attentiveness. Toward that end, we offer the following guidelines for discussion.

Guidelines for Discussion in Class and Online

1. Take time to process the questions your instructor or classmates have posed. Be sure you understand what is being asked before you respond.
2. If the question is unclear, ask for clarification or restate what you understood the question to be.
3. When you offer your answer, speak in an audible, clear voice. Online, quickly proofread your response before posting.
4. In class, listen carefully to answers or comments made by your classmates. Online, read every contribution to a conversation before jumping in.
5. Take notes during the discussion so that you can refer to specific remarks. Also, jot down ideas that will help you express yourself as you give feedback.
6. Refer to comments made by other classmates in your response. Then elaborate on how your ideas agree or disagree with statements made by classmates.

7. In an online or synchronous class discussion, resist the temptation to IM (instant message) friends or visit other websites.

8. Do not interrupt a classmate when he or she is speaking. Give the speaker a chance to finish a thought. Some people need more time than others to articulate their ideas.

9. In an online class discussion, try not to use common IM abbreviations such as "srsly" or "LOL." Your language choices should be thoughtful and engaging.

10. Use context to connect your thoughts to the larger conversation. You may begin your response by saying, "I disagree with Tom's view that . . . because. . . ," or "I agree with what Mary just said and can offer an example. . ." or "In the piece we read by David Plotz, this idea was discussed."

11. Make sure your response addresses the topic being discussed and does not go off on a tangent.

12. Rely on the moderator of the discussion for prompting and direction. It might naturally be your instructor or another student in the class. The moderator's job is to call on individuals to speak, ask new questions, or prompt students to explore new ideas.

13. Regard every speaker with respect—just as you would like to be treated with respect.

14. A spirited answer is acceptable, but not an aggressive, loud, or rude one.

15. If you know the topic your class will be discussing on a given day, jot down your ideas or opinions beforehand. You might want to look up an article on the topic online before your class.

1 | Is the Internet Changing Our Social Lives?

The phrase "social networking," while understood in concept offline, is really a phenomenon of the Internet that has evolved over the last 10 years. While web communities have changed the way many of us think about meeting people and sharing information, social networking sites such as MySpace and Facebook have revolutionized the way we communicate with friends and share information about ourselves.

While there are many social networking sites worldwide, the clear leaders in the industry are Facebook and Twitter. In North America, MySpace and LinkedIn have large followings, while Bebo, Skyrock, StudiVZ, and hi5 lead in different parts of Europe. Orkut and hi5 tend to dominate South America and Central America, and Friendster, once very popular in the United States, still has a strong following in Asia and the Pacific Islands. With over 500 million active users and an average 50 percent of users online on any given day, Facebook now leads the social networking sites in popularity. Twitter processes over 65 million tweets a day among its 200+ million users.

Within these vast numbers, user demographic profiles have emerged. MySpace users tend to be younger and to use the site to network with friends and share music. Facebook has seen a huge boom among adults between 30 and 50 over the last two years. And LinkedIn is growing in popularity among professionals seeking to network. There is even a new emerging area of psychiatric research—cyberpsychology—to address the multifaceted issues connected to social networking and individuals.

Like any space where people gather, the virtual world is not immune to the same set of troubles we face in real life. Teens and children can be targeted by sexual predators. Kids can "cyberbully" classmates, carrying the tortures of the playground onto cell phones and computer screens at home. Illicit romances and online flirting may be taken beyond laptops, ruining relationships and destroying marriages. And, of course, cyber crime is ever present, seeking login numbers, financial data, and credit card information.

CRITICAL THINKING

1. What do you need to know in order to understand the point of this cartoon? Explain.
2. What does the woman in the cartoon mean when she says the man has "no friends in real life"? What is the cartoonist trying to say about the life of the man and his relationship to people?
3. Would this cartoon have made sense 10 years ago? Why or why not?

This unit explores how social networking sites influence our relationships with each other and the ways we relate to the world around us. Is the Internet redefining friendships and what it means to be a "friend"? Does it make it easier to do things we wouldn't do in face-to-face interactions, like bullying and acting inappropriately? How is social networking influencing the way we think and speak? Will Facebook, MySpace, Twitter, or some new web-based network continue to hold such sway over us? Or are they merely a passing fad?

Cam Cardow, *Ottawa Citizen*

MySpace, Facebook, and Other Social Networking Sites: Hot Today, Gone Tomorrow?

This review of popular online social networking sites was published on May 3, 2006, by Knowledge@Wharton, the online business journal of the Wharton School of the University of Pennsylvania. It draws upon the knowledge and expertise of many marketing and business professors at the Wharton School, including David Bell, Peter Fader, Leonard Lodish, and Eric K. Clemons.

CONNECTING TO THE TOPIC

Members of the next generation use the Internet to network for business, friendships, and dating. It is inextricably connected to daily life and social experience. What is still unclear is the sustainability of social networking sites such as Facebook and MySpace. While popular now, will such sites remain a fixture in the lives of the next generation? This essay explores current trends and the future of social networking sites. Will children born today use MySpace and Facebook as teens and young adults, or will such sites be long-distant memories?

WORDS IN CONTEXT

serendipitous (3)   random (adj.)
mercurial (4)   fluid, moving (adj.)
touted (4)   highly praised (v.)
domiciled (5)   housed (adj.)

1   Popular social networking sites, including MySpace and Facebook, are changing the human fabric of the Internet and have the potential to pay off big for investors, but—given their youthful user base—they are unusually vulnerable to the next "new new" thing. As quickly as users flock to one trendy Internet site, they can just as quickly move on to another, with no advance warning, according to Wharton faculty and Internet analysts.

2   MySpace, with 70 million visitors, has become the digital equivalent of hanging out at the mall for today's teens, who load the site with photos, news about music groups and detailed profiles of their likes and dislikes. Other social network sites include Facebook, geared to college students, LinkedIn, aimed at professionals, and Xanga, a blog-based community site. In all, an estimated 300 sites, including smaller ones such as StudyBreakers

for high schoolers and Photobucket, a site for posting images, make up the social network universe.

3   Wharton marketing professor David Bell says the long-term success of these sites will depend on their ability to retain the interest of their members. "There is a fad or a fashion component to all these networks. Some will come and go," says Bell. The classic example, he suggests, is Friendster, which burst onto the Internet in 2003 and soon had 20 million visitors. Late last year, it slipped below a million after MySpace and other sites with better music and video capability lured Friendster users away. "A lot of the [success] is **serendipitous**. These things can have exponential growth. Then, if another community shows up that has better functionality in some way, there can be a mass migration."

4   Wharton marketing professor Peter Fader agrees that social network sites are powerful, but **mercurial**, particularly since most are aimed at teenagers and young adults. "It's a complete crapshoot. Look how many of these have come along and how many were **touted** as the next big thing. How many have disappeared completely or find themselves in some strange little unexplainable niche?"

5   He points to Orkut, an invitation-only service introduced by Google in 2004 that is little known in the United States, but wildly popular in Brazil, where more than 70% of its users are based. Indeed, Orkut has made Portuguese a second language in its interface. "In Brazil it's gold, but in the U.S., where the service is **domiciled**, nobody's even heard of Orkut. And there's no good reason why." While MySpace and Facebook currently rule the popular crowd on the Internet social scene, Fader says the forces that make a hot site are difficult to quantify; any site could become the next outcast. "There is no reason to believe that these, or future ones that are emerging on the radar screen, will be any different. I don't think anyone can come up with a genuine reason why they have become so popular, outside of 20-20 hindsight." Echoing that point, an article in the April 30 *New York Times* reports that AOL plans to launch a social networking site to be called AIM Pages as a competitor to MySpace, Yahoo360 and other such services.

6   One way for investors to benefit from the rise of social networks would be to develop a highly diverse portfolio, Fader adds. "I have no problem with betting on a crapshoot, but you want to hedge your bets carefully and accept the downside in exchange for what could be an incredible upside. You can't control your destiny with these nearly as much as any other web site or portal."

Target: Cell Phones

7 For the moment, MySpace and Facebook are hot. News Corp. paid $580 million last year for MySpace as part of a $1.3 billion Internet acquisition

spree. Facebook just received an additional $25 million in venture capital. Both companies are planning to extend their reach beyond the computer screen to cell phones. Cingular Wireless, Sprint Nextel and Verizon Wireless are starting a service that will allow users to post messages on Facebook's home pages or search for other users' phone numbers and email addresses from a cell phone. MySpace has a pact with Helio, a wireless joint venture between SK Telecom and Earthlink, that will allow users to send photos and update their blogs or profiles by cell phone.

8　　According to ComScore Media Metrix, MySpace, with its 70 million users, ranks second behind Yahoo in pages viewed and time spent on the site. Facebook, founded by a 21-year-old student on leave from Harvard and backed by Silicon Valley venture capitalists, has 7.3 million registered users. Chris Hughes, a spokesperson for Facebook, says the company thinks of itself more as a directory grounded in real life rather than a social network creating connections between strangers. "We model people's real lives at their individual schools in a virtual space that enables them to exchange information about themselves. We are not focused on meeting new people, dating or anything like that. Instead, we want to manage information efficiently so that we can provide our users the information that matters most to them."

9　　Social networking sites in general rely mainly on a simple advertising model—selling banner and text ads (although they ban uncool pop-up ads). Facebook also permits sponsored groups in which a marketer can build communities within the site. *BusinessWeek* recently reported that Facebook had rejected a $750 million buyout offer and was holding out for $2 billion. "That number is nothing but rumor," Hughes says.

10　　When it comes to placing a valuation on the social network sites, Wharton marketing professor Leonard Lodish says traditional tools, such as the discounted present value of the profit stream, apply to these new Internet networks as much as they do to any other business. He recalls an argument he had with marketing students during the Internet boom of 2000 about Internet music seller CDNow. Lodish said the firm would never be able to justify costs of $70 to attain each customer. The following year the firm declared bankruptcy.

11　　In the case of MySpace and Facebook, Lodish points out, the cost of gaining new customers is practically nothing because users join voluntarily and provide their own content through their profiles. In addition, the cost of running the sites' web servers is relatively low. If a classic advertising or subscription revenue model is used, he says, low-cost social network sites could be highly profitable. Yahoo must buy or develop content for its site to attract advertisers and Google has to invest in its search capabilities, Lodish notes. "Yahoo makes a lot of money selling ads on its sites. Why can't Facebook and MySpace do the same thing?"

12　　Nitin Gupta, an analyst with The Yankee Group in Boston, says MySpace is rooted in linking emerging bands to new fans, which makes it a logical partner for a media company, such as News Corp. The company can use the site to test or build buzz around its products. "These have become almost living systems, as the social network has begun to expand beyond a place for people with certain musical tastes and become popular for dating and all sorts of things."

13　　While the MySpace population has grown, the site's roots remain in media, Gupta adds. "Today, it continues to be used to identify individuals interested in, not just music, but television and radio as well." Before News Corp. bought MySpace, NBC used it to show clips of "The Office" before the show was aired on the network. While media companies may be a more logical fit with a social networking site, other businesses might mesh too, according to Gupta. "It's a little more difficult to build a community around a Norelco razor, but it's possible."

14　　Meanwhile, Gupta says, social networks have power beyond ad revenue to act as a customer relationship management (CRM) tool for companies selling products or services. "There's a lot of focus on advertising and banner ads and the amount of traffic. But it's important to look beyond traditional forms of web advertising to see the real potential—which is leveraging the connectivity of the sites and using them to form communities around products, media or services to really be in contact with your users." Still, he acknowledges, it will not be easy to convert those relationships to new revenue sources. "The future is in finding ways to monetize the online community beyond just traditional web advertising, although it's going to be difficult for online communities, even those behemoths like MySpace."

15　　According to Wharton professor of operations and information management Eric K. Clemons, connectivity is nice, but the Internet bust of 2000 showed that revenue is what matters. "As we learned from the first dot-com silliness, value is not in click-through or eyeballs. Value comes from revenues. . . . Can you sell subscriptions to your data or your service? Can you charge for referrals or for purchases that result from referrals? Can you sell stuff? If not, your revenue is zero and your market value is zero."

Safety and Privacy Concerns

16　As MySpace and other social networking sites have grown, so, too, have concerns about Internet safety and privacy. The Center for Missing and Exploited Children reported more than 2,600 incidents of adults using the web to target children online in order to engage in sexual activity. In March, federal prosecutors in Connecticut charged two men with using MySpace to contact youths with whom they later had sexual contact. Following Congressional hearings about online sexual predators, MySpace hired a safety czar to improve the site's protections for young users.

17   The popularity of social networking sites may also have unexpected consequences for users. A gay student attending a Christian college was expelled after administration officials viewed photos of the student in drag on Facebook. Twenty middle school students in California were suspended after participating in a MySpace group where one student allegedly threatened to kill another and made anti-Semitic remarks. In Kansas, authorities arrested five teenagers after one of the suspects used MySpace to outline plans for a Columbine-like attack on the boys' school.

18   Gary Arlen, president of Arlen Communications, a Bethesda, Md., research and consulting firm, says MySpace users may also begin to shy away as they grasp the long-term consequences of putting up photos of wild parties or tales of sexual bravado. "This stuff may come back to haunt you 20 years from now. MySpace runs the risk of a social reaction, but that is part of being the pioneer." Despite those obstacles, he is enthusiastic about social networks' promise, although he says the sites' ultimate value is less clear-cut than other Internet successes, such as eBay and Amazon. "It may be that this is a very slow play because the existing sites, Friendster and now MySpace and Facebook, are building a habit among young users. It will become a part of how they operate in their 20s and 30s. This service will be part of the landscape."

19   According to Bell, there are strategies that social network sites can use to avoid becoming tomorrow's abandoned property. One way to retain a site's aura is to limit membership. For example, Bell notes that when Diesel jeans faced the problem of losing marketing cachet by becoming too popular, the brand cut back on the number of outlets it would sell to. Facebook tries to limit itself to college students. Social networks seem to operate best when they strike a balance between heterogeneity, which provides large numbers of members, and selectivity, which keeps the hordes focused and engaged in the site, he says, adding that social networking sites also must keep pace with technology and provide new features—for example, fast downloads. "To create stickiness you must have functional value and also community value. If either of those becomes diluted, you give people a reason to start looking elsewhere."

20   As a web-based business, social networks do have some advantages over traditional companies in tracking user behavior in order to detect problems early. "If you are sophisticated, you can measure and monitor the rate at which users join and you can detect early warning signs, such as a drop-off in the number of people interacting," says Bell. "There would be metrics to monitor if you are headed in the wrong direction." Bell also cautions that sites will need to remain subtle in their approach to marketing if they are to build on their current success. While they provide banner and

text ads, even more valuable word-of-mouth promotion lurks in the buzz within user profile pages. "Part of the popularity of these things is that they are more credible and not explicitly commercial," he says. "If somebody on the Mac fanatic site tells me about iPod, it's more credible than Mac advertising. If people feel the networks are too corporate, that's a turnoff."

21 Still, no matter how their future takes shape, Bell says these types of networks are ingrained in Internet society. "They're here to stay. Like eBay, they are embedded now. The idea of joining online communities and being able to participate in them is not going to disappear." ◆

CONSIDERING THE ISSUES

1. Which social networking sites do you currently use? Have you ever switched from one site to another? If so, what were the reasons behind the switch? If not, why have you remained loyal to your original site?

2. Wharton marketing professor Leonard Lodish notes, "Yahoo makes a lot of money selling ads on its sites. Why can't Facebook and MySpace do the same thing?" Do you think social networking sites should sell ads? Explain the consequences of doing so.

CRAFT AND CONTENT

1. Review the section on "Safety and Privacy Concerns." How have social networking sites been abused? Should these sites be shut down or does the responsibility lie elsewhere?

2. The essay provides several examples of traditional forms of web advertising and discusses additional ways advertisers can survive in the age of the Internet. Evaluate these examples. Do you have any experience with them? Can you think of other methods to reach consumers online?

CRITICAL THINKING

1. Do you agree with the spokesperson for Facebook who surmises that Facebook is "a directory grounded in real life rather than a social network creating connections between strangers"? On what evidence is this based? Do you agree? Why or why not?

2. In this essay, Wharton marketing professor David Bell observes, "If somebody on the Mac fanatic site tells me about iPod, it's more credible than Mac advertising. If people feel the networks are too corporate, that's a turnoff." Do you agree with this statement? Explain.

WRITING ABOUT THE ISSUES

1. This essay describes the transitory nature of social networking sites (note that Friendster in the United States has dramatically declined in popularity). What other Internet phenomena have experienced "hot today, gone tomorrow" lifespans? Based on your own experiences with the Internet and with social networking sites, do you believe Facebook and Twitter will remain fixtures online, or is social networking likely to be replaced by something else in the near future?

2. Have you ever put anything on Twitter or Facebook that could potentially embarrass you in 5, 10, or even 20 years? Write a brief essay in which you describe the information you have personally shared online (include e-mails) and the ramifications of having a record of your online activity possibly accessible in the future.

As Bullies Go Digital, Parents Play Catch-Up

Jan Hoffman

Jan Hoffman is a Styles reporter for the *New York Times*. She writes about tweens, teens, and modern family dynamics.

CONNECTING TO THE TOPIC —————————

Bullying is taking on a whole new definition with the emergence of the Internet and specifically Facebook. In the past, with schoolyard bullying, we knew who the bullies were; but on the Internet, bullies can remain faceless and do far more damage. The next article recounts how one teenager was accused of bullying through Facebook when, in fact, he was the victim. What happens when others can assume your identity and wreak havoc on the Internet? Or when the torments of the schoolyard follow you home to appear on your personal computer in your own living room? It's called cyberbullying, and it is getting worse.

WORDS IN CONTEXT —————————

forays (7) a venture or an initial attempt, especially outside one's usual area (n.)
gratuitous (11) unnecessary or unwarranted; unjustified (adj.)

inhibitions (12)   impulses or desires (n.)
cavalier (13)   showing arrogant disregard; dismissive (adj.)
subpoena (16)   to serve or summon with an appearance in court to give testimony (v.)
congenital (22)   relating to a condition that is present at birth (adj.)
doted (31)   to show excessive love or fondness (v.)
untoward (35)   improper; unseemly (adj.)

1   Ninth grade was supposed to be a fresh start for Marie's son: new school, new children. Yet by last October, he had become withdrawn. Marie prodded. And prodded again. Finally, he told her. "The kids say I'm saying all these nasty things about them on Facebook," he said. "They don't believe me when I tell them I'm not on Facebook."

2   But apparently, he was.

3   Marie searched Facebook. There she found what seemed to be her son's page: his name, a photo of him grinning while running—and, on his public wall, sneering comments about teenagers he scarcely knew. Someone had forged his identity online and was bullying others in his name.

4   Students began to shun him. Furious and frightened, Marie contacted school officials. After expressing their concern, they told her they could do nothing. It was an off-campus matter. But Marie was determined to find out who was making her son miserable and to get them to stop. In choosing that course, she would become a target herself. When she and her son learned who was behind the scheme, they would both feel the sharp sting of betrayal.

5   It is difficult enough to support one's child through a siege of schoolyard bullying. But the lawlessness of the Internet, its potential for casual, breathtaking cruelty, and its capacity to cloak a bully's identity all present slippery new challenges to this transitional generation of analog parents. Desperate to protect their children, parents are floundering even as they scramble to catch up with the technological sophistication of the next generation.

6   Like Marie, many parents turn to schools, only to be rebuffed because officials think they do not have the authority to intercede. Others may call the police, who set high bars to investigate. Contacting Web site administrators or Internet service providers can be a daunting, protracted process.

7   When parents know the aggressor, some may contact that child's parent, stumbling through an evolving etiquette in the landscape of social awkwardness. Going forward, they struggle with when and how to supervise their adolescents' **forays** on the Internet.

8   Marie finally went to the police. The force's cybercrimes specialist, Inspector Brian Brunault, asked if she really wanted to pursue the matter. "He said that once it was in the court system," Marie said, "they would

have to prosecute. It could probably be someone we knew, like a friend of
D.C.'s or a neighbor. Was I prepared for that?"

9   Marie's son urged her not to go ahead. But Marie was adamant.
"I said yes."

Parental Fears

10 One afternoon last spring, Parry Aftab, a lawyer and expert on cyberbullying, addressed seventh graders at George Washington Middle School in
Ridgewood, N.J. "How many of you have ever been cyberbullied?" she
asked. The hands crept up, first a scattering, then a thicket. Of 150 students, 68 raised their hands. Aftab then asked: How many of your parents
know how to help you? A scant three or four hands went up.

11   Cyberbullying is often legally defined as repeated harassment online,
although in popular use, it can describe even a sharp-elbowed, **gratuitous**
swipe. Cyberbullies themselves resist easy categorization: the anonymity
of the Internet gives cover not only to schoolyard-bully types but to victims themselves, who feel they can retaliate without getting caught.

12   But online bullying can be more psychologically savage than schoolyard bullying. The Internet erases **inhibitions**, with adolescents often
going further with slights online than in person. "It's not the swear words,"
Inspector Brunault said. "They all swear. It's how they gang up on one
individual at a time. 'Go cut yourself.' Or 'you are sooo ugly'—but with
10 u's, 10 g's, 10 l's, like they're all screaming it at someone."

13   The **cavalier** meanness can be chilling. On a California teenage boy's
Facebook wall, someone writes that his 9-year-old sister is "a fat bitch."
About the proud Facebook photos posted by a 13-year-old New York girl,
another girl comments: "hideous" and "this pic makes me throwup a lil."
If she had to choose between the life of an animal and that of the girl in the
photos, she continues, she would choose the animal's, because "yeah, at
least they're worth something."

14   This is a dark, vicious side of adolescence, enabled and magnified
by technology. Yet because so many horrified parents are bewildered by
the technology, they think they are helpless to address the problems it
engenders.

The Bully Next Door

15 Throughout the fall, the Facebook profile set up in D.C.'s name taunted
students: "At least I don't take pics of myself in the mirror like a homosexual midget," wrote "D.C." Also, "you smell weird." And "ur such a
petaphile." At school, students would belligerently ask D.C. why he was
picking fights on Facebook. He would eat lunch alone, and skipped some
school, insisting that he was ill.

16   "I would always ask him, 'Are you having a good day?'" Marie said. "So he stopped talking to me about anything at school. He was afraid I would make more trouble for him. But the real victim was being ostracized more than the kids who were being bullied on his Facebook page." She would call Inspector Brunault weekly. Last fall, the detective had to subpoena Facebook for the address of the computer linked to the forged profile. Then he had to **subpoena** Comcast, the Internet service provider, for the home address of the computer's owner.

17   Finally, in January, Inspector Brunault told Marie he was getting close. He visited the home address supplied by Comcast. When he left, he had two more names and addresses. Two culprits were 14; one was 13. After learning the first two names, D.C. said: "Those guys have never liked me. I don't know why." But the third boy had been a friend since preschool. His father was a sports coach of D.C.'s.

18   D.C. was silent. Then he teared up. Finally, he said, "Do you mean to tell me, Mom, that they hate me so much that they would take the time to do this?"

19   Inspector Brunault asked the boys why they had done it. That summer, they replied, they had been reading Facebook profiles of people's dogs, which they found hilarious. They decided to make up a profile. They picked D.C. "because he was a loner and a follower."

20   Although the police did not release the boys' names because they are juveniles, word seeped through town. In the middle of the night, Marie received anonymous calls. "They told me my son should just suck it up," she recalled. "They said he would be a mama's boy. They would rant and then they would hang up."

Contacting the Other Parent

21 After Marie learned the identities of her son's cyberbullies, she did not call their parents. She was so incensed that she communicated only through official go-betweens, like the police and prosecutors. But some parents prefer to resolve the issue privately, by contacting the bully's family. Psychologists do not recommend that approach with schoolyard bullying, because it can devolve into conflicting narratives. With cyberbullying, a parent's proof of baldly searing digital exchanges can reframe that difficult conversation.

22   Parents who present the other parents with a printout of their child's most repugnant moments should be prepared for minimization, even denial. For example, Major Glenn Woodson's daughter, Sierra, has a shortened leg because of a **congenital** condition. One night, when she was in sixth grade, she received a text message showing a stick figure of her lying prostrate, eyes crossed out, another girl holding a bloody blade over the body. It had been sent by three girls in Sierra's grade.

23   Major Woodson, who lives on an Army base in Monterey, Calif., contacted the military police. They had a stern sit-down with the families of the three girls. Teachers held a workshop on cyberbullying. Two families apologized to the Woodsons.

24   Finally, the mother of the third girl, the instigator, called. "'It isn't her fault,' she said to my wife," Major Woodson said. "The mom said: 'I think this is way overblown. My daughter is being punished and she's not the only one who did it.'" The mother did not apologize.

When the Bully Is Your Child

25 After the police arrested the boys who usurped D.C.'s identity, the parents wrote Marie awkward apology letters. Only one mother phoned, in tears. No matter how parents see their children, learning of the cruelties they may perpetrate is jarring and can feel like an indictment of their child-rearing.

26   One afternoon two years ago, Judy, a recent widow in Palm Beach County, Fla., who had been finishing her college degree, helping a professor research cyberbullying, and working in an office, got a call from the middle school.

27   "Your daughter is involved in a cyberbullying incident," the assistant principal said. "Come down immediately." Her daughter and two others had made a MySpace page about another middle-schooler, saying she was a "whore," with a finger pointing to her private parts. The young teenagers printed out copies and flung them at students.

28   Judy rushed to school. Her daughter, a sweet, straight-A student, was waiting in the guidance counselor's office, her arms crossed defiantly. "I said to her, 'This is a human being,'" Judy recalled. "'This girl will be destroyed for the rest of her life!' And my daughter just said: 'I don't care. It's all true.' And I bawled while she just sat there."

29   The school suspended Judy's daughter for three days. Once Judy got over her shock, she said, "I had to accept that my daughter had really done this and it was so ugly."

30   Judy took away her daughter's computer, television and cellphone for months. She tried talking with her. Nothing. There were weeks of screaming and slammed doors. In time, as Judy took long walks with her daughter, the girl began to resemble the child Judy thought she had known.

31   When things improved, Judy bought her a puppy. "A lot of people will disagree with me," Judy said, "but I thought, this is a way for her to be responsible for something other than herself, something that would be dependent on her for all its needs." The girl **doted** on the puppy. One day, Judy asked: "'Would you want anyone to be mean to your dog? Throw rocks at Foxy?'" Her daughter recoiled. Judy continued: "'How do you

think other parents feel when something mean happens to their children?'
Then she broke down crying. That's when I think she finally understood
what she had done."

Supervisor or Spy?

32   Should teenagers have the same expectation of privacy from parents in
their online accounts that an earlier generation had with their little red diaries and keys? Software programs that speak to parental fears are mani-
fold. Parents can block Web sites, getting alerts when the child searches
for them. They can also monitor cellphones: a program called Mobile Spy
promises to let parents see all text messages, track G.P.S. locations and
record phone activity without the child knowing.

33   Last April in an omnibus review of studies addressing youth, privacy
and reputation, a report by the Berkman Center for Internet and Society
at Harvard noted that parents who checked their children's online communications were seen as "controlling, invasive and 'clueless.'" Young
people, one study noted, had a notion of an online public viewership "that
excludes the family."

34   Conversely, a recent study of teenagers and phones by the Pew Research
Center Internet and American Life Project said that parents regard their children's phones as a "parenting tool." About two-thirds said they checked the
content of their children's phones (whether teenagers pre-emptively delete
texts is a different matter). Two-thirds of the parents said they took away
phones as punishment. Almost half said they used phones to check on their
child's whereabouts.

35   Anne Collier, editor of NetFamilyNews.org, a parenting and technology news blog, noted that stealth monitoring may be warranted in rare
cases, when a parent suspects a child is at serious risk, such as being contacted by an unknown adult. But generally, she said, spying can have terrible repercussions: "If you're monitoring your child secretly," Ms. Collier
said, "what do you say to the kid when you find something **untoward**?
Then the conversation turns into 'you invaded my privacy,' which is not
what you intended to talk about."

36   Last spring, the Essex County, Mass., district attorney's office sent
the three boys who forged D.C.'s Facebook identity to a juvenile diversion
program for first-time nonviolent offenders. If the boys adhere to conditions for a year, they will not be prosecuted. According to a spokesman,
those conditions include: a five-page paper on cyberbullying; letters of
apology to D.C. and everyone they insulted in his name on Facebook; attending two Internet safety presentations; community service; no access to
the Internet except to complete schoolwork.

37   Marie, who reports that D.C. has a new circle of friends and
good grades, is reasonably satisfied with the sentencing conditions. But

compliance is another matter. She believes that at least one boy is already back on Facebook. Overburdened school administrators and, increasingly, police officers who unravel juvenile cybercrimes, say it is almost impossible for them to monitor regulations imposed on teenagers.

38   As with the boys who impersonated D.C. online, a district attorney's spokeswoman said, "That monitoring is up to the parents." ◆

CONSIDERING THE ISSUES

1. Hoffman asserts, "Desperate to protect their children, parents are floundering even as they scramble to catch up with the technological sophistication of the next generation." Are you more technologically sophisticated than your parents? Explain by giving some concrete examples.
2. Have you ever been cyberbullied? Have you ever cyberbullied someone else? Describe your experience.

CRAFT AND CONTENT

1. Review the introduction and conclusion of this article. Which attention-grabbing device does the author use in the introduction? How does she conclude her article? Explain.
2. The author of this essay choses to tell us the story of Marie and her son in spurts throughout the article. Why do you think Hoffman uses this technique and do you find it to be effective?
3. In the article, Judy tells how she bought her daughter a puppy in order to teach her daughter responsibility. Judy says, "A lot of people will disagree" with her decision to buy her daughter a pet. Why does Judy think people would disagree with her decision? Do you disagree? Explain.

CRITICAL THINKING

1. Should it be illegal to open a Facebook account, or that of any other Internet site, under someone else's identity? Explain.
2. As told in this article, Marie's son stopped talking to his mother about anything happening at school. Why do you think children don't talk to their parents about school? Did you speak openly about what was happening in your life during high school? Explain.
3. Do you think it is ethical for parents to "spy" on their children's electronic behavior, such as through blocking websites, getting alerts, monitoring cell phones, and reading text messages? Explain.

WRITING ABOUT THE ISSUES

1. Research the antibullying laws cropping up in most states. Does your state have a law against cyberbullying? Against bullying in general? Write a persuasive paper either for or against establishing antibullying laws.
2. Parry Aftab, a lawyer and expert on cyberbullying, asked a group of middle school children, "How many of your parents know how to help you?" Only a few raised their hands. Write an essay addressed to parents telling them how to help their middle school children with the issues of cyberbullying.

Blog Matters

A blog ("web log") is an online diary or commentary site that features regular entries that describe events, impressions, and viewpoints. Blogs may contain text, images, video, and often link to other websites, blogs, and online media. Most blogs allow readers to comment on the content of the post and respond to each other. As of September 2011, there were over 160 million public blogs in existence. While many blogs are maintained by individuals, some are run by journals, newspapers, and other media outlets. Remember that most blogs are not monitored for factual accuracy and often express the opinion and views of the "blogger" writing the content.

The following blog is by British comedian, writer, and actor Stephen Fry, published by the *Guardian's* column "Dork Talk" on January 12, 2008. In this entry, Fry observes that there is some sort of deep human instinct that compels us to take a wild and open territory and divide it into citadels, independent city-states, MySpaces and Facebooks. Social networking sites, rather than being the next new thing, are subject to the same compartmentalization, rules, and social constructs of more traditional communities.

Networking Through the Ages

Stephen Fry
January 12, 2008

1   **M**uch ink, electronic and atomic, has been expended on the subject of social networking and web 2.0. First, let's decide on how this last is pronounced. "Web two" won't do. "Web two point oh" is common, but I heard it as "web two dot oh."

2   These days web 2.0 refers both to user-generated content and to social networking sites. Rather than passively searching, browsing and eyeballing the billions of pages of the web, millions now contribute their videos, their journals, their music, their photos, their lives.

The Big New Thing

3   Social networking (Facebook, MySpace, Bebo, etc.) has been identified as the Big New Thing. In other words, people who watch My Family have now heard of it and are at last aware of the difference between downloading and uploading. A sure sign, perhaps, that the phenomenon is on the way out. MySpace is already as seriously uncool (and as hideously girlie, pink and spangly) as My Little Pony; Facebook is taking its advantage (openness to having applications written for it) to such extremes that it's in danger of losing the original virtues of elegance, intelligence and simplicity that established it as a classy, upmarket place in which to live a digital life in the first place.

4   I am old enough to remember Prestel and the original bulletin boards and "commercial online services" Prodigy, CompuServe and America Online. These were closed communities. You paid a subscription, dialed in and connected. You made new friends and you chatted in "rooms" designated for the purpose according to special interests, hobbies and propensities. CompuServe and AOL were shockingly late to add what was called an "internet ramp" in the 90s. This allowed those who dialled up to go beyond the confines of the provider's area and explore the strange new world of the internet unsupervised. AOL offered its members a hopeless browser and various front ends that it hoped would keep people loyal to its squeaky-clean, closed world. This lasted through the 90s as it covered the planet in CDs in an attempt to recruit subscribers. A lost cause, naturally, and the company ended up as little more than an ordinary ISP. Made millions for Steve Case on the way as AOL merged with Time Warner, but that's another story.

Opening and Closing Like a Flower

5   My point is this: what an irony! For what is this much-trumpeted social networking but an escape back into that world of the closed online service of

15 or 20 years ago? Is it part of some deep human instinct that we take an organism as open and wild and free as the internet, and wish then to divide it into citadels, into closed-border republics and independent city states? The systole and diastole of history has us opening and closing like a flower: escaping our fortresses and enclosures into the open fields, and then building hedges, villages and cities in which to imprison ourselves again before repeating the process once more. The internet seems to be following this pattern.

6   How does this help us predict the Next Big Thing? That's what everyone wants to know, if only because they want to make heaps of money from it. In 1999 Douglas Adams said: "Computer people are the last to guess what's coming next. I mean, come on, they're so astonished by the fact that the year 1999 is going to be followed by the year 2000 that it's costing us billions to prepare for it."

7   But let the rise of social networking alert you to the possibility that, even in the futuristic world of the net, the next big thing might just be a return to a made-over old thing.

RESPOND TO THE BLOG:

What do you think? Do you participate in online social networks? Do you think they represent a new way of connecting with people, or are they really just a "return to a made-over old thing"?

I Tweet, Therefore I Am
Peggy Orenstein

> Peggy Orenstein is an essayist and author of several books including *Cinderella Ate My Daughter* (2011). Her essays have appeared in such publications as the *Los Angeles Times, USA Today, Vogue, Discover, Mother Jones,* and the *New Yorker,* and she has contributed commentaries to National Public Radio's "All Things Considered." She is a contributing writer for the *New York Times* in which this essay appeared on July 30, 2010.

CONNECTING TO THE TOPIC ───────────

Most people agree that social networking sites have allowed users to connect to people in way they never could before. The social networking site, Twitter, allows people to share, almost instantly, moments in time (as long as they can summarize these moments into 140 characters or fewer). What do our online postings reveal about us and how we view ourselves? More than simply connecting us, social networking sites allow us to present a persona to the world—publicly sharing who we know, what we think, what we do, and even who we wish to be. Are social networking sites distracting us from living fully in the moment? Or are they enabling us to share our moments with our friends? Or is it a little of both?

WORDS IN CONTEXT

quintessential (1)   perfect (adv.)
tweet (1)   to post on Twitter
tacit (3)   implied but not spoken (adj.)
referendum (3)   something decided by popular vote (n.)
Seinfeldian (3)   from the sitcom *Seinfeld*, which focused on the everyday pointless and trivial matters of life (adj.)
empathy (7)   the capacity to recognize and share feelings (n.)
instigated (7)   to urge on (v.)

1   On a recent lazy Saturday morning, my daughter and I lolled on a blanket in our front yard, snacking on apricots, listening to a download of E.B. White reading "The Trumpet of the Swan." Her legs sprawled across mine; the grass tickled our ankles. It was the **quintessential** summer moment, and a year ago, I would have been fully present for it. But instead, a part of my consciousness had split off and was observing the scene from the outside: this was, I realized excitedly, the perfect opportunity for a **tweet**.

2   I came late to Twitter. I might have skipped the phenomenon altogether, but I have a book coming out this winter, and publishers, scrambling to promote 360,000-character tomes in a 140-character world, push authors to rally their "tweeps" to the cause. Leaving aside the question of whether that actually boosts sales, I felt pressure to produce. I quickly mastered the Twitterati's unnatural self-consciousness: processing my experience instantaneously, packaging life as I lived it. I learned to be "on" all the time, whether standing behind that woman at the supermarket who sneaked three extra items into the express check-out lane (you know who you are) or despairing over human rights abuses against women in Guatemala.

3   Each Twitter post seemed a **tacit referendum** on who I am, or at least who I believe myself to be. The grocery-store episode telegraphed that I was tuned in to the **Seinfeldian** absurdities of life; my concern about women's victimization, however sincere, signaled that I also have a soul. Together they suggest someone who is at once cynical and compassionate, petty yet deep. Which, in the end, I'd say, is pretty accurate.

4   Distilling my personality provided surprising focus, making me feel stripped to my essence. It forced me, for instance, to pinpoint the dominant feeling as I sat outside with my daughter listening to E.B. White. Was it my joy at being a mother? Nostalgia for my own childhood summers? The pleasures of listening to the author's quirky, underinflected voice? Each put a different spin on the occasion, of who I was within it. Yet the final decision ("Listening to E.B. White's 'Trumpet of the Swan'

with Daisy. Slow and sweet.") was not really about my own impressions: it was about how I imagined—and wanted—others to react to them. That gave me pause. How much, I began to wonder, was I shaping my Twitter feed, and how much was Twitter shaping me?

5   Back in the 1950s, the sociologist Erving Goffman famously argued that all of life is performance: we act out a role in every interaction, adapting it based on the nature of the relationship or context at hand. Twitter has extended that metaphor to include aspects of our experience that used to be considered off-set: eating pizza in bed, reading a book in the tub, thinking a thought anywhere, flossing. Effectively, it makes the greasepaint permanent, blurring the lines not only between public and private but also between the authentic and contrived self. If all the world was once a stage, it has now become a reality TV show: we mere players are not just aware of the camera; we mug for it.

6   The expansion of our digital universe—Second Life, Facebook, MySpace, Twitter—has shifted not only how we spend our time but also how we construct identity. For her coming book, "Alone Together," Sherry Turkle, a professor at M.I.T., interviewed more than 400 children and parents about their use of social media and cellphones. Among young people especially she found that the self was increasingly becoming externally manufactured rather than internally developed: a series of profiles to be sculptured and refined in response to public opinion. "On Twitter or Facebook you're trying to express something real about who you are," she explained. "But because you're also creating something for others' consumption, you find yourself imagining and playing to your audience more and more. So those moments in which you're supposed to be showing your true self become a performance. Your psychology becomes a performance." Referring to "The Lonely Crowd," the landmark description of the transformation of the American character from inner- to outer-directed, Turkle added, "Twitter is outer-directedness cubed."

7   The fun of Twitter and, I suspect, its draw for millions of people, is its infinite potential for connection, as well as its opportunity for self-expression. I enjoy those things myself. But when every thought is externalized, what becomes of insight? When we reflexively post each feeling, what becomes of reflection? When friends become fans, what happens to intimacy? The risk of the performance culture, of the packaged self, is that it erodes the very relationships it purports to create, and alienates us from our own humanity. Consider the fate of **empathy**: in an analysis of 72 studies performed on nearly 14,000 college students between 1979 and 2009, researchers at the Institute for Social Research at the University of Michigan found a drop in that trait, with the sharpest decline occurring since 2000. Social media may not have **instigated** that trend, but by encouraging self-promotion over self-awareness, they may well be accelerating it.

8   None of this makes me want to cancel my Twitter account. It's too late for that anyway: I'm already hooked. Besides, I appreciate good writing whatever the form: some "tweeple" are as deft as haiku masters at their craft. I am experimenting with the art of the well-placed "hashtag" myself

(the symbol that adds your post on a particular topic, like #ShirleySherrod, to a stream. You can also use them whimsically, as in, "I am pretending not to be afraid of the humongous spider on the bed. #lieswetellourchildren").

9   At the same time, I am trying to gain some perspective on the perpetual performer's self-consciousness. That involves trying to sort out the line between person and persona, the public and private self. It also means that the next time I find myself lying on the grass, stringing daisy chains and listening to E.B. White, I will resist the urge to trumpet about the swan. ◆

CONSIDERING THE ISSUES

1. Do you use Twitter? If so, how often do you tweet, and what do you tweet about? If not, explain why you chose not to participate in this social medium.
2. When you post something online, do you think carefully about what you are about to post and how it might sound to others? Do you consider, as Orenstein does, how people will think about you and react to your post? Or do you shoot from the hip, writing whatever comes to mind? Explain.

CRAFT AND CONTENT

1. What does Orenstein mean when she refers to the "packaged self?" How do we "package" ourselves online? What does this mean for our communication with others?
2. Evaluate Orenstein's style of writing in the first person narrative. How does this style allow her to reach her audience?

CRITICAL THINKING

1. Orenstein notes that when she tweets, she is projecting "who I am—or at least, who I believe myself to be." What does she mean? If we have to critically assess each communication for what it might say about us (and how we believe we are supposed to be), are we reflecting reality, or a constructed image? Explain.
2. In your opinion, does Twitter, and other social networking sites, interfere with our ability to truly engage in the present? Do they distract us from our "live" moments, or do they allow us to live these moments more fully and with more engagement with others? Explain.

WRITING ABOUT THE ISSUES

1. Write an essay exploring the consequences of social networking sites such as Twitter on the future of friendship and community.

2. Orenstein admits that when she tweets, she isn't necessarily conveying the truth of a moment as she lives it. She is, rather, creating tweets for how she imagines and wants people to react to what she says. What does this reveal about her tweeting? Write a short essay exploring the connection between what we tweet and the "self-portraits" we create for our friends through our words.

You Gotta Have (150) Friends
Robin Dunbar

Robin Dunbar is a professor of evolutionary anthropology at Oxford. He is best known for formulating Dunbar's number, roughly 150, a measurement of the "cognitive limit to the number of individuals with whom any one person can maintain stable relationships." He is the author of many books, including *Grooming, Gossip and the Evolution of Language* (1997) and *How Many Friends Does One Person Need?* (2010). This essay appeared in the *New York Times* on December 25, 2010.

CONNECTING TO THE TOPIC

Can social networking sites fulfill the need to connect to others in the same way face-to-face relationships do? Can they really be as meaningful as our in-person interactions with others? In this next essay, anthropologist Robin Dunbar explains that they can, to a certain extent. Social networking sites allow us to broadcast to (and thereby connecting with) a large group of people. But the number of people we can truly handle, offline and on, is capped—at about 150. Which, of course, begs the question, what's the point of having more than 150 "friends" on Facebook?

WORDS IN CONTEXT

proverbial (5)   widely referred to; famous (adj.)
voyeurs (8)   an observer of socially taboo images, especially from a secret vantage point (n.)
disparate (12)   fundamentally distinct or different in kind; entirely dissimilar (adj.)
albeit (14)   even if; although (conj.)

1   **M**ore than anything since the invention of the postal service, Facebook has revolutionized how we relate to one another. But the revolution hasn't

come in quite the way that the people behind it and other social networking sites assume.

2   These sites may have allowed us to amass thousands of "friends," but they have not yet devised a way to cut through the clunky, old-fashioned nature of relationships themselves. Our circle of actual friends remains stubbornly small, limited not by technology but by human nature. What Facebook has done, though, is provide us a way to maintain those circles in a fractured, dynamic world.

3   Social networking and other digital media have long promised to open up wonderful new vistas, all from the comfort of our own homes. The limitations of face-to-face interaction that have, until now, bound us to our small individual worlds—the handful of people we meet in our everyday lives—would be overcome.

4   The critical component in social networking is the removal of time as a constraint. In the real world, according to research by myself and others, we devote 40 percent of our limited social time each week to the five most important people we know, who represent just 3 percent of our social world and a trivially small proportion of all the people alive today. Since the time invested in a relationship determines its quality, having more than five best friends is impossible when we interact face to face, one person at a time.

5   Instant messaging and social networking claim to solve that problem by allowing us to talk to as many people as we like, all at the same time. Like the **proverbial** lighthouse blinking on the horizon, our messages fan out into the dark night to every passing ship within reach of an Internet connection. We can broadcast, literally, to the world.

6   I use the word "broadcast" because, despite Facebook's promise, that is the fundamental flaw in the logic of the social-networking revolution. The developers at Facebook overlooked one of the crucial components in the complicated business of how we create relationships: our minds.

7   Put simply, our minds are not designed to allow us to have more than a very limited number of people in our social world. The emotional and psychological investments that a close relationship requires are considerable, and the emotional capital we have available is limited.

8   Indeed, no matter what Facebook allows us to do, I have found that most of us can maintain only around 150 meaningful relationships, online and off—what has become known as Dunbar's number. Yes, you can "friend" 500, 1,000, even 5,000 people with your Facebook page, but all save the core 150 are mere **voyeurs** looking into your daily life—a fact incorporated into the new social networking site Path, which limits the number of friends you can have to 50.

9   What's more, contrary to all the hype and hope, the people in our electronic social worlds are, for most of us, the same people in our offline social worlds. In fact, the average number of friends on Facebook is 120 to 130, just short enough of Dunbar's number to allow room for grandparents and babies, people too old or too young to have acquired the digital habit.

10   This isn't to say that Facebook and its imitators aren't performing an important, even revolutionary, task—namely, to keep us in touch with our existing friends.

11   Until relatively recently, almost everyone on earth lived in small, rural, densely interconnected communities, where our 150 friends all knew one another, and everyone's 150 friends list was everyone else's.

12   But the social and economic mobility of the past century has worn away at that interconnectedness. As we move around the country and across continents, we collect **disparate** pockets of friends, so that our list of 150 consists of a half-dozen subsets of people who barely know of one another's existence, let alone interact.

13   Our ancestors knew the same people their entire lives; as we move around, though, we can lose touch with even our closest friends. Emotional closeness declines by around 15 percent a year in the absence of face-to-face contact, so that in five years someone can go from being an intimate acquaintance to the most distant outer layer of your 150 friends.

14   Facebook and other social networking sites allow us to keep up with friendships that would otherwise rapidly wither away. And they do something else that's probably more important, if much less obvious: they allow us to reintegrate our networks so that, rather than having several disconnected subsets of friends, we can rebuild, **albeit** virtually, the kind of old rural communities where everyone knew everyone else. Welcome to the electronic village. ◆

CONSIDERING THE ISSUES

1. The author's research indicates that we devote 40 percent of our social time each week to the five most important people we know. First, think about how many people you would define as the "most important people" in your life and then determine how much time per week you actually spend with those people. Does it seem to be about 40 percent of your social time? Does the author's research reflect your life style and experiences? Explain.

2. What is "Dunbar's number"? How many friends do you have on Facebook (or other social networking sites)? Does it fit with "Dunbar's number"?

CRAFT AND CONTENT

1. Consider the author's words: "The emotional and psychological investments that a close relationship requires are considerable, and the emotional capital we have available is limited." Explain what you think the author means here. Have any of your own friendships required emotional and psychological investment? Explain.

2. What point is Dunbar making in the final sentence of his article?

CRITICAL THINKING

1. Do you have any personal examples of long-distance friend-ships? Dunbar asserts, "Emotional closeness declines by around 15 percent a year in the absence of face-to-face contact." Do you find this assertion to be true according to your own examples of long-distance friendship?

2. In the article, Dunbar states that we can only maintain around 150 meaningful relationships, online and off. What does the author likely mean by the word "maintain"? What would your definition of "maintaining a friendship" be? Do you agree that it is impossible to "maintain" more than 150 friends? Explain.

WRITING ABOUT THE ISSUES

1. Watch the film *The Social Network* and do research on the be-ginnings of Facebook. Then write an essay arguing if Robin Dunbar is correct in stating: "Facebook has revolutionized how we relate to one another. But the revolution hasn't come in quite the way that the people behind it assume."

2. According to a blog post of Path's founder Dave Morin, "Path allows you to capture your life's most personal moments and share them with the 50 close friends and family in your life who matter most. Because your personal network is limited to your closest friends and family, you can always trust that you can post any moment, no matter how personal. Path is a place where you can be yourself." Analyze Morin's comments and argue which site is better for college students, Path or Facebook, and state if you think Path will take over Facebook in the future.

Faceless on Facebook
Kate Beals

Kate Beals is a writing instructor in Boston, Massachusetts.

CONNECTING TO THE TOPIC

While social networking sites help people network, connect, and meet new friends, they also project an image of their users online. For people who network or meet online, a user's profile page is their online self—the first impression they present to others. Have you ever thought about what your Facebook profile says about you? What image do you project? What do you hope people will learn about you from what you share? Do you carefully consider what messages you are conveying online about who you are and what you want people to think about you? In this next essay, a newcomer to Facebook describes how the experience forces her to question every word she puts online.

WORDS IN CONTEXT

Epicurious (2)   Website that contains recipes from *Gourmet* and *Bon Appetit* magazines and cooking information (www.epicurious.com)
fraught (7)   filled with something, charged (n.)
covet (9)   to desire or want something to the point of envy (v.)
Xanax (10)   the trade name for a drug of the benzodiazepine class used to treat moderate to severe anxiety and/or panic attacks (n.)

1   After great urging from my younger, hipper friends, I gave into pressure and registered on Facebook. As I am on the other side of 30, they told me to network on Facebook, and leave MySpace to the kids.

2   I consider myself to be quite Internet savvy. I used a blog site to connect my graduating class in order to organize my 20th high school reunion. I read Salon.com and Slate.msn weekly. I prefer email to the telephone, and even text message my twenty-something cousin fairly regularly (but I admittedly spell out all the words). I cannot imagine living without Google, Mapquest, or eBay. I regularly look up recipes on **Epicurious**, and do at least 90 percent of my merchandise shopping online. I suppose you could say that I am young enough to handle technology, but still old enough to be impressed by it and how it has changed my life.

3   So why the holdout on social networking sites? I had poked around on Facebook before, but without registering, you can't see that much. Thus, I didn't see a need. But with my friends raving about how connected it made them feel and how they used it for everything from sharing photographs to blogging, I decided to give it a whirl.

4   I had no idea what I was getting myself into.

5   After registering, I was encouraged to add my friends (or at least try to find them). Right from the get-go I started feeling anxious. What if I didn't have many friends? At least on MySpace, I hear everyone gets Tom. Without friends, would I look like a loser? What if I couldn't get enough? Suddenly, I felt like I was back in eighth grade vying for a place in the popular group (or at least in the "not total geek" group).

6   I am supposed to select and post a photo that represents "me." Do I use a real photo? Taken recently? Should I use some abstract piece of

art that conveys "me" in a more cerebral artistic way? After deciding that my photos looked more like mug shots (and bloated mug shots at that), and waffling over the copyright issues that may be connected to posting a piece of art, I decided to leave this blank (at least for now).

7   Then I needed to fill out a "profile." This is my opportunity to tell the world more about me (presumably one's favorite subject). I found the profile page a bit confusing because I presume that the people I invite to connect on Facebook would already have a handle on this sort of information. The "Personal" area I discovered, however, is less about the real you, and more about what you want people to think about you. And each field is **fraught** with peril.

8   It didn't start off very promising. My first few fields made me look like an insufferable bore. Activities: golf, reading and toddler time; Interests: sociology, culture, medicine, child psychology; Music: classical and 80s punk rock (well, maybe that was a little interesting); TV: *Top Chef*; Movies: They still make those?; Books. . . .

9   Now a book list I can handle, I thought perking up. I love books. I usually have at least three going at one time, so I thought this field would be easy. But wait, umm—should I share that the last thing I read was a trashy regency romance (left in the room of a historic hotel in New Hampshire, and gratefully pounced upon instead of the academic fare I had brought with me). Or should I instead say the *Tipping Point*, which conveyed the image of the sophisticated, well-read woman I imagine myself to be in daydreams? If I owned up to reading *Snoop*— a sociology book about what your stuff says about you, will people think I read it because I am shallow? I just read a great book by Stephen Pinker, but the book hardly projects the persona I **covet**—you know, smart, sexy and quirky in an intriguing way (as opposed to nerdy, dependable, and quirky in a weird way).

10   So I stopped at the book list. In fact, I stopped altogether. My life is too busy to think so much about myself—or worry about what I am saying about myself. I know that I probably was over-thinking this. Most people, I suspect, are able to fill out these fields without looking for a bottle of **Xanax**. But there is my page, woefully barren. No friends. No interests. The question "What are you doing right now" hangs unanswered—for an honest "looking at my empty page" would be hardly inspirational.

11   Let people make their own judgments in person. Let someone find out about that trashy book when *they* admit to a great bodice ripper. I'll jump right in and share. When cocktail conversation turns to linguistics (and it very well may at the parties I attend), I will turn to my companions and explore brain science with some like-minded nerdy types.

12   But at least for now, I've decided to let this area of the Internet remain "Kate free." ◆

CONSIDERING THE ISSUES

1. You have probably heard the expression, "Don't judge a book by its cover." The truth is, however, that most of us do make snap judgments based on what we see. How do Facebook, Twitter, and MySpace (and other social networking pages) serve as our online selves? How do they make that "first impression?"
2. The author of this essay reveals that she is nearing 40 years of age. Do you think older adults should use social networking sites? Based on what you know about such places, would older adults be comfortable networking on pages that have tradition-ally been dominated by teens and twenty-somethings? Explain.

CRAFT AND CONTENT

1. What is the author's tone in this essay? What sort of person do you think she is? How would you describe her based on the information she provides?
2. How does the author use humor to connect with her audience? As a reader, can you better relate to her points because of her humor? Do you think she really takes the issue of Facebook seri-ously, or is she just having some fun with her audience?

CRITICAL THINKING

1. Why is the author "anxious" about what she posts about herself in her Facebook profile?
2. The author is conflicted about the image she wishes to convey and the person she really is. In what ways do we grapple with such issues every day? Why is image so important? Should it be?

WRITING ABOUT THE ISSUES

1. The author argues that the "Profile" section of Facebook is "less about the real you, and more about what you want people to think about you." Does she have a point? If you have a Face-book or MySpace account, share your own perspective on this observation.
2. Go to Facebook or MySpace and visit some random pages. Based on what you see, what conclusions, if any, can you draw about the users? Would you like to get to know them better? Why or why not? What "hooks" do they use to draw you into

their page? How do they engage you? Based on your research and personal experience, write a short essay about what you think makes an effective Facebook or MySpace page.

Visual Connections

CRITICAL THINKING

1. What is happening in this cartoon? What visual clichés does it use to help convey information to the viewer?
2. How does this cartoon relate to the issue of Facebook and the shelf life of information on the Internet? Explain.
3. What is the underlying message in this cartoon? What point is it making? Is it funny? Why or why not?
4. Consider the theme of this cartoon. Is there anything you have already posted on Facebook or online that could come back to haunt you in 20 years?
5. Would knowing that your children could see what you posted years ago on the Internet in any way deter you from posting something online? Why or why not?

Virtual Friendship and the New Narcissism

Christine Rosen

Christine Rosen is a senior editor of *The New Atlantis* and resident fellow at the Ethics and Public Policy Center in Washington, D.C. She writes about the history of genetics, bioethics, the fertility industry, and the social impact of technology. She is the author of *Preaching Eugenics: Religious Leaders and the American Eugenics Movement* (2004). She is widely published in many journals and newspapers including the *New York Times Magazine*, the *Wall Street Journal*, the *Washington Post*, *New Republic*, *National Review*, the *Weekly Standard*, *Commentary*, and the *New England Journal of Medicine*. This essay, abridged for space, appeared in the Summer 2007 issue of *The New Atlantis*, where it can be viewed online in its entirety.

CONNECTING TO THE TOPIC

How are Facebook pages like a self-portrait? What do they reveal about subjects and how they view themselves? More than simply connecting us with each other, social networking sites allow us to present a persona to the world—publicly sharing who we know, what we think, what we do, and even what we own. Are social networking sites raising the bar on our level of self-absorption?

WORDS IN CONTEXT

narcissism (title)   excessive love for or admiration of oneself (n.)
ephemeral (3)   fleeting; brief (adj.)
ubiquity (10)   being everywhere at once (n.)
bureaucratize (16)   placed under formal control, usually government control (v.)
philately (16)   stamp collecting (n.)
debasement (19)   lowered in quality or value (n.)
parochial (19)   limited in scope, restricted (adj.)

1   For centuries, the rich and the powerful documented their existence and their status through painted portraits. A marker of wealth and a bid for immortality, portraits offer intriguing hints about the daily life of their subjects—professions, ambitions, attitudes, and, most importantly, social standing. Such portraits, as German art historian Hans Belting has argued, can be understood as "painted anthropology," with much to teach us, both

intentionally and unintentionally, about the culture in which they were created.

2   Self-portraits can be especially instructive. By showing the artist both as he sees his true self and as he wishes to be seen, self-portraits can at once expose and obscure, clarify and distort. They offer opportunities for both self-expression and self-seeking. They can display egotism and modesty, self-aggrandizement and self-mockery.

3   Today, our self-portraits are democratic and digital; they are crafted from pixels rather than paints. On social networking websites like MySpace and Facebook, our modern self-portraits feature background music, carefully manipulated photographs, stream-of-consciousness musings, and lists of our hobbies and friends. They are interactive, inviting viewers not merely to look at, but also to respond to, the life portrayed online. We create them to find friendship, love, and that ambiguous modern thing called connection. Like painters constantly retouching their work, we alter, update, and tweak our online self-portraits; but as digital objects they are far more **ephemeral** than oil on canvas. Vital statistics, glimpses of bare flesh, lists of favorite bands and favorite poems all clamor for our attention—and it is the timeless human desire for attention that emerges as the dominant theme of these vast virtual galleries.

4   Although social networking sites are in their infancy, we are seeing their impact culturally: in language (where to *friend* is now a verb), in politics (where it is de rigueur for presidential aspirants to catalogue their virtues on MySpace), and on college campuses (where not using Facebook can be a social handicap). But we are only beginning to come to grips with the consequences of our use of these sites: for friendship, and for our notions of privacy, authenticity, community, and identity.

Making Connections

5 The earliest online social networks were arguably the Bulletin Board Systems of the 1980s that let users post public messages, send and receive private messages, play games, and exchange software. Some of those BBSs, like The WELL (Whole Earth 'Lectronic Link) that technologist Larry Brilliant and futurist Stewart Brand started in 1985, made the transition to the World Wide Web in the mid-1990s. (Now owned by Salon.com, The WELL boasts that it was "the primordial ooze where the online community movement was born.") Other websites for community and connection emerged in the 1990s, including Classmates.com (1995), where users register by high school and year of graduation; Company of Friends, a business-oriented site founded in 1997; and Epinions, founded in 1999 to allow users to give their opinions about various consumer products.

6   A new generation of social networking websites appeared in 2002 with the launch of Friendster, whose founder, Jonathan Abrams,

admitted that his main motivation for creating the site was to meet attractive women. Unlike previous online communities, which brought together anonymous strangers with shared interests, Friendster uses a model of social networking known as the "Circle of Friends" (developed by British computer scientist Jonathan Bishop), in which users invite friends and acquaintances—that is, people they already know and like—to join their network.

7   Friendster was an immediate success, with millions of registered users by mid-2003. But technological glitches and poor management at the company allowed a new social networking site, MySpace, launched in 2003, quickly to surpass it. Originally started by musicians, MySpace has become a major venue for sharing music as well as videos and photos. It is now the behemoth of online social networking, with over 100 million registered users. Connection has become big business: In 2005, Rupert Murdoch's News Corporation bought MySpace for $580 million.

8   Besides MySpace and Friendster, the best-known social networking site is Facebook, launched in 2004. Originally restricted to college students, Facebook—which takes its name from the small photo albums that colleges once gave to incoming freshmen and faculty to help them cope with meeting so many new people—soon extended membership to high schoolers and is now open to anyone. Still, it is most popular among college students and recent college graduates, many of whom use the site as their primary method of communicating with one another. Millions of college students check their Facebook pages several times every day and spend hours sending and receiving messages, making appointments, getting updates on their friends' activities, and learning about people they might recently have met or heard about.

9   There are dozens of other social networking sites, including Orkut, Bebo, and Yahoo 360°. Microsoft recently announced its own plans for a social networking site called Wallop; the company boasts that the site will offer "an entirely new way for consumers to express their individuality online." (It is noteworthy that Microsoft refers to social networkers as "consumers" rather than merely "users" or, say, "people.") Niche social networking sites are also flourishing: there are sites offering forums and fellowship for photographers, music lovers, and sports fans. There are professional networking sites, such as LinkedIn, that keep people connected with present and former colleagues and other business acquaintances.

10   Despite the increasingly diverse range of social networking sites, the most popular sites share certain features. On MySpace and Facebook, for example, the process of setting up one's online identity is relatively simple: Provide your name, address, e-mail address, and a few other pieces of information and you're up and running and ready to create your online persona. MySpace includes a section, "About Me," where you can post your name, age, where you live, and other personal details such as your

zodiac sign, religion, sexual orientation, and relationship status. There is also a "Who I'd Like to Meet" section, which on most MySpace profiles is filled with images of celebrities. Users can also list their favorite music, movies, and television shows, as well as their personal heroes; MySpace users can also blog on their pages. A user "friends" people—that is, invites them by e-mail to appear on the user's "Friend Space," where they are listed, linked, and ranked. Below the Friends space is a Comments section where friends can post notes. MySpace allows users to personalize their pages by uploading images and music and videos; indeed, one of the defining features of most MySpace pages is the **ubiquity** of visual and audio clutter. With silly, hyper flashing graphics in neon colors and clip-art style images of kittens and cartoons, MySpace pages often resemble an overdecorated high school yearbook.

11   By contrast, Facebook limits what its users can do to their profiles. Besides general personal information, Facebook users have a "Wall" where people can leave them brief notes, as well as a Messages feature that functions like an in-house Facebook e-mail account. You list your friends on Facebook as well, but in general, unlike MySpace friends, which are often complete strangers (or spammers) Facebook friends tend to be part of one's offline social circle. (This might change, however, now that Facebook has opened its site to anyone rather than restricting it to college and high school students.) Facebook (and MySpace) allow users to form groups based on mutual interests. Facebook users can also send "pokes" to friends; these little digital nudges are meant to let someone know you are thinking about him or her. But they can also be interpreted as not-so-subtle come-ons; one Facebook group with over 200,000 members is called "Enough with the Poking, Let's Just Have Sex."

Won't You Be My Digital Neighbor?

12   According to a survey recently conducted by the Pew Internet and American Life Project, more than half of all Americans between the ages of twelve and seventeen use some online social networking site. Indeed, media coverage of social networking sites usually describes them as vast teenage playgrounds—or wastelands, depending on one's perspective. Central to this narrative is a nearly unbridgeable generational divide, with tech-savvy youngsters redefining friendship while their doddering elders look on with bafflement and increasing anxiety. This seems anecdotally correct; I can't count how many times I have mentioned social networking websites to someone over the age of forty and received the reply, "Oh yes, I've heard about that MyFace! All the kids are doing that these days. Very interesting!"

13   Numerous articles have chronicled adults' attempts to navigate the world of social networking, such as the recent *New York Times* essay in

which columnist Michelle Slatalla described the incredible embarrassment she caused her teenage daughter when she joined Facebook: "everyone in the whole world thinks its super creepy when adults have facebooks," her daughter instant-messaged her. "unfriend paige right now. im serious. . . . i will be soo mad if you dont unfriend paige right now. actually." In fact, social networking sites are not only for the young. More than half of the visitors to MySpace claim to be over the age of 35. And now that the first generation of college Facebook users have graduated, and the site is open to all, more than half of Facebook users are no longer students. What's more, the proliferation of niche social networking sites, including those aimed at adults, suggests that it is not only teenagers who will nurture relationships in virtual space for the foreseeable future.

The New Taxonomy of Friendship

14　There is a Spanish proverb that warns, "Life without a friend is death without a witness." In the world of online social networking, the warning might be simpler: "Life without hundreds of online 'friends' is virtual death." On these sites, friendship is the stated raison d'être. "A place for friends," is the slogan of MySpace. Facebook is a "social utility that connects people with friends." Orkut describes itself as "an online community that connects people through a network of trusted friends." Friendster's name speaks for itself.

15　But "friendship" in these virtual spaces is thoroughly different from real-world friendship. In its traditional sense, friendship is a relationship which, broadly speaking, involves the sharing of mutual interests, reciprocity, trust, and the revelation of intimate details over time and within specific social (and cultural) contexts. Because friendship depends on mutual revelations that are concealed from the rest of the world, it can only flourish within the boundaries of privacy; the idea of public friendship is an oxymoron.

16　The hypertext link called "friendship" on social networking sites is very different: public, fluid, and promiscuous, yet oddly **bureaucratized**. Friendship on these sites focuses a great deal on collecting, managing, and ranking the people you know. Everything about MySpace, for example, is designed to encourage users to gather as many friends as possible, as though friendship were **philately**. If you are so unfortunate as to have but one MySpace friend, for example, your page reads: "You have 1 friends," along with a stretch of sad empty space where dozens of thumbnail photos of your acquaintances should appear.

17　The structure of social networking sites also encourages the bureaucratization of friendship. Each site has its own terminology, but among the words that users employ most often is "managing." The Pew survey mentioned earlier found that "teens say social networking sites help them manage their friendships." There is something Orwellian about the management-speak on social networking sites: "Change My Top Friends," "View All of My Friends" and, for those times when our inner Stalins sense the need for a virtual purge, "Edit Friends." With a few mouse clicks one can elevate or downgrade (or entirely eliminate) a relationship.

18   To be sure, we all rank our friends, albeit in unspoken and intuitive ways. One friend might be a good companion for outings to movies or concerts; another might be someone with whom you socialize in professional settings; another might be the kind of person for whom you would drop everything if he needed help. But social networking sites allow us to rank our friends publicly. And not only can we publicize our own preferences in people, but we can also peruse the favorites among our other acquaintances. We can learn all about the friends of our friends—often without having ever met them in person.

Status-Seekers

19   Of course, it would be foolish to suggest that people are incapable of making distinctions between social networking "friends" and friends they see in the flesh. The use of the word "friend" on social networking sites is a dilution and a **debasement**, and surely no one with hundreds of MySpace or Facebook "friends" is so confused as to believe those are all real friendships. The impulse to collect as many "friends" as possible on a MySpace page is not an expression of the human need for companionship, but of a different need no less profound and pressing: the need for status. Unlike the painted portraits that members of the middle class in a bygone era would commission to signal their elite status once they rose in society, social networking websites allow us to create status—not merely to commemorate the achievement of it. There is a reason that most of the MySpace profiles of famous people are fakes, often created by fans: Celebrities don't need legions of MySpace friends to prove their importance. It's the rest of the population, seeking a form of **parochial** celebrity, that does.

20   But status-seeking has an ever-present partner: anxiety. Unlike a portrait, which, once finished and framed, hung tamely on the wall signaling one's status, maintaining status on MySpace or Facebook requires constant vigilance. As one 24-year-old wrote in a *New York Times* essay, "I am obsessed with testimonials and solicit them incessantly. They are the ultimate social currency, public declarations of the intimacy status of a relationship. . . . Every profile is a carefully planned media campaign."

21   The sites themselves were designed to encourage this. Describing the work of B.J. Fogg of Stanford University, who studies "persuasion strategies" used by social networking sites to increase participation, *The New Scientist* noted, "The secret is to tie the acquisition of friends, compliments and status—spoils that humans will work hard for—to activities

that enhance the site." As Fogg told the magazine, "You offer someone a context for gaining status, and they are going to work for that status." Network theorist Albert-László Barabási notes that online connection follows the rule of "preferential attachment"—that is, "when choosing between two pages, one with twice as many links as the other, about twice as many people link to the more connected page." As a result, "while our individual choices are highly unpredictable, as a group we follow strict patterns." Our lemming-like pursuit of online status via the collection of hundreds of "friends" clearly follows this rule.

22   What, in the end, does this pursuit of virtual status mean for community and friendship? Writing in the 1980s in *Habits of the Heart,* sociologist Robert Bellah and his colleagues documented the movement away from close-knit, traditional communities, to "lifestyle enclaves" which were defined largely by "leisure and consumption." Perhaps today we have moved beyond lifestyle enclaves and into "personality enclaves" or "identity enclaves"—discrete virtual places in which we can be different (and sometimes contradictory) people, with different groups of like-minded, though ever-shifting, friends.

Beyond Networking

23 This past spring, Len Harmon, the director of the Fischer Policy and Cultural Institute at Nichols College in Dudley, Massachusetts, offered a new course about social networking. Nichols is a small school whose students come largely from Connecticut and Massachusetts; many of them are the first members of their families to attend college. "I noticed a lot of issues involved with social networking sites," Harmon told me when I asked him why he created the class. How have these sites been useful to Nichols students? "It has relieved some of the stress of transitions for them," he said. "When abrupt departures occur—their family moves or they have to leave friends behind—they can cope by keeping in touch more easily."

24   So perhaps we should praise social networking websites for streamlining friendship the way e-mail streamlined correspondence. In the nineteenth century, Emerson observed that "friendship requires more time than poor busy men can usually command." Now, technology has given us the freedom to tap into our network of friends when it is convenient for us. "It's a way of maintaining a friendship without having to make any effort whatsoever," as a recent graduate of Harvard explained to *The New Yorker.* And that ease admittedly makes it possible to stay in contact with a wider circle of offline acquaintances than might have been possible in the era before Facebook. Friends you haven't heard from in years, old buddies from elementary school, people you might have (should have?) fallen out of touch with—it is now easier than ever to reconnect to those people.

25 But what kind of connections are these? In his excellent book *Friendship: An Exposé,* Joseph Epstein praises the telephone and e-mail as technologies that have greatly facilitated friendship. He writes, "Proust once said he didn't much care for the analogy of a book to a friend. He thought a book was better than a friend, because you could shut it—and be shut of it—when you wished, which one can't always do with a friend." With e-mail and caller ID, Epstein enthuses, you can. But social networking sites (which Epstein says "speak to the vast loneliness in the world") have a different effect: they discourage "being shut of" people. On the contrary, they encourage users to check in frequently, "poke" friends, and post comments on others' pages. They favor interaction of greater quantity but less quality.

26 This constant connectivity concerns Len Harmon. "There is a sense of, 'if I'm not online or constantly texting or posting, then I'm missing something,'" he said of his students. "This is where I find the generational impact the greatest—not the use of the technology, but the overuse of the technology." It is unclear how the regular use of these sites will affect behavior over the long run—especially the behavior of children and young adults who are growing up with these tools. Almost no research has explored how virtual socializing affects children's development. What does a child weaned on Club Penguin learn about social interaction? How is an adolescent who spends her evenings managing her MySpace page different from a teenager who spends her night gossiping on the telephone to friends? Given that "people want to live their lives online," as the founder of one social networking site recently told *Fast Company* magazine, and they are beginning to do so at ever-younger ages, these questions are worth exploring.

27 The few studies that have emerged do not inspire confidence. Researcher Rob Nyland at Brigham Young University recently surveyed 184 users of social networking sites and found that heavy users "feel less socially involved with the community around them." He also found that "as individuals use social networking more for entertainment, their level of social involvement decreases." Another recent study conducted by communications professor Qingwen Dong and colleagues at the University of the Pacific found that "those who engaged in romantic communication over MySpace tend to have low levels of both emotional intelligence and self-esteem."

28 The implications of the narcissistic and exhibitionistic tendencies of social networkers also cry out for further consideration. There are opportunity costs when we spend so much time carefully grooming ourselves online. Given how much time we already devote to entertaining ourselves with technology, it is at least worth asking if the time we spend on social networking sites is well spent. In investing so much energy into improving how we present ourselves online, are we missing chances to genuinely improve ourselves?

29   We should also take note of the trend toward giving up face-to-face for virtual contact—and, in some cases, a preference for the latter. Today, many of our cultural, social, and political interactions take place through eminently convenient technological surrogates—why go to the bank if you can use the ATM? Why browse in a bookstore when you can simply peruse the personalized selections Amazon.com has made for you? In the same vein, social networking sites are often convenient surrogates for offline friendship and community. In this context it is worth considering an observation that Stanley Milgram made in 1974, regarding his experiments with obedience: "The social psychology of this century reveals a major lesson," he wrote. "Often it is not so much the kind of person a man is as the kind of situation in which he finds himself that determines how he will act." To an increasing degree, we find and form our friendships and communities in the virtual world as well as the real world. These virtual networks greatly expand our opportunities to meet others, but they might also result in our valuing less the capacity for genuine connection. As the young woman writing in the *Times* admitted, "I consistently trade actual human contact for the more reliable high of smiles on MySpace, winks on Match.com, and pokes on Facebook." That she finds these online relationships more reliable is telling: it shows a desire to avoid the vulnerability and uncertainty that true friendship entails. Real intimacy requires risk—the risk of disapproval, of heartache, of being thought a fool. Social networking websites may make relationships more reliable, but whether those relationships can be humanly satisfying remains to be seen. ◆

CONSIDERING THE ISSUES

1. This article makes the bold statement: "public friendship is an oxymoron." From your point of view, discuss the meaning of friendship and decide whether social networking sites are using the term "friend" properly.
2. Rosen compares online networking pages to "self-portraits." Explore this concept in more depth. In what ways is this true? If you have a personal page, discuss what that page says about you and in what ways it is indeed a "self-portrait." How are painted portraits and websites similar, and how are they different?

CRAFT AND CONTENT

1. What does Rosen mean when she uses the term "Orwellian" and the phrase "our inner Stalins" when referring to social networking sites? To what/whom is she referring, and how do these references connect to her point?

2. What does Rosen think of online networking sites? Identify areas in her essay in which she reveals her viewpoint.

CRITICAL THINKING

1. Rosen comments in an aside, "It is noteworthy that Microsoft refers to social networkers as 'consumers' rather than merely 'users' or, say, 'people.'" Why do you think Microsoft uses the term "consumers"? Do you see this as negative or positive? Explain.
2. The author comments, "tech-savvy youngsters [are] redefining friendship while their doddering elders look on with bafflement and increasing anxiety." Do you find this to be true? How do your older family members view social networking sites? Do any of them have MySpace or Facebook pages? Why or why not?

WRITING ABOUT THE ISSUES

1. Write an essay exploring the consequences of social networking sites on the future of friendship and community.
2. This article traces the evolution of social networking sites. Outline this evolution showing how these sites have evolved from "the primordial ooze" of the 1980s to the newest site being planned by Microsoft.

TOPICAL CONNECTIONS

GROUP PROJECTS

1. Track all of your online correspondence—received and sent— for a period of one week. This should include e-mail, IM, text messaging, and postings on social networking sites including Facebook and Twitter. Develop categories for the communication (social, family, work, school, junk, etc.) and chart how many of each you receive and send in each category. Keep track of how much time you spend online. Discuss your personal results with the group. Discuss as a group how the Internet both enhances and complicates life, and whether it is indeed changing your personal relationships for better or for worse.
2. Several of the writers in this chapter are critical of social networking sites, noting that they promote self-centeredness, reduce our ability to cope with emotions, and cheapen what it means to be "a friend." Interview at least 10 people of different age groups about how they use online communication and their

views of social networking sites. Create simple questions, but make them broad enough to allow for the expression of detailed viewpoints and opinions. Discuss the interviews as a group, and write a short essay evaluating the role of social networking in the lives of people today. Include any differences or similarities you noticed between age groups, professions, and/or social backgrounds. Based on your surveys, can you predict the role social networking will have in our lives in the next decade?

WEB PROJECTS

1. Is there a connection between how we communicate and relate to others online and how we develop our own sense of identity? How others perceive us? Print the profiles of at least 10 people you know (you may need to ask for permission if you are not part of a social network) and compare the profiles they present to the people you know in "real life." Alternatively, you could ask an acquaintance to share five profiles of people you don't know for analysis.

2. Research the pages of at least four different social networking sites (many are named in this chapter). Describe how they are similar and how they are different. Do they attract different groups? Are some "cooler" than others? What groups do they attract and how do they promote a sense of belonging and community? Explain.

FOR FURTHER INQUIRY

1. What might the erosion of the real and virtual boundaries that social networking promotes eventually do to the way we communicate with each other? Will the way people define themselves now be different in 20 years as a result of blending online and offline relationships? Explain.

2. A popular television commercial for an Internet employment agency features a man writing an insulting letter to his boss only to have a toy fall off his monitor and hit the "enter" key, sending his message. Have you ever had a mishap with online communication, or found yourself sending a message that you shouldn't have simply because you hit the "enter" key in the heat of the moment? Describe your experience. Did it change your use of online communication?

2 | Does Personal Privacy Have Limits?

"Do what you want, it's a free country!" is an expression that we often hear and would like to believe. Most Americans take personal freedom for granted, and are startled when our rights seem to be threatened. Over the last decade, personal privacy rights have become a subject of concern and controversy. The threat of terrorism, the near universal use of the Internet, and improved technology have raised new questions connected to personal privacy. Should we have national identification cards as a measure to thwart terrorism? Do Internet companies have the right to track our movements online? Do surveillance cameras in stores, parking lots, and public spaces deter criminal activity? Are we giving too much away voluntarily when we post information on blogs and social networking pages such Facebook and Twitter? What about Foursquare, which allows our phones to automatically broadcast our whereabouts to groups of people? Or is less privacy simply the price we pay for more convenience, an enhanced social life, and greater safety?

Most Americans assume that their right to privacy is protected by the Fourth Amendment of the Constitution, which ensures "the right of the people to be secure in their persons, houses, papers, and effects, against unreasonable searches and seizures." But does the Fourth Amendment actually protect our right to privacy in the way that we think? How do we define an "unreasonable" search? And does the Fourth Amendment protect us from things such as Internet cookies, or public surveillance cameras? Police, if they believe there is probable cause, may enter our homes or even tap our phones. Airport security guards may search our bags and our persons. Is privacy something we must sacrifice in order to participate in today's world? This unit takes a closer look at some of the multiple privacy issues Americans face today.

CRITICAL THINKING

1. What is happening in this cartoon? Who are the people in the cartoon, and what are the people doing? What is the meaning of all the objects around them?
2. What is your initial reaction to this cartoon? What do you need to know about the subject to "get" the joke?
3. What is the cartoonist trying to say about the subject matter? What do you need to know in order to understand the point of this cartoon? Explain.

is Slane *http://privacycartoonportfolio.blogspot.com/*

Privacy Is Overrated
David Plotz

David Plotz is a writer and deputy editor for *Slate*. His articles have appeared in many publications, including *Harper's Magazine*, the *New York Times Magazine*, *Rolling Stone,* and the *New Republic*. He is a recipient of the National Press Club's Sandy Hume Award for Political Journalism. This essay first appeared in *GQ* magazine in 2003.

CONNECTING TO THE TOPIC

What privacy rights do we surrender in the name of safety, convenience, and even health? Is this sacrifice a fair exchange? For example, did you know that every time you log on to the Internet, information engines can put "cookies" on your computer to track your movements? When you visit their site again, these cookies are able to remember who you are as well as your preferences. Cookies may also gather information about you as a consumer. Is our privacy the price we pay for the convenience of the Internet? And are the rights that we give up a small price to pay when we consider the benefits we get in exchange?

WORDS IN CONTEXT

cookies (7)   a collection of information stored on an Internet user's computer that identifies visitors of particular websites (n.)

paranoia (11)   extreme, irrational distrust of others (n.)

pundits (11)   critics (n.)

Orwellian (11)   relating to the works of author George Orwell, especially the satirical novel *1984*, which depicts a futuristic totalitarian state (adj.)

Big Brother (13)   a character in George Orwell's novel *1984*, who is an omnipresent figure representing an authoritarian government's total control over individual lives. The figure symbolizes a political or social situation in which one's actions are closely monitored by an authoritarian figure or group (n.).

crusade (14)   a campaign or concerted movement for a cause (n.)

hypocrisy (14)   falseness (n.)

nostalgia (14)   a longing for things, persons, or situations of the past (n.)

entrepreneurship (21)   the act of organizing, operating, and assuming the risk for a business venture (n.)

titanic (21)   enormous (adj.)

stigmatized (25)   marked as disgraceful (adj.)

egocentric (27)   holding the view that oneself is the center, object, and norm of all experience (adj.)
fallacy (27)   incorrect reasoning or beliefs (n.)
monolithic (28)   massive (adj.)
encryption (30)   the process of making information indecipherable by using a secret code to prevent access by unauthorized parties (n.)

1   Let's start by invading my privacy. I own a three-bedroom house on Cortland Place in Washington D.C. I am married to Hanna Rosin. We have a two-year-old child. I drive a 2001 Volkswagen Passat.

2   I have no criminal record. I have never been party to a lawsuit. I have no tax liens against me. I have never declared bankruptcy (unlike 2 of the 11 other David Plotzes in the United States). I have no ties to organized crime, though I do hold stock options in Microsoft.

3   The James Mintz group, a leading corporate investigation firm head-quartered in New York City, learned all this about me in a few hours with a computer, an Internet connection and a single phone call—without even bending the law.

4   If you spent a bit more time, you would discover my Social Security number and how much I paid for the house. You would find out that I bank at Bank of America. You could have my listed home telephone number in two mouse clicks and my unlisted cell phone number if you paid the right data broker.

5   Corporations, meanwhile, are recording my every move. I don't watch what I eat, but Safeway does, thanks to my club card. Telecoms can pinpoint where I am when I make my cell phone calls. Clothing stores analyze my purchases in detail, recording everything from the expansion of my waist (up to 35 from 32) to my recent infatuation with three-button suits.

6   The credit reporting agencies know every time I have made a late payment to my Citibank MasterCard (number 6577 . . . I'm not that stu-pid) and every time I have applied for credit. This is all going on my per-manent record.

7   Surveillance cameras are watching me in malls and sometimes on public streets. Even my own computer is spying on me. A scan of my hard drive turns up 141 **cookies**, deposited by companies that track me around the Web. I recently surfed a porn site (just because a high school friend runs it, I swear). The cookies may know about it. My employer probably does too. After all, my employment contract permits my boss to track all my on-the-job Web surfing, and read all my work e-mail too.

8   If my company isn't watching, perhaps the FBI is: Its Carnivore pro-gram rafts through vast rivers of e-mail flow in search of criminal activity.

9   They—a *they* that includes the feds, a thousand corporations, a million telemarketers, my employer, my enemies and maybe even my friends—know all this about me, and more. And unless you are a techno-phobe hermit who pays for everything in cash, they know all this about you too.

10   To which I say, "Hallelujah!"

11   I'm in the minority. Privacy **paranoia** has become a national obses-sion. **Pundits**, politicians and privacy activists have been shouting about the latest government intrusion on privacy. The Defense Department's office of Total Information Awareness plans to collect massive quantities of information about all Americans—everything from what you buy to where you travel—in gigantic databases, and then sift through the infor-mation for clues about terrorism. Total Information Awareness has been denounced as **Orwellian**, and there are efforts to stop the program.

12   You could fill a library with privacy-alarmism books (*The End of Privacy; Privacy: How to Protect What's Left of It*). Congress and the state legislatures are awash in proposals to protect privacy. Horror sto-ries fuel the fire of anxiety. The sailor the Navy tried to book out after he used the word *gay* in a supposedly confidential AOL profile. The stalker who bought his target's address from a Web information broker, tracked her down, and murdered her. The sale of Social Security numbers by LexisNexis.

13   You can more or less distill the essence of the privacy-rights move-ment to this idea: **Big Brother** and Big Business observe us too often, without our consent. The most intimate details of our lives are being sold and used secretly to make judgments about us, and we have no control over it.

14   It sounds appalling. But in fact, the privacy **crusade** is built on a foundation of **hypocrisy**, paranoia, economic know-nothingism and bogus **nostalgia**.

15   The first flaw of privacy: People care a great deal about their own, but not at all about anyone else's. We figure, why should anyone get to review my real-estate records or get to read my divorce proceedings? My life is my own business.

16   But I bet you want to know if your baby-sitter has ever been convicted of child abuse, if your business partner has a history of bankruptcy, if your boyfriend is still married. When your husband flees the state to duck child support payments, wouldn't you use his Social Security number, driving records, real estate filings and whatever else you could get your hands on to track him down?

17   You don't want the Total Information Awareness office to know what you bought at the hardware store or where you take vacations. But if your neighbor is stockpiling fertilizer and likes to holiday in Iraq, don't you want the government to notice? If government had been using even

basic data-mining techniques before September 11, at least 11 of the hijackers might have been stopped, according to a report by the Markel Foundation. Wouldn't that be worth letting the feds know you bought an Xbox last month?

18   Hysteria is growing that companies are shadowing us constantly. They are. But here, too, privacy is a silly value, both because "protecting" it is enormously costly and because it's not really being violated.

19   Ignorant companies are bankrupt companies. A recent study found that restricting marketing data would raise catalog clothing prices up to 11 percent, costing shoppers $1 billion per year. By buying address lists and consumer profiles, Victoria's Secret knows to send a catalog to my house, and International Male knows not to bother. Their marketing costs plummet. We get less junk mail, lower prices, and catalogs for clothing we might buy.

20   Your father probably shopped with a clothier who knew he wore a 44 long suit and preferred a faint pinstripe. Such friendships are extinct, murdered by megastores and armchair shopping. But today, when I log on to Amazon.com, I am pitched another book about privacy, because Amazon has learned that I am the kind of guy who buys books on privacy. They are saving me time (which is money) by delivering what I like.

21   Information sharing is also an engine of **entrepreneurship**. Thanks to cheap mailing lists, upstarts can challenge **titanic** businesses, lowering prices and bringing clever products to market.

22   Losing privacy has made it much cheaper to use a credit card or buy a house. Credit card and mortgage companies collect and share information about who pays, who doesn't, etc. Because they have an idea who will default, they offer significantly lower rates to people with good records and make credit much more available to poorer customers.

23   It's true that identity theft has become easier. On the other hand, credit card fraud—a much more common crime—is harder. Companies often catch a thief before a customer even notices her card is missing. (Their observant computers notice that her buying habits have suddenly changed.)

24   Similarly, surveillance cameras reduce shoplifting and stop ATM robberies, while cameras in police cars reduce incidents of police brutality. Lack of privacy actually tends to fight crime, not cause it.

25   There is one notable exception to the argument for transparency, however. If medical records are unsealed, especially to employers, people may avoid treatment, fearing they will be **stigmatized** or fired for their health problems.

26   Philosophically, many people don't like the idea that a soulless corporation records that they buy sexy underwear, subscribe to *Penthouse* and collect heavy metal CDs. Friends were freaked out to receive ads for infant formula soon after they gave birth. How did the company know? Is the hospital selling your baby already?

27   But this worry is an example of the **egocentric fallacy**: the belief that because people know something about you, they care. One wonderful, terrible thing about modern capitalism is that companies don't care. You are not a person. You are a wallet.

28   Privacy advocates like to say, "It didn't used to be this way." They hark back to a time—it generally sounds like 19th-century rural America—when stores didn't record your every purchase and doctors didn't report your ailments to a **monolithic** insurance company. You could abandon a bad life in one state, reinvent yourself 50 miles away, and no one needed to know. Nothing went down on your permanent record, because there was no permanent record. This nostalgia imagines a past that never existed. Small town America never guarded anyone's privacy. In small towns, as anyone who lives in one can attest, people can be nosy and punish nonconformity viciously.

29   The right to privacy is not mentioned in the Constitution, and was not even conceived until 1890. Censuses in the 18th and 19th centuries demanded answers to intrusive questions, such as compelling Americans to reveal any history of insanity in the family.

30   Nostalgists fail to recognize that technology is creating a golden age from what they actually care about: real privacy. This is nothing that Amazon.com cares about. Nothing that Total Information Awareness can track down. Nothing that needs to be protected by **encryption**.

31   The opposite of privacy is not invasion of privacy: it is openness. Real privacy is what allows us to share hopes, dreams, fantasies, fears, and makes us feel we can safely expose all our faults and quirks and still be loved. Privacy is the space between us and our dearest—where everything is known and does not matter.

32   There has never been a better time for real privacy. The Internet allows people who have peculiar interests, social awkwardness or debilitating health problems to create communities that never could have existed before. Online, they can find other folks who want to re-enact the Battle of Bull Run or sunbathe nude or whatever your bag is, baby.

33   By surrendering some privacy—that is, by revealing our humanity with all its peculiarity in chat rooms or on e-mail or in newsgroups—we gain a much greater privacy: an intimacy with others, a sense of belonging. To be less private sometimes is to have more privacy. To be less private is to be more ourselves. ◆

CONSIDERING THE ISSUES

1. How much do you value your privacy? Do you ever think about this right? Plotz notes that while we tend to value our own privacy, we do not value the privacy of others. What

do you feel others have a right to know about you? What do you think you have a right to know about other people? Explain.

2. Do you think we have more or less privacy than we did 50 years ago? Discuss with an older adult their perception of privacy in America now and 50 years ago. What factors, such as where we live and the lifestyle we lead, contribute to the level of privacy we have? Explain.

CRAFT AND CONTENT

1. Why does Plotz begin his essay by revealing his personal information? How does it help support the points he outlines in his essay? As a reader, how did you react to his divulging of so much personal information? Explain.

2. Identify specific areas where Plotz uses humor in his essay. Does his use of humor help him connect with his audience, or does it trivialize a serious subject? Explain.

CRITICAL THINKING

1. According to Plotz, why is our concern over privacy rights an "egocentric fallacy"? Do you agree with his argument? Why or why not?

2. What level of privacy do the "nostalgists" believe we enjoyed in the past? Why does Plotz say this memory is incorrect? Explain.

WRITING ABOUT THE ISSUES

1. At the end of his essay, Plotz states, "the opposite of privacy is not invasion of privacy: It is openness." Develop your own definition of privacy. How does it compare to Plotz's viewpoint?

2. Plotz begins his article by revealing information that is easily accessible about him through the Internet. Conduct an Internet search of yourself or a parent and see how much information you can locate. You may try online phone books, a Google search, and other information systems such as www.whowhere.com. After conducting your search, write your own narrative about what someone could find about you and how you feel about the availability of personal information online.

Invading Our Own Privacy
David Schimke

David Schimke is editor-in-chief of *Utne Reader*. His articles and essays have appeared in many newspapers and journals. His essay, "Rack 'Em Up," a profile of a young pool hustler, was recognized in *The Best American Sports Writing* (1999). This essay appeared in the May–June 2007 issue of *Utne Reader*.

CONNECTING TO THE TOPIC

Tell-all blogs, party photos on Twitter and Facebook, cookies and trackers online, GPS systems on our phones that can tell people where we are at any given moment—are we giving away too much information? As members of the digital generation come of age, they bring with them new questions regarding online privacy. Employers are using information gathered online to make hiring decisions. Online tracking devices tell marketing companies what we like to buy, where we like to eat, and with whom we like to socialize—all with the goal of steering the right advertising our way. And most online users give away information without thinking very much about it, which raises this question: are we giving our privacy away?

WORDS IN CONTEXT

grizzled (1)   gray-haired, old (adj.)
caricature (1)   an exaggerated picture or image of a person (n.)
blithely (3)   exceedingly casual and carefree (adv.)
paradigm (4)   a new model (n.)
proclivities (5)   practices or inclinations (n.)
paradoxically (6)   seemingly contradictory (adv.)

1   It's a good guess that the last thing the newly hired editor of an alternative newspaper would want a **grizzled** group of journalists to know is that the person he'd most like to meet is Howard Stern. Yet hours after Kevin Hoffman was tapped to take the helm at *City Pages*, staffers at the Minneapolis weekly, who had yet to meet the 30-year-old in person, were reading all about their new leader's love of Stern, ultimate fighting, and *The Real World* on his MySpace page and sketching a less than favorable **caricature**.

2   That same week in late January, Jessica Blinkerd, a 22-year-old California woman charged with drunken driving and vehicular manslaughter, received a tougher-than-expected sentence, 64 months in prison. Despite having professed deep remorse in court, Blinkerd had posted pictures at MySpace of herself out on the town after the accident, drinking with friends and sporting a shirt advertising a brand of tequila. "Why would probation get your attention?" the judge asked.

3   Both cases, one comical, the other life-altering, illustrate a commercially driven cultural trend whose consequences may not be known until well after debates over the merits of wiretapping, the Patriot Act, and digital spying are resolved in Congress. People of all ages, but especially those between 18 and 34, have become so comfortable with online commerce, instant correspondence, and daily confession that personal privacy is being redefined and, some argue, **blithely** forfeited.

4   "Young people have already embraced the frenzied commercial environment of the digital marketplace," says Jeff Chester, founder and executive director of the Center for Digital Democracy. "The prevailing **paradigm** is a seamless integration of content, communication, data collection, and targeted marketing."

5   The technological assault on our anonymity is gaining speed: Surveillance cameras and now cell phones track physical movement; computer "cookies" transmit buying habits, political affiliations, and sexual **proclivities**. And now, according to *Science News* (Jan. 13, 2007), because computer users have "characteristic patterns of how they time their keystrokes [and] browse websites," researchers are learning how to use "typeprints, clickprints, and writeprints, respectively, as digital forms of fingerprints."

6   *New York* magazine (Feb. 12, 2007) points out that people of all ages are susceptible to these intrusive technologies, but it's twentysomethings who are, **paradoxically**, the most savvy about how they can be watched and the least likely to self-censor. "In essence, every young person in America has become, in the literal sense, a public figure," writes Emily Nussbaum, who posits that online differences represent the first true generation gap in nearly 50 years. "And so they have adopted the skills that celebrities learn in order not to go crazy: enjoying the attention instead of fighting it."

7   It's tempting to write off those darn kids as narcissistic or obsessed with fame, as Lakshmi Chaudhry does in the *Nation* (Jan. 29, 2007). After all, as she points out, "Celebrity has become a commodity in itself, detached from and more valuable than wealth or achievement." What's received little attention, though, is the ways corporations are stacking the digital deck.

8   "Young people are now heavily engaged in identity exploration and development well into their 20s, and the Internet has become their

primary tool," says Kathryn Montgomery, professor of communications at American University and author of *Generation Digital* (MIT Press, 2007). "Companies build brands by purposely cultivating this process, creating spaces where they're encouraging people to pour their hearts out. It's like a diary—but there's no key."

9   In February of 2007, ClickZ.com reported that Fox Interactive Media, a division of Rupert Murdoch's News Corp., which owns MySpace, had hired a high-tech ad firm to mine user profiles, blog posts, and bulletins to "allow for highly refined audience segmentation and contextual microtargeting . . . which might put it in more direct competition with the likes of Yahoo, AOL, and MSN."

10   "I don't think kids understand the long-term consequences of our surveillance culture. I'm not sure any of us do," Montgomery says. "But it's the responsibility of educators and policy makers to make sure we're educating people about the value of privacy and what it really means to give it up."

11   In that spirit, according to the *Chronicle of Higher Education* (Jan. 12, 2007), two professors at Drake University's law school, worried that their students' casual approach to digital correspondence could hinder their careers, started a class stressing online discretion. The lesson, according to one student, is simple: "If you are not comfortable with shouting your comments from a street corner, you probably shouldn't convey them via electronic print." ◆

CONSIDERING THE ISSUES

1. Do you have a page on Facebook, MySpace, or another social networking site? If so, which one did you chose to become a member of, and why? What information do you post, and who can see it? Alternatively, if you do not have a personal page, describe why you prefer not to participate in social networking sites.

2. What unique issues and challenges do young adults growing up with the Internet face that their parents and grandparents did not? How has "growing up digital" affected how you live? Explain.

CRAFT AND CONTENT

1. Evaluate the author's use of examples to support the point of his essay. Can you think of any areas that could be supported with more information or another point of view? Explain.

2. Summarize Schimke's article in a single paragraph. Remember to include the most important points of his article and the point he is trying to make on the subject of online privacy.

CRITICAL THINKING

1. In paragraph 6, Schimke notes that today's young adults are the most savvy about how they can be monitored online, yet they are the least likely group of Internet users to censor themselves. What are the potential pitfalls of this attitude? In your opinion, what accounts for this paradox?
2. This article mentions that ClickZ.com was mining user profiles and posts for marketing purposes. What are your expectations regarding the personal information you choose to put online? Is it free for "data mining"? Do you think it should remain private? Is ClickZ.com violating privacy rights of users of online networking sites? Why or why not?

WRITING ABOUT THE ISSUES

1. Review a few pages on Facebook or MySpace and evaluate the information posted online. If you have your own page, you can discuss the information you post as well. Are the pages you review guilty of making some of the mistakes Schimke notes in his article? For example, how would a potential employer view the pages? A judge? A possible love interest? Parents? Explain.

Who Is Really Stealing Your Privacy?
Amitai Etzioni

Amitai Etzioni is a sociologist and professor of international relations at George Washington University and the author of several books, including *Security First* and *New Common Ground*. He was a senior advisor to the Carter administration and has taught at Columbia and Harvard universities and the University of California, Berkeley. This editorial appeared online on CNN on December 10, 2010.

CONNECTING WITH THE TOPIC

Online privacy advocates tend to focus on the government's interference in our personal lives. In this editorial, Amitai Etzioni explains that businesses are the real threat to our privacy. Corporations track what we buy, read, visit, drink, and who we call, e-mail, even date. Planting cookies in your computer system, some corporations shadow travels on the Internet, keeping detailed reports so that they can sell the information to other corporations, who will in turn, track you online.

WORDS IN CONTEXT

Big Brother (2)   a character in George Orwell's novel *1984*, who is an all-seeing/knowing figure representing an authoritarian government's total control over individual lives. The figure symbolizes a political or social situation in which one's actions are closely monitored by an authoritarian figure or group (n.)

pseudonym (7)   literally, "false name"; a name one assumes that is different from one's true name, usually to conceal one's true identity (n.)

burqa (12)   a loose outer garment plus head-covering, worn by women in some Islamic countries to cover their bodies in public

1   **P**rivacy advocates are up in arms. They say the Obama administration is seeking to increase the government's surveillance powers. The White House is out to require internet companies to keep trapdoors so the government can read any and all messages.

2   Kevin Bankston of the Electronic Frontier Foundation called the proposal "a drastic anti-privacy, anti-security, anti-innovation solution in search of a problem." These privacy advocates remind me of someone who locks his front door only to return home and find that thieves have emptied his home through the back door and the windows he left wide open. These days, the main enemy of privacy is not **Big Brother**, but a whole bunch of Little Brothers: profit-making corporations.

3   Two kinds of corporations keep track of what you buy, read, visit, drink; whom you call, e-mail, and date; and lots more. Some merely track your activity on their site as part of their regular business, to help them sell you stuff. This is true from Amazon to Zappos. Other corporations make shadowing you—and keeping very detailed dossiers on you—their main line of business. They sell this information to all comers. Just one such company, Choicepoint, has records on more than 220 million people.

4   Most Americans probably know corporations are tracking them, but they may well be unaware of the latest ways corporations are carving up whatever remains of their privacy.

5   Cell phone companies offer a service that allows lovers, ex-wives and ex-husbands, lawyers, or anyone else to find out where you are hanging out. We are accustomed to tracking tools like cookies, which are installed on your computer by websites you visit. Cookies are used to identify you and to remember your preferences. They make shopping easier, but they also give sites the power to spy on you.

6   We have learned about devices that allow us to clear cookies from our computer, but corporations are installing "supercookies" that are very difficult to detect, and if removed, can secretly reinstall themselves.

7   You might think you can hide behind **pseudonyms** and use multiple cyber-mailboxes so trackers will be unable to profile you. However, some companies have developed software to match pseudonyms used on message boards and blogs with real names and personal e-mail addresses. The subjects of this tracking—who are unaware that their anonymity has been stripped—include people who use online pseudonyms to discuss sensitive topics, such as mental illness or medical conditions.

8   Beyond tracking and surveillance, select corporations keep dossiers on any crimes you have committed, any divorces, political leanings, the gender and age of any children in the household, as well as interests in topics including religion, the Bible, gambling and adult entertainment.

9   Privacy advocates have sharply objected to proposals for the government to employ "deep packet inspection," a powerful tool used to analyze the contents of data sent on the internet, to fight viruses and cybercrime. But now, private companies offer this service for a fee.

10   If you think that what the private sector knows about you stays in the private sector, I have a bridge in Brooklyn I'd like to sell you. In what must be the ultimate irony, the corporations not only do almost everything the federal government has been banned from doing since the 1974 Privacy Act—as well as Congress' 2003 termination of Total Information Awareness, a Pentagon surveillance program—but they also make the stuff available to the government.

11   For instance, Choicepoint has 35 contracts with government agencies, including the Department of Justice, and through it, the FBI, Drug Enforcement Administration, IRS and the Bureau of Citizenship and Immigration Services.

12   Your options are limited and not very appealing, to put it mildly. Some say, "Get over it; privacy is dead." Or "assume nothing is private anymore." You might try to return to the olden days: Pay only with cash, smash your PC and GPS and cell phone, and wear a **burqa**. Or you may move to Europe, which has much stronger privacy protection laws than the U.S. but, as far as I can tell, often does not enforce them.

13   Or: Take a deep breath and realize that the only one who can protect you is the Big Bad Wolf—the federal government. It is the one that, since 2000, has banned the selling of medical records, previously used by mortgage companies to call in loans of those who got cancer, or by employers in their hiring decisions. It is the government that required banks to keep your financial records private. And it is the government that is working to create new internet privacy laws and methods and a new office to enforce them. For example, the Federal Trade Commission has recommended a "do not track" mechanism that would allow computer users to opt out of surveillance by companies.

14   I grant you that long experience teaches us that the government itself must be watched. However, if you think that it is the main threat to your privacy these days, I humbly suggest that you think again. ◆

CONSIDERING THE ISSUES

1. Most people are aware that companies track their information. When you use the Internet, do you care that your movements might be tracked? Why or why not?
2. Etzioni notes that there are many companies that let us track the online activity of others, even using technology to determine where people are located. Would you ever use such technology to track the movements of a loved one? Have you ever been tracked yourself, such as by a parent using technology to monitor your computer usage or driving habits? Explain.

CRAFT AND CONTENT

1. This article ran on an Internet news site. What style of writing do we expect from online news articles? How is it different from pieces in magazines or journals? Explain.
2. What is the author's opinion of corporations? Of government? Can you tell? Explain.
3. Evaluate Etzioni's tone in this article. Identify specific words or passages that seem to reveal a unique tone or personality in his writing.

CRITICAL THINKING

1. In this essay, Etzioni warns that we might be focusing on the wrong "Big Brother" tracking our online movements. In your opinion, which is worse—a bunch of corporate "Little Brothers" monitoring our activity or a government-backed "Big Brother"?
2. What solution does Etzioni offer to corporate data mining? Do you think his solution is a good one? Why or why not? What steps, if any, do you think we should be taking to protect our privacy online and off?

WRITING ABOUT THE ISSUES

1. Write a short article in which you express your own opinion on whether corporations should be able to put cookies and "super-cookies" on our computers to gather information about us.

2. Write an essay describing your views on personal freedom and the Internet. How does personal freedom connect to privacy rights, if at all? Do you feel your personal freedom has been violated by government and private Internet tracking practices? Explain.

The Case for a National ID Card
Margaret Carlson

Margaret Carlson has been writing the column "Public Eye" for *Time* magazine since 1994. In addition to writing for *Time*, she serves as a panelist on CNN's political programs *Inside Politics* and *The Capital Gang*. Her articles have appeared in many publications, including the *New Republic, Esquire*, and *Washington Weekly*. This column was first published in the January 14, 2002, issue of *Time*.

CONNECTING TO THE TOPIC

Most Americans are used to carrying identification cards: a Social Security card, a library card, a driver's license, a student college ID. Other cards we carry include credit cards, bank cards, even cards to allow us to take out DVDs and video games. After the terrorist attacks of September 11, 2001, discussion over whether we should carry "national identification cards" dramatically increased, with even Larry Ellison, chief of the information mega-giant Oracle, offering to provide the software for such cards. What would a national ID card be used for? Would it make us safer? More open to governmental scrutiny? Is this the next card we can expect to be carrying in our wallets?

WORDS IN CONTEXT

Nazis (2)   the National Socialist German Workers' Party, founded in Germany in 1919 and gaining notoriety in 1933 under the direction of Adolf Hitler. (n.)
trove (2)   a collection of valuable items discovered or found; a treasure trove (n.)
pertinent (3)   relevant to the matter (adj.)
noncommittal (3)   refusing to commit to a particular opinion or idea (adj.)
civil libertarian (3)   someone who advocates for the protection of individual rights guaranteed by law (n.)
anonymity (8)   the state of being unknown or having one's identity unacknowledged (adj.)

1   After Michigan representative John Dingell was asked to drop his pants at Washington's National Airport, some people felt safer. Others, like me, decided that we'd lost our collective minds. A near strip search of a 75-year-old Congressman whose artificial hip has set off a metal detector— while a suspected al-Qaeda operative like Richard Reid slips onto a Paris-to-Miami flight with a bomb in his shoe—doesn't make us safer. It's making us ridiculous for entrusting our security to an unskilled police force that must make split-second decisions on the basis of incomplete data.

2   Incidents like this—and airport waits longer than the flight itself— have pushed me into the camp of the national ID card. Yes, a tamperproof ID smacks of Big Brother and **Nazis** intoning "Your papers, please," but the federal government already holds a **trove** of data on each of us. And it's less likely to mess up or misuse it than the credit-card companies or the Internet fraudsters, who have just as much data if not more.

3   The idea of a national ID card leaped into the headlines just after Sept. 11. Oracle chairman Larry Ellison offered to donate the **pertinent** software. Ellison went to see Attorney General John Ashcroft, who was **noncommittal** despite his obvious enthusiasm for expanding government powers into other areas that trouble **civil libertarians**.

4   Enter Richard Durbin. In concert with the American Association of Motor Vehicle Administrators (yes, the dreaded DMVs have their own trade group), the Illinois Senator proposed legislation that would create a uniform standard for the country's 200 million state-administered driver's licenses. Durbin noticed that the driver's license has become "the most widely used personal ID in the country. If you can produce one, we assume you're legitimate," he says. At present, nearly anyone can get a license; 13 of the 19 hijackers did. Having those licenses "gave the terrorists cover to mingle in American society without being detected."

5   Since we're using the driver's license as a de facto national ID, Durbin argues, let's make it more reliable. As it stands, the chief requirement is that one knows how to drive. This is fine if the only intent is to ensure that someone behind the wheel has mastered turn signals, but it shouldn't be sufficient to get someone into a federal building, the Olympics or an airplane. All a terrorist needs to do is shop around for a lax state (Florida still doesn't require proof of permanent residency) or resort to a forger with a glue gun and laminator.

6   A high-tech, hard-to-forge driver's license could become a national E-ZPass, a way for a law-abiding citizen to move faster through the roadblocks of post-9/11 life. It's no digitalized Supercard, but the states would have uniform standards, using bar codes and biometrics (a unique characteristic, like a palm print) and could cross-check and get information from other law-enforcement agencies. Polls show 70% of Americans support an even more stringent ID. But Japanese-American members of Congress and

Transportation Secretary Norman Mineta are keenly sensitive to anything that might single out one nationality. Yet an ID card offers prospects of less profiling. By accurately identifying those who are in the U.S. legally and not on a terrorist watch list, the card would reduce the temptation to go after random members of specific groups.

7   It is not ideal to leave a national problem to the states, but because of the general squeamishness about federal "papers" in the Congress, Durbin's proposal—congressional oversight of state DMVs—may be the best way to go. And if the government doesn't act, corporations will. Delta and American Airlines already provide separate lines for premium passengers; Heathrow Airport in London has an iris scan for people who have registered their eyeballs. An airline-industry association is at work on a Trusted Traveler card. Do we really want frequent-flyer status to be the basis for security decisions, or more plastic cards joining the too many we already have?

8   This ID would require one virtual strip search instead of many real ones. Durbin says the card would remove the **anonymity** of a Mohamed Atta but not the privacy of others. With a card, Dingell could have confirmed his identity (though he made a point of not pulling rank). With the presumption that he wasn't a terrorist, a once-over with a wand—with his pants on—would have lent credence to his claim that he possessed an artificial hip, not a gun. The Durbin card would at least let us travel with our clothes on. ◆

CONSIDERING THE ISSUES

1. When were you last asked to produce identification? What were the circumstances? Were you asked by a person, or did you need identification of some form to access a building or pick up an item? What form of identification did you produce?

2. What personal information are you willing to give out? For example, if a cashier asks you to provide a zip code or telephone number when making a purchase, do you give out this information? What about online? Do you consider your privacy when responding to requests for personal information? Explain.

CRAFT AND CONTENT

1. What is the position of the author on the issue of national ID cards? Identify specific areas of her essay in which she reveals her position.

2. Carlson notes that national ID cards "smack of Big Brother and the Nazis." Why does she use this reference? Who is "Big Brother"? How does the concept of Big Brother connect to the idea of a national ID card and set the tone of her essay? Explain.

CRITICAL THINKING

1. Carlson presents congressman John Dingell's experience at Washington's National Airport as an example of a security blunder. Evaluate this example. Does it demonstrate her point? Did the security guards act appropriately? Would a national ID card have prevented this situation in the first place? Explain.

2. In paragraph 6, Carlson states that "Japanese-American members of Congress and Transportation Secretary Norman Mineta are keenly sensitive to anything that might single out one nationality." Why are Japanese-American members of Congress particularly cautious of a national ID system? Why would they be more concerned than other groups?

WRITING ABOUT THE ISSUES

1. Do you think that a national identification card is a good idea? Why or why not? Do you think it would deter terrorism? Make U.S. citizens safer? Explain your point of view.

2. In paragraph 6, Carlson notes that polls indicate that 70% of Americans support "more stringent ID." Considering that this article was published only four months after September 11, conduct your own poll to see if Americans still feel this way. Ask at least 40 to 50 people if they support a national identification card. Based on your results, write a short essay analyzing the data. Incorporate any opinions expressed by the people you poll if appropriate.

National ID Cards: Five Reasons Why They Should Be Rejected
ACLU

The American Civil Liberties Union (ACLU) was founded in 1920. Since its beginning, the nonprofit, nonpartisan ACLU has grown from a small group of civil liberties activists to an organization of nearly 400,000 members with offices in almost every state. The ACLU's mission is to fight civil liberties violations wherever and whenever they occur. It is also active in national and state government arenas and is dedicated to upholding the Bill of Rights.

CONNECTING TO THE TOPIC

The preceding essay presented the idea that national ID cards might not be a bad idea in the post-9/11 world. The next piece explains why the ACLU believes national ID cards would be a colossal failure. Not only would such cards *not* solve the very problems that inspire them, but they would ultimately cause more harm than good.

WORDS IN CONTEXT

superficial (2)   only on the surface; insubstantial (adj.)
thwarted (3)   prevented (v.)
naïve (5)   simple; lacking in experience or understanding (adj.)
prohibition (6)   a policy or law that forbids something (n.)
visceral (8)   instinctive (adj.)
aversion (8)   intense dislike or disgust (n.)
totalitarian (8)   referring to a government or political body that exercises total control over the individual lives of citizens within a state, usually with the suppression of all dissenting viewpoints (adj.)
sentries (8)   guards or officials with authority (n.)
stigma (9)   a mark of disgrace (n.)

1   The terrorist attacks of September 11 have revived proposals for a national identity card system as a way to verify the identity of airline passengers and prevent terrorists from entering the country. For example, the Chairman and CEO of Oracle Corp., Larry Ellison, recently called for the creation of a national ID system and offered to provide the software for it without charge.

2   The newest calls for a national ID are only the latest in a long series of proposals that have cropped up repeatedly over the past decade, usually in the context of immigration policy, but also in connection with gun control or health care reform. But the creation of a national ID card remains a misplaced, **superficial** "quick fix." It offers only a false sense of security and will not enhance our security—but will pose serious threats to our civil liberties and civil rights. A national ID will not keep us safe or free.

Reason #1: A National ID Card System Would Not Solve the Problem That Is Inspiring It

3   A national ID card system will not prevent terrorism. It would not have **thwarted** the September 11 hijackers, for example, many of whom reportedly had identification documents on them, and were in the country legally.

4   Terrorists and criminals will continue to be able to obtain—by legal and illegal means—the documents needed to get a government ID, such as birth certificates. Yes, these new documents will have data like digital fingerprints on them, but that won't prove real identity—just that the carrier has obtained what could easily be a fraudulent document.

5   And their creation would not justify the cost to American taxpayers, which according to the Social Security Administration would be at least $4 billion. It is an impractical and ineffective proposal—a simplistic and **naïve** attempt to use gee-whiz technology to solve complex social and economic problems.

Reason #2: An ID Card System Will Lead to a Slippery Slope of Surveillance and Monitoring of Citizens

6   A national ID card system would not protect us from terrorism, but it would create a system of internal passports that would significantly diminish the freedom and privacy of law-abiding citizens. Once put in place, it is exceedingly unlikely that such a system would be restricted to its original purpose. The original Social Security Act contained strict **prohibitions** against use of Social Security cards for unrelated purposes, but those strictures have been routinely ignored and steadily abandoned over the past 50 years. A national ID system would threaten the privacy that Americans have always enjoyed and gradually increase the control that government and business wields over everyday citizens.

Reason #3: A National ID Card System Would Require Creation of a Database of All Americans

7   What happens when an ID card is stolen? What proof is used to decide who gets a card? A national ID would require a governmental database of every person in the U.S. containing continually updated identifying information. It would likely contain many errors, any one of which could render someone unemployable and possibly much worse until they get their "file" straightened out. And once that database was created, its use would almost certainly expand. Law enforcement and other government agencies would soon ask to link into it, while employers, landlords, credit agencies, mortgage brokers, direct mailers, private investigators, civil litigants, and a long list of other parties would begin seeking access, further eroding the privacy that Americans have always expected in their personal lives.

Reason #4: ID Cards Would Function as "Internal Passports" That Monitor Citizens' Movements

8 Americans have long had a **visceral aversion** to building a society in which the authorities could act like **totalitarian sentries** and demand "your papers please!" And that everyday intrusiveness would be conjoined with the full power of modern computer and database technology. When a police officer or security guard scans your ID card with his pocket bar-code reader, for example, will a permanent record be created of that check, including the time and your location? How long before office buildings, doctors' offices, gas stations, highway tolls, subways and buses incorporate the ID card into their security or payment systems for greater efficiency? The end result could be a nation where citizens' movements inside their own country are monitored and recorded through these "internal passports."

Reason #5: ID Cards Would Foster New Forms of Discrimination and Harassment

9 Rather than eliminating discrimination, as some have claimed, a national identity card would foster new forms of discrimination and harassment of anyone perceived as looking or sounding "foreign." That is what happened after Congress passed the Employer Sanctions provision of the Immigration Reform and Control Act of 1985: widespread discrimination against foreign-looking American workers, especially Asians and Hispanics. A 1990 General Accounting Office study found almost 20 percent of employers engaged in such practices. A national ID card would have the same effect on a massive scale, as Latinos, Asians, Caribbeans and other minorities became subject to ceaseless status and identity checks from police, banks, merchants and others. Failure to carry a national ID card would likely come to be viewed as a reason for search, detention or arrest of minorities. The **stigma** and humiliation of constantly having to prove that they are Americans or legal immigrants would weigh heavily on such groups. ◆

CONSIDERING THE ISSUES

1. When asked to provide proof of identity, do you consider this request an invasion of your privacy or simply a reality of modern life? Explain.

2. Many of us take the idea of privacy for granted. Think about the number of times in a given day when your actions may be tracked by others (for example, if you use a student ID card to gain access to the cafeteria or if you purchase something with a credit card). How often is your privacy at risk? Does it matter? Why or why not?

CRAFT AND CONTENT

1. The ACLU lists five reasons why national ID cards are a bad idea. Evaluate the relevancy and logic of the reasons they cite. Are they valid points? Off track? Can you think of any additional reasons that they might have left out? Alternatively, if you do not think their reasons hold merit, explain why.

2. What is a "slippery slope"? Why would national ID cards create a "slippery slope of surveillance"? Explain.

CRITICAL THINKING

1. Why does the ACLU believe that national ID cards would be a "superficial quick fix" that poses a serious threat to our civil liberties? What liberties do they fear will be sacrificed? Do you agree with their position? Why or why not?

2. Both this article by the ACLU and Carlson's essay before it mention the idea of totalitarian governments. In your opinion, would a national ID policy contribute to such a government or legal system? How would a national ID card be different from a driver's license or a Social Security card? A passport? Explain.

WRITING ABOUT THE ISSUES

1. This article by the ACLU lists five arguments that a national ID system would threaten our civil liberties. Assuming the position of Oracle chairman Larry Ellison, who encouraged a national ID system, draft a list of five arguments that a national ID system is a good policy for Americans to adopt.

2. Write an essay exploring the ways a national ID system could be abused. How could it contribute to a society similar to the totalitarian state depicted in George Orwell's novel *1984*? To review this short novel, look it up at www.online-literature.com.

VISUAL CONNECTIONS

Identity Theft

CONNECTING TO THE TOPIC

One privacy concern of many Americans is identity theft. As more websites and retail establishments store information online, it is possible for hackers to access personal information. In 2005, many banks and credit companies reissued thousands of cards after security systems had been breached, exposing an unprecedented number of people to the possibility of identity theft. How do we protect ourselves from identity theft without unnecessarily complicating our lives? Or is this just another reason for being more vigilant than ever in safeguarding our privacy?

CRITICAL THINKING

1. Consider the faces of the people in this ad. What sort of conclusions might a viewer draw from their expressions? Would the ad be as effective if the images were reversed? Why or why not?
2. Can you tell what this ad is trying to accomplish without reading the fine print at the bottom of the ad? Explain.
3. What does this ad imply about your privacy?
4. What is your gut reaction to this ad? How does it play into our fears and insecurities? Are these fears well founded? Why or why not?

The Invasion of the Cookie Monsters
Jack Shafer

Jack Shafer is a *Slate* editor at large. He edited two city weeklies, *Washing-ton City Paper* and *SF Weekly*, before joining *Slate* prior to its 1996 launch. Shafer has written on new media, the press, and drug policy for publications big (the *New York Times Magazine*) and small (*Inquiry*). His "Press Box" column appears several times a week in *Slate*, and this article was posted on November 11, 2010.

CONNECTING TO THE TOPIC

We know there is big money to be made on the Internet. Like most media, advertising is the name of the game on the web. But unlike print media that doesn't know who is looking at it, our online experience is being recorded, analyzed, and sold. On some level, we know we're losing our privacy with modern technology, but do we realize exactly how much privacy we are giving up, and do we even care? In this next editorial, Jack Shafer explains that *we* are to blame for the loss of our Internet privacy and why we might want to think about that.

WORDS IN CONTEXT

vigilant (1)   on the alert; watchful (adj.)
buff (1)   one who is enthusiastic and knowledgeable about a subject (n.)
surreptitiously (4)   doing something secretly, stealthily (adv.)
compulsory (9)   obligatory; required (adj.)
voluminous (10)   large in volume, ample, lengthy (adj.)
candid (10)   impartial; free from prejudice (adj.)
fluke (11)   a chance occurrence; an accident (n.)
lucrative (11)   profitable (adj.)

1   Unless you're a **vigilant** privacy **buff**, you're being watched right now.

2   As you scoot from one Web site to another, you accumulate a swarm of tracking cookies and other bits of computer code ("beacons" or "flash cookies") that report your status to a database that keeps a dossier on you and what you do on the Web.

3   And you thought the Web was "free." You're paying with your privacy.

4   The invasive use of these technologies, documented brilliantly in an ongoing *Wall Street Journal* series titled "What They Know," allows data

miners to collect reams of personal information about you. They know which Web sites you've visited and which ads you've clicked. "Scrapers" know about comments you've added to online forums. They've installed software that tells them what you're doing on the Web in real time. As the *Journal* reports, some of these bits of code "**surreptitiously** re-spawn themselves even after users try to delete them." These dossiers "are bought and sold on stock-market-like exchanges that have sprung up in the past 18 months."

5   I doubt that few who use the Web ever thought they were signing up for a technology whose surreptitious data-gathering can hone in on a user's age, ZIP code, level of education, health data, gender, estimated income, marital status, real estate situation, and more, as the *Journal* reports.

6   Tracking technology has spun so far out of control that Comcast was dropping tracking cookies that it didn't even know about on users' computers. The culprit was some free software Comcast used to build a slide show. Microsoft confessed to the *Journal* that it didn't know why its MSN.com site was planting a powerful tracking file from Targus Information Corp. on users' computers. Dictionary.com, meanwhile, took the cookie prize in the *Journal* series, depositing 168 tracking tools on browsers without giving users a chance to opt out. Even the *Journal* is guilty of tracking without asking. The series noted that the paper's WSJ.com drops 60 tracking files. The *Journal* busted its corporate sibling, MySpace, for shipping users' personal data to outside advertising companies when they clicked on ads.

7   You can cleanse your computer of tracking files if you follow the *Journal's* instructions or those published in the *New York Times* today. But I'm warning you—it's as much work as a part-time job. Some users will decide that deleting cookies is more trouble than it's worth. Cookies, after all, store passwords, preferences, and other settings that make surfing easier. Plus, some tracking done by advertisers can be beneficial if it serves you an advertisement that interests you as opposed to a random pitch.

8   The Web-advertising industry has tried policing itself with programs that allow users to opt out of certain tracking files. Software developers have written nifty programs that help Web surfers minimize unwanted surveillance. But these fixes only ratchet up the arms race between the snooping companies and the blockers. As we've learned from our experiences with spam, viruses, and malware, there are no permanent solutions to our computer annoyances.

9   We could always go to the government for legislation to blunt the snooper. But the Cato Institute's Jim Harper would remind us that the feds have too much in common with the Web spies to be good protectors of our privacy. It's the federal government that wants the Web infrastructure to be reprogrammed, so it can expand its wiretapping powers. It wanted a "clipper chip" that would allow authorities "back-door" entry into encrypted

communications. It's behind the FBI's "Carnivore" system and the Total Information Awareness proposal. It installed those hideous "backscatter" scanning devices at airports. It mandated **compulsory** identification cards. Do we really want to put the Federal Trade Commission in charge of the Internet?

10   As I already noted, the privacy problem is really one of our own making. We're the ones who surrender the privacy of the contents of our e-mail, calendars, and contacts to Gmail, which then sells ads against those contents. We give the mapping services our home addresses and our destinations; we give similar information to free GPS outfits. We share our comings and goings by checking in on Foursquare. We let iTunes catalog our music libraries in exchange for its "Genius" recommendations. We submit volumes of personal information to Facebook for Mark Zuckerberg to monetize. None of these exploitations should come as a surprise. They weren't forced on us. If we read the **voluminous** "terms of service" agreements that we check yes to in return for these free services, we'd see that the providers of "free" services were very **candid** about how they'd use our personal information.

11   Much of the privacy that so many of us cherish has been an economic **fluke**. The comings and goings of city dwellers, their preferences and perversions, and their secrets weren't easily known, because they were too expensive to harvest. But for inhabitants of small towns, this was never true. Those streets have gossiping eyes, which is one reason people moved to cities. Since the Web makes harvesting of personal data so cheap—and **lucrative**—it's hard to imagine village- or city-dwellers enjoying any of their former anonymity unless they're willing to pay for it.

12   As the *Journal* series notes, our privacy dilemma is baked into many of the Web browsers that we either download for free or accept with our operating systems. In 2008, a faction at Microsoft wanted the next version of its browser, Internet Explorer, to "give users a simple, effective way to avoid being tracked online. They wanted to design the software to automatically thwart common tracking tools, unless a user deliberately switched to settings affording less privacy."

13   That set off a debate at the company between user advocates and advertising advocates. Microsoft, Google, and Apple, makers of three top Internet browsers, are also in the advertising business. You can guess which Microsoft faction won. The automatic privacy functions were gutted to make consumer tracking—and hence ad sales—easier. (Here's how to use the "InPrivate Filtering" tool that survived in the shipped version of Internet Explorer 8.)

14   Surfing the Web anonymously is possible, as the *Journal* and *New York Times* primers show, but, as I said, it's a lot of work. So my question is this: Would you be willing to pay for a browser that was designed from the bottom up for privacy, not to serve advertisers? Are you prepared to

pay for all the content (like *Slate!*) and services you now get for "free" in exchange for giving up privacy and anonymity to tracking files?

15   How much is your privacy worth? ◆

CONSIDERING THE ISSUES

1. Do you consider yourself a "vigilant privacy buff"? In other words, do you care if others know what you are doing at any given time either online or offline? Explain.

2. The author doubts that most people when using the web realize the amount of information that databases are gathering on them. Before reading this article, did you know the extent to which your personal information was being used? Did this article surprise you? Explain.

CRAFT AND CONTENT

1. Author Jack Shafer states, "You're paying with your privacy." Is the Internet worth the price of your privacy? Explain.

2. The author says that having cookies can be beneficial. Which examples of these benefits does the author give, and do you agree that each of these examples is in fact positive for the typical Internet user? Explain.

CRITICAL THINKING

1. Have you ever used Dictionary.com? After reading this article, will you ever use it again? Explain why or why not.

2. In the conclusion to this article, the author asks his audience if we would be willing to pay for complete privacy on the Internet, including paying for access to otherwise "free" content on the web and paying for a browser designed to not serve advertisers. How much would the Internet have to cost in order to maintain complete privacy for its users?

WRITING ABOUT THE ISSUES

1. Write a short essay in which you explain both sides of the Microsoft "user advocates" versus "advertising advocates" debate in your own words. In your conclusion, state on which side you would have been.

2. Shafer mentions that everyone who is connected to the Internet has a "dossier." Write a narrative essay explaining what your online dossier says about you.

VISUAL CONNECTIONS

Chicago's Camera Network

CONNECTING TO THE TOPIC

Surveillance cameras monitor us in department stores and at ATMs. They are present in elevators and offices, parking lots, sporting arenas, and police cars. It seems as if cameras are everywhere. All this monitoring can seem intrusive, but when a camera captures child abuse or abduction on film, such surveillance can prove to be a useful law enforcement tool. Is surveillance a price we should pay for a safer society? Is it a fair trade-off for an invasion of our personal privacy? Or is this a case where the ends do not justify the means? The image and text below is an excerpt from a longer article published in the *Wall Street Journal* on November 17, 2009 on Chicago's camera network.

Video feeds at Navy Pier, part of Chicago's camera-surveillance network

A giant web of video-surveillance cameras has spread across Chicago, aiding police in the pursuit of criminals but raising fears that the City of Big Shoulders is becoming the City of Big Brother.

While many police forces are boosting video monitoring, video-surveillance experts believe Chicago has gone further than any other U.S. city in merging computer and video technology to police the streets. The networked system is also unusual because of its scope and the integration of non-police cameras.

The city links the 1,500 cameras that police have placed in trouble spots with thousands more—police won't say how many—that have been installed by other government agencies and the private sector in city buses, businesses, public schools, subway stations, housing projects, and elsewhere. Even home owners can contribute camera feeds.

The system is too vast for real-time monitoring by police staffers. But each time a citizen makes an emergency call, which happens about 15,000 times a day, the system identifies the caller's location and instantly puts a video feed from the nearest camera up on a screen to the left of the emergency operator's main terminal. The feeds, including ones that weren't viewed in real time, can be accessed for possible evidence in criminal cases.

A police spokesman said the system has "aided in thousands of arrests." Video cameras caught 16-year-old Michael Pace, an alleged Chicago gang member, opening fire with a 40-caliber handgun on a city bus in a 2007 incident that claimed the life of 16-year-old honor student Blair Holt and wounded four others. In July, Mr. Pace pleaded guilty to murder on the eve of his trial, and the video was released during a hearing where a judge sentenced him to 100 years in jail.

The city is "allowing first responders access to real-time visual data," said Ray Orozco, executive director of the city department responsible for the system. Former U.S. Homeland Security chief Michael Chertoff has called Chicago's use of cameras "a model for the country."

Mr. Orozco dismisses worries about privacy abuse. The department logs in all users and can monitor what they are doing, he said, assuring accountability. He also said access to the command center is tightly controlled. He declined to discuss specifics of who is allowed inside the center.

Chicago said that it only networks video cameras in public areas where people have an expectation they may be seen. None of the cameras record speech, because that would violate wire-tapping laws, although some can detect the sound of gunfire and breaking glass.

"People want these cameras in their neighborhoods," said Mayor Richard Daley in a prepared statement. "We can't afford to have a police officer on every corner, but cameras are the next best thing."

CRITICAL THINKING

1. Most people are aware that surveillance cameras help loss prevention officers catch shoplifters at department stores. In Chicago, over 1,500 cameras are used to aid law enforcement offices to keep the peace. Would knowing you could be caught on film influence your behavior? How would you feel if you lived in a society that could track you on film? Would you care? Why or why not?

2. Do you think cameras in public places are a good law enforcement tool? If you ran a municipal law enforcement operation, where would you put surveillance cameras, and why? Or would you choose to not use cameras at all? Explain.

3. When you are watched on camera, do you feel your privacy is invaded, or do you accept cameras as a fact of modern life? Do law-abiding citizens need to worry about surveillance cameras at all?

4. Does knowing that surveillance cameras are located at a particular site make you feel safer? Would it make you feel better riding public transportation? Why or why not?

5. What assumptions do we make about cameras in public spaces? For example, who do you think the camera is watching? Is it likely to deter criminal behavior? Explain.

Blog Matters

A blog ("web log") is an online diary or commentary site that features regular entries that describe events, impressions, and viewpoints. Blogs may contain text, images, video, and often link to other websites, blogs, and online media. Most blogs allow readers to comment on the content of the post and respond to each other. As of September 2011, there were over 160 million public blogs in existence. While many blogs are maintained by individuals, some are run by journals, newspapers, and other media outlets. Remember that most blogs are not monitored for factual accuracy, and often express the opinion and views of the "blogger" writing the content.

The blog below is hosted by *The New York Times*' "BITS"—Business-Innovation-Technology-Society—blog pages and was written by Jenna Wortham, who posted this entry on August 20, 2009. In this entry, she explains why what you post on Facebook and other social networking sites really does matter. Research suggests that employers are increasingly looking job candidates up on social networking sites when considering hires. And what you post may just cost you a job.

Employers Use Social Networks to Check Out Applicants

Jenna Wortham
August 20, 2009

> Most job applicants have a general checklist before a job interview—updating a résumé, ironing a professional outfit, rehearsing an explanation for those two years spent bumming around after college. However, if tidying up the Facebook profile isn't on that list, maybe it should be.

1   According to a new study conducted by Harris Interactive for CareerBuilder.com, 45 percent of employers questioned are using social networks to screen job candidates—more than double from a year earlier, when a similar survey found that just 22 percent of supervisors were researching potential hires on social networking sites like Facebook, MySpace, Twitter and LinkedIn.

2   The study, which questioned 2,667 managers and human resource workers, found that 35 percent of employers decided not to offer a job to a candidate based on the content uncovered on a social networking site. (The survey has no margin of sampling error because it was not drawn from a representative nationwide sample but rather from volunteer participants.)

3   The report showed that Facebook was the most popular online destination for employers to do their online sleuthing, followed by LinkedIn and MySpace. In addition, 7 percent followed job candidates on Twitter.

4   More than half of the employers who participated in the survey said that provocative photos were the biggest factor contributing to a decision not to hire a potential employee, while 44 percent of employers pinpointed references to drinking and drug use as red flags.

5   Other warning signs included bad-mouthing of previous employers and colleagues and poor online communication skills.

6   While most of these may seem like obvious stumbling blocks, what constitutes alarming behavior to a particular employer? Would photographs of a trip to the beach be considered inappropriate? What about a racy Halloween costume? As Facebook continues to grow as an essential personal and business networking tool for most of the Web, these issues are only going to get thornier.

7   To be on the safe side, it's probably wise to use the new privacy settings offered by Facebook to keep everything but the most innocuous content away from the public eye.

RESPOND TO THE BLOG:

What do you think? Are we giving away too much information online? Should employers be able to consider the behavior expressed on a social networking site in its hiring decisions? If you have a MySpace or Facebook page, what would an employer learn about *you*?

TOPICAL CONNECTIONS

GROUP PROJECT

1. In the first essay in this section, David Plotz argues that the infringements on our privacy are a small price to pay for the protections we enjoy in return for this sacrifice. As a group, compile a list of ways that you must sacrifice your privacy. You may include airport security checks, locker searches, and even having to produce identification to pay with a check. Is this forfeiture of privacy rights worth it? Are some more invasive than others? Discuss your list and assess the costs and benefits of privacy loss. After group discussion, share your opinions with the rest of the class.

WEB PROJECT

1. This chapter addresses several issues connected to our concept of privacy. Many of us are unclear about what our privacy rights actually are. Visit the Privacy Rights Clearinghouse website at www.privacyrights.org for fact sheets on privacy and your privacy rights. What assumptions do you make about your privacy? Write an essay in which you explore privacy rights in American society.

FOR FURTHER INQUIRY

1. While some authors in this section imply that we are subjected to more invasions of privacy than ever before, others infer that we are more anonymous now than we were a century ago. What are your impressions of this issue? Interview fellow students, parents, grandparents, and older relatives and ask them for their viewpoints on privacy. Assess whether we have more or less privacy today than in the past. Then address how Americans feel about privacy.

2. Watch the movie *The Net,* starring Sandra Bullock, or *The Truman Show,* with Jim Carrey. Write a short review of either film, addressing specifically how the movie illuminates privacy issues in modern life.

3 | How Does Advertising Influence Us?

Advertising surrounds us, permeating our daily lives—on television, billboards, newspapers, magazines, the Internet, the sides of buses and trains, T-shirts, sports arenas, even license plates. Advertising is the driving force behind our consumptive economy, accounting for more than 150 billion dollars worth of commercials and print ads each year in the United States. Commercials fill 15 to 20 minutes of television airtime per hour (more for sporting events such as football games). They form the bulk of most newspapers and magazines. Advertising is everywhere we are, appealing to the root of our desires—our fantasies, hopes, wishes, and dreams—while promising us youth, beauty, social acceptance, power, sex appeal, and happiness. Through carefully selected images and words, advertising may be the most powerful manufacturer of meaning in our society. And many of us are not even aware of how it influences our lives.

Most of us are so accustomed to advertising that we barely notice its presence around us. However, if we stopped to think about how it works on our subconscious, we might be amazed at how powerful and complex a force it is. This chapter examines how advertising tempts us to buy, feeds our fantasies, and convinces us to part with our money.

The chapter closes with some sample ads for popular products and services. Use a critical eye when reviewing these advertisements, and consider some of the points about persuasion and advertising described in this chapter.

CRITICAL THINKING

1. This editorial cartoon features a great deal of visual material. What is happening in this cartoon? What does it seek to demonstrate? How effective is it in relaying its message? Explain.
2. How many scenarios exhibited in this cartoon can you relate to? Cite a few examples of how this cartoon reflects your own life experience.
3. Can you tell how the person in the cartoon feels about the issue depicted? Explain.

A Brand by Any Other Name

Douglas Rushkoff

Douglas Rushkoff is a writer and columnist who analyzes, writes, and speaks about the way people, cultures, and institutions share and influence each other's values. He is the author of many books on new media and popular culture, including *Media Virus* and *Coercion: Why We Listen to What "They" Say*. His column on cyberculture appears monthly in *The New York Times*. This essay appeared in the April 30, 2000, edition of the *London Times*.

CONNECTING TO THE TOPIC

Brand-name products target groups of consumers—Pepsi and Levi appeal to large, diverse populations, while Fendi, Coach, or Gucci appeal to very elite ones. Brands depend on image—the image they promote, and the image consumers believe they will project by using the product. For many teens, brands can announce membership in a particular group, value systems, personality type, and personal style. Today's youth are more consumer and media savvy than previous generations, forcing retailers to rethink how they brand and market goods to this group. While teens like to think that they are hip to advertising gimmicks, marketers are one step ahead of the game—a game that teens are likely to lose as they strive to "brand" themselves.

WORDS IN CONTEXT

affiliation (1)   connection; association (n.)
psycho-physical (2)   mind-body (adj.)
phenomenon (2)   a circumstance or fact that can be felt by the senses (n.)
utilitarian (3)   practical (adj.)
esoteric (3)   confined to and understood by a small group only (adj.)
affinity (3)   natural attraction and liking (n.)
existential (4)   relating to or dealing with existence (adj.)
anthropology (5)   the study of the behavior and physical, social, and cultural development of humans and human groups (n.)
predilections (6)   preferences (n.)
angst (8)   anxiety (n.)
compunction (8)   sense of guilt (n.)
deconstruct (8)   to break down and analyze (v.)
arsenal (9)   a store of weapons of defense (n.)
opaque (10)   impenetrable; difficult to see through and understand (adj.)
sensibility (11)   awareness and sense of feeling (n.)

coerce (12) to force to act or think in a certain way by use of pressure or intimidation; to compel (v.)
conflation (13) a mix of several things together (n.)

1 I was in one of those sports "superstores" the other day, hoping to find a pair of trainers for myself. As I faced the giant wall of shoes, each model categorized by either sports **affiliation**, basketball star, economic class, racial heritage or consumer niche, I noticed a young boy standing next to me, maybe 13 years old, in even greater awe of the towering selection of footwear.

2 His jaw was dropped and his eyes were glazed over—a **psychophysical** response to the overwhelming sensory data in a self-contained consumer environment. It's a **phenomenon** known to retail architects as "Gruen Transfer," named for the gentleman who invented the shopping mall, where this mental paralysis is most commonly observed. Having finished several years of research on this exact mind state, I knew to proceed with caution. I slowly made my way to the boy's side and gently asked him, "What is going through your mind right now?"

3 He responded without hesitation, "I don't know which of these trainers is 'me.'" The boy proceeded to explain his dilemma. He thought of Nike as the most **utilitarian** and scientifically advanced shoe, but had heard something about third world laborers and was afraid that wearing this brand might label him as too anti-Green. He then considered a skateboard shoe, Airwalk, by an "indie" manufacturer (the trainer equivalent of a micro-brewery) but had recently learned that this company was almost as big as Nike. The truly hip brands of skate shoe were too **esoteric** for his current profile at school—he'd look like he was "trying." This left the "retro" brands, like Puma, Converse and Adidas, none of which he felt any real **affinity** for, since he wasn't even alive in the 70's when they were truly and non-ironically popular.

4 With no clear choice and, more importantly, no other way to conceive of his own identity, the boy stood there, paralyzed in the modern youth equivalent of an **existential** crisis. Which brand am I, anyway?

5 Believe it or not, there are dozens, perhaps hundreds of youth culture marketers who have already begun clipping out this article. They work for hip, new advertising agencies and cultural research firms who trade in the psychology of our children and the **anthropology** of their culture. The object of their labors is to create precisely the state of confusion and vulnerability experienced by the young shopper at the shoe wall—and then turn this state to their advantage. It is a science, though not a pretty one.

6 Marketers spend millions developing strategies to identify children's **predilections** and then capitalize on their vulnerabilities. Young people

are fooled for a while, but then develop defense mechanisms, such as media-savvy attitudes or ironic dispositions. Then marketers research these defenses, develop new countermeasures, and on it goes.

7   The battle in which our children are engaged seems to pass beneath our radar screens, in a language we don't understand. But we see the confusion and despair that results. How did we get in this predicament, and is there a way out? Is it your imagination, you wonder, or have things really gotten worse? Alas, things seem to have gotten worse. Ironically, this is because things had gotten so much better.

8   In olden times—back when those of us who read the newspaper grew up—media was a one-way affair. Advertisers enjoyed a captive audience and could quite authoritatively provoke our **angst** and stoke our aspirations. Interactivity changed all this. The remote control gave viewers the ability to break the captive spell of television programming whenever they wished, without having to get up and go all the way up to the set. Young people proved particularly adept at "channel surfing," both because they grew up using the new tool, and because they felt little **compunction** to endure the tension-provoking narratives of storytellers who did not have their best interests at heart. It was as if young people knew that the stuff on television was called "programming" for a reason, and developed shortened attention spans for the purpose of keeping themselves from falling into the spell of advertisers. The remote control allowed young people to **deconstruct** TV.

9   The next weapon in the child's **arsenal** was the video game joystick. For the first time, viewers had control over the very pixels on their monitors. The television image was demystified. Then, the computer mouse and keyboard transformed the TV receiver into a portal. Today's young people grew up in a world where a screen could as easily be used for expressing oneself as consuming the media of others. Now the media was up-for-grabs, and the ethic, from hackers to camcorder owners, was "do it yourself."

10   Likewise, as computer interfaces were made more complex and **opaque**—think Windows—the do-it-yourself ethic of the Internet was undone. The original Internet was a place to share ideas and converse with others. Children actually had to use the keyboard! Now, the World Wide Web encourages them to click numbly through packaged content. Web sites are designed to keep young people from using the keyboard, except to enter in their parents' credit card information.

11   But young people had been changed by their exposure to new media. They constituted a new "psychographic," as advertisers like to call it, so new kinds of messaging had to be developed that appealed to their new **sensibility**.

12   Anthropologists—the same breed of scientists that used to scope out enemy populations before military conquests—engaged in focus groups,

conducted "trend-watching" on the streets, in order to study the emotional needs and subtle behaviors of young people. They came to understand, for example, how children had abandoned narrative structures for fear of the way stories were used to **coerce** them. Children tended to construct narratives for themselves by collecting things instead, like cards, bottlecaps called "pogs," or keychains and plush toys. They also came to understand how young people despised advertising—especially when it did not acknowledge their media-savvy intelligence.

13   Thus, Pokemon was born—a TV show, video game, and product line where the object is to collect as many trading cards as possible. The innovation here, among many, is the marketer's **conflation** of TV show and advertisement into one piece of media. The show is an advertisement. The story, such as it is, concerns a boy who must collect little monsters in order to develop his own character. Likewise, the Pokemon video game engages the player in a quest for those monsters. Finally, the card game itself (for the few children who actually play it) involves collecting better monsters—not by playing, but by buying more cards. The more cards you buy, the better you can play.

14   Kids feel the tug, but in a way they can't quite identify as advertising. Their compulsion to create a story for themselves—in a world where stories are dangerous—makes them vulnerable to this sort of attack. In marketer's terms, Pokemon is "leveraged" media, with "cross-promotion" on "complementary platforms." This is ad-speak for an assault on multiple fronts.

15   Moreover, the time a child spends in the Pokemon craze amounts to a remedial lesson in how to consume. Pokemon teaches them how to want things that they can't or won't actually play with. In fact, it teaches them how to buy things they don't even want. While a child might want one particular card, he needs to purchase them in packages whose contents are not revealed. He must buy blind and repeatedly until he gets the object of his desire.

16   Meanwhile, older kids have attempted to opt out of aspiration altogether. The "15–24" demographic, considered by marketers the most difficult to wrangle into submission, have adopted a series of postures they hoped would make them impervious to marketing techniques. They take pride in their ability to recognize when they are being pandered to, and watch TV for the sole purpose of calling out when they are being manipulated.

17   But now advertisers are making commercials just for them. Soft drink advertisements satirize one another before rewarding the cynical viewer: "image is nothing," they say. The technique might best be called "wink" advertising for its ability to engender a young person's loyalty by pretending to disarm itself. "Get it?" the ad means to ask. If you're cool, you do.

18   New magazine advertisements for jeans, such as those created by Diesel, take this even one step further. The ads juxtapose imagery that actually makes no sense—ice cream billboards in North Korea, for example. The strategy is brilliant. For a media-savvy young person to feel good about himself, he needs to feel he "gets" the joke. But what does he do with an ad where there's obviously something to get that he can't figure out? He has no choice but to admit that the brand is even cooler than he is. An ad's ability to confound its audience is the new credential for a brand's authenticity.

19   Like the boy at the wall of shoes, kids today analyze each purchase they make, painstakingly aware of how much effort has gone into seducing them. As a result, they see their choices of what to watch and what to buy as exerting some influence over the world around them. After all, their buying patterns have become the center of so much attention!

20   But however media-savvy kids get, they will always lose this particular game. For they have accepted the language of brands as their cultural currency, and the stakes in their purchasing decisions as something real. For no matter how much control kids get over the media they watch, they are still utterly powerless when it comes to the manufacturing of brands. Even a consumer revolt merely reinforces one's role as a consumer, not an autonomous or creative being.

21   The more they interact with brands, the more they brand themselves. ◆

CONSIDERING THE ISSUES

1. When you were in junior and senior high school, did you have particular brands to which you were most loyal? Did this brand loyalty change as you got older? Why did you prefer certain brands over others? What cultural and social influences, if any, contributed to your desire for that brand?
2. How would you define your personal style and the image you wish to project? What products and/or brands contribute to that image? Explain.
3. What can a brand tell you about the person who uses it? Explain.

CRAFT AND CONTENT

1. How does Rushkoff support his argument? Evaluate his use of supporting sources. Identify some of the essay's particular strengths.
2. In paragraph 7, Rushkoff notes that things have gotten worse because they have gotten better. What does he mean by this statement? Explain.

CRITICAL THINKING

1. Look up the phrase "Gruen transfer" on the Internet. Were you aware of this angle of marketing practice? Does it change the way you think about how products are sold to you? Explain.
2. In order to stay in business, marketers have had to rethink how they sell products to the youth market. How have they changed to keep pace with the youth market? Explain.
3. In his conclusion, Rushkoff predicts that even media-savvy kids will still "lose" the game. Why will they fail? Explain.

WRITING ABOUT THE ISSUES

1. Rushkoff notes in paragraph 11 that the youth generation "constitutes a new psychographic." First, define what you think "psychographic" means in the advertising industry. What makes this generation different from previous generations of consumers? If you are part of this generation (ages 15–24), explain why you do or don't think you indeed represent a new "psychographic." If you are older than this group, answer the same question based on your own experience and observation of younger consumers.
2. Teens and young adults covet certain brand-name clothing because they believe it promotes a particular image. What defines brand image? Is it something created by the company, or by the people who use the product? How does advertising influence the social view we hold of ourselves and the brands we use? Write an essay on the connection between advertising, image, and cultural values of what is "in" or popular and what is not.
3. Did marketing techniques such as the one described by Rushkoff for the Pokemon trading cards and games influence your consumer habits as a child or teen? Were you aware of such techniques? Write an essay exploring the way advertising targets specific age groups. Support your essay with information from the article and your own experience. You may wish to identify particular products that use specific marketing techniques to target young consumers.

Black Friday . . . Gray Thursday

Benjamin R. Barber

Benjamin R. Barber is a democratic theorist and the author of *Strong Democracy, Jihad vs. McWorld, Consumed: How Markets Corrupt Children,*

Infantilize Adults, and Swallow Citizens Whole (2007). He is a Distinguished Senior Fellow at Demos: A Network for Ideas and Action, and President of CivWorld at Demos. This editorial was posted on *The Huffington Post* on November 26, 2007.

CONNECTING TO THE TOPIC

Black Friday is the name given to the day after Thanksgiving where it is recognized as kicking off the holiday shopping season. While it is not an official holiday, many people take this day off and devote it to shopping, making it one of the most profitable retail days of the year. Many stores open their doors very early (some as early as 5 AM) and hold "early-bird specials," featuring discounts on merchandise that can range from video game consoles to cashmere sweaters. Such great buys can lead to store stampedes when shop doors open. The name originally reflected the huge traffic jams that often developed on that day, but its contemporary meaning is now connected to the concept of "being in the black" (making a profit). The dark phrasing may hold another meaning for some consumers, who are disgusted by the long lines, the mad grabs for merchandise, and the hoarding of popular items for resale online.

WORDS IN CONTEXT

solidarity (2)   a union of among members of a group who share similar views or interests (n.)

mantra (6)   a repeated word or phrase that holds mystical properties (n.)

anomaly (10)   a deviation from what is normal or expected (n.)

incarnate (10)   given a human form, personified (adj.)

compliant (10)   submissive, willing to go along with (adj.)

instigate (10)   to stir up, urge on (v.)

1   **O**n this blue Monday following Black Friday, can anyone remember Thursday?

2   Thanksgiving, once America's holiday of gratitude and family **solidarity**, has become the staging area for Christmas shopping. It is no longer just the day after Thanksgiving—Black Friday (as in "in the black, or profitable")—that is devoted to consumerism, but Thanksgiving Day itself, on which more and more stores are now staying open for pre-Black Friday sales. Call it gray Thursday.

3   America's retail industry, now indistinguishable from its marketing industry, sees in every blank space a billboard, in every suburban meadow, a mall, in every screen—big or small—a banner ad. And in every

"non-working" holiday, a time for more shopping. The Thanksgiving weekend comprises four non-working days: that's ninety-six hours available for non-stop shopping. Ditto for Halloween, Ramadan, Christmas, you name it—the "holy days" are now all shopoholy days.

4   And whose fault is that?

5   I had a half-dozen calls from radio and TV stations over this long shopping weekend asking me to talk about why consumers are so hungry to shop, why housewives were camping out at 3 AM Friday morning to make the 4 AM opening of mega-stores like Target. The assumption of the reporters who called was that Black Friday was a demand-side phenomenon—moms deciding there wasn't enough time in the day for all the shopping they wanted to do, dads insisting that stores stay open on Thanksgiving and open again at midnight on Black Friday cause they just couldn't get enough of those bargains, kids leaping from bed at midnight as if they'd spotted Peter Pan in the window and shouting, "Let's go shopping!"

6   See, the point seems to be, the retail industry is just saying—after all, this is its **mantra**—we're just giving people what they want.

7   Well, not quite: Americans like to shop, but they also like to pray, read, play, talk, make art, make love, take walks, and spend time munching turkey with loved ones. They like to shop but not 24/7. The shopping fanaticism we see on Black Friday, and throughout the year, is a supply-side phenomenon: the result of corporations "pushing," not consumers "pulling."

8   That's why marketing and advertising are capitalism's main industries today, why they expend a quarter of a trillion every year to get people to "want" all the stuff they sell. It's why they target children and encourage shopaholism (a serious problem for more than 20 million Americans who regularly go shopping without a particular purchase in mind).

9   Where capitalism once produced goods and services to meet real needs and wants, today it produces needs and wants to sell all the goods, wanted or not, it must sell to stay in business. Real needs (clean water in the third world) go wanting, while manufactured needs (bottled water) are pushed on first-world consumers who can get free clean water from their taps.

10   So Black Friday is no **anomaly**; it is consumer capitalism **incarnate**. It is not a **compliant** response by polite retailers to consumer demand, it is part of a massive world-wide campaign to **instigate** and sustain consumer demand beyond any reasonable definition of need or want. To satisfy shareholders, not citizens.

11   Our hyper-consumerism is actually consuming us (sub-prime mortgage anyone?). It's time we understand that Black Friday is not something we do; it something being done to us. And comprehend that, left to the

marketplace, Black Friday will eat Thursday as well and annihilate what is left of Thanksgiving and the American spirit it represents. ◆

CONSIDERING THE ISSUES

1. How do you approach the holiday season? Do you plan to shop on the day after Thanksgiving? Why or why not?
2. What is our social attitude about people who spend a lot of money on items they don't really need? Do we send mixed messages that consumerism is a bad thing, but then urge consumers to keep spending?

CRAFT AND CONTENT

1. Evaluate the author's tone in this piece. Identify specific words and phrases that convey his personal opinion on the subject of consumerism and "Black Friday."
2. At various points throughout his editorial, Barber asks his readers a question. What questions does he pose to his reader, and how does he answer these questions? Is this a good writing technique? Explain.

CRITICAL THINKING

1. In his conclusion, Barber asserts, "Black Friday is not something we do; it is something being done to us." What does he mean?
2. Barber argues that corporations are not really giving consumers what they want—rather, they are pushing consumers to buy more than they need. What is your own reaction to this point? Do you feel pushed by advertisers to buy things you don't really want?

WRITING ABOUT THE ISSUES

1. Research the topic of consumer spending during the holiday season. How important is "Black Friday" to the economy? What are the origins of the term, and how has this day changed over the last 20 to 30 years (for example, what is "Cyber Monday"?). Based on what you know already and what you learn from research, how might this day change over the next decade?
2. Write a personal narrative describing your Thanksgiving break and any consumer practices you associate with this four-day period (Thursday to Sunday). Connect your narrative to points Barber raises in his editorial.

On Sale at Old Navy: Cool Clothes for Identical Zombies!

Damien Cave

Damien Cave is a writer and Phillips Foundation Fellow. This article first appeared in the November 22, 2000, issue of the e-zine *Salon*.

CONNECTING TO THE TOPIC

Mass-market retail stores like Old Navy, Gap, Pottery Barn, and Ikea have enjoyed enormous popularity in recent years. Part of their appeal is that they market the concept of "cool." We believe that they represent a "with-it" lifestyle that we literally buy into. But are these stores just marketing conformity under the guise of "cool"? Are they crushing our individuality? Are we moving rapidly to the day where we will all dress the same, have the same furniture, and want the same things? If the things we own and the clothes we wear help create our identity, are chain stores just helping us join the cult of conformity?

WORDS IN CONTEXT

pugnacious (3)   scornful or hostile; disapproving and critical (adj.)

homogenous (5)   of the same or similar nature or kind (adj.)

urbanite (6)   a city dweller (n.)

equate (9)   to consider, treat, or depict as equal or equivalent (v.)

Pavlovianly (11)   referring to Russian scientist Ivan Petrovich Pavlov, known for discovering the conditioned response. In one experiment, by ringing a bell when feeding dogs, he eventually was able to get the dogs to salivate just by hearing the bell, even when no food was present. His experiment proved that animals could be conditioned to expect a consequence on the results of previous experience. (adv.)

commodify (15)   to turn into or treat as a product that can be sold; make commercial (v.)

pessimistic (16)   tending to stress the negative or unfavorable viewpoint (adj.)

duality (19)   state of having two sides (n.)

insidious (20)   sinister; intended to entrap by stealth; having a harmful allure (adj.)

1   Thomas Frank walks by the candy-cane-adorned displays of Old Navy, passing the sign exclaiming "priced so low, you can't say no," and into the chain's San Francisco flagship store.

2   The all-devouring Christmas rush hasn't started yet, but it's clear from the frown on Frank's face that he's not being seduced by the cheap but stylish clothes, the swirling neon and the bass-heavy hip-hop pounding in his ears.

3   "Oh God, this is disgusting," Frank says. This reaction isn't surprising. The bespectacled Midwesterner is a pioneering social critic—one of the first writers to document how, starting in the '60s, American businesses have co-opted cool anti-corporate culture and used it to seduce the masses. His arguments in the *Baffler*, a **pugnacious** review Frank founded in 1988, and in 1997's "The Conquest of Cool" read like sermons, angry wake-up calls for consumers who hungrily ingest hipper-than-thou ("Think Different") marketing campaigns without ever questioning their intent.

4   Old Navy and other cheap but tasteful retailers provide perfect fodder for Frank's critique. Their low prices and hip-but-wholesome branding strategy are supposed to present a healthy alternative to the conspicuous consumption of a Calvin Klein. But critics like Frank and Naomi Klein, author of "No Logo," argue that the formula is really nothing more than the wolf of materialism wrapped in cheaper sheep's clothing.

5   Consumers are being scammed, says Klein, arguing that stores like Old Navy and Ikea are duping millions, inspiring mass conformity while pretending to deliver high culture to the masses. "It's this whole idea of creating a carnival for the most **homogenous** fashions and furniture," says Klein. "It's mass cloning that's being masked in a carnival of diversity. You don't notice that you're conforming because everything is so colorful."

6   Klein and Frank say that few consumers recognize just how conformist their consumption habits have become. And certainly, it's hard to argue that Ikea's and Old Navy's items haven't become icons of **urbanite** and suburbanite imagination. Watch MTV, or rent "Fight Club," to see Ikea's candy-colored décor, then truck down to your local Old Navy flagship store. When you arrive, what you'll find is that hordes of people have beaten you there. At virtually every opening of Old Navy's and Ikea's stores—in the New York, Chicago and San Francisco areas, for example—tens of thousands of people appeared in the first few days. Even now, long after the stores first opened, lines remain long.

7   What's wrong with these people? Nothing, say defenders of the companies. The popularity of brands like Ikea and Old Navy, they argue, derives from the retailers' ability to offer good stuff cheap. "They provide remarkable value," says Joel Reichart, a professor at the Fordham School of Business who has written case studies on Ikea. "They're truly satisfying people's needs."

8   Despite his irritation with the way companies like Old Navy market themselves, Frank acknowledges that businesses have always sought to offer cheap, relatively high-quality merchandise and concedes that there

is some value in their attempts. He even admits that consumerism is good for the economy.

9   But he and other critics argue that in the end we're only being conned into thinking that our needs are being satisfied. What's really happening, they argue, is that clever marketers are turning us into automatons who **equate** being cool with buying cheap stuff that everyone else has. Under the stores' guise of delivering good taste to the general public, any chance we have at experiencing or creating authenticity is being undermined. Ultimately, our brave new shopping world is one in which we are spending more time in the checkout line than reading books, watching movies or otherwise challenging ourselves with real culture.

10   "Shopping is a way of putting together your identity," laments "Nobrow" author John Seabrook. And the "homogenized taste" of today's Old Navy and Ikea shoppers proves, he says, that Americans either are consciously choosing to look and live alike or are determined not to notice that that is what they're doing.

11   According to Christine Rosen, a professor in the Haas School of Business at UC-Berkeley, people who fill their closets, homes and lives with Old Navy and Ikea—or Pottery Barn or a host of other slick stores—are simply new examples of the trend toward conformity that started when the first "brands" appeared in the 1910s and '20s. "We're **Pavlovianly** trained to respond to this," she says.

12   And we're also just too damn lazy. That's the theory floated by Packard Jennings, an anti-consumerism activist who says that stores like Old Navy are designed to numb the brain and remove all semblance of creativity from the purchasing process. "Ikea pre-arranges sets of furniture in its stores, thereby lessening individual thought," he says. Once people are in the store, they can't resist. "Entire households are purchased at Ikea," he says.

13   Indeed, Janice Simonsen, an Ikea spokeswoman, confirmed that a large part of the chain's demographic consists of "people who come in and say, 'I need everything.'" Meanwhile, those who don't want everything usually end up with more than they need, says Fordham's Reichart. "The way they design their stores"—with an up escalator to the showroom and no exit until the checkout—"you end up going through the entire store," he says.

14   Old Navy plays by the same sneaky rules. When Frank and I entered the San Francisco store, clerks offered us giant mesh bags. Ostensibly, this is just good service, but since the bags are capable of holding at least half a dozen pairs of jeans and a few shirts, it's obvious that they're also meant to encourage overconsumption.

15   Frank called the bags "gross" but not out of line with other state-of-the-art retailing practices. But according to Klein, the sacks, in conjunction with Old Navy's penchant for displaying T-shirts in mock-1950s supermarket coolers, prove that the company is aiming to do something more. The idea behind this "theater for the brand" architecture is to **commodify**

the products, to make them "as easy to buy as a gallon of milk," Klein says. "The idea is to create a Mecca where people make pilgrimages to their brand," Klein says. "You experience the identity of the brand and not the product."

16   Old Navy and Ikea, however, are very popular—and, if you believe the more **pessimistic** of their critics, dangerous. Not only are the two chains remaking many closets and homes into one designer showcase, says Klein, but they are also lulling consumers to sleep and encouraging them to overlook some important issues.

17   Such as quality. People think they're getting "authenticity on the cheap," says David Lewis, author of *The Soul of the New Consumer*. But the truth may be that they're simply purchasing the perception of quality and authenticity. "Because [Ikea and Old Navy] create these self-enclosed lifestyles," Klein explains, "you overlook the fact that the products are pretty crappy and fall apart." Adds Jennings, "Things may be cheaper, but you keep going back to replace the faulty merchandise."

18   Then there is the trap of materialism. Survey after survey suggests that people who place a high value on material goods are less happy than those who do not, says Eric Rindfleisch, a marketing professor at the University of Arizona. The focus on bargains, incremental purchases and commodification plays to a uniquely American blind spot.

19   "We operate with a **duality**," explains Rindfleisch, who has conducted studies linking materialism with depression. "Americans know that money doesn't buy happiness, but most people somehow believe that increments in pay or goods will improve our lives. It's a human weakness—particularly in America."

20   The most **insidious** danger may be more abstract. The anti-consumerism critics argue that by elevating shopping to cultural status, we are losing our grip on real culture. We live in a time where college kids think nothing of decorating their rooms with Absolut vodka ads and fail to realize that they're essentially turning their rooms into billboards. Meanwhile, museum stores keep getting larger, Starbucks sells branded CDs to go with your coffee and because Ikea and other stores now look like movie theaters or theme parks, we don't just shop, "we make a day of it," as Klein puts it.

21   This only helps steer us away from other endeavors. When people spend so much time buying, thinking and talking about products, they don't have time for anything else, for real conversations about politics or culture or for real interaction with people.

22   Ultimately, the popularity of Old Navy, Ikea and their ilk proves that we're stuck in what Harvard professor Juliet Schor calls "the cycle of work and spend." Breaking that cycle may not be easy, but if one believes critics like Frank, it's essential if we are to control our own culture, instead of allowing it to be defined by corporations.

23   The cycle may not be possible to break. Frank, for one, is extremely pessimistic about our chances for turning back the tide of conformity and co-opted cool. Maybe that's one reason why he wanted to get out of Old Navy as fast as he could.

24   But I'm not so sure. When "Ikea boy," Edward Norton's character in *Fight Club*, watched his apartment and his Swedish furniture explode in a blaze of glory, I wasn't the only one who cheered. ◆

CONSIDERING THE ISSUES

1. Cave notes several businesses in his essay that he calls "mass-market" sellers of "cool." What stores does he specifically identify? Do you shop at any of these stores? If so, why do you shop there? Because they are "cool"? Affordable? Hip? Popular? Explain.

2. In paragraph 20, Cave observes that "college kids think nothing of decorating their rooms with Absolut vodka ads and fail to realize that they're essentially turning their rooms into billboards." What decorating choices have you made for your personal space? In what ways has your decorating style been influenced by outside forms of advertising? Explain.

CRAFT AND CONTENT

1. Cave quotes many different people in his essay. Identify all of his sources and group them as either "inside advertising/marketing," or "outside critics/academics." Whom does he rely upon more? How do the quotes he uses from both groups support his argument?

2. Can you tell what position Cave supports on the issue of mass consumption and on the stores he describes in his essay? Identify a few specific statements he makes in his essay that reveal his point of view.

3. How does Cave's title connect to his subject matter? What images does it create? How does it influence the reader's interpretation of his argument? Explain.

CRITICAL THINKING

1. In paragraph 3, Cave notes that American businesses have "co-opted cool anti-corporate culture." What does he mean? What is "anti-corporate" culture and why is it "cool"? What started it and how are businesses using it to their advantage? In what ways is this ironic? Explain.

2. What techniques do mass-market stores employ to squeeze the maximum profit from consumers who enter them? Were you aware of these techniques? Have you fallen victim to them yourself? Explain.

WRITING ABOUT THE ISSUES

1. In paragraph 10, author John Seabrook comments, "Shopping is a way of putting together your identity." Consider the ways your shopping habits put together your identity. Are you influenced by some of the techniques described in this essay? Consider in your response not just what you buy, but where you shop, why you shop, and with whom. How do your shopping companions influence your choices? How does advertising appeal to your desire to buy particular things as part of your own personal identity? Explain.

2. Several critics in this essay fear that mass-marketing chains aim to make shopping the primary characteristic of American culture. "By elevating shopping to cultural status, we are losing our grip on real culture. When people spend so much time buying, thinking, and talking about products, they don't have time for anything else, for real conversations about politics or culture or for real interaction with people." Write a response to this assertion, expressing your own point of view.

Consumerism Is "Eating the Future"
Andy Coghlan

Andy Coghlan is a writer for *New Scientist*, in which this opinion essay was published in August of 2009.

CONNECTING TO THE TOPIC

Could our culture of consumerism actually destroy us? The author of this next essay points out a few facts that lead to a disturbing conclusion. Our planet has limited resources, and we are using them up at an alarming rate. Led by consumer-based behaviors of wanting more things, we are using more than our fair share per person in Westernized countries. Combine this trend with our throw-away mentality, and we have a recipe for disaster for our planet. And if something doesn't change soon, argues Andy Coghlan in this next piece, we will run out of time.

WORDS IN CONTEXT

plague (1)   disease that spreads rapidly, often wiping out large populations (n.)
Petri dish (2)   a growing medium used to culture bacteria in labs (n.)
epidemiologist (3)   a person who studies health trends in populations (n.)
inexorable (6)   impossible to stop or prevent (adj.)
redress (6)   remedy or set right (v.)
finite (7)   limited (adj.)
EFA (11)   ecological footprint analysis; EFA generates figures that demonstrate where consumption is least sustainable and how fast finite material resources are being used up (acronym, n.)

1   We're a gloomy lot, with many of us insisting that there's nothing we can do personally about global warming, or that the human race is overrunning the planet like a **plague**. But according to leading ecologists, few of us realise that the main cause of the current environmental crisis is human nature.

2   More specifically, all we're doing is what all other creatures have ever done to survive, expanding into whatever territory is available and using up whatever resources are available, just like a bacterial culture growing in a **Petri dish** till all the nutrients are used up. What happens then, of course, is that the bugs then die in a sea of their own waste.

3   **Epidemiologist** Warren Hern of the University of Colorado at Boulder likened the expansion of human cities to the growth and spread of cancer, predicting "death" of the Earth in about 2025. He points out that like the accelerated growth of a cancer, the human population has quadrupled in the past 100 years and at this rate will reach a size in 2025 that leads to global collapse and catastrophe.

4   But there's worse. Not only are we simply doing what all creatures do, we're doing it better. In recent times we're doing it even faster because of changes in society that encourage and celebrate conspicuous and excessive consumption.

5   "Biologists have shown that it's a natural tendency of living creatures to fill up all available habitat and use up all available resources," says William Rees of the University of British Columbia in Vancouver, Canada. "That's what underlies Darwinian evolution, and species that do it best are the ones that survive, but we do it better than any other species."

Spreading Humans

6   Although we like to think of ourselves as civilized thinkers, we're subconsciously still driven by an impulse for survival, domination and expansion. This is an impulse which now finds expression in the idea that

inexorable economic growth is the answer to everything, and, given time, will **redress** all the world's existing inequalities.

7   The problem with that, according to Rees and Hern, is that it fails to recognize that the physical resources to fuel this growth are **finite**. "We're still driven by growing and expanding, so we will use up all the oil, we will use up all the coal, and we will keep going till we fill the Petri dish and pollute ourselves out of existence," he says.

8   But there's another, more recent factor that's making things even worse, and it's an invention of human culture rather than an evolved trait. According to Rees, the change took place after the second world war in the US, when factories previously producing weapons lay idle, and soldiers were returning with no jobs to go to. American economists and the government of the day decided to revive economic activity by creating a culture in which people were encouraged to accumulate and show off material wealth, to the point where it defined their status in society and their self-image.

9   Rees quotes economist Victor Lebow as saying in 1955: "Our enormously productive economy demands that we make consumption our way of life, that we convert the buying and use of goods into rituals, that we seek our spiritual satisfaction and our ego satisfaction in consumption. We need things consumed, burned up, worn out, replaced and discarded at an ever-increasing rate."

Insecure Society

10   In today's world, such rhetoric seems beyond belief. Yet the consumer spree carries on regardless, and few of us are aware that we're still willing slaves to a completely artificial injunction to consume, and to define ourselves by what we consume. "Lebow and his cronies got together to 'create' the modern advertising industry, which plays to primitive beliefs," says Rees. "It makes you feel insecure, because the advertising industry turned our sense of self-worth into a symbolic presentation of the possessions we have," he told me. "We've turned consumption into a necessity, and how we define ourselves."

11   The result is a world in which rampant consumption in rich countries is rapidly outstripping the resources in the world needed to satisfy demand. For example, Rees developed in 1992 a process called ecological footprint analysis (**EFA**). Produced by combining national consumption statistics with calculations of the resources needed to meet reported consumption patterns, EFA generates figures that conveniently demonstrate where consumption is least sustainable, and how fast finite material resources are being used up.

Big Footprints

12   Rees cited latest figures, taken from the WWF's study Living Planet Report 2008, showing that, globally, we'e already in "overshoot," consuming 30 per cent more material than is sustainable from the world's resources.

At present, 85 countries exceed their domestic "bio-capacities," compensating for their lack of local material by depleting stocks elsewhere, in countries that have "surpluses" because they're not consuming as much.

13   Perhaps not surprisingly, given the encouragement from Lebow, North Americans are the most consumptive, eating resources equivalent to 9.2 global average acres per capita. The world can only supply 2.1 global average acres per person, so already, Americans are consuming four times what the Earth can sustainably supply. "North Americans should be taking steps to lower their eco-footprints by almost 80 per cent, to free up the 'ecological space' for justifiable growth in the developing world," says Rees. The worrying thing is that if everyone on Earth adopted American lifestyles overnight, we would need four extra worlds to supply their needs, says Rees.

14   We haven't yet mentioned climate change or global warming. What's to be done? Marc Pratarelli of Colorado State University at Pueblo believes we need to snap out of our sleepwalking and begin to take real steps to cut consumption. "We have our heads in the sand, and are in a state of denial," he says. "People think: 'It won't happen to me, or be in my lifetime, or be that bad, so what's the point of change'."

What to Do?

15   But there is hope, however slim, according to Rees, both from the top down and the bottom up. The hope from above is that governments will finally realize that never-ending economic growth is incompatible with the finite material resources Earth has to offer, and begin to manage those resources more fairly and equitably through some kind of world government. Without global management, destruction will continue, producing food and energy "crunches" that make the credit crunch look like a tea party.

16   "We need to learn to live within the means of nature," says Rees. "That means sharing and redistribution of wealth, and for that we need leadership at the highest level to understand that the competitive instinct and the drive for power and more resources is mutually destructive, so governments must act in our collective interest."

17   From the bottom up, there are the glimmers of global grassroots organisations campaigning for global justice and global solutions, such as the internet-based justice organisation Avaaz, which collects email votes for petitions on issues of international or personal justice.

Desire to Acquire

18   Solving the other problem—the advertising that feeds our desire to acquire—might be more tricky. In an ideal world, it would be a counter-advertising campaign to make conspicuous consumption shameful.

"Advertising is an instrument for construction of people's everyday reality, so we could use the same media to construct a cultural paradigm in which conspicuous consumption is despised," he says. "We've got to make people ashamed to be seen as a 'future eater'."

19   Whether we're capable of such a counter-revolution is doubtful, both because of our state of personal denial and because of the huge power of industry to continue seducing us. "In effect, globalism and consumerism have succeeded in banishing moderation and sanctifying greed, thereby liberating *Homo economicus* from any moral or ethical constraints on consumption," says Rees.

20   Pararelli is even more pessimistic. The only hope, he says, is a disaster of immense scale that jolts us out of our denial. "My sense is that only when the brown stuff really hits the fan will we finally start to do something." ◆

CONSIDERING THE ISSUES

1. What is your consumer footprint? Do you buy more than you need? Do you tend to throw out a lot of extra food or items that expire before you have a chance to use them? Explain.
2. How much time, if any, do you take to consider the impact of what you purchase on a grander scale, such as described in this article? Do you think consumers are likely to think about their purchases more carefully if they knew what their "fair share" of the earth's resources was?

CRAFT AND CONTENT

1. What is the tone of this essay? How does it make you feel? Identify areas of the text where the tone influences your emotional connection to the author's message.
2. Summarize this article into a single paragraph. What action is the author trying to pursude his readers to do?

CRITICAL THINKING

1. What factors have contributed to the overall practice of Western cultures to use "more than their fair share?" What is fair? How is fairness determined? If you live in a country that has more resources and fewer people, are you entitled to more of the Earth's resources (in the area where you live) than someone living in a more populated area? Why or why not?
2. What is the political and social message and position of this article? Explain.

WRITING ABOUT THE ISSUES

1. When we buy products or consume resources, we usually view our behavior as a personal act with personal consequences. Write an essay in which you explore the psychology of our buying habits as it relates to a larger world. Should we begin to think about how our habits impact others, even people oceans away?
2. Consumerism critics often argue that our buying habits have been manufactured by the advertising industry and even the government. We are taught from birth to consume and buy and that having more things is desirable. How might the world be different if there was no advertising influencing our purchasing decisions? Write an essay in which you envision a culture without advertising. Would your society be better than the one we have now? Or worse?

With These Words I Can Sell You Anything
William Lutz

William Lutz teaches English at Rutgers University and is the author of several books, including *Beyond Nineteen Eighty-Four* (1984) and *Doublespeak Defined* (1999). The following essay is an excerpt from Lutz's book *Doublespeak*.

CONNECTING TO THE TOPIC

Words such as "help" and "virtually" and phrases such as "new and improved" and "acts fast" seem like innocuous weaponry in the arsenal of advertising. But not to William Lutz, who analyzes how such words are used in ads—how they misrepresent, mislead, and deceive consumers. In this essay, he alerts us to the special power of "weasel words"—those familiar and sneaky little critters that "appear to say one thing when in fact they say the opposite, or nothing at all." The real danger, Lutz argues, is how such language debases reality and the values of the consumer.

1   One problem advertisers have when they try to convince you that the product they are pushing is really different from other, similar products is that their claims are subject to some laws. Not a lot of laws, but there are some designed to prevent fraudulent or untruthful claims in advertising.

Generally speaking, advertisers have to be careful in what they say in their ads, in the claims they make for the products they advertise. Parity claims are safe because they are legal and supported by a number of court decisions. But beyond parity claims there are weasel words.

2   Advertisers use weasel words to appear to be making a claim for a product when in fact they are making no claim at all. Weasel words get their name from the way weasels eat the eggs they find in the nests of other animals. A weasel will make a small hole in the egg, suck out the insides, then place the egg back in the nest. Only when the egg is examined closely is it found to be hollow. That's the way it is with weasel words in advertising.

"Help"—The Number One Weasel Word

3 The biggest weasel word used in advertising doublespeak is "help." Now "help" only means to aid or assist, nothing more. It does not mean to conquer, stop, eliminate, end, solve, heal, cure, or anything else. But once the ad says "help," it can say just about anything after that because "help" qualifies everything coming after it. The trick is that the claim that comes after the weasel word is usually so strong and so dramatic that you forget the word "help" and concentrate only on the dramatic claim. You read into the ad a message that the ad does not contain. More importantly, the advertiser is not responsible for the claim that you read into the ad, even though the advertiser wrote the ad so you would read that claim into it.

4   The next time you see an ad for a cold medicine that promises that it "helps relieve cold symptoms fast," don't rush out to buy it. Ask yourself what this claim is really saying. Remember, "helps" means only that the medicine will aid or assist. What will it aid or assist in doing? Why, "relieve" your cold "symptoms." "Relieve" only means to ease, alleviate, or mitigate, not to stop, end, or cure. Nor does the claim say how much relieving this medicine will do. Nowhere does this ad claim it will cure anything. In fact, the ad doesn't even claim it will do anything at all. The ad only claims that it will aid in relieving (not curing) your cold symptoms, which are probably a runny nose, watery eyes, and a headache. In other words, this medicine probably contains a standard decongestant and some aspirin. By the way, what does "fast" mean? Ten minutes, one hour, one day? What is fast to one person can be very slow to another. Fast is another weasel word.

5   Look at ads in magazines and newspapers, listen to ads on radio and television, and you'll find the word "help" in ads for all kinds of products. How often do you read or hear such phrases as "helps stop . . .," "helps overcome . . .," "helps eliminate . . .," "helps you feel . . .," or "helps you look . . ."? If you start looking for this weasel word in advertising, you'll be amazed at how often it occurs. Analyze the claims in the ads using "help," and you will discover that these ads are really saying nothing.

Virtually Spotless

6 One of the most powerful weasel words is "virtually," a word so innocent that most people don't pay any attention to it when it is used in an advertising claim. But watch out. "Virtually" is used in advertising claims that appear to make specific, definite promises when there is no promise. After all, what does "virtually" mean? It means "in essence of effect, although not in fact." Look at that definition again. "Virtually" means not in fact. It does not mean "almost" or "just about the same as," or anything else.

7 The next time you see the ad that says that this dishwasher detergent "leaves dishes virtually spotless," just remember how advertisers twist the meaning of the weasel word "virtually." You can have lots of spots on your dishes after using this detergent and the ad claim will still be true, because what this claim really means is that this detergent does not in fact leave your dishes spotless. Whenever you see or hear an ad claim that uses the word "virtually," just translate that claim into its real meaning. So the television set that is "virtually trouble free" becomes the television set that is not in fact trouble free, the "virtually foolproof operation" of any appliance becomes an operation that is in fact not foolproof, and the product that "virtually never needs service" becomes the product that is not in fact service free.

New and Improved

8 If "new" is the most frequently used word on a product package, "improved" is the second most frequent. In fact, the two words are almost always used together. It seems just about everything sold these days is "new and improved." The next time you're in the supermarket, try counting the number of times you see these words on products.

9 Just what do these words mean? The use of the word "new" is restricted by regulations, so an advertiser can't just use the word on a product or in an ad without meeting certain requirements. For example, a product is considered new for about six months during a national advertising campaign. If the product is being advertised only in a limited test market area, the word can be used longer, and in some instances has been used for as long as two years.

10 What makes a product "new"? Some products have been around for a long time, yet every once in a while you discover that they are being advertised as "new." Well, an advertiser can call a product new if there has been "a material functional change" in the product. What is "a material functional change," you ask? Good question. In fact it's such a good question it's being asked all the time. It's up to the manufacturer to prove that the product has undergone such a change. And if the manufacturer isn't challenged on the claim, then there's no one to stop it. Moreover, the change

does not have to be an improvement in the product. One manufacturer added an artificial lemon scent to a cleaning product and called it "new and improved," even though the product did not clean any better than without the lemon scent. The manufacturer defended the use of the word "new" on the grounds that the artificial scent changed the chemical formula of the product and therefore constituted "a material functional change."

11   Which brings up the word "improved." When used in advertising, "improved" does not mean "made better." It only means "changed" or "different from before." So, if the detergent maker puts a plastic pour spout on the box of detergent, the product has been "improved," and away we go with a whole new advertising campaign. Or, if the cereal maker adds more fruit or a different kind of fruit to the cereal, there's an improved product. Now you know why manufacturers are constantly making little changes in their products. Whole new advertising campaigns, designed to convince you that the product has been changed for the better, are based on small changes in superficial aspects of a product. The next time you see an ad for an "improved" product, ask yourself what was wrong with the old one. Ask yourself just how "improved" the product is. Finally, you might check to see whether the "improved" version costs more than the unimproved one.

12   "New" is just too useful and powerful a word in advertising for advertisers to pass it up easily. So they use weasel words that say "new" without really saying it. One of their favorites is "introducing," as in, "Introducing improved Tide," or "Introducing the stain remover." The first is simply saying, here's our improved soap; the second, here's our new advertising campaign for our detergent. Another favorite is "now," as in, "Now there's Sinex," which simply means that Sinex is available. Then there are phrases like "Today's Chevrolet," "Presenting Dristan," and "A fresh way to start the day." The list is really endless because advertisers are always finding new ways to say "new" without really saying it.

Acts Fast

13 "Acts" and "works" are two popular weasel words in advertising because they bring action to the product and to the advertising claim. When you see the ad for the cough syrup that "Acts on the cough control center," ask yourself what this cough syrup is claiming to do. Well, it's just claiming to "act," to do something, to perform an action. What is it that the cough syrup does? The ad doesn't say. It only claims to perform an action or do something on your "cough control center." By the way, what and where is your "cough control center"? I don't remember learning about that part of the body in human biology class.

14   Ads that use such phrases as "acts fast," "acts against," "acts to prevent," and the like are saying essentially nothing, because "act" is a word

empty of any specific meaning. The ads are always careful not to specify exactly what "act" the product performs. Just because a brand of aspirin claims to "act fast" for headache relief doesn't mean this aspirin is any better than any other aspirin. What is the "act" that this aspirin performs? You're never told. Maybe it just dissolves quickly. Since aspirin is a parity product, all aspirin is the same and therefore functions the same.

Works Like Anything Else

15 If you don't find the word "acts" in an ad, you will probably find the weasel word "works." In fact, the two words are almost interchangeable in advertising. Watch out for ads that say a product "works against," "works like," "works for," or "works longer." As with "acts," "works" is the same meaningless verb used to make you think that this product really does something, and maybe even something special or unique. But "works," like "acts," is basically a word empty of any specific meaning.

Like Magic

16 Whenever advertisers want you to stop thinking about the product and to start thinking about something bigger, better, or more attractive than the product, they use that very popular weasel word, "like." The word "like" is the advertiser's equivalent of a magician's use of misdirection. "Like" gets you to ignore the product and concentrate on the claim the advertiser is making about it. "For skin like peaches and cream" claims the ad for a skin cream. What is this ad really claiming? It doesn't say this cream will give you peaches-and-cream skin. There is no verb in this claim, so it doesn't even mention using the product. How is skin ever like "peaches and cream"? The ad is making absolutely no promise or claim whatsoever for this skin cream. If you think this cream will give you soft, smooth, youthful-looking skin, you are the one who has read that meaning into the ad.

17 The wine that claims "It's like taking a trip to France" wants you to think about a romantic evening in Paris as you walk along the boulevard after a wonderful meal in an intimate little bistro. Of course, you don't really believe that a wine can take you to France, but the goal of the ad is to get you to think pleasant, romantic thoughts about France and not about how the wine tastes or how expensive it may be. That little word "like" has taken you away from crushed grapes into a world of your own imaginative making. Who knows, maybe the next time you buy wine, you'll think those pleasant thoughts when you see this brand of wine, and you'll buy it. Or, maybe you weren't even thinking about buying wine at all, but now you just might pick up a bottle the next time you're shopping. Ah, the power of "like" in advertising.

The World of Advertising

18 A study some years ago found the following words to be among the most popular used in U.S. television advertisements: "new," "improved," "better," "extra," "fresh," "clean," "beautiful," "free," "good," "great," and "light." At the same time, the following words were found to be among the most frequent on British television: "new," "good-better-best," "free," "fresh," "delicious," "full," "sure," "clean," "wonderful," and "special." While these words may occur most frequently in ads, and while ads may be filled with weasel words, you have to watch out for all the words used in advertising, not just the words mentioned here.

19 Every word in an ad is there for a reason; no word is wasted. Your job is to figure out exactly what each word is doing in an ad—what each word really means, not what the advertiser wants you to think it means. Remember, the ad is trying to get you to buy a product, so it will put the product in the best possible light, using any device, trick, or means legally allowed. Your only defense against advertising (besides taking up permanent residence on the moon) is to develop and use a strong critical reading, listening, and looking ability. Always ask yourself what the ad is really saying. When you see ads on television, don't be misled by the pictures, the visual images. What does the ad say about the product? What does the ad not say? What information is missing from the ad? Only by becoming an active, critical consumer of the doublespeak of advertising will you ever be able to cut through the doublespeak and discover what the ad is really saying. ◆

CONSIDERING THE ISSUES

1. Consider the phrases used in advertising such as "new and improved" and "cleans like a dream." Do you think about such advertising phrases? How much do such phrases influence you as a consumer? Explain.

2. Do you think that most people fail to comprehend how advertising works on them? When you read or watch ads, do you see through the gimmicks and weasel words?

CRAFT AND CONTENT

1. What do you think of Lutz's writing style? Is it humorous? Informal? Academic? What strategies does he use to involve the reader in the piece?

2. The author uses "you" throughout the article. Do you find the use of the second person stylistically satisfying? Do you think it is appropriate for the article?

CRITICAL THINKING

1. How did "weasel words" get their name? Does it sound like an appropriate label? Why, according to Lutz, do advertisers use them?
2. According to the author, how can consumers protect themselves against weasel words?

WRITING ABOUT THE ISSUES

1. As Lutz suggests, look at some ads in a magazine or newspaper (or television and radio commercials). Then make a list of all uses of "help" you find over a 24-hour period. Examine the ads to determine exactly what is said and what the unwary consumer thinks is being said. Write up your report.
2. Invent a product and have some fun writing an ad for it. Use as many weasel words as you can to make your product shine.
3. Lutz characterizes the language used in ads as "weasel words," that is, language that pretends to do one thing while really doing another. Explore your campus for examples of "weasel words." Look not only at ads but also at material such as university brochures and pamphlets that are sent to prospective students and/ or any political contests taking place (e.g., students running for the student government or candidates for office speaking at your campus). Write down all examples of weasel words and explain why they are empty words.

The Language of Advertising
Charles A. O'Neill

Charles A. O'Neill is an independent marketing consultant in Boston. This essay first appeared in the textbook *Exploring Language* and was updated for this edition in 2011.

CONNECTING TO THE TOPIC

Taking the minority opinion is marketing consultant Charles A. O'Neill, who disputes the criticism of advertising language by William Lutz in the preceding essay. While admitting to some of the craftiness of his profession, O'Neill defends the huckster's language—both verbal and visual—against claims that it debases reality and the values of the consumer. Examining some familiar commercials and recent print ads, he explains why the language may be seductive but is far from brainwashing.

WORDS IN CONTEXT

vexing (11)   causing irritation or annoyance (adj.)
neocortex (11)   a part of the brain located in the back cerebral cortex region (n.)
titillation (12)   exciting or stimulating (n.)
superficial (15)   without substance or significance, shallow (adj.)
eloquence (21)   forceful and persuasive speech (n.)
debases (23)   lowers in status or esteem (v.)

1   We all recognize the value of advertising, but on some level we can't quite fully embrace it as a "normal" part of our experience. At best, we view it as distracting. At worst, we view it as a pernicious threat to our health, wealth, and social values.

2   How does advertising work? Why is it so powerful? Why does it raise such concern? What case can be made for and against the advertising business? In order to understand advertising, you must accept that it is not about truth, virtue, love, or positive social values. It is about selling a product.

3   But this simple fact does not explain the unique power of advertising. Whatever the product or creative strategy, advertisements derive their power from a purposeful, directed combination of images. Images can take the form of words, sounds, or visuals, used individually or together. The combination of images is the language of advertising, a language unlike any other.

4   Everyone who grows up in the Western world soon learns that advertising language is different from other languages. We may have forgotten the sponsors, but we certainly know that these popular slogans "sound like ads."

"The Real Thing" (Coca Cola)
"The Ultimate Driving Machine" (BMW)
"Intel Inside" (Intel)
"Just Do It" (Nike)
"Have it Your Way" (Burger King)

Edited and Purposeful

5   At heart, advertising is nothing more than the delivery system for sales-manship, something woven into the fabric of our society. There is nothing

a consumer can do to hide from sales messages. This is not limited to what we think of as advertising media. We encounter it face-to-face, too.

6　　For example: When you stop at a fast food restaurant for a cup of breakfast coffee, the young man or woman who takes your order will more than likely try to "upsell" you—Not what you ordered, but something else. The manager of one such restaurant left a laminated card on the counter following an early morning motivational session for his crew. The card shows clerks how to promote items the customers did not know they wanted— i.e., a scripted sales track laced with words designed to make the customer feel *hungrier*. Simply order coffee, for example, and they might offer you "piping hot, fresh pancakes to go with your coffee" or the opportunity to "top off your breakfast with something sweet. Maybe some yummy blueberry biscuits with a dollop of sweet Vermont butter? They're my favorite."

7　　Here perfectly ordinary language is carefully enlisted in the service of sales. Even a small increase in business for a national fast food chain generates hundreds of millions of dollars of new revenue, in this case created by a few clever words delivered with a sparkling smile. Like sales scripts, advertising slogans may seem casual, but in fact they are carefully engineered with a clear purpose: to trigger a specific response.

8　　If you listen to the radio, you have undoubtedly heard an ad for "Kars4Kids." The first verse is sung by a child; and the second verse is the same as the first, but a man sings it. Both are accompanied by a strumming guitar.

1-877-kars for kids
k-a-r-s kars for kids
1-877-kars for kids
Donate your car today

9　　This is followed by the reassurance that Kars4Kids is a registered charity, and donors may be able to claim the value of their car as a tax deduction. It's not a particularly artful ad, but it does attract attention, and it works, principally through mind-numbing repetition. Never mind that some listeners have found it profoundly disturbing.

10　　In a comment on a Topix forum titled, "The most irritating radio commercial of all time" a poster from Houston said, "I couldn't stop it from playing in my head . . . I just wanted to take a power drill to my temple to drill out the awful repetition!"

11　　**Vexing** though it may be, repetition is a reliable tool in advertising. According to Answers.com "the average person needs to hear something twenty times before they truly learn it." So once you have heard about Kars4Kids a 21st time, it has been filed away in your **neocortex**. What else could an advertiser possibly hope to achieve? On its website, "Joy for Our Youth," parent of Kars4Kids, reports 2009 contributions of $23 million.

Rich and Arresting

12 Repetition works, but the all-time favorite advertising device is sex. Why? Because the desire to be sexually attractive is our most powerful instinct. Flip through any popular magazine, and you will find ads that are unabashedly, unapologetically sexual. Victoria's Secret, Calvin Klein, and every other clothing and fragrance marketer uses sex to sell. Popular media is a veritable playground of **titillation**, abounding with images of barely clothed men and women in poses suggesting that if only you would wear one of our little padded brassieres or cologne, a world a sexual adventure will reveal itself to you.

13 Every successful ad uses a creative strategy based on an idea intended to attract and hold the attention of the consumer. This may include a photo of a pretty girl, strong creative execution or a straightforward list of product features, or as we've seen, even mind-numbing repetition. Soft drink and fast-food companies are famous for their "slice of life" ads. Coke or Pepsi ads are often staged in Fourth of July parades or family events, the archetype being a scene of tots frolicking with puppies in the sunlit foreground while their youthful parents play touch football. On the porch, Grandma and Pops are seen smiling as they wait for all of this affection to transform itself in a climax of warmth, harmony, and joy. The intent is to seduced us into feeling that if we drank the right combination of sugar, preservatives, caramel coloring, and secret ingredients, we'd join the crowd that—in the words of Coca-Cola's ad from 1971—would help "teach the world to sing in perfect harmony."

Involving

14 Now that they have our attention, advertisers present information intended to show us that their product fills a need and differs from the competition. It is the copywriter's responsibility to express, exploit, and intensify product differences where they exist.

15 When product differences do not exist, the writer must glamorize **superficial** differences—for example, the packaging. As long as the ad gets our attention, the "action" is mostly in the words and visuals. But as we read or watch an ad, we become more involved. The action starts to take place in us. Our imagination is set in motion, and our individual fears and aspirations, quirks, and insecurities come into play. Consider, again, the running battle among soft drinks. The cola wars have spawned many "look-alike" advertisements, because the product features and consumer benefits are generic, applying to all products in the category. Substitute one cola brand name for another, and the messages are often identical, right down to the way the cans are photographed. This strategy relies on mass saturation and exposure for impact.

16   Another device is the use of famous personalities as product spokes-
people or models. Although ad writers didn't invent the human tendency
to admire famous people, once we have seen a celebrity in an ad, we associate the product with that person. "Britney Spears drinks milk. She's
a hottie. I want to be a hottie, too! 'Hey Mom, Got Milk?'" Celine Dion
pitches her own perfume; Sharon Stone sells Christal watches. The logic
is faulty, but we fall under the spell just the same. Advertising works, not
because Britney is a nutritionist, Celine an expert perfumer-diva or Sharon
a horologist, but because we participate in it. The ads bring the words,
sounds, and pictures. We bring the chemistry.

A Simple Language

17 Advertising language differs from other types of language in its simplicity. To determine how the text of a typical advertisement rates on
a "simplicity index" in comparison with text in a magazine article, for
example, try this exercise: Clip a typical story from the publication you
read. Calculate the number of words in an average sentence. Count the
number of words of three or more syllables in a typical 100-word passage,
omitting words that are capitalized or hyphenated or verbs made into
three syllables words by the addition of *-ed* or *-es*. Add the two figures
(average number of words per sentence and the number of three-syllable
words per 100 words), then multiply the result by .4. According to Robert
Gunning, the result is the approximate grade level required to understand
the content. He developed this formula, the "Fog Index," to determine the
comparative ease with which any given piece of written communication
can be read.

18   Let's apply the Fog Index to the lyrics in the Kars4Kids ad.

1-877-kars for kids
k-a-r-s kars for kids
1-877-kars for kids
Donate your car today

19   Counting each digit in the phone number as a word, the average
sentence in this ad is 6.25 words. There *are no three-syllable words.*
6.25 words per sentence 0 three syllable words/100 6.25 × 4 = 2.5

20   According to Gunning's scale, the language of the Kars4Kids commercial is so simple that even Geico's cavemen—and children half way
through the second grade—could understand it.

21   Why do advertisers favor simple language? The answer lies with the
consumer: People of every age are subject to an overwhelming number of
commercial messages each day. As a practical matter, we would not notice
many of these messages if engaging content or **eloquence** were counted

among their virtues. Today's consumer cannot take the time to focus on anything for long. Every aspect of modern life runs at an accelerated pace. Voice mail, smart phones, tweets, Facebook updates, text messages—the world is always switched-on, feeding our hunger for more information, now. Time generally, and TV-commercial time in particular, is experienced in increasingly smaller segments. Fifteen-second commercials are no longer unusual.

22   Advertising language is simple; in the engineering process, difficult words or images—which in other forms of communication may be used to lend color or shades of meaning—are replaced by simple words or images less vulnerable to misinterpretation.

Who Is Responsible?

23 Some critics view the advertising business as a cranky, unwelcome child of the free enterprise system. In reality, advertising mirrors the fears, quirks, and aspirations of the society that creates it (and is, in turn, sold by it). This fact alone exposes advertising to parody and ridicule. The overall level of acceptance and respect for advertising is also influenced by the varied quality of the ads themselves. Some ads are deliberately designed to provoke controversy. But this is only one of the many charges frequently levied against advertising. Others include:

1. Advertising encourages unhealthy habits.
2. Advertising feeds on human weaknesses and exaggerates the importance of material things, encouraging "impure" emotions and vanities.
3. Advertising sells daydreams—distracting, purposeless visions of lifestyles beyond the reach of most people exposed to advertising.
4. Advertising warps our vision of reality, implanting groundless fears and insecurities.
5. Advertising downgrades the intelligence of the public.
6. Advertising **debases** English.
7. Advertising perpetuates racial and sexual stereotypes.

24   What can be said in advertising's defense? First, it's only a reflection of society.

25   What about the charge that advertising debases the intelligence of the public? Those who support this particular criticism would do well to ask themselves another question: Exactly how intelligent is the public? Sadly, evidence abounds that "the public" at large is not particularly intelligent, after all. Johnny can't read. Susie can't write. And the entire family spends the night in front of the television, watching one mindless reality show after another. Ads are effective because they sell products. They would not succeed if they did not reflect the values and motivations of the real world.

Advertising both reflects and shapes our perception of reality. Consider prominent brand names and the impressions they create: Absolut is cool. Mercedes represents quality. BMW is the ultimate driving machine. Our sense of what these brand names stand for has as much to do with advertising as with the objective "truth."

26   That said, advertising shapes our perception of the world as surely as architecture shapes our impression of a city. It is part of our environment. Good, responsible advertising can serve as a positive influence for change, and encourage product innovation, while generating profits. Of course, the problem is that the obverse is also true: Advertising, like any form of mass communication, can be a force for both "good" and "bad." It can just as readily reinforce or encourage irresponsible behavior, ageism, sexism, ethnocentrism, racism, homophobia—you name it—as it can encourage support for diversity and social progress. People living in society create advertising. Society isn't perfect.

27   Perhaps, by learning how advertising works, we can become better equipped to sort out content from hype, product values from emotions, and salesmanship from propaganda. No one is forcing you to buy yummy biscuits just because they're the server's favorite. No one is holding you hostage until you call 1-877-kars for kids and give away your grandfather's car in exchange for a tax deduction and a vacation voucher. You must listen. You must read. And finally you must think— all by yourself. ◆

CONSIDERING THE ISSUES

1. O'Neill says that advertisers create in consumers a sense of need for products. Do you think it is ethical for advertisers to create such a sense when their products are "generic" and do not differ from the competition? Do you feel that you "need" one particular product over another, such as Starbucks coffee instead of Dunkin Donuts brand?

2. O'Neill believes that advertising language mirrors the fears, quirks, and aspirations of the society that creates it. Do you agree or disagree with this statement? Explain your view.

CRAFT AND CONTENT

1. William Lutz teaches English and writes books about the misuse of language. Charles O'Neill is a professional advertiser. How do their views about advertising reflect their occupations? Which side of the argument do you agree with?

2. In paragraph 16, O'Neill claims that celebrity endorsement of a product is "faulty" logic. What is faulty logic? Why do people buy products sold by famous people?

3. O'Neill anticipates potential objections to his defense of advertising. What are some of these objections? What does he say in defense of advertising? Which set of arguments do you find stronger?

CRITICAL THINKING

1. O'Neill notes that symbols have become important elements in the language of advertising. Can you think of some specific symbols from the advertising world that you associate with your own life? Are they effective symbols for selling? Explain your answer.

2. O'Neill describes several ways that advertising language differs from other kinds of language. Briefly list the ways he mentions. Can you think of any other characteristics of advertising language that set it apart?

WRITING ABOUT THE ISSUES

1. Obtain a current issue of each of the following publications: *The New Yorker, TIME, GQ, Vogue,* and *People.* Choose one article from each and calculate its Fog Index according to the technique described above. Choose one ad from each periodical and figure out its Fog Index. What different reading levels do you find among the publications? What do you know about the readers of these periodicals from your survey of the reading difficulty of each? Write up your findings in a paper.

2. Working with a group of classmates, develop a slogan and advertising campaign for one of the following products: sneakers, soda, a candy bar, or jeans. How would you apply the principles of advertising, as outlined by O'Neill, to market your product? After completing your marketing strategy, "sell" your product to the class. If time permits, explain the reasoning behind your technique.

SAMPLE ADS AND STUDY QUESTIONS

The following section features five magazine advertisements. Diverse in content and style, some ads use words to promote the product, while others depend on emotion, name recognition, visual appeal, or association. They present a variety of sales pitches and marketing techniques.

Following each ad is a list of questions to help you analyze how the ads work their appeal to promote their products. When studying them, consider how they target our social perception and basic desires for happiness, beauty, and success. Approach each as a consumer, an artist, a social scientist, and a critic with an eye for detail.

DOLCE AND GABBANA

1. Examine this advertisement carefully. What is happening in this ad? How does it sell the product? Can you tell what product the ad promotes?
2. What is the woman doing in the ad? How is she dressed and where is she located? Do these elements connect to the product? Are they confusing? Entertaining? Explain.
3. Would you know what this ad was selling if there were no brand names mentioned in the ad? Explain.
4. If you were leafing through a magazine and saw this ad, would you stop to read it? Why or why not?
5. Dolce & Gabbana is known for creating controversial ads, including ones that imply that women are second-class citizens. Could this ad be viewed in this light? Why or why not?

VISA

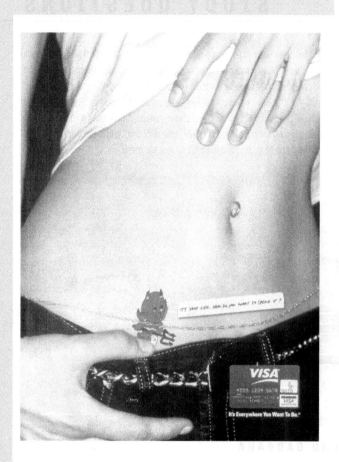

1. Would you know what this ad was promoting if the logo and the copy were not provided? Would there be any ambiguity about what was being sold? How much does this ad depend on name and image recognition? Explain.
2. This ad uses a fairly racy image to promote the product. What does this image say about Visa? About their feelings about the ad's target audience? Who are they hoping to attract to use their product?
3. In what sort of magazines and other print media would this ad be best placed? For example, would it work in *People* magazine or *Good Housekeeping?* Explain.
4. Would this ad be as effective if the tattoo were located on a different part of the body? On an arm or shoulder, for example? Why or why not?

BURGER KING

1. Who is the woman in the ad? What is she wearing, and why?
2. Where would you expect to see an ad like this, and why? If you were an advertising executive, where would you place this ad? How would you target your public? Explain.
3. What connection does the tag line, "The Lunch Battle Is Over" have to the product? What association or product image is the company trying to promote?
4. What is Burger King trying to do with this ad? Who are they targeting? Is there a primary audience and a secondary one? Explain.

STOLICHNAYA

1. How do the young women in the photograph connect to the product being promoted in this ad?
2. Who is the likely target audience for this ad? In what magazines would you expect to see it? Is it an effective ad? Explain.
3. What are the young women doing in the ad? What lifestyle does the ad promote? What is the product's implied promise? Explain.
4. What does the text below the photograph say about the product? Is the text about the women, or directed to the reader? Who do we presume the reader to be?

VANS

1. Analyze the different images featured in the ad. What do they depict? How do the different photos contribute to the overall tone of
   the ad?
2. Do you know who the man is in the ad? How does he connect to
   the product—sneakers? Is it important that he connect at all?
3. What is the meaning of the skull photo behind the man? Would the
   tone of the ad be different without it? Why or why not?
4. Who would you say is the target audience for this ad, and why?
   Consider age, gender, lifestyle, etc., in your response.

VISUAL CONNECTIONS

Corporate Crackdown

CONNECTING TO THE TOPIC ————————————

Adbusters magazine is a nonprofit, reader-supported, 120,000-circulation journal that provides critical commentary on consumer culture and corporate marketing agendas. Articles and issues from the magazine have been featured on MTV and PBS, *The Wall Street Journal, Wired,* and in hundreds of other newspapers, magazines, and television and radio shows around the world. They are "dedicated to examining the relationship between human beings and their physical and mental environment" and striving to create a "world in which the economy and ecology resonate in balance." This ad appeared both in its magazine and on its website at www.adbusters.org.

CONSIDERING THE ISSUES

1. What expectations do we have of brand names and brand-name products? Do we expect them to be better quality? To promote an image? To convey status? To be admired by others? Explain.
2. What brands do you use and why?

CRITICAL THINKING

1. What message is *Adbusters* trying to convey with this ad? Explain.
2. How many of the brands on the flag can you identify? As a challenge, can you name the 50 U.S. states that are represented by the stars on the real U.S. flag?

Blog Matters

A blog ("web log") is an online diary or commentary site that features regular entries that describe events, impressions, and viewpoints. Blogs may contain text, images, video, and often link to other websites, blogs, and online media. Most blogs allow readers to comment on the content of the post and respond to each other. As of September 2011, there were over 160 million public blogs in existence. While many blogs are maintained by individuals, some are run by journals, newspapers, and other media outlets. Remember that most blogs are not monitored for factual accuracy and often express the opinion and views of the "blogger" writing the content.

The blog below "Branding and Pop Culture," is maintained by Winthrop & Weinstein, P.A. Guest blogger, David Mitchel, Vice President of Marketing at Norton Mitchel Marketing, posted this entry on March 10, 2010.

Branding in Pop Culture

David Mitchel
March 10, 2010

Branding is an intricate and complicated process. Every aspect of the marketing mix must be handled with care. Brand managers watch their brands in
the same manner that most parents care for a newborn child. However, there
is an element of marketing communications that brand management teams
are unable to directly control: pop culture references about the brands in
what appear to be non-product placement contexts. These pop culture references can come from both old and new media. They are often found in music, and frequently occur in the hip hop genre. In recent years, brands have
been prominent parts of popular YouTube videos. As social media evolves,
it has the potential to present new threats for brands. With regard to pop
culture references, it is a challenging minefield that brands must negotiate
carefully in order to prevent them from detracting from marketing strategy.

1   In 2003, hip hop artist 50 Cent became a huge sensation with the album
"Get Rich or Die Tryin'," One of the many hit songs from that album
was "In Da Club." Near the beginning of the song, the lyric "we gon' sip
Bacardi like it's your birthday" appears. This is not the only time that the
Bacardi brand has been mentioned in song lyrics, but it is certainly one of
the more prominent references. In its advertising over the years, Bacardi
has crafted an image of being a fun brand, as their ads often feature a party
scene. This may have inspired 50 Cent to write the lyric in the way that
he did. In the late 1990s and early 2000s, Bacardi featured a "Bacardi by
Night" print advertising campaign. These ads clearly targeted individuals
with serious jobs and emphasized that Bacardi was a part of their work-life
balance. Additionally, Bacardi has also used their long standing and rich
history as a selling proposition in advertising. Bacardi's association with
fun and partying may have attracted the hip hop element, as extravagant
partying is a common theme of hip hop imagery. However, this association is tenuous at best and does not appear to be widely perceived. Bacardi
has strongly withstood unsolicited pop culture references and its well-
refined marketing communication messages have helped to ensure that
they remain the world's largest spirits brand.

2   Heineken is another alcohol brand that has received an unsolicited pop
culture reference. In 2007, a YouTube video entitled "My New Haircut"
(Warning: Contains Adult Language) was a tremendous sensation. One
could surmise that the success of the video may have been an inspiration

for MTV's *Jersey Shore*. In this video, a stereotypical New York/New Jersey young male in his 20s is shown in a variety of situations. He brags about his lifestyle, how awesome he is and professes his love for alcohol, particularly Heinekens and Jagerbombs. The Heineken brand is mentioned overtly twice in this video and is shown in the background for a significant portion of the video. The product placement in this video is the antithesis of the image that Heineken attempts to convey in its advertising. It would not desire to be associated with out-of-control, crass youths such as the one portrayed in "My New Haircut." Through its marketing communications, Heineken wishes to be perceived as a brand for those with a greater degree of class and sophistication (as seen here, here, here and here).

3   Although many of the ads are aimed at different global markets, they are tied together by the theme of Heineken being an upscale brand for the discerning palette. It is clear that Heineken has disassociated itself from the type of consumer portrayed in "My New Haircut," a strong strategic move given its history and positioning in the beer market.

4   Alcohol isn't the only product category that is referred to in pop culture. In 2004, hip hop artist Juvenile scored a huge hit with the song "Slow Motion." Juvenile makes a reference to Victoria's Secret with the lyric, "I like how that Victoria Secret sit in that (rear end)." In this situation, Victoria's Secret could not take the same approach as Heineken and completely disassociate the brand from the reference. Victoria's Secret has long been known as a lingerie brand that accentuates the sensual aspects of a woman's figure. As a result, the brand positioning was aligned with the meaning of the lyric. This pop culture reference was utterly inconsequential for the brand and Victoria's Secret never clearly addressed it. It continues to have the same positioning in the market and charges a price premium for this positioning as compared to underwear brands like Hanes and Playtex.

5   Brands in the upper end of the pricing spectrum are regularly mentioned in hip hop. Luxury brand references are as ubiquitous as inexpensive beer brands at frat parties. Gucci and Prada are common targets. In general, luxury brands try to distance themselves from hip hop culture for fear of damaging brand equity. Luxury brands will never use marketing communications messages to appeal to hip hop artists and their ardent community of followers. In fact, Burberry once refused to let rapper Ja Rule wear any of their clothing products for an Esquire magazine photo shoot.

6   All of these brands all have to deal with these references in one way or another, as pop culture references can influence how these brands are perceived by their target markets. Brand managers at each of these brands were able to successfully steer their brands away from any potential negative repercussions. An approach of distancing the brand's communication messages from the pop culture reference and focusing on advertising to strengthen the brand's positioning has repeatedly proven to be the correct strategic approach.

RESPOND TO THE BLOG:

What do you think? How does pop culture "brand" certain products? Do you find that you gravitate toward one product over another, similar one because of the pop culture branding associated with it? Explain.

TOPICAL CONNECTIONS

GROUP PROJECTS

1. Working in a group, develop a slogan and advertising campaign for one of the following products: sneakers, soda, a candy bar, or jeans. How would you apply the principles of advertising language to market your product? After completing your marketing plan, "sell" your product to the class. If time permits, explain the reasoning behind your selling technique.
2. With your group, think of some advertising campaigns that created controversy (Camel cigarettes, Calvin Klein, Carl's Jr., etc.) What made them controversial? What was the impact on sales?

WEB PROJECTS

1. Access the websites for several popular soft drinks, such as www.pepsi.com, www.coke.com, www.drpepper.com, etc. How do the websites promote the product? Who is the target audience, and how do the sites reflect this audience? What techniques do they use to sell? Write an essay on the differences between online and paper advertising for soft drinks. Will the web be the next great advertising venue? Will paper ads become obsolete? What considerations are unique to each? Is advertising on the web a passing fad or the wave of the future? Consider the information on advertising provided in this chapter when developing your response.
2. *Adbusters* addresses the unethical ways advertisers manipulate consumers to "need" products. However, if we consider ads long enough, we can determine for ourselves the ways we may be manipulated. Write a paper in which you consider the techniques of advertising. Support your evaluation with examples of advertising campaigns with which you are familiar. Make an argument for the effectiveness or exploitative nature of such campaigns. You may draw support from the articles by authors such as Rushkoff, Barber, Cave, and Lutz, as well as from your personal experience as a consumer.

FOR FURTHER INQUIRY

1. You are an advertising executive. Select one of the products featured in the sample ads section and write a new advertising campaign for it. Do you use "weasel words" or tap into popular consciousness? Do you use sex appeal or power to promote your product? How do you create a need or desire for the product? Defend your campaign to your supervisors by explaining what motivates your creative decisions.

2. Write an essay evaluating advertising techniques in the twentieth and twenty-first centuries. Have ads changed over the last 50 years or so? If you wish, view some old ads online at www .advertisingarchives.co.uk. What accounts for similarities or differences? Has advertising become more or less ethical? Creative? Focused? Be sure to explain your position and support it with examples from real advertisements.

4 | Do the Media Promote a Culture of Fear and Violence?

We live in a media-driven world. We are constantly under the influence of newspapers, magazines, television and radio programs, music, the Internet, and advertising. The mass media competes for our eyes and ears to ensure that we are exposed to the advertising that forms its backbone. Newspapers, television programs, magazines, and most radio programs are all supported by the marketing industry. The goal is getting us to pay attention. And in today's world, we seem to pay attention to scary stories.

It is human nature to pay attention to that which is distressing—whether a car wreck on the freeway, a mass murder in a restaurant in the Midwest, or a child abduction a few states away. And while such incidents are indeed distressing, we also pay attention to other "horror" stories—from moldy basements making people sick, to high mercury levels in tuna, to exploding cigarette lighters, to dangerous trans fats in our doughnuts. We are drawn to violent programs and music, even though many of us feel that such media can cause harm—especially to impressionable children.

To sift through the hype, it is important that we understand how to critically analyze different media, to use and maximize its many benefits, and to defend ourselves against its sneaky manipulations. The articles in this chapter examine the ways the media grabs our attention and preys on our deepest fears and natural tendency to worry about what a dreadful world we live in. These pieces also raise questions about violence on television and in music and the impressions such violence can make on us. Do the media have a responsibility to the public to balance hype with fact? Are the media creating a culture of fear and violence in order to sell airtime, music, magazines? And how do we distinguish fact from fiction?

CRITICAL THINKING

1. What is the effect of the four panels? What is happening? Explain.
2. Is there more than one possible interpretation of this cartoon? What do you think the cartoonist is trying to say here? Can you think of other interpretations in addition to your first one? Explain.
3. How does this cartoon connect to the larger theme of "media hype"? Explain.
4. What do the expressions on the faces of the people in the cartoon convey? Who is reacting in which panel? How might the cycle of media hype begin afresh?

http://townhall.com/political-cartoons/lisabenson/2009/02/06/20599

Extreme Reality: How Media Coverage Exaggerates Risks and Dangers
John Stossel

John Stossel is host of a weekly Fox News program, and a former coanchor of ABC's *20/20* and the recipient of 19 Emmy awards for reporting. He is the author of *Give Me a Break: How I Exposed Hucksters, Cheats, and Scam Artists and Became the Scourge of the Liberal Media* (2004). The article that follows was part of a *20/20* segment airing on July 12, 2002.

CONNECTING TO THE TOPIC

News programs such as *20/20, Dateline, 60 Minutes*, and *48 Hours*, and news magazines such as *TIME* and *Newsweek*, tend to rely on sensational stories to grab viewers' attention and keep it for the hour. Sometimes the information they provide can be quite helpful and illuminating. Yet sometimes they twist an obscure incident into a national epidemic. The trick for the audience, of course, is to figure out which is which.

WORDS IN CONTEXT

amid (4) surrounded by; in the middle of (prep.)

circular logic (8) a fallacy in reasoning in which the premise is used to prove the conclusion, and the conclusion used to prove the premise—e.g., *steroids are dangerous because they ruin your health* (n.)

conglomerate (10) a corporation made up of a number of different companies that operate in diversified fields (n.)

infinitesimally (11) immeasurably or incalculably (adv.)

mundane (12) relating to or concerned with the commonplace and the ordinary (adj.)

ramp up (14) to increase, usually in violence (v.)

rivet (14) to engross or hold (as in one's attention) (v.)

1   If you watch television news regularly, you can't help but think that the world is a very scary place.

2   You'll be hammered with a whole host of frightening stories about crime, terror threats, strange new diseases, or scary old ones. It's the media's job to inform us of these dangers, but does the amount of coverage reflect the risk we really face?

3   Remember 2001's coverage of shark attacks? It seemed everywhere you looked someone in the press was talking about the "Summer of the Shark." You may have believed that shark attacks were on the rise. That's what some television stations reported. But it wasn't true.

4   In 2002, shark attacks off American beaches were hardly different from previous years. Most of the reports mentioned that, but that important truth got lost **amid** the blare and blur of frightening headlines and images. While the media were busy scaring us out of the water, scientists said there was no increase in the number of sharks off our beaches and stressed that sharks were so unlikely to kill you that you're about 25 times more likely to be killed by lightning.

5   If television isn't frightening you, then news magazines are ready to step in and fill that void. *Newsweek*, for example, claimed Americans were being "driven to destruction" by road rage. In their report, they quoted a study saying we were "increasingly being shot, stabbed, beaten and run over." Then television echoed with its own flurry of road-rage reports. On *20/20*, ABC NEWS introduced a story by telling viewers that they're surrounded by "strangers in their cars, ready to snap." We called road rage a frightening trend and a growing American danger.

6   The hype surrounding the reporting blew the real dangers out of proportion. Bob Lichter, president of the Center for Media and Public Affairs, which studies media coverage, has concluded that the media often distort or exaggerate threats. He said, "If road rage is something that's increasing . . . we should see more fatalities on the road. There should be more reports of reckless driving. But these things are going down instead of up."

7   A justification for the media hype surrounding road rage was a study sponsored by the American Automobile Association (AAA) that chronicled reports of aggressive driving. According to a *Time* magazine story, which based its information on the AAA report, road rage was up 51 percent in the first half of the 1990s.

8   Stefanie Faul, a spokeswoman for the AAA, said the consumer group based its analysis mostly on the number of road rage and aggressive driving incidents reported in the press. It was a strange sort of **circular logic** that fueled the spiraling coverage of road rage. The AAA study looked at police reports as well, but was largely based on media accounts.

9   Lichter said people have been yelling at each other in their cars for years. Journalists just found a term for it. A few years back, Lichter noted, a person might come and complain that somebody yelled at them from his car. Today, people go home and say they're victims of "road rage."

10   AAA's Faul said that the idea of violent death by strangers is a very common topic in news reports. "You know that if you get people excited about an issue . . . that's what makes it appealing as a topic." She also added that small organizations like hers can't take on huge media **conglomerates**.

Still, she admits that she didn't make an effort to correct the mischaracterization she saw in the press.

11   And before there was road rage, there were carjackings. The media told us that carjackings were making a comeback on Americans streets in the '90s. Greg McCrary, of the Threat Assessment Group, which works to point out that life's real dangers are far less dramatic than what the media may lead you to believe, said the chance of being killed in a carjacking is **infinitesimally** small.

12   McCrary said the **mundane** things pose greater risks on the road—things like drunken driving and failing to fasten our seat belts. Like Faul, McCrary said these sorts of things just aren't attention-grabbing. "It doesn't sell on TV. Sex and violence sells," he said.

13   Lichter agrees with McCrary's assessment. His organization noted that press coverage of murders increased by 700 percent in the 1990s, but the murder rate had fallen by half during the decade. Lichter said, "It's easier to point a camera at a blood-stained wall where a victim has just been taken away, than it is to dig into a book of dull, dry statistics."

14   According to Lichter, when there's not a major news story that has some dramatic element to it, newspapers and television stations will **ramp up** their coverage of things like shark attacks and carjackings to keep us buying papers and tuning in. Lichter said, "Journalists unconsciously train themselves to look for the story that really **rivets** your attention. And that story is, 'Wow, here's a disaster, oh my God.'"

15   A few years ago, for example, there were as many shark attacks, but it wasn't a summer of the shark. Perhaps because the media were busy covering the election. Back in 1995 there were 46 shark attacks, but the spotlight was on O.J. Simpson's murder trial. In 1998, the Monica Lewinsky story kept the shark attacks in the shadows.

16   Lichter said that reporters may have the best of intentions when they pursue a story, but often they stir up problems that really aren't there. This, Lichter said, poses a real danger to the public. Lichter said, "Bad journalism is worse than no journalism, because it leaves people thinking they know something that is, in fact, wrong." ◆

CONSIDERING THE ISSUES

1. In his article, Stossel notes several media-hyped issues: shark attacks, road rage, and carjackings. Coverage of these issues contributes to our perception that it is a very dangerous world out there. What fears do you have regarding the society in which we live? For example, are you afraid that you could be a victim of road rage? Murder? Make a list of the things that worry you about today's society. Include even small things that may not seem dangerous but concern you nonetheless.

2. Have you ever changed your behavior based on a news report? For example, did you avoid swimming because of shark attacks or avoid driving in a certain area for fear of road rage or carjackings? Or stop eating a particular food because it might cause cancer or another disease? Explain.

CRAFT AND CONTENT

1. What was the "circular logic" of the media hype surrounding road rage (paragraphs 5–7)? What was faulty about this logic, and how did it mislead the public's perception of road rage?
2. Review Stossel's last paragraph in which he paraphrases Bob Lichter: "[The media] stir up problems that really aren't there . . . this . . . poses a real danger to the public." Can this paragraph be viewed as making some of the same media errors Stossel challenges in his essay? Explain.

CRITICAL THINKING

1. John Stossel is a media journalist. Does the fact that he is reporting on a problem in his own industry make his comments seem more credible? Why or why not?
2. Greg McCrary, of the Threat Assessment Group, observes, "Sex and violence sells." Why do we find these things more interesting than more mundane things? What is it about sex and violence that holds such appeal?

WRITING ABOUT THE ISSUES

1. In the closing paragraph, Bob Lichter states, "Bad journalism is worse than no journalism, because it leaves people thinking they know something that is, in fact, wrong." Write a response to this statement from the viewpoint of a television journalist. You may agree or disagree with his comment. (Remember that Stossel seems to agree and he is a television journalist himself.)
2. Stossel notes that the summer of 2002 was "the summer of the shark." Review the news from the past year and try to identify the sensationalized stories that marked certain seasons. For example, some people may think that the winter of 2004 was marked by stories about Lacey Peterson and the Atkins diet ("Carb Wars"). Visit websites such as www.cnn.com and www. msnbc.com/top10.asp for current hot news topics. After compiling your list, try to determine which topics were likely hyped up for the consumer audience.

The Female Fear Factor

Myrna Blyth

Myrna Blyth served as the editor for the magazine *Ladies' Home Journal* from 1981 to 2002. Before joining *Ladies' Home Journal*, Blyth was the executive editor of the women's magazine *Family Circle*. This article is excerpted from her 2004 exposé book, *Spin Sisters: How the Women of the Media Sell Unhappiness and Liberalism to the Women of America.*

CONNECTING TO THE TOPIC

American women today are the most prosperous, healthy, well-educated, and advantaged ever. Yet many feel unhappy—overwhelmed, unsafe, stressed, and even victimized. From morning shows to women's magazines, journalists influence how women see the world. As a member of the female journalistic elite, Myrna Blyth knew firsthand just how to twist a story to sell magazines. This twisting of information, or *spin* as it is known in the industry, promotes sensationalized stories in order to get women to watch a program, read an article, or listen to a news broadcast. Do the media feed on women's natural insecurities? If so, is such manipulation unethical, or simply part of media culture? And, to take a page out of the media hype playbook, could spin be creating a culture of fear?

WORDS IN CONTEXT

solemnly (2)   earnestly, with grave seriousness (adv.)
wont (4)   likely (adj.)
chaser (4)   something closely following another thing, from the informal reference to a drink, such as beer or water, taken after hard liquor (n.)
incensed (5)   extremely angry; infuriated (adj.)
Alar (12)   the trade name for daminozide, a chemical plant growth regulator, formerly used to increase the storage life of fruit (n.)
asbestos (12)   a chemical-resistant, fibrous mineral form of impure magnesium silicate used for fireproofing, electrical insulation, building materials, brake linings, and chemical filters (n.)
Alzheimer's (13)   a degenerative brain disease marked by memory loss and dementia (n.)
mitigate (16)   to moderate (a quality or condition) in force or intensity; alleviate (v.)
tuberculosis (18)   an infectious disease usually of the lungs (n.)
diluted (18)   made thinner or less concentrated by adding a liquid such as water (adj.)

1 **W**hen Diane Sawyer looks me in the eye and tells me "sleeping on a conventional mattress is like sleeping on kerosene," she gets my attention—and that's the point. It was a March 30, 2000, *Good Morning America* segment. I stopped making the bed, grabbed my coffee, and sat glued to the set watching a fairly typical and typically scary network report on the dangers of non-flame-resistant mattresses.

2 Watching, with a pro's eye—hey, maybe this is a story for my magazine, too—I noted that the report had everything a woman needs . . . to start the day wrong. It had:

1. **Fear**—"This is a mattress study called 'The Big Burn' conducted by the California Bureau of Home Furnishings back in 1991." (Meaning nine whole years had passed before the show, but who's counting?) "It was a test to see how long it would take for a fire to consume a mattress like the one you just spent the night on. Firefighters . . . say they are well aware of the risk," **solemnly** intoned reporter Greg Hunter.
2. **A threat that endangers children**—"Stacey Hernandez's son, Damon, set a polyurethane foam mattress on fire in California back in 1993 . . ." (Seven years before the show.) "Third-degree burns over half his body."
3. **A distraught mother**—"If I had known that that was so unsafe I would rather we had slept on the floor."

3 The story also featured a bit of a debate and a doubter or two, but any and all criticisms of the story's basic premise were passed over faster than a size 14 at a fashion shoot. "The Consumer Product Safety Commission and the mattress industry insist that the greater fire hazard is what's on the mattress, [namely] the bedclothes. Not the polyurethane on the inside." Great. Now, what are the odds of finding a comforting little fire-resistant tag still on those sheets I've slept on through at least three presidents?

4 Then, as television is **wont** to do, we were given a **chaser** of reassurance after the scare session: "The federal government has required mattresses to be cigarette resistant since 1973," which I had already guessed is the cause of most bedroom fires.

5 Still, I sat there watching a terribly disfigured child, a weeping mom, and an **incensed** Diane. "This is really stunning," she said.

6 But what should be done about it? If I wanted to get a flame-retardant mattress right away, like before tonight when I might once again be "sleeping on kerosene," where do I find one?

7 "Only in some state prisons," Greg tells me.

8 Now, that's very helpful. Let me run right out and rob a bank.

9 That short *Good Morning America* piece was pretty standard fare, and a good illustration of the way editors and television producers construct

human interest stories and consumer reports that are the bread and butter of media aimed at women. Next time you watch *48 Hours* or *Dateline NBC*, look at the way the story is told. They all tend to have the same format: High volume on the emotions, low volume on everything else (facts, balance, debate, assessment of risks, advice you can really use).

10   But even knowing how the media overdoes stories, my basic reaction to the *GMA* piece was probably just what yours would have been. How very sad about that child. And even though I know that most safety officials are neither uncaring nor unwise, I was left with the uneasy feeling that we are often in danger, even in our own beds.

11   And that's what *GMA*, *20/20*, *Today*, *Dateline*, *Lifetime*, and other network series—all of them—want you to feel. Afraid. Worried that the next victim might be you or your child. When it comes to selling fear, television and women's magazines live by one rule—there's no such thing as overkill, no pun intended.

12   For years, we have been warned and warned again about so many terrible things—benzene in our bottled water, Alar on our apples. We may not have **Alar** to be afraid of anymore but never fear, there's always **asbestos** in our school buildings, secondhand smoke in our environment, the hole in the ozone layer, the ozone in the ozone layer, high-tension power lines, cell phones that cause brain cancer, and lead paint peeling off our walls. That old lead paint fear was recycled in a recent *Redbook* article that claimed that living in any house built before 1978—which means 40 percent of all homes in America—could be a serious danger to your children. So now I know my kids spent their entire childhood in danger, not just when they came home after curfew.

13   We have also been warned by the Center for Science in the Public Interest, a.k.a. the food police, that popcorn, margarine, red meat, Chinese, Italian, French, and Mexican food along with McDonald's French fries contribute to heart disease. Still ordering fettuccine Alfredo? Heart attack on a plate, sister! Aluminum and zinc may contribute to **Alzheimer's**. And almost everything else including alcohol, birth control pills, bottled water, silicone breast implants, exhaust fumes, chlorine, caffeine, dairy products, diet soda, hot dogs, fluoridation, grilled meat, hair dyes, hydrogen peroxide, incense, jewelry, kissing, laxatives, low-fiber diets, magnetic fields, marijuana, olive oil, orange juice, peanut butter, playground equipment, salt, "sick" buildings, sun beds, sunlight, sunscreen, talc, testosterone, tight bras, toast, tooth fillings, vinyl toys, and wallpaper may cause cancer.

14   More than twenty years ago, political scientist Aaron Wildavsky looked around America and wrote, "How extraordinary! The richest, longest-lived, best-protected, most resourceful civilization with the highest degree of insight into its own technology is on its way to becoming the most frightened." We have arrived.

15   And the media is largely to blame; even media reporters fess up to that. As David Shaw wrote in the *Los Angeles Times*, "The media, after all, pays the most attention to those substances, issues and situations that most frighten their readers and viewers. Thus, almost every day, we read and see and hear about a new purported threat to our health and safety."

16   Says TV commentator Jeff Greenfield, "It's a basic rule of journalism—to get the human angle. But with a complicated technical story . . . the concerns, the worries, the fears of people . . . will always carry more weight than the disputes and the cautions of the experts." In other words, let's not clutter up a perfectly good horror story with any **mitigating** facts.

17   Human drama, human emotions are what work. And pictures—dramatic pictures of a sobbing mother, an injured child, a disfigured teenager. Such pictures and the stories that go with them are easy for women to empathize with and understand. And that's the name of the game—attracting women. So why should we be surprised that so many of these pieces are for and about women. For example, on *20/20* there was a segment, in the early summer of 2001, introduced by Barbara Walters telling us:

> How do you like to be pampered? For millions . . . especially women, especially as summer approaches, the answer is a visit to a nail salon. Maybe you're headed there tomorrow. Well, we have to warn you, you may come home with more than beautiful fingers and toes, because there is something ugly going on at some nail salons. Customers who don't know how to protect themselves are really getting nailed.

18   "Getting Nailed" was about a California nail salon where a group of women were infected by **tuberculosis**-related bacteria that were found in the drain of the foot basin, which had not been carefully cleaned. The rest of the piece took us along as undercover inspectors raided other salons in various states. Many, owned by immigrants, were found to be violating local health codes, reusing emery boards and swabbing counters down with **diluted** disinfectant. Only one salon was shown to have seriously injured any clients, but the legs of the women who had become infected did, I grant you, look quite gruesome.

19   At the end of the piece, Barbara Walters shared that "I wanted to have a pedicure this week," but she said she didn't. Why not? Did the *20/20* piece make her as fearful as it was supposed to make us? Not really. Barbara told us, "Once and again I've been too busy." She didn't say she would be sure to do a safety check the next time she hits Frederic Fekkai's exclusive salon as she advised her loyal viewers to do.

20   Still, e-mails flew around my office and across the Internet—the world's biggest party line—as women warned their sister sandal wearers of the newly discovered dangers of the pedicure. This was real news we

can use from one of television's most respected women journalists warning us that pampering can be hazardous to your health.

21   And we do depend on media to tell us what's important in the world, good news and bad. Whether it's *Dateline NBC* or Peter Jennings or *Ladies' Home Journal*, the media is our information source, and we want the truth. And there's the rub. Although we might like to think so, journalists and editors don't just transmit the facts, ma'am. They select and shape it and make facts fit into emotional stories that tug at our heartstrings or send a chill up our spines. I've done it myself. That's because news is most effective when it tells a story that confirms our deep-seated beliefs and stokes our deep-seated fears. As psychology professor Paul Slovic of the University of Oregon says, "We trust people who tell us we're in danger more than people who tell us we're not in danger." And when we hear someone is harmed, we want a simple explanation for her pain. A very simple explanation. Editors and producers know that.

22   Look, I'm not telling you that all these "fear factor" pieces you read in magazines and see on the networks are untrue. Those women on *20/20* did get a nasty infection from their pedicures. Through the years I published many articles about wrongs against women and families, and stories about health that were fair and honest. I believed I was giving good sensible information. But there is always the temptation to play gotcha! To simplify and dramatize in order to hold the attention of the reader or viewer. And I can't deny that those of us in media, like a little girl who keeps crying long after her stubbed toe has stopped hurting, tend to exaggerate and do a lot of it for effect.

23   That's why even though women and men are safer and healthier than we have ever been, we are also more afraid of what we eat, drink, touch, and breathe. Eleanor Singer and Phyllis Endreny, two social scientists, did a study of risk coverage by the media and concluded, "A direct comparison between hazards as topics of news stories and as causes of death show essentially no relationship between the two." So we're really okay, but we are being told not to feel okay. That's because the media, in order to attract readers and viewers, "often overplays risks of dubious legitimacy. Scientific studies show that many of the alleged hazards the media trumpet are either misstated, overstated, nonexistent or there just is not enough scientific evidence yet to yield reliable guidance on the true risk for the average American." Which, I admit, is a kind of shabby way to get readers or ratings. ◆

CONSIDERING THE ISSUES

1. Blyth's introduction describes a television program segment that drew her to sit and watch. What types of news story "hooks" are likely to get your attention? Have you stayed up

later than you intended or watched a news program because the "hook" statement before the show or news segment grabbed your interest? Explain.

2. What makes you buy a particular magazine? Is it the content? The advertisements? The stories? The layout? Do the headlines on the magazine influence you to buy it? Do you ever think about how the headlines might be manipulating you? Explain.

CRAFT AND CONTENT

1. In paragraph 2, Blyth notes three things that Diane Sawyer's story used to hold a woman riveted to the television set. Analyze these elements and explain why they work to capture the intended audience. Would they work on you to grab and hold your attention? Why or why not?

2. Like John Stossel at the beginning of this chapter, Myrna Blyth is an "insider" to the journalism industry. Drawing from your experience with the format of most stories in popular magazines, in what ways does Blyth's article resemble the story format typical in many women's magazines? Does this format make her argument more accessible to her readers? (If you are unfamiliar with this format, take a look at some articles from the magazines she cites in your library or at a newsstand, and then review the article again.)

CRITICAL THINKING

1. In paragraph 15, Blyth quotes *Los Angeles Times* reporter David Shaw, "The media, after all, pays the most attention to those substances, issues, and situations that most frighten their readers and viewers. Thus, almost every day, we read and see and hear about a new purported threat to our health and safety." Respond to Shaw's statement with your own opinion. Is this practice acceptable? Does it allow the reader to determine what information is important, and what is not? Explain.

2. Blyth reveals how women's magazines target women's fears in order to sell magazines. What techniques are used to hook men's attention on magazines? How do men and women's magazines differ? Can the same principles be applied to popular men's magazines such as *Details, Maxim, GQ,* and *Esquire*? Explain.

WRITING ABOUT THE ISSUES

1. Blyth notes that "When it comes to selling fear, television and women's magazines live by one rule—there's no such thing as overkill, no pun intended." Visit your local library and scan the headlines on some popular women's magazines. Write down any headlines that seem to fit Blyth's assertion. How does the magazine twist the story to grab the viewer's attention? Is this technique ethical? Is it simply the way magazines market their material? Explain.

2. Create your own magazine cover for a women's magazine presenting stories in a factual and unsensationalized way. Select a real magazine and create an alternative cover for it after reading the articles and analyzing them with a critical eye.

Blog Matters

A blog ("web log") is an online diary or commentary site that features regular entries that describe events, impressions, and viewpoints. Blogs may contain text, images, video, and often link to other websites, blogs, and online media. Most blogs allow readers to comment on the content of the post and respond to each other. As of September 2011, there were over 160 million public blogs in existence. While many blogs are maintained by individuals, some are run by journals, newspapers, and other media outlets. Remember that most blogs are not monitored for factual accuracy and often express the opinion and views of the "blogger" writing the content.

The blog below is maintained by danah boyd, a social media researcher at Microsoft Research New England and a fellow at Harvard University's Berkman Center for Internet and Society. Her research examines social media, youth practices, tensions between public and private, social network sites, and other intersections between technology and society.

Growing Up in a Culture of Fear: From Columbine to Banning of MySpace

danah boyd*
November 2, 2005

1   'm tired of mass media perpetuating a culture of fear under the scapegoat of informing the public. Nowhere is this more apparent than how they discuss youth culture and use scare tactics to warn parents of the safety risks about the Internet. The choice to perpetually report on the possibility or rare occurrence of kidnapping/stalking/violence because of Internet sociability is not a neutral position—it is a position of power that the media chooses to take because it's a story that sells. There's something innately human about rubbernecking, about looking for fears, about reveling in the possibilities of demise. Mainstream media capitalizes on this, manipulating the public and magnifying the culture of fear. It sells horror films and it sells newspapers.

2   A few days ago, I started laying out how youth create a public in digital environments because their physical publics are so restricted. Since then, I was utterly horrified to see that some school officials are requiring students to dismantle their MySpace and Xanga accounts or risk suspension. The reason is stated simply in the article: "If this protects one child from being near-abducted or harassed or preyed upon, I make no apologies for this stance." OMG, this is insane.

3   In some ways, I wish that the press had never heard of these sites. . . . I wish that I had never participated in helping them know of its value to youth culture. I wish that it remained an obscure teenage site. Because I'm infuriated at how my own participation in information has been manipulated to magnify the culture of fear. The culture of fear is devastating; it is not the same as safety.

4   Let's step back a few years. Remember Columbine? I was living in Amsterdam at the time and the coverage was brilliant—the Dutch press talked about how there was a school shooting by kids who felt alienated from their community. And then the US coverage started pouring in. Goths (or anyone wearing black, especially black trench coats) were marked as the devil incarnate. Video games were evil and were promoting killing. Everything was blamed except the root cause: alienation. There were exceptions though. I remember crying the first time I read Jon Katz's *Voices from the Hellmouth* where numerous youth poured out their souls about how they were treated in American education systems. Through his articles, he was able to capture the devastation of the culture of fear. My professor Henry Jenkins testified in Washington about how

dangerous our culture has become, not because there are tools of rage, but an unchecked systematic creation of youth alienation. He pleaded with Congress: "Listen to our children. Don't fear them." And yet, we haven't. In response, youth went underground. Following one of his talks, a woman came up to him dressed in an array of chaotic pink. She explained to Henry that she was a goth, but had to go underground. What kind of world do we live in where a color symbolizes a violent act?

5   We fear our children. We fear what they might do in collectives. We ban them from public spaces. We think that we are protecting them, but we're really feeding the media industry and guaranteeing the need for uncountable psychiatrists. Imagine the weight that this places on youth culture. Imagine what it's like to grow up under media scrutiny, parental protectionism and formalist educational systems.

6   During the summer of 1999, I was driving cross-country and ended up at an outdoor rave outside of Denver, Colorado. I was sitting in my tent, writing in my diary when a group of teens rapped at my door asking if they could come in and smoke because it was too windy outside to light the damn thing. I invited them in and we started talking. They were all from Littleton and had all dropped out of school shortly following Columbine and were now at a loss for what to do. I asked them why they dropped out, expecting that they would tell me about how eerie the school was or how they were afraid of being next. No. They dropped out because the media was hounding them everywhere they went. They couldn't get into the school without being pestered; they couldn't go to the mall or hang out and play basketball. They found underground venues for socialization. Here we were, in the middle of a field outside town at a rave, the only place that they felt safe to be themselves. The underground rave scene flourished in the summer of 1999 outside Denver because it was a safe haven for teens needing to get away from adult surveillance and pressure. Shortly later, the cops busted the party. I went and pleaded with them, asking them to let the kids camp there without the music; they had the permits for camping. No; they had heard that there were kids doing ecstasy. Let's say they are—you want them to drive on drugs? Why not let them just camp? The cops ignored me and turned on bright lights and told the kids that they needed to leave in 10 minutes or they would be arrested. Argh! I'm not going to condone teenage drug use, but I also know that it comes from a need to find one's identity, to make sense of the world removed from adult rules. These kids need a safe space to be themselves; overzealous police don't help a damn thing.

7   How do youth come of age in this society? What good is it to restrict every social space that they have? Does anyone actually think that this is a good idea? Protectionist actions tend to create hatred, resentment. It destroys families by failing to value trust and responsibility. Ageist rhetoric alienates the younger generation. And for what purpose?

8   The effects are devastating. Ever wonder why young people don't vote? Why should they? They've been told for so damn long that their voices don't matter, have been the victims of an oppressive regime. What is motivating about that? How do you learn to use your voice to change power when you've been surveilled and controlled for so long, when you've made an art out of subversive engagement with peers? When you've been put on drugs like Strattera that control your behavior to the point of utter obedience?

9   We drug our children the whole way through school as a mechanism of control and wonder why drug abuse and alcoholism is rampant when they come of age. I've never seen as many drugs as I did at pristine prestigious boarding schools. The wealthy kids in our society are so protected, pampered. When given an ounce of freedom, they go from one extreme to the other instead of having healthy exploratory developments. Many of the most unstable, neurotic and addicted humans I have met in this lifetime come from a position of privilege and protectionism. That cannot be good.

10   We need to break this culture of fear in order to have a healthy society. Please, please . . . whenever you interact with youth culture (whether you're a parent, a schoolteacher or a cafe owner), learn from them. Hear them from their perspectives and stop trying to project your own fears onto them. Allow them to flourish by giving them the freedom to make sense of their identity and culture. It doesn't mean that there aren't risks—there are. But they are not as grandiose as the press makes them out to be. And besides, youth need to do stupid things in order to learn from their own mistakes. Never get caught up in the "I told you so" commentary that comes after that "when I was your age" bullshit. People don't learn this way—they learn by putting their hand in the fire and realizing it really is hot and then stepping back.

11   Post-Columbine, we decided to regulate the symptoms of alienation rather than solve the problem. Today, we are trying to regulate youth efforts to have agency and public space. Both are products of a culture of fear and completely miss the point. We need to figure out how to support youth culture, exploration and efforts to make sense of the social world. The more we try to bottle it into a cookie-cutter model, the more we will destroy that generation.

12   In line with Henry's claim to Congress, I want to plead to you (and ask you to plead to those you know): Listen to the youth generation—don't fear them and don't project your fear onto them.

13   *(Note: My use of the term "kids" references the broader youth population using a slang very familiar to subcultures where an infantilized generation reclaimed the term for personal use. I am 27 and I still talk about my friends as kids. What I'm referencing is youth culture broadly, not children and not just teens.)*

RESPOND TO THE BLOG:

What do you think? Are the media programming us to fear American life? Are they promoting a world that is cold, heartless, violent, corrupt, and dangerous? Why? How do we slog through the hype to get to the truth? Present your own view here.

Violent Media Numbs Viewers to Pain of Others
Diane Swanbrow

Diane Swanbrow is Communications Director at University of Michigan Institute for Social Research. This next piece is a press release describing the research of University of Michigan professor Brad Bushman and Iowa State University professor Craig Anderson. The results of their research into media violence were later published in the March 2009 issue of *Psychological Science.*

CONNECTING TO THE TOPIC

A recent study appearing in the March 2009 issue of *Psychological Science* reported that violent video games and movies make people numb to the pain and suffering. Although previous research has suggested that people can become more aggressive and desensitized to real-life violence after repeatedly viewing violent media—including movies, television, and video games—little is known about how the extent of watching such programs and the severity of the aggression displayed affects the brains of children and adults. Should the media industry be more responsible for its programming? Is society as a whole at risk?

WORDS IN CONTEXT

physiological (1)   relating to the biological study of living organisms (adj.)
desensitization (1)   numbness, inability to feel (n.)

1   **V**iolent video games and movies make people numb to the pain and suffering of others, researchers say. Two studies, conducted by Institute for Social Research at the University of Michigan professor Brad Bushman and Iowa State University professor Craig Anderson, fill an important research gap in the literature on the impact of violent media. In earlier work, Bushman and Anderson demonstrated that exposure to violent media produces

physiological desensitization—lowering heart rate and skin conductance—when viewing scenes of actual violence a short time later. But the current research demonstrates that violent media also affect someone's willingness to offer help to an injured person, in a field study as well as in a laboratory experiment.

2   "These studies clearly show that violent media exposure can reduce helping behavior," says Bushman, professor of psychology and communications and a research professor at ISR. "People exposed to media violence are less helpful to others in need because they are 'comfortably numb' to the pain and suffering of others, to borrow the title of a Pink Floyd song."

3   In one of the studies, 320 college students played either a violent or a nonviolent video game for approximately 20 minutes. A few minutes later, they overheard a staged fight that ended with the victim sustaining a sprained ankle and groaning in pain. People who had played a violent game took significantly longer to help the victim than those who played a nonviolent game—73 seconds compared to 16 seconds. People who had played a violent game also were less likely to notice and report the fight. And if they did report it, they judged it to be less serious than did those who had played a nonviolent game.

4   In the second study, the participants were 162 adult moviegoers. The researchers staged a minor emergency outside the theater in which a young woman with a bandaged ankle and crutches dropped her crutches and struggled to retrieve them. The researchers timed how long it took moviegoers to retrieve the crutches. Participants who had just watched a violent movie took over 26 percent longer to help than either people going into the theater or people who had just watched a nonviolent movie.

5   The studies are part of an on-going research program into the causes and consequences of human aggression. ◆

CONSIDERING THE ISSUES

1. Think about the level and frequency of violence in the programs you watch on television. Is violence a common theme? What types of television programs do you like to watch, and why?
2. This press release reports that when people view violent media, they are less swift to help others, especially people who are in pain or who are obviously suffering. In your opinion, do you think this phenomenon has translated into our daily lives? Why or why not?

CRAFT AND CONTENT

1. This article is a press release—that is, it reports on research that will appear in another publication. What information does this document convey most strongly? What organizational devices does it use to make certain points stand out? Explain.

2. What authorities and sources does Swanbrow use to support her report? Who are the authorities in this release, and how likely are you to agree with their research conclusions?

CRITICAL THINKING

1. The American Psychological Association has warned that research indicates that children who watch violent television programs are more likely to think that the world is "a mean and dangerous place." What effect might such a belief have on a child? What about when that child grows up? Explain.
2. What are the broader uses of the information conducted by Bushman and Anderson? How might a teacher use this information? A psychologist? A criminal lawyer? A military leader? Explain.

WRITING ABOUT THE ISSUES

1. Despite significant evidence indicating that violence influences our psychology, the issue continues to be debated. Why do you think that is? Why is this issue so controversial?
2. Locate the study published by *Psychological Science* (you will need to use your library resources to do this) and review the entire report. Based on what you learn, write an essay exploring the social implications of violent media and its impact on our culture today and in the next 10 years.

Hate Violence? Turn It Off!

Tim Goodman

Columnist Tim Goodman is a television and media critic for the *San Francisco Chronicle,* in which this article first appeared on April 29, 2001.

CONNECTING TO THE TOPIC

Not everyone agrees that television violence is a problem. Some people argue that if you don't like what you see on television, you should change the channel or turn it off. The author of the next piece is tired of critics complaining that television violence is damaging to children. He says, "Vote with your remote" and stop trying to ruin television for everyone else.

WORDS IN CONTEXT

plethora (2)   a superabundance; an excess (n.)

censorship (4)   the practice of restricting, suppressing, or removing material that is considered morally, politically, or socially objectionable (n.)

scapegoat (4)   one that is made to bear the blame of others (n.)

lax (4)   lacking in strictness; overly permissive; negligent (adj.)

vaunted (5)   boasted or bragged about (adj.)

pap (6)   material lacking real value or substance (n.)

prominent (10)   immediately noticeable; conspicuous (adj.)

ratcheted (11)   increased or decreased by increments (v.)

erode (13)   wear away (v.)

chaos (13)   condition or place of great disorder or confusion (n.)

1   Perhaps it's a sign of progress that Americans are becoming just as concerned about violence on television as they are about sex. For years, a barely concealed nipple or a tame bed scene was deemed worse than hundreds of people being brutally shot down on cop shows and the like.

2   Now you can't pick up the paper without some watchdog group denouncing Hollywood for ruining their children's lives with a **plethora** of violent images nightly. Some kid goes postal at his high school and *Starsky and Hutch* is the root cause.

3   We're getting our priorities right and wrong simultaneously. If sexuality is now not the enemy, great. But to continue to demonize Hollywood for its portrayals of violence is to put our heads in the sand about the world we live in.

4   Worse, it's just plain wrong, reeks of **censorship** and, in the context of parents worried about their children, it's looking for a **scapegoat** when **lax** parenting skills are more to blame.

5   For example, parents have put pressure on their elected officials to "do something" about violence, and the result has been a ratings system that surveys suggest most parents never use. And then there's the **vaunted** "V-chip," which effectively shifted parental responsibility to the government and doesn't consider the simplest way for everyone to solve this problem: Vote with your remote.

6   Some of us like violence. Some of us like shows that have a gritty realism to them, rather than the glossy **pap** offered up by most networks. And think of all the people without children who, as grown-ups, choose to watch programming clearly geared to adults. Just because you've given little Jimmy his own TV set upstairs and now you can't stop him from watching *Jackass* on MTV or *Oz* on HBO, don't cry foul and ruin it for the rest of us.

7   This is an old and now increasingly tired defense of art, anti-censorship and the need for parents to take more responsibility for what their children are watching. Don't like it? Don't watch it. There are enough elements in place now—blocking devices, ratings, V-chips, etc.—that to whine about how Hollywood should tone it down (as you allow the blood-and-guts nightly news to waft over dinner) completely misses the point about whose kid it is.

8   Then again, many adults also dislike violence. Fine. Vote with the remote. Go to PBS, the History Channel, Disney—whatever—just stop writing letters to politicians who have already had a chilling effect (thus a watering- and dumbing-down of content) on what we already see.

9   Most recently, there has been a backlash against *The Sopranos*, with many people thinking there's been an amping up of the violence and at least two very disturbing episodes filled with violence toward women.

10   First off, yes, those were difficult to watch. But HBO runs a very **prominent** content advisory at the front of every episode. And, more important, *The Sopranos* is not *Leave It to Beaver*, despite near universal acclaim from critics and an almost scary loyalty among viewers.

11   It's just a hunch, but perhaps creator David Chase, sensing this weird, uncomfortable embracing of—let's be honest here—bad people, **ratcheted** up the violence as a reminder of what exactly it is we're watching.

12   If this moved people out of their comfort zones, they should stop watching. Many have. Others have complained to HBO and some are asking that such behavior be toned down. The short answer to that is this: No. *The Sopranos* is art. As a viewer, your reaction to that art can be anything you want it to be, but restricting it instead of looking away is not the right course.

13   This goes beyond freedom of expression, of course, and those who do not embrace their own freedom to choose other programming. People assume that television has somehow helped **erode** the social contract that keeps **chaos** and horror at bay. They blame television for the downfall of the nation's morals.

14   But we have always been a violent country. People were killed at a pretty good clip before television appeared. It's the dark side of our nature, but it didn't come out of the bogeyman's closet 50 years ago.

15   Violence as entertainment, or as a realistic expression of what is really going on in our world, will never appeal to some people. But no one is forcing them to watch. There are dozens of other channels, hundreds of other programs.

16   There's also an off button. Sometimes that gets forgotten.

17   Television is not the problem in our society. It may always be the scapegoat, but it's nothing more than a bastard machine, not half as disturbing as the real thing. ◆

CONSIDERING THE ISSUES

1. Goodman states that pressuring Hollywood to change violent programming "reeks of censorship." Do you agree with Goodman? What do you think censorship means? Are you opposed to censorship of this kind? Why or why not?
2. Do you enjoy watching violent television programs? Would you be upset if a "watchdog" group forced one of your favorite programs off the air? Explain.

CRAFT AND CONTENT

1. Evaluate the author's use of language in paragraphs 6, 7, 16, and 17. What does it reveal about people who wish to change television programming? Is this language likely to appeal to or anger his readers? Or does the answer depend on who is reading his column? Explain.
2. What phrases does Goodman repeat in his essay? Why do you think he repeats certain words?

CRITICAL THINKING

1. What is Goodman's opinion of parents who want to influence television programming? Do parents have a right to pressure Hollywood to change violent shows?
2. How might the other side respond to Goodman's claim that he has a right to watch violent programs if he wants to?
3. Goodman urges people to "vote with your remote." Is changing the channel the equivalent of "voting" on what programs should air on television? Is it a solution that could work, or is it just a catchy phrase? Explain.
4. Goodman notes that "we have always been a violent country" (paragraph 14). Does this statement justify television violence? Why or why not?

WRITING ABOUT THE ISSUES

1. Goodman argues that if parents or other adults object to a television program, they should change the channel or just turn off the television. Is this a reasonable solution? Why or why not? Write about your thoughts on this issue in a short essay.
2. What is "art"? Are violent television programs, such as the ones Goodman cites, art? Does the claim that these programs are a form of artistic expression support Goodman's argument? Explain.

3. Write a short essay exploring the connection between censorship and television programming. Who is likely to control the
airwaves? What programs would survive, and what would be
cut? Explain.

VISUAL CONNECTIONS

It's a Scary World

Pulitzer Prize–winner Jim Borgman's comic strip "Zits" has described the teen-angst-ridden life of 15-year-old Jeremy and his family and friends since its debut in July 1997. The syndicated strip appears in 875 newspapers around the world and is translated into at least seven languages, including German, Chinese, Spanish, and Finnish.

ZITS   ***BY JERRY SCOTT AND JIM BORGMAN***

CONSIDERING THE ISSUES

1. Can you recall a time when you knew your parents were frightened? How did you react? Explain.
2. Usually, children end up in their parents' room after having a night-mare. Is it significant that the parents turn to their teenage son for "protection" from their "nightmare"? Explain.

CRITICAL THINKING

1. What is this cartoon about? What cultural theme does it employ? What does the audience need to understand in order to "get" the comic's twist?
2. Who is the audience for this cartoon? How does it tap into popular fears? Explain.

In Search of Notorious Ph.D.s
Lindsay Johns

Lindsay Johns is a social commentator and cultural critic on Colourful Radio, London. This essay appeared in the *New Black Magazine* in the Spring 2007 issue.

CONNECTING TO THE TOPIC

Deadly shootings both on the street and in the schools are putting kids—especially young males—in front of and behind the trigger. Music glorifying violence and promoting "gangsta life" is giving a soundtrack to the violent street dramas that unfold daily in the nation's neighborhoods and suburbs. Could hip-hop music and its preoccupation with violence be fueling the fire? In this next essay, Lindsay Johns takes a look at the connection between hip-hop, violence, and black masculinity.

WORDS IN CONTEXT*

priapic (2)   phallic; having to do with male sexuality (adj.)
über (3)   German, "ultra" or "over" (adj.)
hackneyed (3)   cliched, boring (adj.)
malaise (3)   weariness, boredom, lack of energy or initiative (n.)
histrionic (10)   overly dramatic (adj.)
trope (10)   a rhetorical use of words in anything other than their literal sense (n.)
redolent (10)   fragrant, suggestive of something (adj.)
striations (10)   parallel lines or grooves (n.)
hyperbolized (13)   to exaggerate (v.)
tranche (14)   French, "slice" (n.)
elegiac (14)   like an elegy; expressing sadness (adj.)
carapace (14)   a hard, protective covering or shell (n.)
misogynistic (15)   anti-woman or anti-female; disrespecting of women (adj.)
ensconced (16)   firmly settled in or nested in a place (adj.)
concomitants (16)   accompanying (n.)
churlish (24)   rude, unpleasant, vulgar (adj.)

---

*The vocabulary in this essay is challenging but part of the author's unique style. Some words are defined. Students may look up additional words (also bolded in the text) as necessary.

ostracism (24)   boastful display or attitude (n.)
alacrity (28)   speed, alertness (n.)
antediluvian (31)   literally, "before the Flood," before the time of Noah in
the Bible
Cornell West and DuBois (32)   Cornell West (b. 1953) is a prominent
African-American philosopher and civil rights activist who teaches at
Princeton University; W.E.B. Du Bois (1868–1963) was an African-American civil rights activist and author of the hugely influential *The Souls of
Black Folk* (1903).

1   ook around. It only takes a nano-second of exposure to modern mass
media to discern a dazzlingly disturbing trend.

2   From the glistening pecs and ridiculously chiseled abs of LL Cool
J on a billboard to the cringingly pimpilicious demeanor of Snoop Dogg
on MTV Base, or the tediously **priapic** and rabidly homophobic lyrics of
Beenie Man, we are constantly bombarded by stylized images of hypermasculine black men.

3   Name your cliché. **Über**-physical, über-feral or über-sexually potent:
they all apply. It doesn't take a genius to see what trite, **hackneyed** and
ultimately depressing images of blackness these all are. What is more,
they are unfortunately symptomatic of a much greater social and racial
malaise, one which, like a rotten timber supporting the **precariously**
balanced **edifice** of our society, threatens to bring it crashing down upon
our heads very soon.

4   Heterosexual black masculinity, as a social construction in the twenty-
first century, is at best deeply problematic, and at worst hideously flawed.

5   From Mike Tyson to Tupac, via 50 Cent, Shaquille O'Neill and
Shabba Ranks, black male icons (invariably from the arenas of sport or
music) are right now **indubitably** doing more harm than good.

6   But what's wrong with the likes of Fifty, Beenie Man, I hear you cry?
What's so wrong with being big 'n' buff or being able to handle your business
in the bedroom and, in the memorable words of Sean Paul, able *to do the wuk*?

7   The answer is devastatingly simple, yet is constantly ignored.

8   Black musicians who indulge in representations of hypermasculinity are simply conceding much-sought-after gains in racial equality. Icons
such as 50 Cent, Snoop Dogg, and Elephant Man persist in trading racial
dignity for a quick buck, and are willingly conforming to the oldest, most
pernicious (but perhaps the most **lucrative**) racial stereotype of all: the
most execrable of old chestnuts: that black is wholly physical, and that by
implication in the system of **binary** opposition, white is cerebral.

9   Why does so much contemporary black music persist in presenting
to the world at large such a limiting and psychologically harmful (not to
mention erroneous) caricature of black hypermasculinity?

10   The **histrionic** (and oh-so-easy to be ridiculed by white people) hip-hop hand gestures, the tedious and repetitive physical and verbal posturing, based on empty self-aggrandizement, the **trope** of mythical sexual prowess, all are images **redolent** of ignorance, and all are indicative of a deeply troubled psyche, a psyche visibly manifesting the scars and **striations** of centuries of slavery and oppression.

11   Where power, control and authority (traditional definitions of masculinity) have been historically denied to black men since slavery, it is perhaps historically understandable that the knee-jerk reaction is to present oneself as all that one has lacked.

12   Thus, the rapper or the reggae singer's conscious embrace of a hypermasculine image as a means of resisting the emasculation of racism is understandable, but ultimately misguided. Unwittingly he plays into the arms of the oppressor yet again. At the risk of gaining the physical, he spectacularly concedes the cerebral.

13   The **ubiquitous** and seemingly **omnipotent** MTV-based culture which peddles *ad nauseam* this **hyperbolized** and grossly distorted image of black masculinity simply reinforces these negative stereotypes in the most harmful, demeaning and detrimental of ways. Thus a whole generation of both white and black kids has now been successfully indoctrinated to think that the only way for black masculinity to manifest itself is through physical posturing, sexual **braggadocio**, **feral** violence, and general anti-social behavior.

14   Very soon (if not already) a massive **tranche** of white people will only be able to relate to black men through the prism of hypermasculinity, not to mention the generation of young black men, some barely into their teens, for whom the *pimp roll*, the *Yo, bitch!* and the *bedroom bully* persona are sadly now the only ways of relating to themselves: the **elegiac carapaces** behind which they hide from an unforgiving, hostile universe.

15   New York rapper Nas' hit song "Oochie Wally" (despite its infectious hook and chorus) exemplifies the long list of anthemic songs built upon deeply troubling **misogynistic** and hypermasculine foundations. Let's be honest: "*I long dicked the bitch all night*" might be a great line to share with your boys at the gym in a moment of locker room bravado or *esprit de corps masculin* when regaling them with tales of your bedroom exploits, but seriously people . . . are we making any progress here?

16   Similarly, Mad Cobra, another legendary luminary firmly **ensconced** in the **pantheon** of dancehall deities (famous for hits such as "Flesh Dagger" and "Plant It") is one of the most sexually brutal lyricists in the reggae business. Yet he is hailed as an **avatar** of all that is good about dancehall music. Hypermasculinity (and its **concomitants** misogyny and homophobia) are all decidedly de rigueur in reggae culture, and, what is worse, continue to go unchallenged.

17   And where does this depiction of black hypermasculinity ultimately lead?

18   Well, in the first instance, it leads to [the youth who want to play the "bad boy"] **ostentatiously** pimp rollin' down the streets, bouncing along as if he has dislocated his pelvis, belligerently kissing his teeth in some old granny's face because he thinks his *respect* has been compromised by her accidental nudge or stray glance. Result: intimidating or laughable, depending on your point of view.

19   On another level, the **endemic** gun violence in the black community can be directly traced back to the wholly irresponsible image of black masculinity which is fed to us through music.

20   I will happily wager that Miles Davis "Birth of Cool" or George Benson's "The Guitar Man" are not the musical accompaniments of choice in the majority of drive-by shootings (auto-tuning into Classic FM by accident notwithstanding).

21   Ceaseless macho posturing and the absorption of violent imagery results in the playing out of violence in real life. Art mirrors life, but also life mirrors art.

22   As a direct result of the hypermasculine lyrics in garage, grime, hip-hop or reggae music, we are witnessing a culture of deeply-ingrained self-loathing which is **imbuing** in black youngsters the notion that to be black means to be physical, violent, homophobic, and über macho (with at least three women). From Ludacris' *I've got hos in different area codes* to Beenie Man's "Nuff Gal," the hypermasculine predominates. Anything else is seen as quite frankly effeminate.

23   These **nefarious** lies of black masculinity, no doubt **expediently propagated** over the centuries by white opportunists (first anti-abolitionists, and now, in their most contemporary guise, the music executives who control the distribution and marketing of black music, knowing that these raw ingredients will ensure more record sales to the white teenagers who are their target audience) need to be swiftly exposed, dispelled and eradicated.

24   Is the hypermasculinity expounded in black music a mask for historical pain? It would be both **churlish** and naive to say that it isn't. It clearly functions as a mask for the pain engendered by centuries of social **ostracism**, oppression and cultural alienation dating back to slavery and also as a mask for chronically low self-esteem.

25   [But] The days of slavery are over. And what may have been once a *bona fide* psychological crutch is now being lucratively peddled as an expedient sales gimmick. Is it any wonder that so much of the educated Black American middle class has a healthy disdain for hip-hop?

26   It is time to smell the coffee and to realize that, although the physical shackles of slavery are off, we still need liberating from the debilitating mental shackles, and that by falling into the trap of complying with and buying into these heinous stereotypes, black people are themselves setting back the notion of racial equality decades, if not centuries.

27   So what next?

28   We need to redefine notions of black masculinity with **alacrity** and to directly incorporate more progressive ideas of what it means to be black and male into our music. There is, of course, no one **monolithic** notion of black masculinity. There are as many manifestations of black masculinity as there are shades of black.

29   But of paramount importance is the need to present more viable and more visibly cerebral alternatives. We urgently need to create new **paradigms** of black masculinity which do not give voice to the old lie of black as physical and by implication, white as cerebral.

30   The sooner we acknowledge that the black male hip-hop or reggae **aesthetic** is fundamentally limiting and ironically intellectually emasculating, as opposed to actually empowering, then, and only then, we will begin to progress as a people.

31   Because, hard though it is to hear, while these **antediluvian** beliefs persist, we are still simply playing ourselves. As the conscious rapper Jeru The Damaja so eloquently said back in 1996:
     "With all that big willy talk, ya playin' yaself.
     With all that big gun talk, ya playin' yaself."

32   At the dawn of the twenty-first century, if we are to stand even a chance of leveling the playing field and making tangible progress, we need (as was said of the teaching methods of **Cornell West** at Harvard) less of *da boyz* and more of **DuBois**.

33   In short, we need much less Notorious B.I.G. and much more Notorious Ph.D. ◆

CONSIDERING THE ISSUES

1. In this essay, Johns notes that MTV "peddles *ad nauseam*" distorted images that reinforce negative stereotypes. In your opinion, is Johns taking MTV culture too seriously, or can this medium be harmful to society? Explain.

2. Do you think that music can influence behavior? Write about a time when music—or another medium such as drama in a film or image in a piece of art—influenced the way you behaved. Describe the incident and your behavior, and discuss why the medium influenced you the way it did.

CRAFT AND CONTENT

1. What does the author's title mean? What do you need to know about hip-hop to understand the title?

2. What can you guess about the author based on his language, word choice, and style of writing? Explain.

3. What is Johns's argument? Who is he trying to convince? Do you think his sophisticated use of vocabulary reaches his target audience, or could it miss the mark? Explain.

CRITICAL THINKING

1. Johns comments "Heterosexual black masculinity, as a social construction in the twenty-first century, is at best deeply problematic, and at worst hideously flawed." In your own words, describe what image of black masculinity is promoted in the media in America today. Do you agree or disagree with Johns's assessment? Why or why not?
2. Why does Johns feel hip-hop artists who cash in on hypermasculinity are setting back racial equality? Explain.

WRITING ABOUT THE ISSUES

1. In this essay, Lindsay Johns expresses his concern about the way some hip-hop artists glorify music that conveys the message that "to be black means to be physical, violent, homophobic, and über macho." Write an essay expressing your own viewpoint on this issue. Can lyrics and images be harmful? Are they just in fun, or maybe intended to shock but not to be taken seriously? Explain.
2. Compare the images of females on hip-hop music covers and videos with real women. What images of women are they promoting? Imagine you are a foreign visitor to the United States who has never seen a music video or listened to hip-hop music. What might you assume about the cultural attitude toward American women based on what you see and hear? Explain.

VISUAL CONNECTIONS

Young Jeezy

CONNECTING TO THE TOPIC

In the preceding article, Lindsay Johns discussed the violence, sexism, and hypermasculinity promoted by some very popular hip-hop artists. The lyrics in this type of music and the glorification of violence, he fears, send a message to youth that such traits are not only permissible, they are cool. Do we take such images seriously, or are they just a marketing ploy? Do they hurt anyone? Consider this photo of rapper Young Jeezy in the audience at the 2008 BET Awards held at the Shrine Auditorium on June 24, 2008, in Los Angeles, California. As you analyze the image, consider the points Johns makes in his essay as well as your own personal perspective.

CONSIDERING THE ISSUES

1. Who are your favorite music artists? How are men and women portrayed in videos and music jackets by these artists? How do the artists portray themselves?
2. Despite warnings to the contrary, we often judge people by how they look and the images they project. How does the body language of the recording artist in this photo reinforce points that Johns makes in his essay? For example, what sort of personality do you expect the young men in the photo to have and why?

CRITICAL THINKING

1. Do you think men would react differently than women to this photo? Why or why not?
2. What is happening in this photo? If you were leafing through a magazine and were unfamiliar with Young Jeezy, would you stop and take a closer look at the picture? Why or why not?

Violent Media Is Good for Kids

Gerard Jones

Gerard Jones is an award-winning American author and comic book writer. Jones is author of the *Men of Tomorrow: Geeks, Gangsters, and the Birth of the Comic Book* (2004), *Killing Monsters: Why Children Need Fantasy, Superheroes and Make-Believe Violence* (2002), and *Honey I'm Home: Sitcoms Selling the American Dream* (1993).

Jones wrote many comic books for a diverse group of publishers, including *Green Lantern, Justice League, Prime, Ultraforce, El Diablo, Wonder Man, Martian Manhunter, Elongated Man, The Shadow, Pokémon,* and *Batman.* This essay appeared in *Mother Jones* in June of 2008.

CONNECTING TO THE TOPIC

In this next essay, renowned comic-book author Gerard Jones argues that bloody videogames, gun-glorifying gangsta rap, and other forms of 'creative violence' help far more children than they hurt by giving kids a tool to master their rage. Is he insightful, or insane?

WORDS IN CONTEXT

bumptious (1)   noisily self-assertive or disruptive (adj.)
juvenility (3)   immaturity, acting juvenile (n.)
benevolence (3)   act of kindness or generosity (n.)
overgendered (4)   state in which the traits of feminine or masculine are heightened or made extreme (adj.)
integrating (5)   mixing many elements into one, blending
derision (6)   using ridicule or scorn to show contempt (n.)
vicariously (9)   experiencing something imaginatively through the actions of another (adv.)
resilient (9)   tending to recover quickly from challenges or change (adj.)
protagonist (12)   the main character in story (n.)

1   **A**t 13 I was alone and afraid. Taught by my well-meaning, progressive, English-teacher parents that violence was wrong, that rage was something to be overcome and cooperation was always better than conflict, I suffocated my deepest fears and desires under a nice-boy persona. Placed in a

small, experimental school that was wrong for me, afraid to join my peers in their **bumptious** rush into adolescent boyhood, I withdrew into passivity and loneliness. My parents, not trusting the violent world of the late 1960s, built a wall between me and the crudest elements of American pop culture.

2   Then the Incredible Hulk smashed through it.

3   One of my mother's students convinced her that Marvel Comics, despite their apparent **juvenility** and violence, were in fact devoted to lofty messages of pacifism and tolerance. My mother borrowed some, thinking they'd be good for me. And so they were. But not because they preached lofty messages of **benevolence**. They were good for me because they were juvenile. And violent.

4   The character who caught me, and freed me, was the Hulk [1]: **over-gendered** and undersocialized, half-naked and half-witted, raging against a frightened world that misunderstood and persecuted him. Suddenly I had a fantasy self to carry my stifled rage and buried desire for power. I had a fantasy self who was a self: unafraid of his desires and the world's disapproval, unhesitating and effective in action. "Puny boy follow Hulk!" roared my fantasy self, and I followed.

5   I followed him to new friends—other sensitive geeks chasing their own inner brutes—and I followed him to the arrogant, self-exposing, self-assertive, superheroic decision to become a writer. Eventually, I left him behind, followed more sophisticated heroes, and finally my own lead along a twisting path to a career and an identity. In my 30s, I found myself writing action movies and comic books. I wrote some Hulk stories, and met the geek-geniuses who created him. I saw my own creations turned into action figures, cartoons, and computer games. I talked to the kids who read my stories. Across generations, genders, and ethnicities I kept seeing the same story: people pulling themselves out of emotional traps by immersing themselves in violent stories. People **integrating** the scariest, most fervently denied fragments of their psyches into fuller senses of selfhood through fantasies of superhuman combat and destruction.

6   I have watched my son living the same story—transforming himself into a bloodthirsty dinosaur [2] to embolden himself for the plunge into preschool, a Power Ranger to muscle through a social competition in kindergarten. In the first grade, his friends started climbing a tree at school. But he was afraid: of falling, of the centipedes crawling on the trunk, of sharp branches, of his friends' **derision**. I took my cue from his own fantasies and read him old Tarzan comics, rich in combat and bright with flashing knives. For two weeks he lived in them. Then he put them aside. And he climbed the tree.

7   But all the while, especially in the wake of the recent burst of school shootings, I heard pop psychologists insisting that violent stories are harmful to kids [3], heard teachers begging parents to keep their kids away from "junk culture," heard a guilt-stricken friend with a son who loved Pokémon lament, "I've turned into the bad mom who lets her kid eat sugary cereal and watch cartoons!"

8   That's when I started the research.

9   "Fear, greed, power-hunger, rage: these are aspects of our selves that we try not to experience in our lives but often want, even need, to experience **vicariously** through stories of others," writes Melanie Moore, Ph.D., a psychologist who works with urban teens. "Children need violent entertainment in order to explore the inescapable feelings that they've been taught to deny, and to reintegrate those feelings into a more whole, more complex, more **resilient** selfhood."

10   Moore consults to public schools and local governments, and is also raising a daughter. For the past three years she and I have been studying the ways in which children use violent stories to meet their emotional and developmental needs—and the ways in which adults can help them use those stories healthily. With her help I developed Power Play, a program for helping young people improve their self-knowledge and sense of potency through heroic, combative storytelling.

11   We've found that every aspect of even the trashiest pop-culture story can have its own developmental function. Pretending to have superhuman powers helps children conquer the feelings of powerlessness that inevitably come with being so young and small. The dual-identity concept at the heart of many superhero stories helps kids negotiate the conflicts between the inner self and the public self as they work through the early stages of socialization. Identification with a rebellious, even destructive, hero helps children learn to push back against a modern culture that cultivates fear and teaches dependency.

12   At its most fundamental level, what we call "creative violence"—headbonking cartoons, bloody videogames, playground karate, toy guns—gives children a tool to master their rage. Children will feel rage. Even the sweetest and most civilized of them, even those whose parents read the better class of literary magazines, will feel rage. The world is uncontrollable and incomprehensible; mastering it is a terrifying, enraging task. Rage can be an energizing emotion, a shot of courage to push us to resist greater threats, take more control, than we ever thought we could. But rage is also the emotion our culture distrusts the most. Most of us are taught early on to fear our own. Through immersion in imaginary combat and identification with a violent **protagonist**, children engage the rage they've stifled, come to fear it less, and become more capable of utilizing it against life's challenges.

13   I knew one little girl who went around exploding with fantasies so violent that other moms would draw her mother aside to whisper, "I think you should know something about Emily. . . . " Her parents were separating, and she was small, an only child, a tomboy at an age when her classmates were dividing sharply along gender lines. On the playground she acted out "Sailor Moon" [4] fights, and in the classroom she wrote stories about people being stabbed with knives. The more adults tried to control her stories, the more she acted out the roles of her angry heroes: breaking rules, testing limits, roaring threats.

14   Then her mother and I started helping her tell her stories. She wrote them, performed them, drew them like comics: sometimes bloody, sometimes tender, always blending the images of pop culture with her own most private fantasies. She came out of it just as fiery and strong, but more self-controlled and socially competent: a leader among her peers, the one student in her class who could truly pull boys and girls together.

15   I worked with an older girl, a middle-class "nice girl," who held herself together through a chaotic family situation and a tumultuous adolescence with gangsta rap. In the mythologized street violence of Ice T, the rage and strutting of his music and lyrics, she found a theater of the mind in which she could be powerful, ruthless, invulnerable. She avoided the heavy drug use that sank many of her peers, and flowered in college as a writer and political activist.

16   I'm not going to argue that violent entertainment is harmless. I think it has helped inspire some people to real-life violence. I am going to argue that it's helped hundreds of people for every one it's hurt, and that it can help far more if we learn to use it well. I am going to argue that our fear of "youth violence" isn't well-founded on reality [5], and that the fear can do more harm than the reality. We act as though our highest priority is to prevent our children from growing up into murderous thugs—but modern kids are far more likely to grow up too passive, too distrustful of themselves, too easily manipulated.

17   We send the message to our children in a hundred ways that their craving for imaginary gun battles and symbolic killings is wrong, or at least dangerous. Even when we don't call for censorship or forbid "Mortal Kombat," [6] we moan to other parents within our kids' earshot about the "awful violence" in the entertainment they love. We tell our kids that it isn't nice to play-fight, or we steer them from some monstrous action figure to a pro-social doll [7]. Even in the most progressive households, where we make such a point of letting children feel what they feel, we rush to substitute an enlightened discussion for the raw material of rageful fantasy. In the process, we risk confusing them about their natural aggression in the same way the Victorians confused their children about their sexuality. When we try to protect our children from their own feelings and fantasies, we shelter them not against violence but against power and selfhood. ◆

Links:

1. http://www.marvel.com/hero/hulk/hulk.html
2. http://www.calvinandhobbes.com/strips/89/02/ch8902052207.gif
3. http://motherjones.com/news/feature/1999/11/quake.html
4. http://www.projectanime.com/sailormoon/
5. http://www.cjcj.org/schoolhousehype/shh2pr.html
6. http://www.mortalkombat.com/
7. http://motherjones.com/news/exhibit/1999/09/feral_cheryl.html

CONSIDERING THE ISSUES

1. In this essay, Jones describes his experience as a child dealing with feelings of powerlessness. Recall your own childhood. Can you relate to the feelings Jones describes? How did you deal with feelings of rage, anger, or helplessness? Explain.

2. Jones notes that many children like superheroes with secret identities because they relate to the duality within themselves. Have you ever pretended to be a superhero? If so, which one? In what situations did you drawn upon the superhero fantasy, and why?

CRAFT AND CONTENT

1. Why does the author share his own experience and that of several other children in his essay? How do these stories support his point? Explain.

2. Why do you think Jones self-identifies himself as a "geek"? What is a geek? What effect does this definition have upon the reader's perception of the author?

3. What is Jones's argument? Who is he trying to convince? Is he persuasive? Why or why not?

CRITICAL THINKING

1. Jones admits that violent media, in certain cases, can incite certain people to commit violent acts. But he also argues that it has helped far more children than it has harmed. Do you agree with this argument? Why or why not?

2. What is appealing about comic book violence and violent action heroes? Is there a difference between the genre of comic books and movies featuring comic book heroes? For example, is one more socially acceptable than another?

WRITING ABOUT THE ISSUES

1. Jones notes that many parents encourage their children to engage in nonviolent play and discourage the use of violent toys, media, games, and role-playing. Yet, social anthropologists have observed that children are exposed a great deal of violence in their daily lives. How might these conflicting messages—from parents and the media—impact a child's view of the world? An adult's view? Explain.

2. In his conclusion, Jones notes, "We act as though our highest priority is to prevent our children from growing up into murderous thugs—but modern kids are far more likely to grow up too passive, too distrustful of themselves, too easily manipulated." Write an essay in which you respond to this assessment, expressing your own viewpoint and personal experience.

TOPICAL CONNECTIONS

GROUP PROJECTS

1. Visit the Media Awareness website and read more about the television violence debate (www.media-awareness.com). Each member of your group should evaluate a different current argument posted on this site. Are there any perspectives with which members particularly agree or disagree? Evaluate the arguments and discuss them as a group.

2. With your group, view the clips and read about the independent movie *HIP-HOP: Beyond Beats and Rhymes* by lifelong hip-hop fan and former college football quarterback turned activist Byron Hurt. Hurt decided to make a film about the gender politics of hip-hop, the music and the culture that he grew up with. "The more I grew and the more I learned about sexism and violence and homophobia, the more those lyrics became unacceptable to me," he says. After visiting all parts of the website (www.pbs.org/independentlens/hiphop/), give a presentation to the class on this issue.

3. Using a major metropolitan newspaper, make a list of the headlines in each section. Using this list, conduct a poll on which stories grab attention or seem the most interesting. Ask the participants of your survey to rank the headlines from most to least interesting. Then, ask them to explain why they picked the top three headlines they ranked as most compelling. Based on the information you gather, what conclusions can you make about the media and the public's appetite for information?

4. Question 3 asked you to make a list of all the headlines included in a major metropolitan newspaper. Working with such a list, analyze the language used in each headline. Are the headlines straightforward and factual, or do they put some "spin" on language in order to hook the reader? How does the headline connect to the actual content of the story? As a group, rewrite each headline in your own words to better reflect the content of the corresponding story.

WEB PROJECT

1. The evening news broadcast that is a staple in many American homes is more than simply a recounting of the day's events. Most programs carefully consider what they will present in order to catch—and hold—viewers' attention. Visit the PBS website "Inside the Local News," which examines how media pick and present stories to the public. Examine the entire site, but carefully read the sections entitled "Behind the Story" and "The Ratings Game." Based on research gathered on this site, design your own news broadcast based on current events and explain in detail the reasons behind your design and story selection.

FOR FURTHER INQUIRY

1. While a critical eye may be able to cut through media hype that helps "sell" a story, media bias may be harder to decipher. Read the article on bias featured on the Rhetorica Network's website at http://rhetorica.net/bias.htm. Apply the questions Rhetorica lists in its six "Critical Questions for Detecting Media Bias" to a television, newspaper, or magazine journal article. Choose a "hot" issue that has received a great deal of press coverage in recent weeks. How does the article stand up to the test? What media bias can you detect, if any?

5 What Does Freedom of Speech Really Mean?

"Congress shall make no law . . . abridging the freedom of speech, or of the press." With these simple words, the writers of the Constitution created one of the pillars of our democratic system of government—the First Amendment guarantee of every American's right to the free exchange of ideas, beliefs, and political debate. Many students arrive on campus eager to learn and eager to debate issues that matter. But are college campuses truly a haven for the exchange of ideas and free expression, or are some ideas more acceptable than others? And what happens if you express an unpopular point of view? Administrators on many campuses are imposing limits on the right to free expression when the exercise of that right imposes hardship or pain on others. How should administrators respond when free expression runs counter to community and university values? Are campus speech codes appropriate, or are they a violation of free speech? This chapter focuses on this issue in depth.

Most students support their right to express themselves without fear of government reprisal. However, over the years questions have arisen about whether limits should be imposed on our right to free expression when the exercise of that right imposes hardship or pain on others. What happens when the right of one person to state his or her beliefs conflicts with the rights of others to be free from verbal abuse? What happens when free expression runs counter to community or university values? At what point does the perceived degree of offensiveness warrant censorship? Do parents have the right to demand a book be banned because its contents offend them? Who decides what is acceptable speech, and what happens to society when controversial books and speakers are opposed and speech itself is challenged? In this chapter, we look at the issue of censorship and free speech, both on and off campus.

CRITICAL THINKING

1. What is happening in this cartoon? Where is the man and what is he doing?
2. How does this cartoon relate to the issue of free speech? Explain.
3. What point is the cartoonist trying to make with this cartoon? Is it funny? Ironic? Explain.

Free Inquiry? Not on Campus
John Leo

Writer John Leo is contributing editor at the Manhattan Institute's *City Journal*, in which this essay appeared in the Winter 2007 issue. He is a former syndicated columnist and author of three books, *How the Russians Invented Baseball and Other Essays of Enlightenment* (1989), *Two Steps Ahead of the Thought Police* (1994), and *Incorrect Thoughts* (2001). For many years his commentary appeared in *TIME* magazine and *U.S. News and World Report*. He is currently working on a book about colleges and universities.

CONNECTING TO THE TOPIC

In only a generation, claims John Leo in the next essay, college campuses have transformed from havens supporting the sanctity of free speech to "politically correct" asylums in which conservative points of view are silenced. Campus speech codes protect students' feelings. Liberal administrators covertly support—and even finance—the disruption of conservative speeches and demonstrations. Students are learning to keep their mouths shut out of fear of expressing the "wrong" point of view. Are the college speech police threatening the liberty of us all?

WORDS IN CONTEXT

Right (1) politically right wing, conservative (n.)
Left (1) politically left wing, liberal (n.)
secular (1) not relating to the spiritual but to the worldly (adj.)
tacit (2) not spoken but implied (adj.)
partisan (6) biased in support of a party or group (adj.)
academe (8) the academic community (n.)
dogma (9) a principle or belief (n.)
effusive (10) excessively emotional expression (adj.)
proliferate (12) to grow rapidly, spread (v.)
reproof (13) criticism, correction (n.)
satirical (17) of or relating to sarcasm (adj.)

1 **R**emember when the **Right** had a near-monopoly on censorship? If so, you must be in your sixties, or older. Now the champions of censorship are mostly on the **Left**. And they are thickest on the ground in our col-

leges and universities. Since the late 1980s, what should be the most open, debate-driven, and tolerant sector of society has been in thrall to the diversity and political correctness that now form the aggressive **secular** religion of America's elites.

2   The censors have only grown in power, elevating antidiscrimination rules above "absolutist" free-speech principles, silencing dissent with antiharassment policies, and looking away when students bar or disrupt conservative speakers or steal conservative newspapers. Operating under the **tacit** principle that "error has no rights," an ancient Catholic theological rule, the new censors aren't interested in debates or open forums. They want to shut up dissenters.

3   In October 2007, for instance, a student mob stormed a Columbia University stage, shutting down speeches by two members of the Minutemen, an anti-illegal-immigration group. The students shouted: "They have no right to speak!" Campus opponents of Congressman Tom Tancredo, an illegal-immigration foe, set off fire alarms at Georgetown to disrupt his planned speech, and their counterparts at Michigan State roughed up his student backers. Conservative activist David Horowitz, black conservative columnist Star Parker, and Daniel Pipes, an outspoken critic of Islamism, frequently find themselves shouted down or disrupted on campus.

4   School officials seem to have little more interest in free speech. At Columbia this fall, officials turned away most of a large crowd gathered to hear former PLO terrorist-turned-anti-jihadist Walid Shoebat, citing security worries. Only Columbia students and 20 guests got in. Colleges often cite the danger of violence as they cancel controversial speeches—a new form of heckler's veto: shrinking an audience so that an event will seem unimportant is itself a way to cave to critics. In 2003, Columbia, facing leftist fury at the scheduled speeches of several conservatives (myself included), banned scores of invited non-students who had agreed to attend. Though some schools cancel left-wing speakers, too—including Ward Churchill and Michael Moore, or abortion-supporters Anna Quindlen and Christie Whitman at Catholic universities—right-of-center speakers are the campus speech cops' normal targets.

5   Official censorship—now renamed speech codes and anti-harassment codes—pervades the campuses. The Foundation for Individual Rights in Education (FIRE) recently surveyed more than 300 schools, including the top universities and liberal arts colleges, and found that over 68 percent explicitly prohibit speech that the First Amendment would protect if uttered off campus. At 229 schools, FIRE found clear and substantial restriction of speech, while 91 more had policies that one could interpret as restricting speech. Only eight permitted genuine free expression.

6   A 2002 *New York Times* article reported that today's college kids seem more guarded in their views than previous generations of students. The writer suggested several possible explanations—disgust with

partisan politics and uncivil debates on cable news shows, perhaps, or simple politeness. A more likely reason is that universities have made honest disagreement dangerous, making students fearful of saying what they think.

7   Much campus censorship rests on philosophical underpinnings that go back to social theorist Herbert Marcuse, a hero to sixties radicals. Marcuse argued that traditional tolerance is repressive—it wards off reform by making the status quo . . . well, tolerable. Marcuse favored intolerance of established and conservative views, with tolerance offered only to the opinions of the oppressed, radicals, subversives, and other outsiders. Indoctrination of students and "deeply pervasive" censorship of others would be necessary, starting on the campuses and fanning out from there.

8   By the late 1980s, many of the double standards that Marcuse called for were in place in **academe**. Marcuse's candor was missing, but everyone knew that speakers, student newspapers, and professors on the right could (make that should) receive different treatment from those on the left. The officially oppressed—designated race and gender groups—knew that they weren't subject to the standards and rules set for other students.

9   Confusing speech and action has a long pedigree on the PC campus. At the time of the first wave of speech codes 20 years ago, Kenneth Lasson, a law professor at the University of Baltimore, argued that "racial defamation does not merely 'preach hate'; it is the practice of hatred by the speaker"—and is thus punishable as a form of assault. Indeed, the Left has evolved a whole new vocabulary to blur the line between acts and speech: "verbal conduct" and "expressive behavior" (speech), "non-traditional violence," and "anti-feminist intellectual harassment" (rolling one's eyeballs over feminist **dogma**).

10   Campus censors frequently emulate the Marcusian double standard by combining **effusive** praise for free speech with an eagerness to suppress unwelcome views. "I often have to struggle with right and wrong because I am a strong believer in free speech," said Ronni Santo, a gay student activist at UCLA in the late nineties. "Opinions are protected under the First Amendment, but when negative opinions come out of a person's fist, mouth, or pen to intentionally hurt others, that's when their opinions should no longer be protected."

11   In their 1993 book, *The Shadow University*, Alan Charles Kors and Harvey Silverglate turned some of the early speech codes into national laughingstocks. Among the banned comments and action they listed: "intentionally producing psychological discomfort" (University of North Dakota), "insensitivity to the experience of women" (University of Minnesota), and "inconsiderate jokes" (University of Connecticut). Serious nonverbal offenses included "inappropriate laughter" (Sarah Lawrence College), "eye contact or the lack of it" (Michigan State University), and

"subtle discrimination," such as "licking lips or teeth; holding food pro-vocatively" (University of Maryland). Later gems, added well after the courts struck down campus codes as overly broad, included bans on "inap-propriate non-verbals" (Macalester College), "communication with sexual overtones" (Lincoln University), and "discussing sexual activities" (State University of New York–Brockport). Other codes bar any comment or gesture that "annoys," "offends," or otherwise makes someone feel bad. Tufts ruled that attributing harassment complaints to the "hypersensitiv-ity of others who feel hurt" is itself harassment. Brockport, which banned "cartoons that depict religious figures in compromising situations," "jokes making fun of any protected group," and "calling someone an old hag," helpfully described for students what does not constitute sexual harass-ment: "non-coercive interaction(s) . . . that are acceptable to both parties." Commented Greg Lukianoff of FIRE: "The wonder is that anyone would risk speaking at all at SUNY Brockport."

12   Despite numerous court decisions overturning these codes, they have **proliferated**. College officials point to the hurt feelings of women or minorities as evidence that a violation must have occurred, in part because they want to avoid charges of racism, sexism, and homophobia—an over-riding fear in today's academe, where diversity offices can swarm with 40 or 50 administrators. Georgia Tech went so far as to ban "denigrating" comments on "beliefs," which would make almost any passionate argu-ment over ideas a violation. Needless to say, the targets here are usually conservative. Ohio State University at Mansfield launched a sexual harass-ment investigation of a research librarian, Scott Savage, for recommend-ing the inclusion of four conservative books, including popular works by David Horowitz and ex-senator Rick Santorum, on a freshman reading list. Two professors had complained that one of the books, *The Marketing of Evil*, by journalist David Kupelian, was "homophobic tripe" and "hate literature." This may have been the first time that a campus charged that a book recommendation qualified as sexual harassment. After a burst of publicity and a threat to sue, the university dropped the investigation.

13   Student censors regularly spirit away whole print runs of conservative student newspapers, almost always without **reproof** from administrators. Over the years, campus officials, including a few university presidents, have even encouraged such stealing. After repeated thefts of the *Dart-mouth Review*, an official egged on the thieves by calling the paper "litter" and "abandoned property." In a commencement speech, former Cornell president Hunter Rawlings III praised students who seized and burned copies of the conservative *Cornell Review* in retaliation for printing a gross parody of Ebonics.

14   Once in a blue moon, a college president vigorously defends free speech. At Northern Kentucky University, president James Votruba rebuked and suspended a tenured feminist professor, Sally Jacobsen,

who led a group that demolished a campus-approved right-to-life display. Jacobsen cited two justifications: her deep feelings and her alleged free-speech right to tear down displays that offend her. "I did invite students to express their freedom of speech rights to destroy the display if they wished," she said. "Any violence perpetrated against that silly display was minor compared to how I felt when I saw it."

15   Nothing makes the campus censors angrier than someone who dares to question race and gender preferences, especially if he uses satire to do it. That's why the anti-affirmative-action bake sales that conservative students have sponsored at many schools—white male customers can buy cookies for $1, with lower prices for women and various minorities—have provoked such ferocious responses from campus authorities.

16   Grand Valley State University in Allendale, Michigan, provides a typical example. A Republican club there staged a bake sale, and several students then said that they felt offended. This amounted to a powerful argument, since hurt feelings are trump cards in the contemporary campus culture. Next came the usual administrative scramble to suppress free speech while expressing great respect for it. The university charged the club with a violation of the student code and threatened sanctions. The students folded under administrative pressure and apologized. When the Republican club president refused to back down, club members asked him to resign, and he did. The students' retreat was understandable, if not very courageous. The university in effect was trying them for bias, with the likelihood that a notation of racism would become part of their academic record and follow them to post-college job interviews.

17   The College Republicans at Northeastern Illinois University canceled an announced affirmative-action bake sale after the administration threatened punishment. Dean of Students Michael Kelly announced that the cookie sellers would be violating university rules and that "any disruption of university activities that would be caused by this event is also actionable." This principle—politically incorrect speakers are responsible for attacks on them by students who resent their speech—is dear to campus censors' hearts. The university didn't view itself as engaging in censorship—and double-standard censorship at that, since it freely allowed a **satirical** wage-gap bake sale run by feminists. Absurdly, Kelly said that the affirmative-action sale would be fine—if cookie prices were the same for whites, minorities, and women. Other administrators complained that differential pricing of baked goods is unfair, thus unwittingly proving the whole point of the parody.

18   Schools will use almost any tactic to shut the bake sales down. At the University of Washington, the administration said that the sponsor had failed to get a food permit. At Grand Valley, the university counsel argued that the sale of a single cupcake would convert political commentary into forbidden campus commerce. At Texas A&M, the athletics director

argued that a satirical bake sale would damage the sports teams by making
it harder to recruit minorities. [. . .]

19   We are very lucky to have the First Amendment. Without it, our
chattering classes would be falling all over themselves to ban speech that
offends sensitive groups. We know this because our campus speech codes,
the models for the disastrous hate-speech laws elsewhere, were the inven-
tions of our own elites. Without a First Amendment, the distortions and
suppressions of campus life would likely have gone national. Mel Gibson,
Michael Richards, and many rap artists would be in jail, or at least facing
charges.

20   The cause of free speech can no longer expect much help from the
American Civil Liberties Union, more concerned today with civil rights
and multicultural issues than with civil liberties and free speech. True, the
ACLU still takes some censorship cases—it led the fight against the first
wave of campus speech codes circa 1990, for instance. But the rise of the
ACLU's internal lobbies or "projects," such as the Lesbian and Gay Project
and the Immigrants' Rights Project, has made the organization look more
and more like a traditional left-wing pressure group, with little passion for
the First Amendment. The ACLU is also following the money: funds flow
in because the group responds to concerns of feminist, gays, and other
identity groups, not because of its historical defense of free speech and
civil liberties.

21   These days, the ACLU visibly stands aloof from obvious First
Amendment cases—such as the college speech and harassment codes—
and even comes down on the anti-free-speech side. Consider the group's
stance in *Aguilar v. Avis Rent-A-Car System,* a case involving ethnic epithets aimed by supervisors at Latino employees of Avis in San Francisco.
A California court ruled that Avis had permitted a hostile environment.
The California Supreme Court, abetted by both the northern Californian
and the national ACLU, agreed, and upheld the lower court's startling
speech restriction: prior restraint on workers' speech, forbidding a judge-
made list of specific words. These words, not yet revealed or promulgated,
will soon be taboo in every California workplace, even outside the earshot
of Latino employees, and even if they are welcome. As civil libertarian
Nat Hentoff wrote: "This may be the broadest and vaguest restriction of
speech in American legal history."

22   Even with the ACLU, the mainstream media, school officials, and
much of the professorate AWOL, the speech police haven't gone unop-
posed. Just ask former Clinton official Donna Shalala. As chancellor of
the University of Wisconsin in the late eighties, she proved a fervent
early advocate of campus speech restrictions. Though Shalala occasionally praised free speech, she and her team imposed not only a full-
fledged student speech code, later struck down in federal court, but also
a faculty code that provoked the first (and so far, only) pro-free-speech

campus campaign strong enough to repeal such repressive restrictions. The Wisconsin faculty code was a primitive, totalitarian horror. Professors found themselves under investigation, sometimes for months, without a chance to defend themselves or even to know about the secret proceedings. One female professor said: "It was like being put in prison for no reason. I had no idea what it was that I was supposed to have done."

23 A small group of free-speech-minded faculty formed the Committee for Academic Freedom and Rights (CAFR). The group asked for help from the Wisconsin chapter of the pro-free-speech National Association of Scholars, which enlisted as speakers such celebrated allies as Alan Dershowitz and *National Journal* columnist Jonathan Rauch.

24 The First Amendment forces got a lucky break when the university signed a foolish contract with Reebok, in which it received millions of dollars in exchange for the use of the company's footwear by campus sports teams. The contract included a clause forbidding negative comments on Reebok products by any "University employee, agent or representative." The clause greatly irritated the anticorporate campus Left, which had usually been lukewarm or indifferent to free-speech concerns, helping convert some of its members to the anti-speech-code side. Later, a strong defense of free speech by a homosexual professor, called a traitor to his identity group for his courage, brought in other campus leftist allies. CAFR was amazed at how quickly many would-be censors backed down when confronted with controversy and threatened lawsuits. Wisconsin rescinded its faculty code—the first university to do so without a court order.

25 New national groups have joined the fight for free speech on campus (and off), among them the Center for Individual Rights, the Alliance Defense Fund, and FIRE, the most relentless of the newcomers. FIRE usually starts a campaign with a polite letter to a university president, noting that some policy is either unconstitutional or a clear violation of civil liberties. If it doesn't get the change it wants, it will then write to trustees, parents, and alumni, and take its case to the media.

26 FIRE now has an extensive network of campus free-speech "spies," as its cofounder, Harvey Silverglate, jauntily calls them (Alan Charles Kors, the other cofounder, prefers "concerned members of the community"). The organization is seeking new ways to open up closed campus systems, too, such as suing administrators as individuals, which FIRE believes will get their full attention. Another new tactic is to publicize what colleges spend on fighting for unconstitutional speech codes. Most of all, FIRE is trying to show stubborn administrators that the era of hiding gross civil liberties violations behind a PC wall of silence is over: the group wins more than 95 percent of its cases.

27 Political correctness took hold when there were 40 radio talk shows, three networks, and no bloggers. Today, the cross-referencing of PC outrages among bloggers, radio talkers, and rights groups makes it hard to

run an old-fashioned repressive campus. University presidents now understand that their reputations do not rest entirely with the PC platoons.

28   Perhaps the battle to release the campuses from the iron grasp of PC will take decades, but the struggle for free speech is being fought—and won—now. ◆

CONSIDERING THE ISSUES

1. Have you ever participated in or witnessed a demonstration on campus? What was the demonstration about? Was it restricted to a particular area? Could the participants speak freely, or were they restricted in what they could say? Were they of a liberal or conservative viewpoint?
2. Should leaders of controversial groups be allowed to speak on campus? For example, should a person with extremist views, such as a member of the Ku Klux Klan or Hammas be allowed to speak? What about staunchly pro-life and pro-choice groups? Anti-war demonstrators? Who decides what is extremist? Students? Administrators? What do you think?

CRAFT AND CONTENT

1. What is Leo's opinion of college administrators? Identify areas of his essay that use "us" and "them" rhetoric.
2. Review the list of speech codes (paragraph 11). Explain whether you feel any or all of the "banned comments and actions" are justifiable and should indeed be banned from public discourse.
3. What does the phrase "error has no rights" mean? How does it connect to censorship and free speech? Explain.

CRITICAL THINKING

1. Why does Leo think that censorship is "thickest on the ground" at colleges and universities? How does he support this view? Do you agree?
2. Leo points out that the voices of conservatives are being censored from campus. In your view, is this fair? Should a university setting support all viewpoints, or is the nature of a university simply more liberal and thus, less welcoming to conservative views? Can there be a balance between the two that promotes a climate of mutual respect? Why or why not?
3. Who is Herbert Marcuse? How have his theories influenced modern campuses today?

WRITING ABOUT THE ISSUES

1. Imagine that a controversial or conservative speaker was going to speak at your school. Explain why you would or would not protest such a speaker. Alternatively, you could explain why you would support his or her right to speak.
2. In paragraph 6, Leo comments, "Universities have made honest disagreement dangerous, making students fearful of saying what they think." Respond to his statement with your own viewpoint. Reference instances on campus or from your personal experience that support or challenge this assessment.

Hate Cannot Be Tolerated

Richard Delgado

Richard Delgado is a law professor at the University of Pittsburgh. He is widely published and often appears on television and radio programs including *Good Morning America*, NPR, and the *MacNeil-Lehrer Report*. He has authored 15 books and has published articles in the *Nation*, *The New Republic*, *The New York Times*, *The Washington Post*, and *The Wall Street Journal*. His most recent book is *Race and Races, Cases and Resources for a Diverse America* (2007). This article appeared in *Insight on the News*, a national biweekly news magazine published as the sister publication of *The Washington Times*.

CONNECTING TO THE TOPIC ─────────────

Speech codes and harassment policies have been adopted by many U.S. colleges and universities in an effort to stop racist, sexist, or other types of offensive language. The rationale is that racial and other offensive slurs are violent verbal assaults that interfere with students' rights. Many civil liberties activists, students, college faculty, and administrators fear that such codes violate First Amendment rights. Who decides what is offensive language and what is not? Should "hate speech" be protected, or can it lead to violence? Are there limits to free speech in favor of greater good and greater safety for the campus body?

WORDS IN CONTEXT ─────────────

epithet (1)   abusive, disdainful, or condescending word or phrase (n.)
elicit (3)   to provoke or draw out (v.)

revile (4)   to assault or attack with abusive language (v.)

evolution (5)   in biology, the gradual change in the genetic composition of a species over generations, resulting in the improvement of existing species or the development of new ones (n.)

hone in (6)   to focus on or advance toward a target or goal (v.)

1   Anonymous vandals scrawl hate-filled graffiti outside a Jewish student center. Black students at a law school find unsigned fliers stuffed inside their lockers screaming that they do not belong there. At a third campus, a group of toughs hurls **epithets** at a young Latino student walking home late at night.

2   In response to a rising tide of such incidents, some colleges have enacted hate-speech codes or applied existing rules against individuals whose conduct interferes with the educational opportunities of others. Federal courts have extended "hostile environment" case law to schools that tolerate a climate of hate for women and students of color.

3   Despite the alarm these measures sometimes **elicit**, nothing is wrong with them. In each case, the usual and preferred response—"more speech"—is unavailable to the victim. With anonymous hate speech such as the flier or graffiti, the victim cannot talk back, for the hate speaker delivers the message in a cowardly fashion. And talking back to aggressors is rarely an option. Indeed, many hate crimes began just this way: The victim talked back—and paid with his life.

4   Hate speech is rarely an invitation to a conversation. More like a slap in the face, it **reviles** and silences. College counselors report that campuses where highly publicized incidents of hate speech have taken place show a decline in minority enrollment as students of color instead choose to attend schools where the environment is healthier.

5   A few federal courts have declared overly broad hate-speech codes unconstitutional, as well they should. Nothing is gained by a rule so broad it could be construed as forbidding the discussion of controversial subjects such as **evolution** or affirmative action.

6   But this is not what most people mean by hate speech, nor are colleges barred from drafting narrow rules that **hone in** on the conduct they wish to control. And when they do, courts are very likely to find in their favor. Recent Supreme Court rulings striking down laws upholding affirmative action and approving punishment for cross-burning show that the court is not unaware of current trends. Society is becoming more diverse. Reasonable rules aimed at accommodating that diversity and regulating the conduct of bullies and bigots are to be applauded—not feared. ◆

CONSIDERING THE ISSUES

1. Does the saying "sticks and stones may break my bones, but names will never hurt me" apply to racist and hate speech? Have you ever witnessed or experienced a verbal assault based on race or gender? What was the impact, if any, on you? How did you react?

2. In your opinion, when racist or hate speech is used on campus, should it be ignored or dealt with formally? If you feel racist or hate speech should be banned from campus, do you think *all* such speech should be prohibited in *any* situation, or only in public forums? Explain your point of view.

CRAFT AND CONTENT

1. This piece is called an opinion editorial that allows the writer to offer an opinion or viewpoint on an issue. Summarize Delgado's opinion in this editorial. What is his position on hate speech and on campus speech codes, and why?

2. Delgado identifies several "cowardly" methods people use to promote hate speech. What are they? Why does Delgado feel such speech is cowardly? Does he object to the speech itself, or the method of delivery, or both?

CRITICAL THINKING

1. What reasons does Delgado offer for banning hate speech from campus and from general public discourse? Do you agree? Explain.

2. Do you think hate speech deserves First Amendment protection? If not, why? If so, can you think of any circumstances when hate speech should be protected? Explain.

3. Delgado observes that "hate speech is rarely an invitation to a conversation." Why do you think he makes this comment? To what free speech argument is he referring? Explain.

WRITING ABOUT THE ISSUES

1. Many legal scholars view restrictions on hate speech as a form of censorship and contrary to the democratic spirit of pluralism and tolerance. Write a paper in which you argue that hate speech should be protected if we are to remain a legitimate democracy.

2. Taking an opposing view expressed in the last assignment, write a paper in which you argue that hate speech should be banned. In your discussion, explain what types of hate speech should be banned, and why. How would bans on hate speech be enforced?

Academic Bill of Rights
David Horowitz

David Horowitz is president of the Center for the Study of Popular Culture and the author of *Left Illusions: An Intellectual Odyssey* (2003).

CONNECTING TO THE TOPIC

In an effort to curtail criticism of campus speech codes, some colleges and universities have adopted speech codes that define acceptable speech. Critics of such codes argue that they curtail campus discourse and erode the very foundation of a college education, posing a dangerous threat to ideals of free speech. Speech code advocates counter that certain types of language can create uncomfortable situations for some students, that this interferes with learning and the right to pursue an education without fear of intimidation. But who decides what is acceptable speech? Are campus speech codes going too far? In this next piece, David Horowitz presents the rights he feels every student should have on campus.

WORDS IN CONTEXT

faction (2) a small group within a larger group (n.)
transcendent (3) encompassing all (adj.)
orthodoxy (5) beliefs or practices (n.)
admonished (5) criticized, rebuked (v.)
indoctrinate (5) to instruct with a point of view or promote a body of beliefs (v.)
substantive (6) considerable (adj.)

I. The Mission of the University

1 The central purposes of a University are the pursuit of truth, the discovery of new knowledge through scholarship and research, the study and reasoned criticism of intellectual and cultural traditions, the teaching and general development of students to help them become creative individuals and productive citizens of a pluralistic democracy, and the transmission of knowledge and learning to a society at large. Free inquiry and free speech within the academic community are indispensable to the achievement of these goals. The freedom to teach and to learn depend upon the creation of appropriate conditions and opportunities on the campus as a whole as well as in the classrooms and lecture halls. These purposes reflect the

values—pluralism, diversity, opportunity, critical intelligence, openness and fairness—that are the cornerstones of American society.

II. Academic Freedom

2   1. *The Concept.* Academic freedom and intellectual diversity are values indispensable to the American university. From its first formulation in the General Report of the Committee on Academic Freedom and Tenure of the American Association of University Professors, the concept of academic freedom has been premised on the idea that human knowledge is a never-ending pursuit of the truth, that there is no humanly accessible truth that is not in principle open to challenge, and that no party or intellectual **faction** has a monopoly on wisdom. Therefore, academic freedom is most likely to thrive in an environment of intellectual diversity that protects and fosters independence of thought and speech. In the words of the General Report, it is vital to protect "as the first condition of progress, [a] complete and unlimited freedom to pursue inquiry and publish its results."

3   Because free inquiry and its fruits are crucial to the democratic enterprise itself, academic freedom is a national value as well. In a historic 1967 decision (*Keyishian v. Board of Regents of the University of the State of New York*) the Supreme Court of the United States overturned a New York State loyalty provision for teachers with these words: "Our Nation is deeply committed to safe-guarding academic freedom, [a] **transcendent** value to all of us and not merely to the teachers concerned." In *Sweezy v. New Hampshire* (1957) the Court observed that the "essentiality of freedom in the community of American universities [was] almost self-evident."

4   2. *The Practice.* Academic freedom consists in protecting the intellec-tual independence of professors, researchers and students in the pur-suit of knowledge and the expression of ideas from interference by legislators or authorities within the institution itself. This means that no political, ideological or religious orthodoxy will be imposed on professors and researchers through the hiring or tenure or termination process, or through any other administrative means by the academic institution. Nor shall legislatures impose any such orthodoxy through their control of the university budget.

5   This protection includes students. From the first statement on aca-demic freedom, it has been recognized that intellectual independence means the protection of students—as well as faculty—from the imposition of any **orthodoxy** of a political, religious or ideological nature. The 1915 General Report **admonished** faculty to avoid "taking unfair advantage of

the student's immaturity by **indoctrinating** him with the teacher's own opinions before the student has had an opportunity fairly to examine other opinions upon the matters in question, and before he has sufficient knowledge and ripeness of judgment to be entitled to form any definitive opinion of his own." In 1967, the AAUP's Joint Statement on Rights and Freedoms of Students reinforced and amplified this injunction by affirming the inseparability of "the freedom to teach and freedom to learn." In the words of the report, "Students should be free to take reasoned exception to the data or views offered in any course of study and to reserve judgment about matters of opinion."

6   Therefore, to secure the intellectual independence of faculty and students and to protect the principle of intellectual diversity, the following principles and procedures shall be observed. These principles fully apply only to public universities and to private universities that present themselves as bound by the canons of academic freedom. Private institutions choosing to restrict academic freedom on the basis of creed have an obligation to be as explicit as is possible about the scope and nature of these restrictions.

7   1. All faculty shall be hired, fired, promoted and granted tenure on the basis of their competence and appropriate knowledge in the field of their expertise and, in the humanities, the social sciences, and the arts, with a view toward fostering a plurality of methodologies and perspectives. No faculty shall be hired or fired or denied promotion or tenure on the basis of his or her political or religious beliefs.

8   2. No faculty member will be excluded from tenure, search and hiring committees on the basis of their political or religious beliefs.

9   3. Students will be graded solely on the basis of their reasoned answers and appropriate knowledge of the subjects and disciplines they study, not on the basis of their political or religious beliefs.

10   4. Curricula and reading lists in the humanities and social sciences should reflect the uncertainty and unsettled character of all human knowledge in these areas by providing students with dissenting sources and viewpoints where appropriate. While teachers are and should be free to pursue their own findings and perspectives in presenting their views, they should consider and make their students aware of other viewpoints. Academic disciplines should welcome a diversity of approaches to unsettled questions.

11   5. Exposing students to the spectrum of significant scholarly viewpoints on the subjects examined in their courses is a major responsibility of faculty. Faculty will not use their courses for the purpose of political, ideological, religious or anti-religious indoctrination.

12   6. Selection of speakers, allocation of funds for speakers programs and other student activities will observe the principles of academic freedom and promote intellectual pluralism.

13 7. An environment conducive to the civil exchange of ideas being an essential component of a free university, the obstruction of invited campus speakers, destruction of campus literature or other effort to obstruct this exchange will not be tolerated.

14 8. Knowledge advances when individual scholars are left free to reach their own conclusions about which methods, facts, and theories have been validated by research. Academic institutions and professional societies formed to advance knowledge within an area of research, maintain the integrity of the research process, and organize the professional lives of related researchers serve as indispensable venues within which scholars circulate research findings and debate their interpretation. To perform these functions adequately, academic institutions and professional societies should maintain a posture of organizational neutrality with respect to the **substantive** disagreements that divide researchers on questions within, or outside, their fields of inquiry. ◆

CONSIDERING THE ISSUES

1. Have you ever felt uncomfortable in class or while participating in an online class newsgroup because of something a professor or student said? What were the circumstances, and how did you react? If this has never happened, can you think of any circumstances that might make you feel uncomfortable in class? Explain.

2. Some schools now require that incoming students sign an agreement that they will not use racist, sexist, or offensive language on campus or face suspension or expulsion. Weighing the social benefits against the restrictions of your freedom of expression, would you have any problem signing such an agreement? Why or why not?

3. Freedom of speech is a fundamental right that many Americans hold sacred. Does it surprise you that many college campuses restrict free speech? Explain.

CRAFT AND CONTENT

1. Critics of the Academic Bill of Rights say that it could be used by students who oppose birth control or deny the Holocaust to sue professors. Review the Academic Bill of Rights and explain why you agree or disagree that this is a valid concern.

2. What style and format does Horowitz chose to present his "Bill of Rights?" Why do you think he chose this style and format?

CRITICAL THINKING

1. The Academic Bill of Rights has been used as the basis of legislation in Congress and has been introduced on the state level to state governments. Write a letter to your state's representative explaining why you support or do not support the Academic Bill of Rights from the perspective of a college student.
2. Read Stanley Fish's response to the Academic Bill of Rights, "'Intellectual Diversity': The Trojan Horse of a Dark Design," printed in the *Chronicle of Higher Education* on February 13, 2004, at http://chronicle.com/free/v50/i23/23b01301.htm (if the link is broken, search for the article by its title online). Why does Fish object to the Academic Bill of Rights? What evidence does he provide that the bill is flawed? Explain.

WRITING ABOUT THE ISSUES

1. Research the arguments for and against campus speech codes as expressed in university publications available online for at least four colleges or universities. How are the codes similar and how are they different? Are they open for interpretation? In your opinion, do they unfairly restrict freedom of speech on campus? Write a short essay on this issue. If your own campus has a speech code, include it in your discussion.

VISUAL CONNECTIONS

Silencing Free Speech

On March 6, 2006, members of Students for a Democratic Society at the University of Central Florida (UCF) gathered on the "free speech lawn"—an area designed for organized demonstrations. Caution tape was put up around the lawn, defining the boundaries within which students could demonstrate. Students "gagged" themselves with the caution tape, while still remaining within the "free speech lawn." Students carried signs that read "abolish the free expression zones."

CONNECTING TO THE TOPIC ————————————

Student-run organizations and campus magazines often serve as the voice of the student body, or at least a segment of it. Find out more about your school's campus newspapers, journals, and student organizations. How many, if any, are politically or socially focused? What issues do they represent? Do they promote a particular agenda or point of view? Are they free to share their views openly on campus, ore are they hampered by free speech codes or "zones?"

Photo by Kyle Fasanella

CONSIDERING THE ISSUES

1. Consider how this photograph relays a message to the viewer. What can you determine about campus speech codes based upon what you see in the photo? What is the meaning of the tape on the young man's mouth? What does this symbol mean? What if the man were gagged? Explain.
2. If you saw this photograph on your own campus newsletter or magazine, would you be led to read the article? Why or why not?

CRITICAL THINKING

1. How does this photograph make you feel, and why? Explore the implications of this photograph and the ways it is designed to elicit a response from the viewer.
2. Freedom of speech is a fundamental right that many Americans hold sacred. Does it surprise you that many college campuses restrict free speech? Explain.

Blog Matters

A blog ("web log") is an online diary or commentary site that features regular entries that describe events, impressions, and viewpoints. Blogs may contain text, images, video, and often link to other websites, blogs, and online media. Most blogs allow readers to comment on the content of the post and respond to each other. As of September 2011, there were over 160 million public blogs in existence. While many blogs are maintained by individuals, some are run by journals, newspapers, and other media outlets. Remember that most blogs are not monitored for factual accuracy and often express the opinion and views of the "blogger" writing the content.

The Torch is the blog maintained by the free speech organization FIRE. In 1998, Alan Charles Kors and Harvey A. Silverglate, coauthors of *The Shadow University: The Betrayal of Liberty on America's Campuses*, founded FIRE to defend American liberties on behalf of thousands of students and faculty on U.S. campuses. In addition to individual case work, FIRE works nationally to inform the public about the fate of liberty on our campuses.

Sixth Circuit Orders Federal District Court to Rule on Student Blogger's Free Speech and Due Process Claims

Ari Cohn
April 14, 2011

1   On Monday, the United States Court of Appeals for the Sixth Circuit reversed a 2009 federal district court decision (full opinion here) in which a student claimed that the University of Louisville wrongfully dismissed her based on the contents of her personal blog. The district court had refused to rule on the student's free speech and due process claims, and instead created a contractual claim on which to resolve the case. Now, thanks to the Sixth Circuit, that court will have to rule on important constitutional issues regarding the regulation of student speech.

2   The case originated when Nina Yoder, a University of Louisville nursing student who observed a live birth as part of a clinical assignment, posted her views of the experience on her personal blog. A dean later told Yoder that the blog post violated the school's honor code and patient confidentiality, and she subsequently received a letter dismissing her from the university, citing violations of the honor code. After an appeals process in which Yoder was not allowed to participate, the dismissal was upheld.

3   Yoder sued the school, arguing that the school violated her First Amendment right to free speech, that the honor code and confidentiality agreement were unconstitutionally broad and vague, respectively, and that the school denied her due process by not giving her adequate notice or a proper hearing.

4   Believing itself constrained to first decide the case on any possible non-constitutional grounds, the district court created an entirely new claim based on contract law and resolved the case on those grounds instead. Examining the language of the honor code and the confidentiality agreement, the court found that Yoder had violated neither and as such was wrongfully dismissed—without reaching the constitutional issues.

5   On appeal, the Sixth Circuit made quick work of the district court's decision to avoid the constitutional issues and insert its own contract theory. Finding that the contract claim was invented by the district court with little support, the appellate court reversed the lower court's findings and remanded the case for further proceedings.

6   Fortunately, though it never originally reached the constitutional questions, the district court did use language supportive of students' constitutional rights. Particularly, the court said:

7   If the [School of Nursing] wishes for its students' confidentiality obligations to extend to the giving of non-identifiable information about patients, it must give fair notice.

8   and

9   'Professionalism' is not defined anywhere within the [School of Nursing]'s rules and regulations. [The associate dean] could not provide a definition of 'professionalism' when asked at her deposition. . . . [I]f the SON wishes for the professionalism affirmation in the Honor Code to apply to every act or all conduct of a SON student everywhere and at all times in all contexts, it must give fair notice by explaining such obligation clearly.

10   These acknowledgments provide hope that, in the face of overbroad and vague restrictions on student speech, the district court will come out on the side of the First Amendment and due process, and the principles which allow true learning to take place.

11   FIRE opposes the overreaching of student conduct codes and honor codes that purport to regulate student conduct and speech in all places and at all times. Public colleges and universities like Louisville should not restrict protected student speech at all, let alone speech that occurs off-campus and on the Internet. The University of Louisville's application of its codes and agreements make it impossible for students to know what speech is subject to those regulations and what is ultimately prohibited. This will almost certainly lead to the chilling of student speech—a truly unacceptable result for an institution of higher education.

RESPOND TO THE BLOG:

What do you think? Should schools have the power to dismiss a student for what he or she posts online? What rights should students have to express themselves online? What recourse should they have if their school objects to their content?

Is Harry Potter Evil?
Judy Blume

Judy Blume is the author of more than 20 books, including the popular and often challenged *Are You There God? It's Me, Margaret; Tiger Eyes; Then Again, Maybe I Won't;* and *Blubber.* She is the editor of *Places I Never Meant to Be: Original Stories by Censored Writers.* This editorial first appeared in *The New York Times.*

CONNECTING TO THE TOPIC

The Harry Potter series written by J.K. Rowling is one of the most popular series of children's books ever written. With over 400 million copies sold, this record-setting series has been translated into 67 languages. But not everyone is a fan of the series. Critics argue that the books are better suited to adults, who can handle their complex themes and morals. Others have argued that Rowlings's world of witchcraft and wizardry promoted sorcery among children. In fact, according to the ALA, the Harry Potter books are often in the top 10 most challenged books, year after year. In this next editorial, author Judy Blume explains why it is dangerous to ignore book censorship. Objecting to books like Harry Potter and the more recently popular Twilight series harms not just children, but the foundations of literary freedom that we hold most dear.

WORDS IN CONTEXT

zealots (3)   fanatics (n.)
befuddled (7)   confused (v.)
subversive (8)   attempting to challenge or destroy the status quo or that which is in legal or political control (adj.)

1   I happened to be in London last summer on the very day *Harry Potter and the Prisoner of Azkaban*, the third book in the wildly popular series by J. K. Rowling, was published. I couldn't believe my good fortune. I rushed to the bookstore to buy a copy, knowing this simple act would put me up there with the best grandmas in the world. The book was still months away from publication in the United States, and I have an 8-year-old grandson who is a big Harry Potter fan.

2   It's a good thing when children enjoy books, isn't it? Most of us think so. But like many children's books these days, the Harry Potter series has recently come under fire. In Minnesota, Michigan, New York, California and South Carolina, parents who feel the books promote interest in the occult have called for their removal from classrooms and school libraries.

3   I knew this was coming. The only surprise is that it took so long — as long as it took for the **zealots** who claim they're protecting children from evil (and evil can be found lurking everywhere these days) to discover that

children actually like these books. If children are excited about a book, it must be suspect.

4 I'm not exactly unfamiliar with this line of thinking, having had various books of mine banned from schools over the last 20 years. In my books, it's reality that's seen as corrupting. With Harry Potter, the perceived danger is fantasy. After all, Harry and his classmates attend the celebrated Hogwarts School of Witchcraft and Wizardry. According to certain adults, these stories teach witchcraft, sorcery and satanism. But hey, if it's not one "ism," it's another. I mean Madeleine L'Engle's *A Wrinkle in Time* has been targeted by censors for promoting New Ageism, and Mark Twain's *Adventures of Huckleberry Finn* for promoting racism. Gee, where does that leave the kids?

5 The real danger is not in the books, but in laughing off those who would ban them. The protests against Harry Potter follow a tradition that has been growing since the early 1980s and often leaves school principals trembling with fear that is then passed down to teachers and librarians.

6 What began with the religious right has spread to the politically correct. And now the gate is open so wide that some parents believe they have the right to demand immediate removal of any book for any reason from school or classroom libraries. The list of gifted teachers and librarians who find their jobs in jeopardy for defending their students' right to read, to imagine, to question, grows every year.

7 My grandson was bewildered when I tried to explain why some adults don't want their children reading about Harry Potter. "But that doesn't make any sense!" he said. J.K. Rowling is on a book tour in America right now. She's probably **befuddled** by the brouhaha, too. After all, she was just trying to tell a good story.

8 My husband and I like to reminisce about how, when we were 9, we read straight through L. Frank Baum's Oz series, books filled with wizards and witches. And you know what those **subversive** tales taught us? That we loved to read! In those days I used to dream of flying. I may have been small and powerless in real life, but in my imagination I was able to soar.

9 At the rate we're going, I can imagine next year's headline: "*Goodnight Moon* Banned for Encouraging Children to Communicate With Furniture." And we all know where that can lead, don't we? ◆

CONSIDERING THE ISSUES

1. As a child or teenager, did you ever encounter the banning of books in your own school or library? If so, what was the book and why was it challenged?
2. Do you think it is ever permissible to ban books? Why or why not?

CRAFT AND CONTENT

1. How does Blume engage her audience? What techniques does she use to connect with her readers and encourage them to see her point of view?
2. What is a "zealot"? Why does Blume use this word to describe people who don't want their children to read certain books, including the Harry Potter series?

CRITICAL THINKING

1. What is the "perceived danger" of the Harry Potter series? How does the author react to this "danger"? Do you think the fact that her own books have been banned influenced her response to the criticism surrounding the Harry Potter books?
2. Consider Blume's concluding comments on book censorship. What is the tone of her hypothetical example of a headline featuring *Goodnight Moon*? Is it an effective ending to her editorial? Why or why not?

WRITING ABOUT THE ISSUES

1. Should schools listen and heed parental objections to certain books used as part of the curriculum? Who decides curriculum? What books are purchased for the public by a library? If a parent objects to a book, for example, *Huckleberry Finn*, do they have a right to ban the book's use from the entire class? Write an essay exploring the rights of parents to influence reading curriculum.
2. In your opinion, does any one person have the right to restrict the reading material of others? What would you do if there were a book to which you strongly objected—for religious, moral, or ethical ground—scheduled to be used as part of your child's reading program?

Why Stop with Mark Twain's 'Huckleberry Finn'?
Alex Beam

Alex Beam is a writer and journalist. His work has appeaered in *Newsweek* and *BusinessWeek*, as well as *The Boston Globe*, where his twice-weekly column has appeared since 1987. He is the author of several books, including *Gracefully Insane: Life and Death Inside America's Premier Mental Hospital* (2002) and *A Great Idea at the Time: The Rise, Fall and Curious Afterlife of the Great Books* (2008). This essay first appeared in the January 11, 2011, edition of *The Boston Globe.*

CONNECTING TO THE TOPIC

Even when it was first published in 1885, Mark Twain's *The Adventures of Huckleberry Finn* was a topic of controversy. That year, the public library in Concord, Massachusetts, banned it as "rude, coarse, and inelegant." Over a 120 years later and a new version of the book is raising the issue of the role of language in literature and education. At issue are the concept of slavery and the use of the "n-word" which appears throughout the book. Attempts to change the words of the book or to ban it altogether raise many questions. Do we ignore parts of American history that make us feel uncomfortable? Do we change "bad" words in works of literature because some people feel they are hurtful? In this essay, Alex Beam asks, why should we stop at Huck Finn? Perhaps other great works of literature could be tweaked for "modern" sensibilities.

WORDS IN CONTEXT

derogatory (2)   with a critical or disrespectful attitude (adj.)
palatable (2)   pleasant or satisfactory (adj.)
bluestocking (2)   educated intellectuals (n.)
emendations (3)   alternations designed to correct or improve (n.)
inveterate (7)   something that is long-standing and unlikely to change (adj.)
archaic (8)   old-fashioned (adj.)
epithet (8)   an insulting or abusive word or phrase (n.)
bowdlerized (11)   modified, as in a book, so that offensive parts are removed or modified (v.)

1   **D**arned writers! Where does Mark Twain get off, calling African-Americans the N-word? Who does he think he is? Kanye West?

2   The hot news in Literature World is NewSouth Books' controversial decision to publish the classic novel *Huckleberry Finn* minus the 219 occurrences of the **derogatory** term for blacks, which was current in 1885, when the book first appeared. The word "slave'' will stand in, immediately rendering the novel **palatable** to the **bluestocking** book-banners in school districts across the country.

3   Everything old is new again, and the august Auburn University scholar who had this brainstorm, Alan Gribben, is treading the well-trod footsteps of the oft-ridiculed British physician Thomas Bowdler, who rendered the works of William Shakespeare and Edward Gibbon safe for the delicate sensibilities of English schoolchildren. His famous **emendations** included eliminating Ophelia's suicide from *Hamlet* — she dies in an accidental drowning; maiden overboard!—and changing Lady Macbeth's "Out, damned spot!" to "Out, crimson spot!"

4   I was reasonably sure he would deny Mr. Macbeth the "spur to prick the sides of my intent," and I was right. Out, darned prick! In Bowdler, the "bawdy hand of the dial" is most certainly not on "the prick of noon," as the Bard artfully punned. Mr. Bowdler's watch is on the point of noon.

5   Now that Professor Gribben has blazed the path, we can think of reworking more classics for the delicate sensibility of the modern American schoolchildren. Or, more probably, their modern American parents.

6   Some texts are hopeless. They might as well cut the Song of Solomon right out of the Bible. "Your breasts are like two fawns, twins of a gazelle." "Your navel is a rounded goblet that never lacks blended wine." Now scholars tell us that may not actually be her navel. . . . Time to move on!

7   Out with the all-too-suggestive "intercourse," which will more or less put Adam Smith, **inveterate** analyzer of social, um, exchanges, out of business. Ditto Karl Marx. That will enable us to de-smut-ify John Milton's "Paradise Lost." When pre-Fall Adam starts jabbering to Eve about the "sweet [exchange] of looks and smiles," who knows what's really on his mind? That goes double for Charles Dickens, who wrote tenderly to his longtime correspondent Mrs. Watson of yearning for "years of unchanged [exchange]."

8   J.D. Salinger's *The Catcher in the Rye* has dropped off many a school library shelf, damned—sorry, darned—for its gamey language. The **archaic epithet** "goddam" appears 137 times in the relatively short novel. Alas, the word will have to go, along with "crap," another staple of the Holden Caulfield lexicon. That pretty much de-fangs the book's famous opening, where Holden vows not "to tell you my whole [darned] autobiography or anything . . . all that David Copperfield kind of [junk.]"

9   I suspect that journalist Hunter Thompson doesn't grace many middle school library shelves, partly because he relies so heavily on Salingerspeak, and worse. *Fear and Loathing in Las Vegas* has some wonderful moments, especially when the author seeks divine absolution at Wild Bill's Cafe, uttering the immortal lines: "Is there a priest in this tavern? I want to confess! I'm [an accursed] sinner! Venal, mortal, carnal. . ."

10   "Queer," "on Queer Street" and to be "queer for" have interesting etymologies. The latter phrase, now used only ironically, once meant "attracted to." One of the characters in *Giovanni's Room*, James Baldwin's 1956 novel about gay life in Paris, says: "Actually, I'm sort of queer for

girls myself." But who needs ambiguity? Let's pack the offending adjective off to the discard pile, with all those other terrible words.

11   Herewith a couplet from Robert Frost's lovely poem, "Stopping by Woods on a Snowy Evening," appropriately **bowdlerized** for modern ears:

12   My little horse must think it [strange] To stop without a farmhouse [within range].

13   Not pretty, but it will have to do. ◆

CONSIDERING THE ISSUES

1. Did you read any of the literature that Beam cites in this essay in your school career (such as *The Adventures of Huckleberry Finn*, *Hamlet*, *Macbeth*, or *Catcher in the Rye*)? If so, what were your impressions of the controversial work? Do you recall any objections you, your peers, or your parents or teachers had over the work? If any of these works were banned at your school, discuss why the school leadership felt such a measure was necessary.

2. Many of the people who call for either banning or changing words in *The Adventures of Huckleberry Finn* are concerned with children's exposure of racial epithets. Do you think protecting children and teens from hurtful words that were used at particular points in history is a good idea? Why or why not?

CRAFT AND CONTENT

1. Beam opens his essay with the jest, "[Mark Twain] who does he think he is, Kayne West?" What does this reference mean? Why does he use it in connection with *The Adventures of Huckleberry Finn*? What point is he trying to make?

2. What is Beam's tone in this essay? Identify specific phrases or words that convey his tone and the way he hopes his readers will receive his argument.

3. Beam proposes several changes to classic works of literature. Do you think he believes these changes will make the works better? Why or why not?

CRITICAL THINKING

1. Beam gives several examples of how offensive words have been changed with less offensive ones (as in Lady Macbeth's famous line, "Out, damned spot" to "Out, crimson spot"). Does the language substitution change the meaning and impact of the original? Explain.

2. What does Beam mean when he uses the phrase "terrible words"? What are terrible words? Why do people object to their use?

WRITING ABOUT THE ISSUES

1. Go to the University of Virginia's Mark Twain archives and examine some of the reviews and illustrations of the first edition of *The Adventures of Huckleberry Finn*. Discuss these reviews and illustrations in the context of society then, and now.

The Dark Side of Web Anonymity
Catherine Holahan

Catherine Holahan covers technology and the web for BusinessWeek. com. She was previously a reporter and columnist for *The Record* in New Jersey. She is a winner of the 2000 New Jersey Press Association's Robert P. Kelly Memorial Award for Reporting and Writing for first-year reporters. This article was published in the May 1, 2008, issue of *Business Week*.

CONNECTING TO THE TOPIC

JuicyCampus.com was a website that promoted gossip and campus rumors from colleges in the United States. Readers could vote on which posts they found "juiciest." The gossip posted by unidentified users, much of it malicious, sparked a new debate about free speech online. While freedom of speech is protected by the Constitution, slander and lies are not. However, the Communications Decency Act of 1996 shields web publishers from liability for libelous comments posted by third parties. The section states "no provider or user of an interactive computer service shall be treated as the publisher or speaker of any information provided by another information content provider." Did JuicyCampus go too far? In 2009, JuicyCampus shut down its site, claiming that economic challenges forced it to close.

WORDS IN CONTEXT

defamatory (6)   damaging one's reputation (adj.)
slander (6)   false and malicious statements (n.)
unfettered (8)   free, unrestricted (adj.)
elicit (9)   draw out (v.)
proliferation (10)   rapid growth (n.)
subpoena (10)   command one to appear in court and give testimony (v.)
akin (14)   similar, alike (adj.)

1   elissa heard the gossip about her Princeton University classmates on JuicyCampus.com even before she saw the Web site.

2   She's anorexic.

3   He's a closeted homosexual.

4   She's spreading sexual diseases.

5   Since it was set up last year, JuicyCampus has become a popular place for college kids around the country to share such gossip. Melissa ultimately found her own name connected with the malicious rumors. But the Princeton junior couldn't do anything about it. All the comments were anonymous and JuicyCampus won't remove posts based on students' objections. "The second someone's name appears on the site, it's a death sentence," she says.

6   She's not the only one who feels that way. Complaints about the site have poured into the office of New Jersey Attorney General Anne Milgram, and Milgram has opened an investigation into JuicyCampus. She wants the site to provide a way to remove **defamatory** posts, but the problems go beyond **slander**. Milgram worries the Web site's guarantee of anonymity could lead to harassment, assault, or worse. One young woman said strange men started knocking on her door at night after comments were posted on the site detailing her alleged sexual activities and giving her home address. "There are public safety issues," says Milgram. Her effort has generated support among legal authorities from Connecticut to California.

7   JuicyCampus denies any wrongdoing. Founder and Chief Executive Matt Ivester says the site has no legal responsibility to police or remove comments based on claims of defamation. "We are confident that we haven't violated any laws," he says, "and we're disappointed that this is where [the attorney general] is focusing her time." The Web site doesn't charge its users any fees, instead generating revenue from advertising.

8   Ivester has plenty of support. Many tech executives and legal experts argue that anonymous, **unfettered** speech is essential on the Internet. It's not just the principle; it's the business. Web sites such as Amazon.com, YouTube, and MySpace depend on user participation to generate content. Monitoring or screening users could prove costly or impossible for some sites. "To shift the burden [of screening content] to Web site operators is precisely the opposite of what has led to a well-developed Internet," says Matt Zimmerman, senior staff attorney with the Electronic Frontier Foundation, a nonprofit civil liberties advocate.

9   Adeo Ressi has seen the controversy at first hand. He founded a Web site called TheFunded, which allows entrepreneurs to anonymously rate venture capital firms and provide comments on firm employees. He says cloaking participants' identities is essential to **elicit** candid assessments, and allows the Web site to provide valuable information about the venture industry. "Anonymity is necessary in order to get to the truth," he says.

10   The **proliferation** of such interactive Internet sites is what's given rise to the current debate. In the past, there were a relatively small number of sites that allowed user comments, players such as Yahoo! and America Online. If needed, prosecutors like Milgram could **subpoena** a site's host to discover a user's identity. But now there are thousands of Web sites that allow comments, and many wipe out or fail to store the records necessary to track down visitors to the site. "It used to be that if someone slammed you anonymously, you subpoenaed AOL and they got his home address and his full name," says Michael Fertik, chief executive of ReputationDefender, which tracks commentary for clients online. "But that's no longer the case."

11   Melissa understands the issues only too well. The confident 20-year-old welcomes a reporter to her dorm room dressed for the gym. She talks about JuicyCampus dismissively. She doesn't believe the site deserves any attention and is annoyed that it has gotten so much of hers. "It is just a mean concept and no one uses it for anything more than reporting mean things," she says.

12   The posts about her, with her full name, include attacks on her integrity, accusing her of backstabbing friends and social climbing. Normally, she would have shrugged it off. But because the posts could stay online for years, she frets about their effect on her reputation, perhaps even as she interviews for jobs. "It's not funny," she says. "I don't know if an employer would consider this a reliable source of anything, but if they went on and found a prospective employee's name, it's worrisome." She asked that her last name not be used for this story to avoid calling more attention to the posts.

13   Milgram believes JuicyCampus' own terms of service could require it to remove such material. The site asks users not to post content that is abusive, defamatory, or invasive of privacy, among other things. Not upholding those terms could violate New Jersey's Consumer Fraud Act, Milgram says.

14   There are few legal means to compel Web sites to police message boards. For more than a decade, section 230 of the Communications Decency Act of 1996 has protected sites from suits concerning user comments, defining such sites as **akin** to public parks rather than publications. Now some lawmakers are saying those protections are too broad. One member of California's state assembly has called for suggestions to change state law to address the problem.

15   The growing dangers of online speech have been illustrated by tragic cases, such as the suicide of 13-year-old Megan Meier in October. The young teen hanged herself a day after being insulted online by a person she believed to be Josh Evans, a 16-year-old boy with whom she had formed a friendship on MySpace. Evans didn't exist. He was later revealed to be a false profile allegedly created by a neighbor.

16   As the legal debate rages, Princeton students are trying another tactic to shut down anonymous gossip online: attacking the sites' business

model. They're organizing boycotts of JuicyCampus and similar ventures, to cut off traffic and, by extension, ad revenue.

17 Behind the movement at Princeton is Connor Diemand-Yauman, 20-year-old president of the 2010 class. He created a new Web site, Own-WhatYouThink.com, that asks students to pledge not to visit anonymous gossip sites and to stand behind their online statements. "This is about changing the way our generation and our culture look at the way we communicate with one another," he says. Since the campaign's launch on Apr. 1, 2008 nearly 1,000 students have signed the pledge. Ivester says the boycott won't have any damaging effect on the site.

18 One warm afternoon, Diemand-Yauman and dozens of other students held a rally to promote their cause. As an antidote to abusive content online, hundreds of positive statements about students from their classmates were projected onto a massive screen.

19 She gives the best hugs.

20 He is sweet and smart.

21 She is always around when I need a friend.

22 Some wore shirts, emblazoned with a retort to JuicyCampus and sites like it: "Anonymity = Cowardice." ◆

CONSIDERING THE ISSUES

1. In your opinion which of the following arguments has more validity: "Milgram worries the Web site's guarantee of anonymity could lead to harassment, assault, or worse" or "Many tech executives and legal experts argue that anonymous, unfettered speech is essential on the Internet"? Explain.

2. Who should be protected more by governmental policies: a person posting comments on the Internet or a person who is written about on the Internet? What types of governmental policies should be in place to protect this person?

CRAFT AND CONTENT

1. Catherine Holahan opens and ends her essay with sample comments about students. Is this "full-circle" approach to her writing effective? Does it keep her reporting objective or does it strengthen one of the arguments about which she is reporting? Explain.

2. The author uses the suicide of Megan Meier to illustrate the "growing dangers of online speech." By using this example, is Holahan giving a fair representation of these dangers or an overly sensational one? Explain.

CRITICAL THINKING

1. In this essay, Adeo Ressi asserts that "Anonymity is necessary in order to get to the truth." What "truth" is Ressi referring to? Is truth commonly viewed as objective or subjective? How is truth viewed when applied to websites such as Juicycampus.com?
2. The author tells us that Melissa "frets about" the comments posted about her on JuicyCampus.com and "their effect on her reputation, perhaps even as she interviews for jobs." Do you believe that Melissa has anything to worry about? Do companies view Juicycampus.com and other websites looking for information on their applicants, and if so, would they see this information as valid or important? Are there other ways that the comments on JuicyCampus.com could potentially affect Melissa's reputation? Explain.

WRITING ABOUT THE ISSUES

1. JuicyCampus closed in 2009, claiming the economy forced it to shut down. Do you think the site users would have written what they did if they were required to attach their names to their words? A similar blog called the College Anonymous Confession Board (ACB) has replaced JuicyCampus, providing unrestricted message boards for students nationwide. Explore other ways in which being given anonymity could possibly change our actions or behaviors.
2. Think back to a time when you were gossiped about or when you gossiped about someone else. Reflect on what was said, how you felt during that time, and what consequences, if any, were enacted. How do you feel about gossip now, and what consequences, if any, should be enacted on those who gossip regularly?
3. Has Facebook taken on the more sordid side of JuicyCampus? Why or why not?

TOPICAL CONNECTIONS

GROUP PROJECT

1. Imagine that you have been chosen to be members of a student committee asked to draft a speech code for your university or college. As a group, draft such a code. Consider students' rights to free speech, what constitutes hate speech, and what limits

can be placed on hate speech. Write a prologue to your code explaining and supporting its tenets.

WEB PROJECTS

1. Several authors in this chapter observe how some students are fighting speech codes on their campuses. Visit the Foundation for Individual Rights in Education, Inc. (FIRE) website at www.thefire.org/index.php and review the cases it is currently fighting. Select one case that you find particularly compelling and state your own position on the issue. Research the issue as thoroughly as possible, reviewing student newspapers, any administrative commentary, and press received in local newspapers.

2. In a January 2003 article in *Boston* magazine, "The Thought Police," Harvey Silverglate states that the First Amendment should protect your right to say what you wish, but that you are not immune to what happens as a result of your speech. You may be subjected to anger, public shunning, and social pressure, but you should not be officially punished for your language. Write a response to Silverglate expressing your own opinion on this assessment of the First Amendment. You may review the article at *Boston* magazine's website at www.bostonmagazine.com.

FOR FURTHER INQUIRY

1. In 1996, Robert B. Chatelle, cochair of the Political Issues Committee National Writers Union, wrote a letter to Wesleyan University President Douglas Bennet to express concern about a Wesleyan student who had been suspended by the university's student judicial board for violating the Wesleyan speech code. Read Chatelle's argument at http://users.rcn.com/kyp/schools/bennet2.html. After determining for yourself both sides of the conflict, write your own views in an essay. Support your position using information from the readings in this chapter as well as from your own personal experience.

6 | What's the Big Deal About Immigration?

The United States of America is a union predicated on similar moral values, political and economic self-interest, a common legal system, and a democratic form of government. While we have much in common, we are also a nation of immigrants—people of different ethnic backgrounds, religions, traditions, languages, and cultures. We are a nation whose motto *e pluribus unum* ("one out of many") bespeaks a pride in its multicultural heritage. But we are also a nation divided by race and ethnicity. We may glorify the memory of our own immigrant ancestors, but we do not always welcome new waves of immigrants. This chapter explores current issues connected with immigration and immigration reform, especially with respect to immigrants coming from Mexico and South America.

Most of the arguments involving immigration focus on illegal aliens circumventing U.S. laws. Some critics argue that immigrants themselves have changed—that the current wave of newcomers is different from those of the past, that this group refuses to assimilate, threatens the American way of life, and expects free handouts. Immigration advocates counter that all immigrant groups resist integration to a certain extent at first and then are assimilated into mainstream culture. They also contend that immigrants promote diversity, revitalize the workforce, and are good for the economy. With such diverse perspectives and positions, the issue can be challenging to navigate. Should new immigrants be required to learn English? What happens when illegal immigrants have children in the United States? Are immigrants changing American culture? If so, is that a bad thing? And what does the United States owe, if anything, to the thousands of people who seek a better life here?

CRITICAL THINKING

1. What is happening in this cartoon? What has happened to the Statue of Liberty, and why?
2. What do you need to know about immigration—both past and present—in order to understand the point the cartoonist is trying to make?
3. On what side of the immigration debate do you think the cartoonist is? In what type of publication would you expect this cartoon to be successful?

Kidding Ourselves About Immigration

Michael Kinsley

Michael Kinsley is a political journalist and television commentator. For many years, he served as a co-host on the political news program *Crossfire*. He is frequently published both in traditional print media and online. He is a former editor of *The New Republic* and started the online news journal *Slate*. This article appeared in the December 6, 2007, issue of *TIME* magazine.

CONNECTING TO THE TOPIC

Most of us can trace our roots to an ancestor who left his or her country and immigrated to the United States. In many cases, this relocation was legal— that is, the government legally allowed this person to enter the United States and live and work here. Today, the United States seems to be very selective about to whom they extend immigrant status. The thousands left in line must find another way across the border. In this next essay, Michael Kinsley attempts to force Americans to own up to what they really mean when they say they are against illegal immigration. And the truth isn't very nice.

WORDS IN CONTEXT

agin (4) (*Chiefly Upper Southern U.S.*) against; opposed to: *I'm agin him.*
(prep.)
queue (7) line (n.)

1   What you are supposed to say about immigration—what most of the political candidates say, what the radio talk jocks say—is that you are not against immigration. Not at all. You salute the hard work and noble aspirations of those who are lining up at American consulates around the world. But that is legal immigration. What you oppose is illegal immigration.

2   This formula is not very helpful. We all oppose breaking the law, or we ought to. Saying that you oppose illegal immigration is like saying you oppose illegal drug use or illegal speeding. Of course you do, or should. The question is whether you think the law draws the line in the right place. Should using marijuana be illegal? Should the speed limit be raised—or lowered? The fact that you believe in obeying the law reveals nothing about what you think the law ought to be, or why.

3   Another question: Why are you so upset about this particular form of lawbreaking? After all, there are lots of laws, not all of them enforced

with vigor. The suspicion naturally arises that the illegality is not what bothers you. What bothers you is the immigration. There is an easy way to test this. Reducing illegal immigration is hard, but increasing legal immigration would be easy. If your view is that legal immigration is good and illegal immigration is bad, how about increasing legal immigration? How about doubling it? Any takers? So in the end, this is not really a debate about illegal immigration. This is a debate about immigration.

4　　And it's barely a debate at all. Immigration has long divided both parties, with advocates and opponents in each. Among Republicans, support for immigration was economic (corporations), while opposition was cultural (nativists). Among Democrats, it was the reverse: support for immigration was cultural (ethnic groups), while opposition was economic (unions). Now, for whatever reason, support for immigration is limited to an eccentric alliance of high-minded Council on Foreign Relations types, the mainstream media, high-tech entrepreneurs, Latinos, and the *Wall Street Journal* editorial page. Everyone else, it seems, is **agin**.

5　　Maybe the aginners are right, and immigration is now damaging our country, stealing jobs and opportunity, ripping off taxpayers, fragmenting our culture. I doubt it, but maybe so. Certainly, it's true that we can't let in everyone who wants to come. There is some number of immigrants that is too many. I don't believe we're past that point, but maybe we are. In any event, a democracy has the right to decide that it has reached such a point. There is no obligation to be fair to foreigners.

6　　But let's not kid ourselves that all we care about is obeying the law and all we are asking illegals to do is go home and get in line like everybody else. We know perfectly well that the line is too long, and we are basically telling people to go home and not come back.

7　　Let's not kid ourselves, either, about who we are telling this to. To characterize illegal immigrants as **queue**-jumping, lawbreaking scum is seriously unjust. The motives of illegal immigrants—which can be summarized as "a better life"—are identical to those of legal immigrants. In fact, they are largely identical to the motives of our own parents, grandparents and great-grandparents when they immigrated. And not just that. Ask yourself, of these three groups—today's legal and illegal immigrants and the immigrants of generations ago—which one has proven most dramatically its appreciation of our country? Which one has shown the most gumption, the most willingness to risk all to get to the U.S. and the most willingness to work hard once here? Well, everyone's story is unique. But who loves the U.S. most? On average, probably, the winners of this American-values contest would be the illegals, doing our dirty work under constant fear of eviction, getting thrown out and returning again and again.

8　　And how about those of us lucky enough to have been born here? How would we do against the typical illegal alien in a "prove how much you love America" reality TV show? ◆

CONSIDERING THE ISSUES

1. In his essay, Kinsley says, "To characterize illegal immigrants as queue-jumping, lawbreaking scum is seriously unjust." Do you agree or disagree with this assertion? How should we characterize illegal immigrants? How would the illegal immigrants probably characterize themselves?
2. What are American values? Kinsley states, "the winners of this American-values contest would be the illegals." Does this statement express your view of American values? Explain.

CRAFT AND CONTENT

1. The author makes many assumptions about his audience in this essay. First of all, explain who Kinsley believes his audience is and then find at least three examples in his writing in which he makes assumptions about his readers. What are those assumptions?
2. According to this article, how have illegal immigrants shown their appreciation for the United States? In what other ways do or could immigrants show their appreciation for their newly adopted nation?

CRITICAL THINKING

1. Kinsley mentions that "support for immigration is limited to an eccentric alliance of high-minded Council on Foreign Relations types, the mainstream media, high-tech entrepreneurs, Latinos, and *The Wall Street Journal* editorial page." Do you think this statement is accurate? Why do you think these groups would support immigration?
2. If the United States could decrease illegal immigration to our country by doubling legal immigration, should that be done? What would be other pros and cons of doubling legal immigration?

WRITING ABOUT THE ISSUES

1. Kinsley ends his essay by asking his presumably American audience, "How would we do against the typical illegal alien in a 'prove how much you love America' reality TV show?" Develop this reality TV show idea by explaining how native-born Americans would compete with illegal immigrants in proving how much each group loves the United States. In other words, write a premise for this reality TV show.

2. This essay makes a bold statement: "There is no obligation to be fair to foreigners." Make a list of situations in which this statement would prove to be accurate and then make a list of situations in which this statement would not be accurate. If you were traveling to another country and were considered a "foreigner," how would you expect to be treated?

Educating Illegal Immigrants

Todd Rosenbaum

The next essay, an editorial by student Todd Rosenbaum, was published in the March 14, 2006 issue of the *Cavalier Daily*, the student newspaper of the University of Virginia. Rosenbaum, a political philosophy and American studies major, wrote this article during his senior year.

CONNECTING TO THE TOPIC

Many students take for granted their right to an education. Rosenbaum asks his fellow students to consider the immigration argument from a different perspective—that of students who are children of illegal aliens. Should the children of illegal immigrants be entitled to the same educational benefits as legal U.S. residents? And if not, who suffers more? By barring such children from the education that may help make them productive members of society, are laws such as the one Rosenbaum challenges doing more harm than good?

WORDS IN CONTEXT

ubiquitous (4)   very common, found everywhere (adj.)
naturalization (6)   the process of becoming a citizen (n.)
viable (6)   likely, plausible (adj.)

1   Imagine that you're a 20-year-old University student—this should be a relatively easy exercise for many of you. You've got the entire world at your feet, a wealth of opportunities which are not afforded to those without a college degree. Now imagine that you're suddenly forced to withdraw from school because you can no longer afford tuition. Suddenly, all of those opportunities you had a split-second ago vanish. If only you were granted in-state tuition, you could afford to stay. But you're not, and here's the clincher: You've lived in Virginia for the past 10 years.

2   Sadly, this is reality for many students who reside in the Common-
wealth of Virginia. They are the sons and daughters of illegal immigrants,
who came to the United States as children with no say in their destinies.
And a few Virginia lawmakers are doing all they can to make it difficult
for them to enroll in Virginia's public colleges and universities. By not
extending in-state tuition to these students, most of them are effectively
barred from attending our public institutions of higher education because
they cannot afford to. As non-U.S. citizens, they do not qualify for student loans or grants. Chances for them to improve their own situations are
starkly limited.

3   It should not be our lawmakers' prerogative to discriminate against
them because of their parents' decisions. Instead, they should focus on
helping young illegal immigrants in Virginia to establish legal status. This
also means affording them opportunities which will allow them to develop
as productive and responsible members of our society.

4   Comforted by our **ubiquitous** diversity statements and antidiscrimination clauses, we are often fooled into thinking that discrimination like this no longer exists in the United States. But some Virginia
lawmakers have tried unsuccessfully in the past to ban outright the enrollment of illegal immigrants in Virginia's institutions of higher education.
Now, they are seeking to keep most illegal immigrants out of our
colleges and universities by ensuring that in-state tuition rates are never
extended to them. Federal statute backs this discriminatory attitude: states
are forbidden to extend higher-education benefits to students who reside
here illegally, if the benefits are not extended to all non-U.S. citizens.
Any state law that violates this statute would require a successful legal
challenge in federal court in order to be upheld.

5   But why should we extend these benefits to those who have chosen to
disregard our immigration laws? Again, young illegal immigrants rarely
make the choice to immigrate on their own. More importantly, there is
also federal constitutional precedent for affording illegal immigrants educational benefits.

6   A 1982 Supreme Court case ensured that those residing in the United
States are able to attend public primary and secondary schools regardless
of their legal statuses. Many of the students who have benefited from that
decision are now graduating from our nation's public high schools—fully
capable of excelling in college, but unable to afford to do so. Many of them
have taken steps towards **naturalization** and are awaiting approval, which
can take years. Others are unable to afford the application costs which
accompany the naturalization process. Returning to their countries of origin,
after having made so much educational progress, is hardly a **viable** option.

7   At the same time, lawmakers must be sensitive to how a law which
extends in-state tuition to illegal immigrants residing in Virginia could
impact its general policy on who qualifies for in-state rates. Offering

reduced tuition for undocumented residents of the state could legally bind Virginia to extend in-state rates to all out-of-state students, hardly a realistic option.

8   A compromise worthy of attention has been proposed which would not extend in-state tuition to illegal immigrants in general, but would make an exception for those who have a history in Virginia. For example, graduating from high school here, belonging to a family that pays taxes and actively seeking legal residency could together form acceptable criteria. According to the *Washington Post*, this could allow up to a few thousand illegal immigrants who reside in Virginia a chance to attend college here.

9   For those who worry about illegal immigrants' drain on our state and national resources, it seems counterintuitive to oppose such legislation. In the long term, allowing these immigrants improved access to higher education is likely to improve their contributions to our society and reduce the burdens they place on it. It will only aid us to help those who are willing and eager to improve their own situations to do so. ◆

CONSIDERING THE ISSUES

1. Rosenbaum states, "It should not be our lawmakers' prerogative to discriminate against them because of their parents' decisions." Should children of illegal immigrants be penalized for their parents' choices?
2. Should the children of illegal immigrants be granted the same rights as children of U.S. citizens? Is this a moral/ethical issue of extending opportunities to all children in this country? Or is it a legal one? Explain.

CRAFT AND CONTENT

1. Rosenbaum encourages his readers to "imagine" they are university students. How does this introductory exercise help lead into his argument? Explain.
2. Summarize Rosenbaum's argument and outline his supporting points.

CRITICAL THINKING

1. Rosenbaum asks, "Why should we extend benefits to those who have chosen to disregard our immigration laws?" What answer does he give for this rhetorical question? Do you agree with his viewpoint?
2. What reasons does Rosenbaum give for extending state funding for education to the children of illegal immigrants?

WRITING ABOUT THE ISSUES

1. Write a response to Rosenbaum's editorial in the form of a letter to the editor of the student newspaper, the *Cavalier Daily*.
2. Rosenbaum raises an important and interesting question—why should we, in effect, punish the children of illegal immigrants for decisions made by their parents? Imagine you were raised in the United States but not afforded citizenship because of your parents' status. What rights would you expect? How would you react if you were barred from the rights enjoyed by your peers?

Anchor Babies
USA Today and Roy Beck

On August 30, 2010, *USA Today* ran a pro/con opinion piece on the issue of "anchor babies." *USA Today* supported the opinion expressed in the first editorial "Our View" while also running another viewpoint expressed by Roy Beck. *USA Today*'s editorials are decided by its editorial board, a demographically and ideologically diverse group that is separate from *USA Today*'s news staff. Roy Beck is executive director of Numbers USA, an immigration-reduction organization. He is the author of *The Case Against Immigration* (1996).

CONNECTING TO THE TOPIC

"All persons born or naturalized in the United States, and subject to the jurisdiction thereof, are citizens of the United States and of the state wherein they reside." So reads the 14th Amendment of the U.S. Constitution. This amendment has led to some controversy concerning children born in the United States to illegal immigrants. The term "anchor baby" is a derogatory phrase used for a child born in the United Sates to an illegal immigrant parent, who supposedly can be then used to facilitate the naturalizing or immigration process for his or her parents' relatives still outside the United States. In reality, a U.S. citizen child cannot file for a visa for his or her parents until 21 years of age and must be earning at least 125 percent above the poverty threshold to be able to apply. Thus, illegal immigrants who have babies in the United States must technically remain in the United States illegally.

WORDS IN CONTEXT

confer (3)   grant, give (v)
fraught (4)   filled with (adv.)
polarized (5)   two contrasting or conflicting positions (v.)

encumbered (7)   burdened or impeded by (v.)

pernicious (8)   having a harmful effect, especially in a gradual or subtle way (adj.)

divisive (10)   ending to cause disagreement or hostility between people (adj.)

Should being born in the USA make you a citizen?

1 With the economic recovery faltering and midterm elections approaching, simmering anger against illegal immigrants seems to be reaching a new boiling point.

2 Polls show most Americans back Arizona's controversial new law aimed at arresting undocumented immigrants, and now support is growing for an even more drastic move to deny citizenship to babies born in the U.S. unless their parents are here legally. Several leading Republican lawmakers, including Senate Minority Leader Mitchell McConnell, have called for hearings into the issue.

3 Any effort to repeal what's known as "birthright citizenship" faces a big obstacle: the 14th Amendment. Ever since the amendment was ratified in 1868, the Constitution has repeatedly been held to **confer** automatic American citizenship on anyone born in the USA.

4 The repealers' argument—logical and enticing—is that an amendment written to ensure that the children of slaves received citizenship rights is obsolete in a modern era of illegal immigration, jetliner travel and international tourism. As a solution to the nation's illegal immigration problem, though, it is at best an unworkable distraction, one so **fraught** with practical difficulties as to make the effort impractical and unwise.

5 For one thing, amending the Constitution is difficult to do, and deliberately so. It takes a vote of two-thirds of both the House of Representatives and the Senate to propose an amendment, and then three-quarters of the states to ratify it. In today's **polarized** political environment, it's hard to imagine that happening.

6 Some opponents of birthright citizenship say that an amendment isn't necessary, that Congress could do the same thing merely by passing a law to "clarify" the 14th Amendment. But such a law would no doubt be challenged, and birthright citizenship has consistently withstood court tests.

7 The opponents also tend to give short shrift to the practical difficulties of enforcement. It's not difficult to envision the joy of childbirth being **encumbered** by bureaucratic red tape. Is it worth inflicting citizenship tests on the parents of all 4.3 million children born in the USA each year in an effort to identify the estimated 8% born to illegal immigrants? And any sort of delivery-based enforcement mechanism would undoubtedly cause some women to avoid hospitals, endangering the health of mother and child.

8 If babies were really the problem, perhaps it would make more sense to change the 14th Amendment. But charges that "anchor babies" begin

a **pernicious** "chain migration" ignore the fact that a baby born a citizen here has to wait 21 years before trying to bring in most relatives. The undocumented parents of a U.S.-born baby are still illegal immigrants; they should not be allowed to plead the citizenship of their child to stave off deportation.

9   The real ways to fight illegal immigration are the same as they've always been: Tighten the border. Make it harder for immigrants to work here illegally. Fix the E-Verify system that lets employers check whether job applicants are here legally. Set up a temporary worker system. And establish a path to legality for undocumented aliens already here who pay taxes and stay out of trouble.

10   Repealing birthright citizenship is so **divisive**, and so far down the list of solutions, as to make it an unworthy addition to the national debate on immigration.

Reject Birthright Citizenship

11   Birthright citizenship is a powerful anchor for keeping illegal workers in a country—and for keeping the jobs they fill out of reach of unemployed legal residents. It is incompatible with a modern age of easy transportation and organized people smuggling. Every developed nation, except the USA and Canada, has rejected citizenship for births to tourists and unlawful foreign residents.

12   An estimated 4 million U.S. residents have received this type of citizenship. Who's hurt by this? Millions of poor American children live in families suffering from unemployment or depressed wages because an estimated 7 million illegal foreign workers are holding construction, manufacturing, service and transportation jobs.

13   Anything that slows the decision of illegal workers to go back home prolongs the disadvantaging of the 30 million less-educated Americans and legal immigrants who don't have a job and who generally seek work in the same non-agricultural industries where most illegal workers are found.

14   Birthright citizenship is a major anchor for illegal workers already here who are led to feel that their birthright citizen children may give them a claim to remain. Note that one of the loudest arguments for giving illegal workers permanent work permits is that it would be wrong to make them go back home if they have U.S. citizen children.

15   Of course, ending birthright citizenship is not enough. Congress should pass the SAVE Act to impede outlaw businesses from hiring illegal workers, and take other actions to protect legal U.S. workers from an immigration system that is importing hundreds of thousands of working-age immigrants annually during a jobs depression. With unemployment high and wages stagnant in most occupations, we don't have labor shortages and don't need additional foreign labor (or the illegal labor already here).

16   Scholars make strong arguments on both sides of what the 14th Amendment's birthright citizenship provision means. Only the Supreme Court can say, and it has never ruled about tourists and illegal residents. For now, Congress should leave the Constitution alone and pass legislation (H.R. 1868) that simply clarifies the birthright provision in immigration law—and then see how the court rules. ◆

CONSIDERING THE ISSUES

1. Do you think there are too many people living in the United States? Too few? Is your view of immigration laws and trends influenced at all by your understanding of U.S. population numbers?
2. What problems does U.S. immigration create today? Where do people settle? What challenges do we face that our forebearers did not?

CRAFT AND CONTENT

1. Both of these articles are opinion pieces. Which one makes the most compelling argument, and why?
2. Summarize each side's position that the U.S. Constitution should or should not be amended regarding birthright citizenship.

CRITICAL THINKING

1. *USA Today* argues that children born to illegal immigrants cannot secure their parents' legal status until they are 21 years of age. Roy Beck argues that while this may be true, green cards are often granted when a child exists because the government doesn't want to separate parents from their children. What do you think? Should illegal immigrants with U.S.-born children be granted green cards? Why or why not?
2. If citizenship were no longer granted to all children born on U.S. soil, would it deter illegal immigration? Why or why not?
3. How might requiring proof of citizenship complicate birth? Explain.

WRITING ABOUT THE ISSUES

1. Write a opinion response to either *USA Today* or Roy Beck in which you either agree or disagree with their position, either in whole or in part.
2. Research the SAVE Act, and write an essay in which you take your own position on this issue. Explain why you feel that the SAVE Act should or should not pass.

America's Real Dream Team

Thomas L. Friedman

Thomas L. Friedman is a three-time Pulitzer Prize winning writer for *The New York Times*. He became the paper's foreign-affairs columnist in 1995. Previously, he served as chief economic correspondent in the Washington bureau, and before that, he was the chief White House correspondent. The author of several books, his latest was the best selling *The World Is Flat: A Brief History of the 21st Century* (2005).

CONNECTING TO THE TOPIC

Controversial immigration laws conjure images of illegal aliens swimming across the Rio Grande and sneaking through tunnels through border crossings. But what about children of immigrants living in states across the United States? While their parents may not speak English, many children of immigrants are excelling in school and participating in the American dream. And many do not come from south of the border. How are stereotypes influencing our view of immigration? What impact do children of immigrants have on our economy, culture, and educational systems? Do we need to rethink our viewpoints?

WORDS IN CONTEXT

spectral (8)   ghostly; phantom-like (adj.)

1   Went to a big Washington dinner last week. You know the kind: large hall; black ties; long dresses. But this was no ordinary dinner. There were 40 guests of honor. So here's my Sunday news quiz: I'll give you the names of most of the honorees, and you tell me what dinner I was at. Ready?

2   Linda Zhou, Alice Wei Zhao, Lori Ying, Angela Yu-Yun Yeung, Lynnelle Lin Ye, Kevin Young Xu, Benjamin Chang Sun, Jane Yoonhae Suh, Katheryn Cheng Shi, Sunanda Sharma, Sarine Gayaneh Shahmirian, Arjun Ranganath Puranik, Raman Venkat Nelakant, Akhil Mathew, Paul Masih Das, David Chienyun Liu, Elisa Bisi Lin, Yifan Li, Lanair Amaad Lett, Ruoyi Jiang, Otana Agape Jakpor, Peter Danming Hu, Yale Wang Fan, Yuval Yaacov Calev, Levent Alpoge, John Vincenzo Capodilupo and Namrata Anand.

3   No, sorry, it was not a dinner of the China-India friendship league. Give up?

4   O.k. All these kids are American high school students. They were the majority of the 40 finalists in the 2010 Intel Science Talent Search, which, through a national contest, identifies and honors the top math and science high school students in America, based on their solutions to scientific problems. The awards dinner was Tuesday, and, as you can see from the above list, most finalists hailed from immigrant families, largely from Asia.

5   Indeed, if you need any more convincing about the virtues of immigration, just come to the Intel science finals. I am a pro-immigration fanatic. I think keeping a constant flow of legal immigrants into our country—whether they wear blue collars or lab coats—is the key to keeping us ahead of China. Because when you mix all of these energetic, high-aspiring people with a democratic system and free markets, magic happens. If we hope to keep that magic, we need immigration reform that guarantees that we will always attract and retain, in an orderly fashion, the world's first-round aspirational and intellectual draft choices.

6   This isn't complicated. In today's wired world, the most important economic competition is no longer between countries or companies. The most important economic competition is actually between you and your own imagination. Because what your kids imagine, they can now act on farther, faster, cheaper than ever before—as individuals. Today, just about everything is becoming a commodity, except imagination, except the ability to spark new ideas.

7   If I just have the spark of an idea now, I can get a designer in Taiwan to design it. I can get a factory in China to produce a prototype. I can get a factory in Vietnam to mass manufacture it. I can use Amazon.com to handle fulfillment. I can use freelancer.com to find someone to do my logo and manage my backroom. And I can do all this at incredibly low prices. The one thing that is not a commodity and never will be is that spark of an idea. And this Intel dinner was all about our best sparklers.

8   Before the dinner started, each contestant stood by a storyboard explaining their specific project. Namrata Anand, a 17-year-old from the Harker School in California, patiently explained to me her research, which used **spectral** analysis and other data to expose information about the chemical enrichment history of "Andromeda galaxy." I did not understand a word she said, but I sure caught the gleam in her eye.

9   My favorite chat, though, was with Amanda Alonzo, a 30-year-old biology teacher at Lynbrook High School in San Jose, Calif. She had taught two of the finalists. When I asked her the secret, she said it was the resources provided by her school, extremely "supportive parents" and a grant from Intel that let her spend part of each day inspiring and preparing students to enter this contest. Then she told me this: local San Jose realtors are running ads in newspapers in China and India telling potential immigrants to "buy a home" in her Lynbrook school district because it produced "two Intel science winners."

10   Seriously, ESPN or MTV should broadcast the Intel finals live. All of
the 40 finalists are introduced, with little stories about their lives and aspirations. Then the winners of the nine best projects are announced. And finally,
with great drama, the overall winner of the $100,000 award for the best
project of the 40 is identified. This year it was Erika Alden Debenedictis of
New Mexico for developing a software navigation system that would
enable spacecraft to more efficiently "travel through the solar system." After
her name was called, she was swarmed by her fellow competitor-geeks.

11   Gotta say, it was the most inspiring evening I've had in D.C. in
20 years. It left me thinking, "If we can just get a few things right—
immigration, education standards, bandwidth, fiscal policy—maybe we'll
be o.k." It left me feeling that maybe Alice Wei Zhao of North High School
in Sheboygan, Wis., chosen by her fellow finalists to be their spokeswoman,
was right when she told the audience: "Don't sweat about the problems our
generation will have to deal with. Believe me, our future is in good hands."

12   As long as we don't shut our doors. ◆

CONSIDERING THE ISSUES

1. Friedman notes that most of the students in the 2010 Intel
   Science Talent Search were of Chinese and Indian descent.
   What stereotypes exist about the children of Asian immigrants?
   Do you think this article reinforces these stereotypes? Can a
   stereotype ever be good?
2. Friedman argues that ESPN or MTV should air the Intel finals
   live. Do you think such a program would be watched by either
   station's typical audience? Why or why not?

CRAFT AND CONTENT

1. How does the author get his audience's attention in his article's introduction? Did you find this device effective in grabbing your attention?
2. Which sentence would you describe as the author's thesis statement? Explain.
3. Thomas L. Friedman asserts that he is pro-immigration. Which
   reasons does he give to support his viewpoint? Do you think of
   yourself as pro- or anti-immigration?

CRITICAL THINKING

1. The author states that the United States needs to "get a few things
   right—immigration, education standards, bandwidth, fiscal policy."
   If you had to prioritize the top four issues that the U.S. government needs to "get right," what would be on your list and why?

2. Thomas L. Friedman refers to the Intel science contestants as "competitor-geeks." How do you feel about the use of the word *geek* in this context? What is a geek? Is it a derogatory term, or has it changed to be socially acceptable? Explain.

WRITING ABOUT THE ISSUES

1. In this article, Friedman maintains that the United States needs immigration reform. Write an essay in which you focus on one reform that the U.S could make regarding immigration and then support your essay with two to three reasons why this reform needs to be made.
2. Create a proposal to air a new program on the Intel Science Talent Search. Include the program format, how it would track the progress of the contestants, and what network it would air on and why.

Blog Matters

A blog ("web log") is an online diary or commentary site that features regular entries that describe events, impressions, and viewpoints. Blogs may contain text, images, video, and often link to other websites, blogs, and online media. Most blogs allow readers to comment on the content of the post and respond to each other. As of September 2011, there were over 160 million public blogs in existence. While many blogs are maintained by individuals, some are run by journals, newspapers, and other media outlets. Remember that most blogs are not monitored for factual accuracy and often express the opinion and views of the "blogger" writing the content.

The blog below is written by Michael Ford, founding director of Xavier University's Institute for Politics and the American Dream. Ford has a 37-year career in politics, government, and business at all levels of American public life. He has held senior staff and senior advisory positions in nine presidential campaigns. This entry appeared on April 26, 2011 on Cincinati.com.

Immigrants Are Crucial to the American Dream

Mike Ford
April 26, 2011

1   No nation, not even the United States, has the in-house creative talent to rule the economic world forever. That's why immigrants are crucial to sustaining the American economy.

2   And despite widely reported anti-immigrant sentiment in the U.S., 60 percent of Americans believe that immigration is important to keeping the American Dream alive, according to the second annual Xavier University Survey of the American Dream.

3   Look at the legendary creative fire given to our nation by immigrants. Immigrants have traditionally supplied the oxygen necessary to igniting and fueling that fire. Perhaps the greatest measurable impact of immigrants can be found in the entrepreneurial world, where success requires a certain fearlessness, vision and determination, which many immigrants bring with them.

4   Immigrants provide those qualities to the United States. Not vice versa.

5   Nevertheless, some people falsely believe that immigrants get handouts from the U.S. government, such as free housing and business loans unavailable to native-born Americans. Indeed, our American Dream Survey shows that immigrants overwhelmingly believe that "hard work" is the way to get ahead in America.

6   If not for immigrants, the U.S. would not be so wildly successful in developing technology. Research at the Kauffman Foundation, which supports entrepreneurship and education, found that, in 25 percent of the U.S. science and technology companies, the chief executive or lead technologist was foreign-born. In Silicon Valley, more than 50 percent of the startups have been founded by immigrants. These immigrant founders are highly educated—96 percent have bachelor's degrees and 74 percent held graduate or postgraduate degrees, mostly in science, technology, engineering and mathematics-related fields.

7   The vast majority of these didn't come to the United States as entrepreneurs. More than 50 percent came to study and 40 percent came to work. Only 1.6 percent came to start companies. But they typically ended up starting companies within a decade after arriving.

8   According to Nobel Prize-winning physicist Robert Richardson of Cornell University, the U.S. has a serious shortage of scientists that's been developing since the 1970s. We rank 23rd in the world in the percentage

of our college graduates who become scientists and engineers. Thirty years ago, we ranked third. Without immigrants, that problem would be even worse.

9   Our ability to attract immigrants is challenged by our own prejudices and our fears that immigrants will take our jobs and our children's slots in colleges. In an economy committed to growth, the number of jobs and educational opportunities are not limited. Rather, as immigration helps to expand our economy, the number of jobs and educational opportunities will grow.

10   And that economic growth will make our nation even more attractive to smart hard-working immigrants who want to pursue the American Dream.

RESPOND TO THE BLOG:

What do you think? Are immigrants essential to the success of the United States? What role do they play in the U.S. economy?

The Problem With Question 36
Dafna Linzer

Dafna Linzer is a Canadian-American reporter at *ProPublica*, a nonprofit investigative newsroom. She was a national security reporter for *The Washington Post*. Before joining the *Post*, she spent 10 years as a foreign correspondent for Associated Press. Based in Jerusalem, New York, and the United Nations, she reported from more than a dozen countries covering terrorism, nonproliferation, and conflict. This article was first published in *Slate* magazine, February 23, 2011.

CONNECTING TO THE TOPIC ─────────────

What does it take to become an American citizen? Dafna Linzer, the author of this article, found out the hard way—by going through the process herself. What befuddled her the most? Why were so many of the official answers on the U.S. citizenship test wrong?

WORDS IN CONTEXT ─────────────

aghast (20)   struck by shock, terror, or amazement (adj.)
explicitly (21)   fully and clearly expressed (adv.)

polygamist (33)   having more than one spouse at a time (n.)
prominently (40)   immediately noticeable; conspicuous; widely known (adv.)
nitpicky (45)   finding fault with insignificant details (adj.)

1   ast month, I became an American citizen, a tremendous honor and no easy accomplishment, even for a Canadian. After living here for 12 years, I thought I knew everything. Then I learned how we mint Americans.

2   After years of steep filing fees and paperwork (including one letter from Homeland Security claiming that my fingerprints had "expired"), it all came down to a test. I passed, and, my fellow Americans, you could, too—if you don't mind providing answers that you know are wrong.

3   Friends told me I didn't need to study, the questions weren't that hard. But I wanted to and so for months I lugged around a set of government-issued flashcards, hoping to master the test. I pestered my family and friends to quiz me. Sometimes I quizzed my sources. I learned things (there are 27 amendments to the Constitution) and they learned things (there are 27 amendments to the Constitution). But then we began noticing errors in a number of the questions and answers.

4   Take Question 36. It asks applicants to name two members of the president's Cabinet. Among the correct answers is "Vice President." The vice president is a cabinet-level officer but he's not a Cabinet member. Cabinet members are unelected heads of executive departments, such as the Defense Department, or the State Department.

5   The official naturalization test booklet even hints as much: "The president may appoint other government officials to the cabinet but no elected official may serve on the cabinet while in office." Note to Homeland Security: The vice president is elected.

6   Still, a wonderful press officer in the New York immigration office noted that the White House's own Web site lists the vice president as a member of the Cabinet. It's still wrong, I explained. I told her that my partner wrote an entire book about the vice president and won a Pulitzer Prize for the stories. I was pretty sure about this one. A parade of constitutional scholars backed me up.

7   In fact, the Constitution aligns the vice president more closely with the legislative branch as president of the Senate. Not until well into the 20th century did the vice president even attend Cabinet meetings.

8   Then there is Question 12: What is the "rule of law"?

9   I showed it to lawyers and law professors. They were stumped.

10   There are four acceptable answers: "Everyone must follow the law"; "Leaders must obey the law"; "Government must obey the law"; "No one is above the law."

11   Judge Richard Posner, the constitutional scholar who serves on the U.S. Court of Appeals in Chicago, was unhappy. "These are all incorrect,"

he wrote me. "The rule of law means that judges decide cases 'without re-spect of persons,' that is, without considering the social status, attractive-ness, etc. of the parties or their lawyers."

12   So, where do these questions come from?

13   U.S. Citizenship and Immigration Services, a department within Homeland Security, spent six years consulting scholars, educators, and historians before the current test was introduced in 2008. The result: 100 questions and answers designed to provide an in-depth treatment of U.S. history and government.

14   "The goal of the naturalization test is to ensure America's newest citizens have mastered a basic knowledge of U.S. history and have a solid foundation to continue to expand their understanding as they embark on life as U.S. citizens," said Christopher Bentley, a spokesman for USCIS.

15   During the citizenship interview, applicants are asked a randomly selected 10 questions from the test and must answer six correctly. In addition to the questions, there is a reading and writing test for English proficiency.

16   My immigration lawyer accompanied me to my interview. In the security line, I told her I was bothered by Question 16: Who makes the federal laws?

17   Each of the three possible answers, it seemed, was incomplete. The official answers were: "Congress"; "Senate and House (of representatives)"; "(U.S. or national) legislature." I'm not a lawyer but even Canadians watched Schoolhouse Rock. Where, I wondered, was the president, whose signature is what makes a bill into a law?

18   My lawyer sighed, she agreed. But: "If you get asked that question, just give the official answer," she said. I didn't get that question.

19   I also wasn't asked Question 1: What is the supreme law of the land?

20   The official answer: "the Constitution." A friend and legal scholar was **aghast**. That answer, he said, is "no more than one-third correct." He's right.

21   Article VI, clause 2 in the Constitution, known as the Supremacy Clause, **explicitly** says that three things—the Constitution, federal laws, and treaties—together "shall be the supreme law of the land."

22   Question 96 asks: Why does the flag have 13 stripes? The official an-swer: "because there were 13 original colonies." In fact, the flag has 13 stripes for the 13 original states.

23   Many of the test questions, organized under topics such as "system of government," "geography," and "American history" are correct and infor-mative. Since I'm a reporter, one tugged at my heart.

24   Question 55 asks: What are two ways that Americans can participate in their democracy? Among the correct answers: "write to a newspaper."

25   At my interview, I was asked questions on presidential succession, the Cabinet, Senate terms, and the Supreme Court. I was asked to name a branch of government. (I went with the executive.)

26   I was asked Question 8: What did the Declaration of Independence do?

27   Heeding my lawyer's advice, I went with the official answer: "declared our independence."

28   I answered six consecutive questions correctly and moved on to the language section of the exam. Native English speakers are not exempt from this section and I was asked to read aloud the following sentence: "Columbus Day is in October."

29   I was then asked to write a sentence in English. Remarkably, it was the same sentence: "Columbus Day is in October."

30   Next, I reaffirmed answers I had given on my citizenship application.

31   Was I a member of the Communist Party? Was I member of a totalitarian party? Am I a terrorist? Although I was born in 1970, I was asked: Between March 23, 1933 and May 8, 1945, did I work for or associate in any way with the Nazi government of Germany? Had I worked at a concentration camp?

32   The officer who interviewed me, Sandy Saint Louis, had to ask me the questions. But she didn't even look up or wait for my responses. She checked off "No" after each one.

33   She did pay attention when she asked whether I was a habitual drunkard, a **polygamist**, a drug-smuggler, a felon, a tax-evader.

34   My paperwork was in order, my background check was complete. When the interview was over, Saint Louis pressed a large wooden seal into a red ink pad and stamped "approved" across my application. A wave of relief washed over me and my lawyer shot me a sweet smile. Ten days later, when I returned for the swearing-in, a brief and final questionnaire asked if I had engaged in prostitution since the interview. I checked "No."

35   On Friday, January 28, accompanied by my family, I was among 160 citizens-in-waiting who filed into a 3rd-floor auditorium in lower Manhattan to be sworn in as Americans. On our seats were an American flag, a copy of the Constitution, a booklet featuring the stories of prominent naturalized Americans, and a welcome letter from President Obama.

36   Reading the letter, I began to cry. I had spent more than one-quarter of my life hoping to become American, and I was suddenly overwhelmed by the honor and the significance of the moment. The place I have called home for 12 years was finally claiming me, as well.

37   I looked around the room and saw other fortunate souls with long journeys now behind them, quietly weeping with joy.

38   An immigration official asked us all to stand, and to remain standing, when the name of our country of origin was called out. After he read through the names of 44 countries, we were all standing, waving our flags.

39   Together, we took the Oath of Allegiance and were then seated as citizens of one nation.

40   Everyone in the room that day had scored a perfect 100 percent on the test and, for fun, an official decided to test us all once more. Who wrote

"The Star Spangled Banner"? he asked. Only a few called out "Francis Scott Key," perhaps because that question is no longer on the test. It was **prominently** removed four years ago.

41   A newly sworn-in citizen led us in the Pledge of Allegiance. We sang the national anthem and then watched a video message from the president shown at every swearing-in ceremony across the country.

42   "It's an honor and a privilege to call you a fellow citizen of the United States of America," Obama told us. "This is now officially your country."

43   There were more tears. At the end of the hour, we received certificates of naturalization and were given instructions on how to obtain U.S. passports.

44   My family and I left soon afterward. It was 10:30 a.m. and cold outside. We took the subway uptown. Three children got off at three different stops, headed to their schools or the library. We took the youngest up to his school. He walked in clutching his American flag and announced proudly to his teachers that "Mommy is American."

45   At a party that evening, I displayed the letter from Obama and laid out the flashcards. Over Sam Adams beer and mini-burgers, I spoke about the ceremony and test. The host led us all in the Pledge of Allegiance, my second of the day. Looking around the room, I realized that a significant number of my friends are journalists, writers, academics, and lawyers. It's a **nitpicky** crowd and during three hours of celebration they noticed additional errors in the questions.

46   At the end of the night, one of the catering staff gathered up the flash cards and as she held them out to me, she revealed that next month she too will take her citizenship test. I was thrilled. I closed my first day as an American citizen by handing them over to her. "Which ones did you say were wrong again?" she asked. "Just give the official answer," I said, "and you'll do fine." ◆

CONSIDERING THE ISSUES

1. Why do you think so many of the answers for the naturalization test are wrong? What might this imply about "how we mint Americans"?

2. Review the questions that Dafna Linzer says are on the naturalization test. Would you have been able to answer them correctly? Explain.

CRAFT AND CONTENT

1. Look up the White House's own web site: does it still list the vice president as a member of the cabinet? Does it matter to you if it does or doesn't?

2. How would you describe the tone of this article? Give textual evidence to prove your point.

CRITICAL THINKING

1. Describe the "language section" of the naturalization test according to the author. Do you find this part of the test to be effective? Explain.
2. Why do you think the author chose to give the "wrong" answer to the test? Should immigrants taking the test be allowed to argue with the "published answers" without failing?

WRITING ABOUT THE ISSUES

1. Rewrite the naturalization test by choosing six questions that you think would "provide an in-depth treatment of U.S. history and government." Make sure to also write answers to your questions. Share your questions (and answers) with the rest of the class.
2. Write a letter to the U.S. Citizenship and Immigration Services stating what you think about the current naturalization test and if it should or should not be revised.

VISUAL CONNECTIONS

Two Views of U.S. Immigration

CONNECTING TO THE TOPIC

In 2005, over 1.2 million illegal immigrants were apprehended by the Border Patrol along the 2,000 mile U.S.–Mexico border. The Border Patrol itself admits a certain impotence in the situation, estimating that they catch only about one out of every four illegal border-crossers. Proposed solutions range from opening the borders and broadening immigration quotas to building walls and deporting entire families. Current debate centers on what should be done to prevent illegal immigration and what to do with the immigrants who are already here. Should children receive health care? Education? Does providing such services unfairly tax legal residents? Who decides? The cartoons below consider two different viewpoints on illegal immigration.

Border Fence
Daryl Cagle

The Enemy Within?
John Cole

CONSIDERING THE ISSUES

1. Consider the point of view of an immigrant to the United States by imagining your own journey to another country. Focusing on your feelings and goals, would you seek to assimilate and integrate in your new country, or merely live there for a while with the intention of one day returning to the United States? Would you learn the language? What employment, if any, would you seek? How would you raise a family? What concerns and fears might you have?

CRITICAL THINKING

1. What is happening in each of these cartoons? What position does each cartoonist take on the issue of illegal immigration? How do their cartoons reflect current debate over immigration today?
2. What was your reaction to each of these cartoons? Do you think they fairly depict the issues at hand? Why or why not?
3. What visual elements contribute to the impression of each cartoon? What clichés do they use, and how do they twist visual clichés to make a point? Explain.

The Next Americans
Tomás R. Jiménez

Tomás R. Jiménez teaches sociology at the University of California, San Diego. His research and teaching focus on immigration, assimilation, social mobility, and identity. His writing has appeared in many scholarly journals. He is a Fellow at the New American Foundation, where he writes about the role of government in immigrant assimilation. This article was published in *The Los Angeles Times* on May 27, 2007.

CONNECTING TO THE TOPIC

Critics of immigration often assert that an influx of foreigners threatens the American way of life and our national identity. By refusing to assimilate, and demanding multicultural acceptance in government and in the classroom, immigrants are forcing Americans to be more like them, instead of the other way around. A June 2006 *NBC/Wall Street Journal* poll found the public evenly divided on the fundamental question of whether immigration helps or hurts the country, with 44 percent saying it helps and 45 percent saying it hurts the United States. Are immigrants changing America's identity? Are they likely to hurt or help America in the long run? In the next article, sociology professor Tomás R. Jiménez explains why he thinks immigrants don't destroy our national identity—but, rather, they renew it.

WORDS IN CONTEXT

anarchist (4)   an advocate of the overthrow of compulsory government (n.)
cohesive (8)   well integrated, unified (adj.)
polyglot (9)   someone able to speak or write many languages, multilingual (adj.)
ubiquitous (10)   being everywhere at once, omnipresent (adj.)
prodigal (12)   wasteful, recklessly extravagant with money (adj.)
palpable (13)   plainly seen or perceived; evident; tangible (adj.)

1   **B**ehind the outcry over the controversial immigration reform legislation making its way through the Senate lies an unsettling question for many Americans. Should the bill become a reality, an estimated 12 million unauthorized immigrants, the vast majority of whom are Latino, would become eligible for citizenship immediately, and opportunities for millions of others to follow them would be created. What effect will these permanently settled immigrants have on American identity?

2   Some critics of the legislation are already arguing that inviting millions of immigrants to stay permanently in the U.S. and become citizens will hasten the fading of a cohesive nation. They say that immigrants may become more interwoven into the fabric of the United States, but the ethnic patches to which they bind their identities will remain all too distinguishable from the rest of the American quilt.

3   How immigrants and their descendants see themselves will change over time, and they will simultaneously transform many aspects of what it means to be an American. This is undoubtedly an uncomfortable process, fraught with tension between newcomers and established Americans that can occasionally become explosive. But the real issue is whether the United States can provide opportunities for upward mobility so that immigrants can, in turn, fortify what is most essential to our nation's identity.

4   History is instructive on whether immigrants will create a messy patchwork of ethnicities in the U.S. About a century ago, a tide of Southern and Eastern European immigrants arriving on our shores raised fears similar to those we hear today. Then, as now, Americans worried that the newcomers were destroying American identity. Many were certain that Catholic immigrants would help the pope rule the United States from Rome, and that immigrant **anarchists** would destroy American democracy. Some eugenicists thought that the dark-skinned immigrants from Southern Europe would contaminate the American gene pool.

5   None of this came to pass, of course. The pope has no political say in American affairs, the United States is still a capitalist democracy, and there is nothing wrong with the American gene pool. The fact that these fears never materialized is often cited as proof that European-origin immigrants and their descendants successfully assimilated into an American societal monolith.

6   However, as sociologists Richard Alba and Victor Nee point out, much of the American identity as we know it today was shaped by previous waves of immigrants. For instance, they note that the Christian tradition of the Christmas tree and the leisure Sunday made their way into the American mainstream because German immigrants and their descendants brought these traditions with them. Where religion was concerned, Protestantism was the clear marker of the nonsecular mainstream. But because of the assimilation of millions of Jews and Catholics, we today commonly refer to an American "Judeo-Christian tradition," a far more encompassing notion of American religious identity than the one envisioned in the past.

7   Immigrants are also redefining American identity today, though there are differences. For one, assimilation no longer exclusively means shedding all remnants of ethnicity and adopting a way of life largely identified

with Anglo Protestants. For instance, it was not at all uncommon in the early 20th century for teachers to give young immigrant pupils a stern rap across their knuckles for speaking their parents' mother tongue in school. By contrast, multiculturalism and the value of diversity are now widely adopted.

8   Although some see this as undercutting a **cohesive** U.S., we nonetheless regularly celebrate, even if sometimes superficially, the various ethnic strands in our multicultural nation. Education, business and political leaders tout the virtues of diversity, and the world of commerce affirms ethnic identity through ethnically oriented marketing aimed at selling everything from laundry detergent to quinceañera celebration packages at Disneyland.

9   These differences from the past have not—and are not—reversing the course of assimilation, even if they have given it a new tone. There are notable signs that immigrants and their children are already adopting features of American identity as their own. Consider, for instance, language, a central front in debates over assimilation. The growth of non-English-speaking immigrant populations, particularly those that speak Spanish, and the explosive rise in commercial services and media that cater to them have led commentators such as Pat Buchanan to pronounce the coming of a **polyglot** society. But nothing appears to be further from the truth.

10   Even in Los Angeles County, where 36% of the population is foreign-born and more than half speak a language other than English at home, English is not losing out in the long run. According to a recent study by social scientists Rubén Rumbaut, Douglas Massey and Frank Bean, published in the *Population and Development Review,* the use of non-English languages virtually disappears among nearly all U.S.-born children of immigrants in the county. Spanish shows more staying power among the U.S.-born children and grandchildren of Mexican immigrants, which is not surprising given that the size of the Spanish-speaking population provides near-**ubiquitous** access to the language. But the survival of Spanish among U.S.-born descendants of Mexican immigrants does not come at the expense of their ability to speak English and, more strikingly, English overwhelms Spanish-language use among the grandchildren of these immigrants.

11   An equally telling sign of how much immigrants and their children are becoming "American" is how different they have become from those in their ethnic homelands. Virtually all of today's immigrants stay connected to their countries of origin. They send money to family members who remain behind. Relatively inexpensive air, rail and bus travel and the availability of cheap telecommunication and e-mail enable them stay in constant contact, and dual citizenship allows their political voices to be heard from abroad. These enduring ties might lead to the conclusion that continuity between here and there threatens loyalty to the Stars and Stripes.

12   But ask any immigrant or their children about a recent visit to their country of origin, and they are likely to tell you how American they

felt. The family and friends they visit quickly recognize the **prodigal** children's tastes for American styles, their American accents and their declining cultural familiarity with life in the ethnic homeland—all telltale signs that they've Americanized. As sociologist David Fitzgerald puts it, their assimilation into American society entails a good deal of "dissimilation" from the countries the immigrants left behind.

13   American identity is absorbing something quite significant from immigrants and being changed by them. Language, food, entertainment and holiday traditions are **palpable** aspects of American culture on which immigrants today, as in the past, are leaving their mark. Our everyday lexicon is sprinkled with Spanish words. We are now just as likely to grab a burrito as a burger. Hip-hop is tinged with South Asian rhythms. And Chinese New Year and Cinco de Mayo are taking their places alongside St. Patrick's Day as widely celebrated American ethnic holidays.

14   But these are not the changes to American identity that matter most. At its core, American identity is a shared belief in the United States as a land of opportunity—a place where those who work hard and display individual effort realize their ambitions. Today's immigrants, including the estimated 12 million that may soon become authorized, have the potential to fortify the idea of the United States as a land of opportunity. Their willingness to risk their lives to come here and the backbreaking work many of them do attest to their ambition.

15   But their capacity to refresh what is essential to American identity depends a great deal on our ability to stay true to its essence—to be a land of opportunity. This means that we should be, above all, concerned that the rungs on the ladder of economic mobility are sturdy and closely spaced.

16   If we are going to take on the formidable challenge of further integrating 12 million mostly poor immigrants, we have to provide better public schools, a more affordable college education, healthcare and jobs that offer a decent wage and benefits so that they and their children are able to rejuvenate the American dream. The real threat is not that immigrants will fail to buy into what's essential to American identity, but that we will fall short in providing them the tools to do so. ◆

CONSIDERING THE ISSUES

1. Why does the prospect of 12 million Latino immigrants becoming citizens make so many people nervous? Do you think racism is a factor? What if 12 million Danish immigrants or 12 million Italian immigrants were at issue? Do you think critics of immigration would voice the same concerns? What if the 12 million immigrants were not poor? Explain.

2. What is "American identity"? When immigration critics refer to the "American identity" what do they mean?

CRAFT AND CONTENT

1. At the end of his essay, Jiménez provides a list of things the United States must do if it is to successfully integrate its 12 million illegal, mostly poor immigrants. Review this list and evaluate how it would be implemented. What are the economic and social costs of implementing such a list? Is it easy to say, but hard to do? Is the list missing anything you think is important?
2. How does Jiménez apply history and statistics to support his viewpoint? Explain.

CRITICAL THINKING

1. Jiménez notes that throughout American history, citizens have feared that the next wave of immigrants would change America for the worse. What really happened? Can history predict what we can expect in the future?
2. Some Americans fear that the close connections between today's immigrant populations and their countries of origin threaten their loyalty to the United States and their commitment to American culture and society. What response does Jiménez provide to this concern? Do you agree with his argument? Why or why not?

WRITING ABOUT THE ISSUES

1. Jiménez observes that past waves of immigrants—from Germany, Ireland, and Italy, for example—subtly left their mark on American identity. Icons such as the Christmas tree, Italian food, and St. Patrick's Day celebrations have become part of the "American fabric." Using the data in the table on the next page (based on data on *legal* immigration to the United States from the 2000 U.S. Census and *2004 Yearbook of Immigration Statistics*) and what you have read about immigration and national identity in the essays in this chapter, write an essay projecting the impact current groups of immigrants will make on American identity. What will be considered "American" 100 years from now?

Top 10 Foreign Countries—Foreign Born Population Among U.S. Immigrants

Country	Number per year	2004	2010 (projected)
Mexico	175,900	8,544,600	9,600,000
India	59,300	1,244,200	1,600,000
Philippines	47,800	1,413,200	1,700,000
El Salvador	33,500	899,000	1,100,000
Dominican Republic	24,900	791,600	941,000
Canada	24,200	774,800	920,000
Korea	17,900	772,600	880,000
Cuba	14,800	1,011,200	1,100,000

2. Visit PBS's website for the program *Independent Lens: The New Americans* at http://www.pbs.org/independentlens/newamericans/index.html. Read some of the immigrant stories and pick one to write about. Explain why you feel that story is particularly compelling. Connect the story to points Jiménez raises in his article.

TOPICAL CONNECTIONS

GROUP PROJECTS

1. Interview a number of people who either immigrated to the United States or are in the country as legal residents (on student visas, etc.). Ask them to discuss their experiences as foreigners coming to live in the United States. Were they welcomed? Did they find a community to support them?

2. Are there particular traditions, practices, and behaviors that we expect new immigrants to adopt when they arrive in the United States? If so, what are they? Write an essay describing the things you think new immigrants should be willing to do in order to live in the United States.

3. Listen to Richard Gonzales's radio commentary, "Mexican Immigrants Weigh Issues of Assimilation," which aired on NPR October 8, 2004 (you can access this broadcast at the NPR website). Gonzales explains that Mexican immigrants, who make up 37 percent of all recent immigrants, differ substantially from other immigrants in many categories. After listening to the report, discuss your reactions as a group. Like several other

authors in this section, Gonzales focuses on issues connected to assimilation. What questions would you have liked to ask if you were allowed to call in to his program? As a group, prepare three questions and share them with the class.

WEB PROJECT

1. Explore how ethnic and racial characteristics divide and unite us as a nation. According to the report *Changing America* by the President's Initiative on Race, the gaps among races and ethnic groups in the areas of education, jobs, economic status, health, housing, and criminal justice are substantial. Access this report online. Choose one subject area from its table of contents, and read through that chapter and charts. Then, summarize the information you have learned about the differences among the different racial and ethnic groups and discuss how you think these disparities affect our chances of creating a society in which all Americans can participate equally.

FOR FURTHER INQUIRY

1. Several authors in this chapter observe that every immigrant population was met with prejudice and suspicion. Research this phenomenon in greater depth with a particular immigrant group. For example, you could research impressions of the Irish arriving on the East Coast during the early nineteenth century, or Japanese and Chinese groups arriving on the West Coast in the late nineteenth century. What challenges did these groups face? How were they viewed by then-current citizens? How can their experience inform the current debate over immigration reform?
2. Research the Immigration and Nationality Act of 1952. Why was this act implemented, and whom did it affect? How did the act change after 2001 and why? Discuss the act and whether it is in need of reform again. Offer suggestions for change, or support its tenets as currently outlined.

7 Why Do We Work?

While the answer to the question of why we work may seem obvious on the surface—to support ourselves and our loved ones—there are many reasons why we work. Some reasons, such as ambition, a drive to succeed and excel, and the desire to make the world a better place are considered noble reasons to work. They can help determine the career paths we take and how we will ultimately measure our success. But there are some reasons we might be less willing to admit, such as the ability to buy more expensive luxuries, drive better cars, support a particular lifestyle, or even to get away from our chaotic home lives.

Most college students enter their two- or four-year training programs in order to develop skills that will allow them to compete more successfully in the working world. But what are our expectations of the working world? What do we hope to get out of a job besides a regular paycheck? What satisfaction do you expect from a job? What defines a career? What is your idea of "making it"—of achieving success? An early retirement? Fame? Respect? This chapter explores some of the issues connected with why we work.

CRITICAL THINKING

1. What is happening in this cartoon? Can you tell who the people are in the cartoon? What are they discussing? Explain.
2. Do you think this cartoon presents a stereotype of the American employment landscape? What issue does it intend to hold up for public scrutiny? Explain.
3. Have you ever had a "quitting fantasy"? Was it like what the cartoonist describes here, or something else? Why do we harbor such fantasies? Do we dislike work or the powerlessness that accompanies so many jobs? Explain.

Andy Singer – Politicalcartoons.com – Posted 08/23/2007

Why We Work
Andrew Curry

Andrew Curry is a general editor of *Smithsonian* magazine. His articles have appeared in many publications, including *The Washington Post*, *The Christian Science Monitor*, *The Miami Herald*, and *The Guardian*. This article appeared in the February 24, 2003, issue of *U.S. News and World Report* when Curry was an associate editor for that publication.

CONNECTING TO THE TOPIC

Although most of us work because we have to, we also assume that this work will ultimately improve our lives. But is the pursuit of the American dream becoming just that—a dream? It seems as if Americans are working harder than ever before, with less leisure time. Today, American society is dominated by work. But there was a time when people could have followed a different path, when we could have opted as a nation to actually work *less*. When did the American workforce make the choice to have more stuff but less time? And was it the right choice?

WORDS IN CONTEXT

eccentric (3)   behaving differently from the norm, as an oddball (adj.)
starkly (5)   bluntly (adv.)
precarious (6)   lacking in stability (adj.)
affluent (7)   wealthy (adj.)
smelter (10)   an iron works (n.)
ample (10)   in large number or quantity (adj.)
apex (13)   highest point (n.)
propaganda (14)   methodical and persistent distribution of a message
   advocating a particular cause or idea (n.)
persistence (16)   refusal to give up (n.)
autonomy (19)   ability to make one's own decisions; independence (n.)

1   **S**ome do it for love. Others do it for money. But most of us do it because we have no other choice.

2   In 1930, W.K. Kellogg made what he thought was a sensible decision, grounded in the best economic, social, and management theories of the time. Workers at his cereal plant in Battle Creek, Michigan, were told to go home two hours early. Every day. For good.

3   The Depression-era move was hailed in *Factory and Industrial Management* magazine as the "biggest piece of industrial news since [Henry] Ford announced his five-dollar-a-day policy." President Herbert Hoover summoned the **eccentric** cereal magnate to the White House and said the plan was "very worthwhile." The belief: Industry and machines would lead to a workers' paradise where all would have less work, more free time, and yet still produce enough to meet their needs.

4   So what happened? Today, work dominates Americans' lives as never before, as workers pile on hours at a rate not seen since the Industrial Revolution. Technology has offered increasing productivity and a higher standard of living while bank tellers and typists are replaced by machines. The mismatch between available work and those available to do it continues, as jobs go begging while people beg for jobs. Though Kellogg's six-hour day lasted until 1985, Battle Creek's grand industrial experiment has been nearly forgotten. Instead of working less, our hours have stayed steady or risen—and today many more women work so that families can afford the trappings of suburbia. In effect, workers chose the path of consumption over leisure.

5   But as today's job market shows so **starkly**, that road is full of potholes. With unemployment at a nine-year high and many workers worried about losing their jobs—or forced to accept cutbacks in pay and benefits—work is hardly the paradise economists once envisioned.

6   Instead, the job market is as **precarious** today as it was in the early 1980s, when business began a wave of restructurings and layoffs to maintain its competitiveness. Many workers are left feeling insecure, unfulfilled, and under-appreciated. It's no wonder surveys of today's workers show a steady decline in job satisfaction. "People are very emotional about work, and they're very negative about it," says David Rhodes, a principal at human resource consultants Towers Perrin. "The biggest issue is clearly workload. People are feeling crushed."

7   The backlash comes after years of people boasting about how hard they work and tying their identities to how indispensable they are. Ringing cell phones, whirring faxes, and ever-present E-mail have blurred the lines between work and home. The job penetrates every aspect of life. Americans don't exercise, they work out. We manage our time and work on our relationships. "In reaching the **affluent** society, we're working longer and harder than anyone could have imagined," says Rutgers University historian John Gillis. "The work ethic and identifying ourselves with work and through work is not only alive and well but more present now than at any time in history."

8   It's all beginning to take a toll. Fully one third of American workers—who work longer hours than their counterparts in any industrialized country—felt overwhelmed by the amount of work they had to do, according to a 2001 Families and Work Institute survey. "Both men and

women wish they were working about 11 hours [a week] less," says Ellen Galinsky, the institute's president. "A lot of people believe if they do work less they'll be seen as less committed, and in a shaky economy no one wants that."

9   The modern environment would seem alien to pre-industrial laborers. For centuries, the household—from farms to "cottage" craftsmen—was the unit of production. The whole family was part of the enterprise, be it farming, blacksmithing, or baking. "In pre-industrial society, work and family were practically the same thing," says Gillis.

10   The Industrial Revolution changed all that. Mills and massive iron **smelters** required **ample** labor and constant attendance. "The factory took men, women and children out of the workshops and homes and put them under one roof and timed their movements to machines," writes Sebastian de Grazia in *Of Time, Work and Leisure.* For the first time, work and family were split. Instead of selling what they produced, workers sold their time. With more people leaving farms to move to cities and factories, labor became a commodity, placed on the market like any other.

11   Innovation gave rise to an industrial process based on machinery and mass production. This new age called for a new worker. "The only safeguard of order and discipline in the modern world is a standardized worker with interchangeable parts," mused one turn-of-the-century writer.

12   Business couldn't have that, so instead it came up with the science of management. The theories of Frederick Taylor, a Philadelphia factory foreman with deep Puritan roots, led to work being broken down into component parts, with each step timed to coldly quantify jobs that skilled craftsmen had worked a lifetime to learn. Workers resented Taylor and his stopwatch, complaining that his focus on process stripped their jobs of creativity and pride, making them irritable. Long before anyone knew what "stress" was, Taylor brought it to the workplace—and without sympathy. "I have you for your strength and mechanical ability, and we have other men paid for thinking," he told workers.

13   The division of work into components that could be measured and easily taught reached its **apex** in Ford's River Rouge plant in Dearborn, Michigan, where the assembly line came of age. "It was this combination of a simplification of tasks . . . with moving assembly that created a manufacturing revolution while at the same time laying waste human potential on a massive scale," author Richard Donkin writes in *Blood, Sweat and Tears.*

14   To maximize the production lines, businesses needed long hours from their workers. But it was no easy sell. "Convincing people to work 9 to 5 took a tremendous amount of **propaganda** and discipline," says the University of Richmond's Joanne Ciulla, author of *The Working Life: The Promise and Betrayal of Modern Work.* Entrepreneurs, religious leaders, and writers like Horatio Alger created whole bodies of literature to glorify the work ethic.

15   The first labor unions were organized in response to the threat of technology, as skilled workers sought to protect their jobs from mechanization. Later, semi- and unskilled workers began to organize as well, agitating successfully for reduced hours, higher wages, and better work conditions. Unions enjoyed great influence in the early 20th century, and at their height in the 1950s, 35 percent of U.S. workers belonged to one.

16   Union **persistence** and the mechanization of factories gradually made shorter hours more realistic. Between 1830 and 1930, work hours were cut nearly in half, with economist John Maynard Keynes famously predicting in 1930 that by 2030 a 15-hour workweek would be standard. The Great Depression pressed the issue, with job sharing proposed as a serious solution to widespread unemployment. Despite business and religious opposition over worries of an idle populace, the Senate passed a bill that would have mandated a 30-hour week in 1933; it was narrowly defeated in the House.

17   Franklin Delano Roosevelt struck back with a new gospel that lives to this very day: consumption. "The aim . . . is to restore our rich domestic market by raising its vast consuming capacity," he said. "Our first purpose is to create employment as fast as we can." And so began the modern work world. "Instead of accepting work's continuing decline and imminent fall from its dominant social position, businessmen, economists, advertisers, and politicians preached that there would never be 'enough,'" says University of Iowa Professor Benjamin Hunnicutt, author of *Work Without End: Abandoning Shorter Hours for the Right to Work.* "The entrepreneur and industry could invent new things for advertising to sell and for people to want and work for indefinitely."

18   The New Deal dumped government money into job creation, in turn encouraging consumption. World War II fueled the fire, and American workers soon found themselves in a "golden age"—40-hour workweeks, plenty of jobs, and plenty to buy. Leisure was the road not taken, a path quickly forgotten in the postwar boom of the 1950s and 1960s.

19   Decades of abundance, however, did not bring satisfaction. "A significant number of Americans are dissatisfied with the quality of their working lives," said the 1973 report "Work in America" from the Department of Health, Education and Welfare. "Dull, repetitive, seemingly meaningless tasks, offering little challenge or **autonomy**, are causing discontent among workers at all occupational levels." Underlying the dissatisfaction was a very gradual change in what the "Protestant work ethic" meant. Always a source of pride, the idea that hard work was a calling from God dated to the Reformation and the teachings of Martin Luther. While work had once been a means to serve God, two centuries of choices and industrialization had turned work into an end in itself, stripped of the spiritual meaning that sustained the Puritans who came ready to tame the wilderness.

20   By the end of the '70s, companies were reaching out to spiritually drained workers by offering more engagement while withdrawing the promise of a job for life, as the American economy faced a stiff challenge from cheaper workers abroad. Employees were given more control over their work and schedules, and "human relations" consultants and motivational speakers did a booming business. By the 1990s, technology made working from home possible for a growing number of people. Seen as a boon at first, telecommuting and the rapidly proliferating "electronic leash" of cellphones made work inescapable, as employees found themselves on call 24/7. Today, almost half of American workers use computers, cellphones, E-mail, and faxes for work during what is supposed to be non-work time, according to the Families and Work Institute. Home is no longer a refuge but a cozier extension of the office.

21   The shift coincided with a shortage of highly skilled and educated workers, some of whom were induced with such benefits as stock options in exchange for their putting the company first all the time. But some see a different explanation for the rise in the amount of time devoted to work. "Hours have crept up partly as a consequence of the declining power of the trade-union movement," says Cornell University labor historian Clete Daniel. "Many employers find it more economical to require mandatory overtime than hire new workers and pay their benefits." Indeed, the trend has coincided with the steady decline in the percentage of workers represented by unions, as the labor movement failed to keep pace with the increasing rise of white-collar jobs in the economy. Today fewer than 15 percent of American workers belong to unions.

22   In a study of Silicon Valley culture over the past decade, San Jose State University anthropologist Jan English-Lueck found that skills learned on the job were often brought home. Researchers talked to families with mission statements, mothers used conflict-resolution buzzwords with their squabbling kids, and engineers used flowcharts to organize Thanksgiving dinner. Said one participant: "I don't live life; I manage it."

23   In some ways, we have come full circle. "Now we're seeing the return of work to the home in terms of telecommuting," says Gillis. "We may be seeing the return of households where work is the central element again."

24   But there's still the question of fulfillment. In a recent study, human resources consultants Towers Perrin tried to measure workers' emotions about their jobs. More than half of the emotion was negative, with the biggest single factor being workload but also a sense that work doesn't satisfy their deeper needs. "We expect more and more out of our jobs," says Hunnicutt. "We expect to find wonderful people and experiences all around us. What we find is Dilbert." ◆

CONSIDERING THE ISSUS

1. In this essay, Curry traces the historical origins of the American workforce and observes that there was a time before World War II when Americans made a choice to have more material things instead of having more leisure time. Which would you rather have? More money or more time? Explain.

2. Curry observes that e-mail, voice mail, cell phones, faxes, and computers have created "electronic leashes" that blur the boundaries between home and work. How much do you rely on this equipment? Would your quality of life be less if you did not have access to a cell phone? To e-mail? Do such devices keep us "on" 24/7? Why or why not?

CRAFT AND CONTENT

1. Curry quotes several authors and professors who have researched transformations in the American workforce and work ethic. How do these authors, and the quotes he cites, support his overall point that American workers have "chosen a path of consumption over leisure"? Explain.

2. In paragraph 14, professor Joanne Ciulla observes that it "took a tremendous amount of propaganda" to convince people to work 9 to 5. What is propaganda? What do we associate with the word *propaganda*? What does it imply? Does it seem to fit this context? Why or why not?

CRITICAL THINKING

1. Who was Frederick Taylor? How do his theories, and the science of management, relate to the state of the modern worker?

2. Participants in a study on Silicon Valley culture noted how they brought work-culture home in the form of "family mission statements," conflict resolution "buzzwords," and even flowcharts to organize Thanksgiving gatherings. Is work intruding on family life?

WRITING ABOUT THE ISSUES

1. What is your definition of "the American Dream"? How important is money in your version of the dream? What priorities do you give to leisure time? Write an essay in which you compare the points Curry makes in his essay on the nature of the modern American workforce and your own lifestyle choices, now and in the future.

2. At the end of his article, Curry quotes consultants Towers Perrin, who found Americans in general to be deeply dissatisfied with work. Today's Americans expect more and get less out of their jobs. Write an essay about your expectations of job satisfaction now and in the future. Have you ever held a job that you truly loved? Do you expect to find one that provides you with a sense of achievement and satisfaction? How has your experience in the workforce thus far measured up to your expectations? Explain.

VISUAL CONNECTIONS

Mean Occupational Groups and Mean Annual Wages

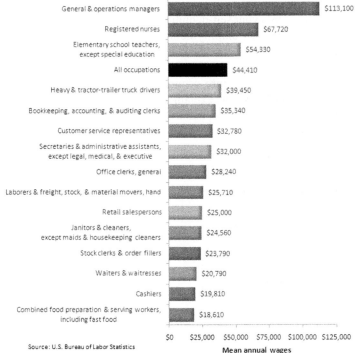

Mean annual wages, selected occupations, May 2010

Occupation	Mean annual wage
General & operations managers	$113,100
Registered nurses	$67,720
Elementary school teachers, except special education	$54,330
All occupations	$44,410
Heavy & tractor-trailer truck drivers	$39,450
Bookkeeping, accounting, & auditing clerks	$35,340
Customer service representatives	$32,780
Secretaries & administrative assistants, except legal, medical, & executive	$32,000
Office clerks, general	$28,240
Laborers & freight, stock, & material movers, hand	$25,710
Retail salespersons	$25,000
Janitors & cleaners, except maids & housekeeping cleaners	$24,560
Stock clerks & order fillers	$23,790
Waiters & waitresses	$20,790
Cashiers	$19,810
Combined food preparation & serving workers, including fast food	$18,610

Source: U.S. Bureau of Labor Statistics

Mean annual wages

General and operations managers earned, on average, $113,100 per year in May 2010; registered nurses had average annual earnings of $67,720; and elementary school teachers, except special education, earned $54,330. In contrast, waiters and waitresses, cashiers, and combined food preparation and serving workers, including fast food, all had average annual earnings of less than $21,000. These three occupations not only had the lowest wages among the 15 largest occupations, they were also among the lowest-paying occupations overall.

Note: http://www.bls.gov/opub/ted/2011/ted_20110523.htm. Data extracted on May 15, 2011.

CONSIDERING THE ISSUES

1. Do you have a full- or part-time job? If so, how much time do you spend working? Do you work more than you would like to? Less?
2. Think of the aspects that define you as a person. Describe how these characteristics help create your personal identity. Does work or career factor into your self-definition? Why or why not?
3. This chart outlines employment in the United States based on occupational groups. Visit the U.S. Department of Labor's website at http://www.bls.gov/ and read more about what people earn. Research your own future occupation. Based on what you read online and already know, explain why you think you will go into a particular industry or occupation, and what you expect in the future for this career.

America's Bizarre Secret to Happiness: More Work
Daily Mail

This April 19, 2011 news article was published in the *Daily Mail*, a British newspaper. Here, writers for the *Daily Mail* provide a synopsis of a psychology article appearing in the April issue of the *Journal of Happiness Studies*.

CONNECTING TO THE TOPIC

It would seem that Americans really do love to work and equate work with their level of happiness. Europeans, however, seem to be much happier if they are not working. A study on happiness revealed that Americans often associated long work hours with a greater level of happiness overall, while Europeans prefer to keep working hours to the absolute minimum. Why the difference? Is it simple work ethic? The pursuit of the American dream? Or something bigger than that?

WORDS IN CONTEXT

correlation (6)   relationship of two or more things (n.)
causation (6)   relationship of cause and effect (n.)

1   **H**appiness for U.S. workers stays at 43 percent, regardless of working hours. Americans really do live to work, it seems. A new study on happiness has shown that those who work longer hours in the U.S. are actually happier. In Europe, on the other hand, the more hours you work, the more unhappy you are.

2   Researchers think the data shows a fundamental difference between the goals held by Europeans and Americans. The study's authors at the University of Texas in Dallas said that working hours do not have a statistically significant impact on Americans' happiness, but that there is a distinct boost in bliss as the amount of working hours increases. "Those who work longer hours in Europe are less happy than those who work shorter hours, but in the U.S. it's the other way around," study author Adam Okulicz-Kozaryn told LiveScience.com.

3   The study could not conclude that work actually causes happiness. Researchers speculated that instead, the results have to do with expectations and how a person measures success.

4   European and American respondents were asked to identify if they were "very happy," "pretty happy" or "not too happy." The survey found that the likelihood of Europeans describing themselves as "very happy" dropped from around 28 percent to 23 percent as work hours climbed from under 17 a week to more than 60.

5   It was not clear what percentage of Europeans described themselves as merely "happy" when compared to working hours. For Americans, however, overall happiness held steady at about 43 percent, regardless of working hours.

6   The results stood up even after researchers had accounted for other factors such as age, marital status and household income. The study warned that without more research, it was difficult to argue if the results represented a **correlation** or **causation**. Other experts said the discrepancy between Americans and Europeans could be accounted for by examining the goals held by each group.

7   University of Southern California economics professor Richard Easterlin, who was not part of the study, told LiveScience.com: "Europeans are more inclined to enjoy life and enjoy leisure. There's a difference in the structure of aspirations." Mr Okulicz-Kozaryn and Professor Easterlin agreed that perceptions could also play a big part, as those who think their hard work has a greater impact on their success or upward mobility may be happier to work longer.

8   Professor Easterlin added: "In some countries in Europe, the income mobility may be higher, for instance in Germany. It's not really that hard work brings more success in the U.S. than in Europe—it's what people believe in."

9   The difference could be down to the American dream: That Americans simply believe that hard work has a greater impact on their success and upward mobility, and when they achieve it, buy in to that dream even more.

10   Previous studies have shown that wealth can result in happiness—especially if a person's earnings are greater than their peers. But an overall satisfaction with life was shown to depend more on social and physical factors, such as whether a person smoked or spent the day alone. ◆

CONSIDERING THE ISSUES

1. What motivates you to work? Do you do it for the love of the job? For the money? Because you must? A little of each? Explain.
2. What makes you happy? What do you need in order to be happy? Money? Time? A feeling of contribution or satisfaction? Explain.

CRAFT AND CONTENT

1. This article was prepared by a reporter working for a British newspaper. Can you detect any bias in the reporting? Explain.
2. What is the author's opinion of the state of the American worker? Identify specific statements in this essay that reveal his viewpoint.

CRITICAL THINKING

1. The author of this article conjectures that one reason Americans are happier working longer hours is their belief in the pursuit of the "American dream." What is the American dream? Why would working longer hours help us achieve it? Explain.
2. What factors could have influenced the results of this study? If possible, try to locate the original study.

WRITING ABOUT THE ISSUES

1. Write a personal narrative in which you describe your ideal job situation. How long would you work? Why would this job make you happy? Explain.
2. This article notes that Americans and Europeans have different views on the connection between work and happiness. Interview some international students—from Europe and other areas of the world—and ask them to consider the connection between happiness (and unhappiness) and hours worked. Summarize and share your findings as part of a class discussion on work and happiness.

Measuring Success

Renée Loth

Renée Loth has been editor of *The Boston Globe*'s editorial page since 2000. She has served on the *Globe*'s staff for over 15 years. She previously wrote for *New England Monthly* magazine and worked as a political reporter for the *Boston Phoenix*. Loth is a frequent political commentator on local and national radio and TV programs and has been an undergraduate study group leader at Harvard's Kennedy School of Government. This essay was first published in *The Boston Globe* on March 14, 1999. Although her essay is over 10 years old, the observations she makes are as true today as they were then.

CONNECTING TO THE TOPIC

The Declaration of Independence describes our inalienable right to "life, liberty, and the pursuit of happiness." But what exactly is "the pursuit of happiness"? As the document has been interpreted, it often means the right to financial independence and success. Many college students enter the workforce with just such a sense of idealism. Time and experience often test this optimism, forcing many to redefine "the pursuit of happiness" along more realistic and mature lines. What is success? Does our definition change with time? What could college students learn about success from their more experienced friends and family?

WORDS IN CONTEXT

callow (1)   young; lacking in experience and maturity (adj.)
approbation (2)   expressions of approval or appreciation (n.)
mutable (3)   changeable (adj.)
superfluous (5)   more than is necessary or than what is required (adj.)
optimist (8)   one who sees the positive side of things, who expects a favorable outcome (n.)
fickle (9)   highly changeable or unstable (adj.)
chagrined (11)   embarrassed (adj.)

1   **B**ack when I was a **callow** college student, I devised a neat grid system for what I hoped would be my life's achievements. I could count my life a good one, I thought, if I could attain both success and happiness. So I set about analyzing the component parts of each: Happiness I subdivided into sections labeled health and love; success, I determined, was composed of wealth and fame.

2   Once I actually entered the world of work, however, I learned that success is not so easy to define. For one thing, when I made my simple calculation, I never took into account the joy of creation; the **approbation** of one's peers; the energy of collaboration; or the sheer satisfaction of a job well done. These are real qualities of success that live outside of wealth or fame.

3   Also, I found that definitions of success are **mutable**, shifting along with our changing values. If we stick with our chosen fields long enough, we sometimes have an opportunity to meet our heroes, people we thought wildly successful when we were young. A musician friend told me that he spent most of his youth wanting to play like the greats, until he started getting to know some of them. To his surprise, many turned out to be embittered, dulled by drink or boredom, unable to hold together a marriage, or wantonly jealous of others. That's when he realized he wanted to play like himself.

4   Success is defined differently by different people. For some, it is symbolized by the number of buttons on the office phone. For others, it is having only one button—and a secretary to field the calls. Some think the more nights and weekends they spend at the office, the more successful they must be. For others, success is directly proportional to time off.

5   And what about those qualities I did include in my handy grid system? Wealth—beyond what is needed to provide for oneself and one's family, with a little left over for airfare to someplace subtropical in January— turned out to be **superfluous**. And the little experience I had with fame turned out to be downright scary.

6   Several years ago, I had occasion to appear on a dull but respected national evening television news show. My performance lasted exactly six minutes, and my name flashed only twice. But when I got home from the live broadcast, my answering machine had maxed-out on messages.

7   I heard from a woman I had last seen in Brownie Scouts. I heard from former boyfriends, conspiracy theorists, and celebrity agents. I even got an obscene phone call—what kind of pervert watches PBS?—from someone who might have been an old friend pulling my leg. At least, I hope so.

8   For weeks afterward, I received tons of what an **optimist** might call fan mail. One fellow insisted that if I froze a particular frame of a political campaign ad I had been discussing, I could see the face of Bill Clinton in the American flag. Somebody sent me a chapter of a novel in progress with a main character disturbingly like me. Several people sent me chain letters.

9   I was relieved when the **fickle** finger of fame moved on to someone else.

10   When I was young and romanticizing about success, I liked a particular Joni Mitchell lyric: "My struggle for higher achievement and my search for love don't seem to cease." Ah, but the trouble with struggling and searching is that it keeps us in a permanent state of wanting—always reaching for more. The drive to succeed keeps us focused on the future, to the detriment of life in the moment. And the moment is all we ever really have.

11   When I look back at my simplistic little value system, I am a bit **chagrined** at how absolute I thought life was. But I am also happy to report that the achievements that have come my way are the ones that count. After 20 years of supercharged ambition, I have stumbled upon this bit of wisdom. Who needs wealth and fame? Two out of four ain't bad. ◆

CONSIDERING THE ISSUES

1. Loth begins her essay by explaining how, as a college student, she developed a grid system that she felt would define her life's achievements. Following Loth's example, create your own list or grid in which you define what you think your life's achievements might be. How do you define *happiness*? How do you define *success*?

2. What is your definition of wealth? To what extent is it connected to your definition of success? How important is it to your definition of success? Explain.

CRAFT AND CONTENT

1. In paragraph 1, Loth recalls the days when she was "a callow college student." How does this word choice help establish both the tone and the theme of this essay? Explain.
2. In paragraph 10, Loth says in reference to the Joni Mitchell lyric she quotes, "The trouble with struggling and searching is that it keeps us in a permanent state of wanting." What does she mean by this statement? How does it relate to the point of this essay overall?

CRITICAL THINKING

1. How did Loth redefine her early notion of success? Why do you think this happened?
2. Loth also changed her definition of fame and abandoned it as a goal of success. Why did she do this? Why do you think she wanted fame? Do you? Why or why not? Explain.

WRITING ABOUT THE ISSUES

1. Write your own essay defining happiness and/or success. Be sure to employ the same strategies Loth does: think of your own experience, the things that make you feel happy and successful, and ask friends and family for their insights.
2. Since you too might be described as "a callow college student" at this point in your life, create a series of questions that you will ask older and more experienced friends, family, and acquaintances about happiness and success. Ask all sorts of people your questions, regardless of your own opinions of their happiness or success. Review your notes and write an essay in which you argue what success and happiness really mean based upon your interviews.

Blog Matters

A blog ("web log") is an online diary or commentary site that features regular entries that describe events, impressions, and viewpoints. Blogs may contain text, images, video, and often link to other websites, blogs, and online media. Most blogs allow readers to comment on the content of the post and respond to each other. As of September 2011, there were over 160 million public blogs in existence. While many blogs are maintained by individuals, some are run by journals, newspapers, and other media outlets. Remember that most blogs are not monitored for factual accuracy, and often express the opinion and views of the "blogger" writing the content.

The blog below was written by Jason Lee Miller, a *WebProNews* editor and writer covering business and technology, on April 6, 2007. He explains what the data collected by Yahoo!'s HotJobs might mean. Are Americans really working too much?

Yahoo Says Americans Work Too Much

Jason Lee Miller

April 6, 2007

1 Usually, when I go home for the day, I unplug. Unplugging means not even jacked in wirelessly: cell phone is off; computer (if I can help it) is off; laptop is off. The same goes for the weekend; if you want to get a hold of me, it can wait until Monday. Home is home, work is work, and I'm quite strict about their separation.

2 One day, I imagine I'll have to violate my own rules. I've already caved in regard to using a cell phone at all. I have an answering machine. Sometimes I'm not home. Deal with it, I'll call you back. Unfortunately, that plan didn't completely stick. My cell number is the only number some people have. Ho hum.

3 Yahoo HotJobs just released new data showing that around a quarter of survey respondents felt that wireless devices kept them "on a permanent corporate leash" and that they were easily distracted by work-related email and calls during personal time.

4 That's not as many as I thought would feel that way, especially since two-thirds of American respondents said they jack into work even while on vacation. Now, vacation is where I really draw the line. Work doesn't exist on vacation. Period.

5 It turns out most people seem to like the flexibility—but Yahoo worries we might be overdoing it.

6 "Wireless devices have become a professional reality," said vice president of marketing for Yahoo! HotJobs Susan Vobejda, "so it's important for people to set limits on when and how to disengage in order to maintain work-life balance."

7 "With 67 percent of respondents admitting to having used a wireless device to connect with work while on vacation, signs indicate that the American workforce may be facing burnout."

8 Vobejda says all that connectivity has changed the physical parameters of the workplace, and has extended the workday. And she be right about burnout.

9 An American in the 21st Century has to work 25 years to get the same number of paid vacation days that are mandatory minimums in Europe. In all, American workers put in almost 400 more hours per year than their European counterparts. That's TEN weeks. Well, eight weeks, if we're talking Stateside hours.

10   Wireless connectivity is only increasing the work-a-holism. Twenty-seven percent of respondents admitted being so attached to their wireless device that the only time they're not texting, talking, emailing, or monitoring work is when they're sleeping.

11   Bet the missus doesn't like that much, either. A third said they found it more difficult to get their point across through electronic means than conversation. So next time you tell her you love her and want her, it may be a good idea to use your voice box instead of your inbox.

12   Despite the reservations of the admitted few, most respondents to Yahoo! HotJobs' survey appreciated the flexibility wireless connectivity offered them. Almost half reported they volunteered for virtual work access. Eighty-one percent stay connected with work via mobile phone; 65 percent via laptop; and 19 percent use smartphones.

13   Interestingly, they say the always-on lifestyle they've adopted "enhances" the work-life balance—something I'll take their words for and continue to turn off when I get home:

14   The rest of Yahoo! HotJobs findings:

> The majority (61 percent) agree that wireless devices make them feel like they have more freedom;
>
> Sixty-five percent say wireless devices allow them to work remotely and have a more flexible schedule;
>
> Almost half (48 percent) report that wireless devices allow them to spend more time with family and friends; and
>
> An overwhelming 70 percent agree that they are more productive thanks to a wireless device.

RESPOND TO THE BLOG

What do you think? Is your work your life? Do we work because we have to, or because we want to? Are we indeed working too hard, as Yahoo suggests, or are we doing what we want? Explain.

The Most-Praised Generation
Goes to Work
Jeffrey Zaslow

Jeffrey Zaslow is a senior writer and columnist for *The Wall Street Journal* in which his column, "Moving On," appears in the Personal Journal section. In 2000, he received the Will Rogers Humanitarian Award, given to a newspaper columnist who exemplifies the ideals and public service work of the noted humorist and columnist. He was honored for using his column to run programs that benefited 47,000 disadvantaged Chicago children, and for raising millions of dollars for Chicago charities. Zaslow's writing has appeared in many other newspapers and journals, including *TIME,* and *USA Today,* and he has appeared on *The Tonight Show, The Oprah Winfrey Show, Larry King Live,* and *The Today Show.* This editorial appeared in the April 20, 2007, edition of *The Wall Street Journal.*

CONNECTING TO THE TOPIC

Über-stroked kids are reaching adulthood—and now their bosses (and spouses) have to deal with them. As Jeffrey Zaslow explains, the newest generation to enter the workforce is used to praise and encouragement. Older managers, ones who believed in sucking it up and doing your time in order to climb the corporate ladder, are befuddled by this group of twentysomethings who demand more attention and approval. Is it time for this coddled group to realize the world isn't all "Good job!" written on an essay, or should employers realize that in order to attract new talent, they are going to have to bring out the smiley stickers?

WORDS IN CONTEXT

calibrating (22)   measuring (v.)
moratorium (27)   ban on; end to proceedings (n.)

1   ou, You, You—you really are special, you are! You've got everything going for you. You're attractive, witty, brilliant. "Gifted" is the word that comes to mind.

2   Childhood in recent decades has been defined by such stroking— by parents who see their job as building self-esteem, by soccer coaches who give every player a trophy, by schools that used to name one "student of the month" and these days name 40. Now, as this greatest generation grows up, the culture of praise is reaching deeply into the adult world. Bosses, professors and mates are feeling the need to lavish praise on young adults, particularly twentysomethings, or else see them wither under an unfamiliar compliment deficit.

3   Employers are dishing out kudos to workers for little more than showing up. Corporations including Lands' End and Bank of America are hiring consultants to teach managers how to compliment employees using email, prize packages and public displays of appreciation. The 1,000-employee Scooter Store Inc., a power-wheelchair and scooter firm in New Braunfels,

Texas, has a staff "celebrations assistant" whose job it is to throw confetti—25 pounds a week—at employees. She also passes out 100 to 500 celebratory helium balloons a week. The Container Store Inc. estimates that one of its 4,000 employees receives praise every 20 seconds, through such efforts as its "Celebration Voice Mailboxes."

4   Certainly, there are benefits to building confidence and showing attention. But some researchers suggest that inappropriate kudos are turning too many adults into narcissistic praise-junkies. The upshot: A lot of today's young adults feel insecure if they're not regularly complimented.

5   America's praise fixation has economic, labor and social ramifications. Adults who were overpraised as children are apt to be narcissistic at work and in personal relationships, says Jean Twenge, a psychology professor at San Diego State University. Narcissists aren't good at basking in other people's glory, which makes for problematic marriages and work relationships, she says.

6   Her research suggests that young adults today are more self-centered than previous generations. For a multiuniversity study released this year, 16,475 college students took the standardized narcissistic personality inventory, responding to such statements as "I think I am a special person." Students' scores have risen steadily since the test was first offered in 1982. The average college student in 2006 was 30% more narcissistic than the average student in 1982.

Praise Inflation

7   Employers say the praise culture can help them with job retention, and marriage counselors say couples often benefit by keeping praise a constant part of their interactions. But in the process, people's positive traits can be exaggerated until the words feel meaningless. "There's a runaway inflation of everyday speech," warns Linda Sapadin, a psychologist in Valley Stream, N.Y. These days, she says, it's an insult unless you describe a pretty girl as "drop-dead gorgeous" or a smart person as "a genius." "And no one wants to be told they live in a nice house," says Dr. Sapadin. "'Nice' was once sufficient. That was a good word. Now it's a put-down." The Gottman Institute, a relationship-research and training firm in Seattle, tells clients that a key to marital happiness is if couples make at least five times as many positive statements to and about each other as negative ones. Meanwhile, products are being marketed to help families make praise a part of their daily routines. For $32.95, families can buy the "You Are Special Today Red Plate," and then select one worthy person each meal to eat off the dish.

8   But many young married people today, who grew up being told regularly that they were special, can end up distrusting compliments from their spouses. Judy Neary, a relationship therapist in Alexandria, Va., says it's

common for her clients to say things like: "I tell her she's beautiful all the time, and she doesn't believe it." Ms. Neary suspects: "There's a lot of insecurity, with people wondering, 'Is it really true?'"

9   "Young married people who've been very praised in their childhoods, particularly, need praise to both their child side and their adult side," adds Dolores Walker, a psychotherapist and attorney specializing in divorce mediation in New York.

10   Employers are finding ways to adjust. Sure, there are still plenty of surly managers who offer little or no positive feedback, but many with-holders are now joining America's praise parade to hold on to young workers. They're being taught by employee-retention consultants such as Mark Holmes, who encourages employers to give away baseball bats with engravings ("Thanks for a home-run job") or to write notes to employees' kids ("Thanks for letting dad work here. He's terrific!")

11   Bob Nelson, billed as "the Guru of Thank You," counsels 80 to 100 companies a year on praise issues. He has done presentations for managers of companies such as Walt Disney Co. and Hallmark Cards Inc., explaining how different generations have different expectations. As he sees it, those over age 60 tend to like formal awards, presented publicly. But they're more laid back about needing praise, and more apt to say: "Yes, I get recognition every week. It's called a paycheck." Baby boomers, Mr. Nelson finds, often prefer being praised with more self-indulgent treats such as free massages for women and high-tech gadgets for men.

12   Workers under 40, he says, require far more stroking. They often like "trendy, name-brand merchandise" as rewards, but they also want near-constant feedback. "It's not enough to give praise only when they're exceptional, because for years they've been getting praise just for showing up," he says.

13   Mr. Nelson advises bosses: If a young worker has been chronically late for work and then starts arriving on time, commend him. "You need to recognize improvement. That might seem silly to older generations, but today, you have to do these things to get the performances you want," he says. Casey Priest, marketing vice president for Container Store, agrees. "When you set an expectation and an employee starts to meet it, absolutely praise them for it," she says.

14   Sixty-year-old David Foster, a partner at Washington, D.C., law firm Miller & Chevalier, is making greater efforts to compliment young associates—to tell them they're talented, hard-working and valued. It's not a natural impulse for him. When he was a young lawyer, he says, "If you weren't getting yelled at, you felt like that was praise."

15   But at a retreat a couple of years ago, the firm's 120 lawyers reached an understanding. Younger associates complained that they were frustrated; after working hard on a brief and handing it in, they'd receive no praise. The partners promised to improve "intergenerational communication."

Mr. Foster says he feels for younger associates, given their upbringings. "When they're not getting feedback, it makes them very nervous."

Modern Pressures

16 Some younger lawyers are able to articulate the dynamics behind this. "When we were young, we were motivated by being told we could do anything if we believed in ourselves. So we respond well to positive feedback," explains 34-year-old Karin Crump, president of the 25,000-member Texas Young Lawyers Association.

17 Scott Atwood, president-elect of the Young Lawyers Division of the Florida Bar, argues that the yearning for positive input from superiors is more likely due to heightened pressure to perform in today's demanding firms. "It has created a culture where you have to have instant feedback or you'll fail," he says.

18 In fact, throughout history, younger generations have wanted praise from their elders. As Napoleon said: "A soldier will fight long and hard for a bit of colored ribbon." But when it comes to praise today, "Gen Xers and Gen Yers don't just say they want it. They are also saying they require it," says Chip Toth, an executive coach based in Denver. How do young workers say they're not getting enough? "They leave," says Mr. Toth.

19 Many companies are proud of their creative praise programs. Since 2004, the 4,100-employee Bronson Healthcare Group in Kalamazoo, Mich., has required all of its managers to write at least 48 thank-you or praise notes to underlings every year.

20 Universal Studios Orlando, with 13,000 employees, has a program in which managers give out "Applause Notes," praising employees for work well done. Universal workers can also give each other peer-to-peer "S.A.Y. It!" cards, which stand for "Someone Appreciates You!" The notes are redeemed for free movie tickets or other gifts.

21 Bank of America has several formal rewards programs for its 200,000 employees, allowing those who receive praise to select from 2,000 gifts. "We also encourage managers to start every meeting with informal recognition," says Kevin Cronin, senior vice president of recognition and rewards. The company strives to be sensitive. When new employees are hired, managers are instructed to get a sense of how they like to be praised. "Some prefer it in public, some like it one-on-one in an office," says Mr. Cronin.

No More Red Pens

22 Some young adults are consciously **calibrating** their dependence on praise. In New York, Web developer Mia Eaton, 32, admits that she loves being complimented. But she feels like she's living on the border between

a twentysomething generation that requires overpraise and a thirtysomething generation that is less addicted to it. She recalls the pre-Paris Hilton, pre-reality-TV era, when people were famous—and applauded—for their achievements, she says. When she tries to explain this to younger colleagues, "they don't get it. I feel like I'm hurting their feelings because they don't understand the difference."

23   Young adults aren't always eager for clear-eyed feedback after getting mostly "atta-boys" and "atta-girls" all their lives, says John Sloop, a professor of rhetorical and cultural studies at Vanderbilt University. Another issue: To win tenure, professors often need to receive positive evaluations from students. So if professors want students to like them, "to a large extent, critical comments [toward students] have to be couched in praise," Prof. Sloop says. He has attended seminars designed to help professors learn techniques of supportive criticism. "We were told to throw away our red pens so we don't intimidate students."

24   At the Wharton School of the University of Pennsylvania, marketing consultant Steve Smolinsky teaches students in their late 20s who've left the corporate world to get M.B.A. degrees. He and his colleagues feel handcuffed by the language of self-esteem, he says. "You have to tell students, 'It's not as good as you can do. You're really smart, and can do better.'"

25   Mr. Smolinsky enjoys giving praise when it's warranted, he says, "but there needs to be a flip side. When people are lousy, they need to be told that." He notices that his students often disregard his harsher comments. "They'll say, 'Yeah, well . . .' I don't believe they really hear it."

26   In the end, ego-stroking may feel good, but it doesn't lead to happiness, says Prof. Twenge, the narcissism researcher, who has written a book titled *Generation Me: Why Today's Young Americans Are More Confident, Assertive, Entitled—and More Miserable than Ever Before.*

27   She would like to declare a **moratorium** on "meaningless, baseless praise," which often starts in nursery school. She is unimpressed with self-esteem preschool ditties, such as the one set to the tune of "Frère Jacques": "I am special/ I am special/ Look at me . . ."

28   For now, companies like the Scooter Store continue handing out the helium balloons. Katie Lynch, 22, is the firm's "celebrations assistant," charged with throwing confetti, filling balloons and showing up at employees' desks to offer high-fives. "They all love it," she says, especially younger workers who "seem to need that pat on the back. They don't want to go unnoticed."

29   Ms. Lynch also has an urge to be praised. At the end of a long, hard day of celebrating others, she says she appreciates when her manager, Burton De La Garza, gives her a high-five or compliments her with a cellphone text message.

"I'll just text her a quick note—'you were phenomenal today,'" says Mr. De La Garza. "She thrives on that. We wanted to find what works for her, because she's completely averse to confetti." ◆

CONSIDERING THE ISSUES

1. In your opinion, what is the culprit of "the Most-Praised Generation"? In other words, why did parents, schools, and communities of the last few decades decide that they needed to start praising their children more than earlier generations?
2. Whom do you agree with more: author Twenge who asserts that there should be a moratorium on "meaningless, baseless praise" or businesswoman Casey Priest who states, "When you set an expectation and an employee starts to meet it, absolutely praise them for it"?

CRAFT AND CONTENT

1. Throughout this essay, Zaslow cites more than 20 examples of giving praise. Locate at least 10 ways to show appreciation, according to this article, and state which ones would and would not work best for you.
2. What attention-getting strategy does Zaslow use in his introduction? Did this make you interested in reading this article? Explain. How does the conclusion mirror the introduction?

CRITICAL THINKING

1. Compare earlier generations with the later generations on how praise is required and received. Be sure to refer to the examples given in Zaslow's article as well as your own experiences.
2. In your opinion, will companies continue to pander to the new generation's need for praise or will the rise of a narcissistic culture cause a backlash?

WRITING ABOUT THE ISSUES

1. Would you consider yourself narcissistic? Research which traits make up a narcissistic person and write a brief essay showing how your own personality compares or contrasts with that of a typical narcissist.
2. Zaslow states, "A lot of today's young adults feel insecure if they're not regularly complimented." Do you agree or disagree? Make a brainstorming list of other reasons for young adults to feel insecure.

VISUAL CONNECTIONS

The Office

CONNECTING TO THE TOPIC

The Office is a television sitcom developed by Greg Daniels airing on NBC. *The Office* is shot in a single-camera setup, without a studio audience or a laugh track, and airs like a documentary. Set in Scranton, Pennsylvania, it portrays the everyday lives of office employees of a fictional paper company, Dunder Mifflin. The humor in *The Office* resonates with many viewers, as the cast represents the different archetypal personalities found in many offices across the country. Since first airing in 2005, the program has won several Golden Globe and Emmy awards.

CONSIDERING THE ISSUES

1. What are our expectations of work? What sort of place do we hope to work in? What consideration, if any, do we give to our future work environment when choosing a major?
2. Have you watched *The Office?* View the program's website for a description of the program. What accounts for its popularity? What drives the humor in the program? Explain.

CRITICAL THINKING

1. Who is in the photo? How does the picture demonstrate a moment in office life? Explain.
2. How does this photo tap into office clichés? Explain.
3. Watch an episode of *The Office* and summarize its plot. As you view the program, try to identify moments in which it holds up the office/work/life dynamic for ridicule.

TOPICAL CONNECTIONS

GROUP PROJECTS

1. Interview friends, family members, and acquaintances who work in corporations and industry about the reasons they work. As a group, develop a list of questions and interview at least five to eight people each about why they work outside the home. Make sure your questions are likely to elicit truthful responses. Prepare a short report on your findings.

2. Thirty years ago, men were expected to earn more than women. Do we still hold such beliefs? Poll your classmates to find out their opinions regarding income status. Do males feel that they should earn more? Would they feel less masculine if their girlfriends or wives earned more than they did? Do females look for higher incomes when they consider a partner? Analyze your results and write an argument that draws conclusions from your survey and connects the results to feminism in the twenty-first century.

WEB PROJECTS

1. In his essay, Andrew Curry mentions author Horatio Alger and his works that "glorified the work ethic." Who was Horatio Alger? Look up more information on this nineteenth-century author and the genre that became synonymous with his name. For Alger's heroes, what was the defining principle of work? Explain.

2. Visit the Work to Live website (http://www.worktolive.info) and read more about the state of the American workweek. Visit the "World Desk" and view information on the number of vacation days many nations afford workers. Write an essay in which you explore the concept of vacation time and its importance—or nonimportance—to the average American worker.

FOR FURTHER INQUIRY

1. Watch a movie that explores different aspects of the American dream—*Death of a Salesman, The Great Gatsby, Wall Street, Field of Dreams*, etc. What arguments does the movie put forth about why we work and the connection between work and happiness?

2. Few teenagers have escaped the question "What are you going to do with your life?" from a curious, perhaps even concerned,

relative. What they are really asking is what sort of work do you intend to do as an adult. Many people never find the answer. Author Po Bronson has written a book asking this very question, interviewing hundreds of successful and struggling people for their perspective on life, work, and happiness. Visit his website and read some of the testimonials at http://www.pobronson.com under the link "What Should I Do with My Life?" After reading a few excerpts and other material on his web page, write your own essay exploring this question.

8 | Is Fast Food Responsible for a Crisis in Public Health?

In 2008, the Centers for Disease Control reported that Americans were becoming more obese and faster than when last measured only a few years before. Over 65 percent of U.S. adults, reports the Trust for America's Health, are considered either overweight or obese as defined by U.S. body mass index guidelines. And the future looks grim . . . especially for children. As of 2011, almost 20 percent of children were considered obese—defined as having body mass index (BMI) of 30 or more. Obesity is a major cause of various heart diseases and certain types of cancers, and now children are developing the traditionally adult disease of type 2 diabetes when they are as young as six.

American physicians describe the situation as "epidemic." Perhaps even more distressing is the fact that despite the proliferation of health clubs and new exercise equipment, Americans are getting fatter, and the effects of all the excess weight are apparent. An estimated 300,000 Americans die of obesity-related causes each year, and the direct medical costs of obesity are over $100 billion annually.

In addition to the proliferation of fast-food restaurants, America has become more sedentary—physical education programs have been cut from many schools, we spend more time in front of computers and television screens than we do engaging in activities outdoors, and time constraints often require that we grab a bite at the local fast-food chain rather than go home and fix a nutritious meal. The result of this combination of factors is visible—America has a weight problem on its hands.

But who is responsible for this crisis in public health? Is it the junk-food companies advertising to young kids? Is it the fast food industry with its high-caloric offerings and encouragement to increase the portion size for a few more cents? Should we consider suing the fast-food companies? This chapter examines the continuing controversy over the connection between the expanding American waistline and the perceived crisis in public health.

CRITICAL THINKING

1. Who are the people in the drawing? How are they depicted? What do you need to know in order to identify these people and understand what is happening? Explain.
2. Summarize your overall feelings regarding this editorial cartoon. Is the message funny? Disturbing? Explain.
3. Would this cartoon have worked well 20 years ago? Explain.

"The handle on your recliner does not qualify as an exercise machine."

What's to Blame for the Surge in Super-Size Americans?

Tori DeAngelis

Tori DeAngelis is a freelance writer who has written for *Psychology Today*, *Common Boundary*, the *APA Monitor*, and other publications. This article appeared in the January 2004 issue of *Monitor on Psychology*, a publication of the American Psychological Association.

CONNECTING TO THE TOPIC

Are Americans relentlessly marching toward their own doom? Researchers are increasingly connecting today's fast-food culture and human biology to an epidemic of obesity. Human biology seems to have hard-wired us to store fat—just in case food runs out. That might have made sense when humans were out hunting for their next meal, but we no longer live in caves, and getting food often requires only a short walk to the kitchen. What is to blame for the obesity explosion, and can we do anything about it?

WORDS IN CONTEXT

debilitating (4)   detrimental to heath and vitality (adj.)
vigor (4)   energy and intensity (n.)
virulent (6)   toxic or poisonous (adj.)
facet (7)   aspect (n.)
lauded (13)   praised (v.)
subcutaneous (14)   just beneath the skin (adj.)
propensity (15)   tendency, inclination (n.)
endocrine (16)   relating to endocrine glands or the hormones they secrete (adj.)
hypothalamus (17)   a part of the brain located beneath the thalamus that regulates body temperature and certain metabolic processes (n.)
countervailing (18)   counteracting, compensating for (adj.)
premise (21)   the idea on which an argument is based or from which a conclusion is drawn (n.)
disseminated (22)   distributed, widely spread (v.)

1   It's a little hard to grasp, but the majority of us—about 65 percent, according to current government estimates—are obese or overweight. Compare that with 1960, when only 45 percent of Americans fell into those categories and proportionally far fewer were obese.

2   What's happened? Is it overindulgence—too much Ben & Jerry's and too little exercise? Maybe. But science is finding it's not so simple. In a special section of the Feb. 7, 2003, issue of *Science* (Vol. 299, No. 5608), some of the nation's top obesity experts agreed that multiple, complex factors—environmental, biological and genetic—make losing and even maintaining weight in today's environment an uphill battle.

3   "When you look at the big picture, there is really a mismatch between our physiology and our environment," says physiological psychologist and obesity expert James O. Hill, PhD, of the University of Colorado Health Sciences Center, who wrote one of the articles featured in *Science.* "We have an environment that provides food everywhere—it's inexpensive, good-tasting and served in large portions—and we have a physiology that says, 'Eat whenever food's available,'" Hill says.

4   Other environmental factors related to a lack of physical activity, such as sit-down jobs with ever-longer hours, further increase the odds we'll put on pounds, he says. Those extra pounds, as amply noted by the media, can lead to diabetes, stroke, heart attacks and other **debilitating** conditions, and such problems associated with obesity now cost the health-care system an estimated $117 billion per year. While solutions to the problem differ and much remains to be proven, there's already enough information to tackle the problem with **vigor**, psychologists concur.

Environmental Causes?

5 Scientists of all stripes now agree that environmental factors such as easy access to junk food, sedentary jobs and high stress rates—once considered a radical and even ridiculous proposition by some—play a major role in the obesity epidemic.

6   "I think we can make the case that the epidemic is environmental in origin," says nutritional biochemist and pediatric expert William H. Dietz, MD, PhD, director of the Division of Nutrition and Physical Activity at the U.S. Centers for Disease Control and Prevention (CDC). "What we can't be very specific about is which of those environmental factors is most **virulent**." Data on direct cause and effect are still pretty scarce, he notes, and besides, many factors, are probably at play.

7   Indeed, says Yale University psychologist Kelly Brownell, PhD, an internationally known obesity expert who was the first to finger environmental causes for the epidemic, you could take almost any **facet** of modern life and find a possible culprit. His villain of choice is the food industry. In his new book, *Food Fight: The Inside Story of the Food Industry, America's Obesity Crisis and What We Can Do About It* (McGraw-Hill, 2003), Brownell cites several factors he thinks give the convenience-food industry an edge in the fight for consumers' taste buds. Unhealthy foods, he argues, are accessible, convenient, engineered with fat and sugar to be tasty, heavily promoted and cheap. By contrast, healthy foods are less

accessible, less convenient, less tasty, not promoted and more expensive. "If you came down from Mars and didn't know anything about our country but those factors, you'd predict an epidemic of obesity," as he puts it.

8   Other features of the food business promote weight gain, too, Brownell maintains. More people are eating out than ever, and restaurant food tends to be higher in fat and calories and served in bigger portions than meals made at home. In addition, while research shows that people tend to eat the amount put in front of them, food manufacturers compete with one another to offer ever-larger sizes of low-cost, calorie-laden foods like French fries and soft drinks.

9   Other researchers are looking at how unhealthy eating may pair with other modern habits, such as television-viewing. CDC's Dietz began looking at the association in children 15 years ago, and others have since picked up the ball, finding what Dietz calls "a clear and significant association between TV-viewing and obesity in kids," and, in some cases, adults. What's not clear, Dietz says—and is an example of the cause-and-effect conundrum—is whether the relationship exists because TV-viewing promotes greater food intake, or because it represents sedentary time that children would otherwise spend being active.

10   Stanford University pediatric specialist Thomas N. Robinson, MD, is testing these variables, and in a still-unpublished study, shows that youngsters consume about 25 percent of their daily food in front of the television. When they decrease their viewing time, he posits, they eat less.

Enter the Beer Belly

11   Researchers also are looking at eating habits and obesity in relation to another modern ill: stress. In the November issue of *Health Psychology* (Vol. 22, No. 6), Debbie Ng, then a graduate student at the University of Minnesota and now at the Fred Hutchinson Cancer Research Center in Seattle, and University of Minnesota psychology professor Robert Jeffery, PhD, examined self-report data from 12,110 mostly white, middle-aged workers employed in a range of settings who took part in an earlier smoking-cessation program at 26 work sites in the Minneapolis and St. Paul, Minn., area.

12   Those reporting higher levels of stress—measured on a four-item scale asking how often in the past month they'd felt difficulties piling up and getting out of control, for example—also said they ate less healthy, fattier diets and exercised less often than those reporting less stress, the team found. (Stressed workers also reported smoking more.) The study is one of the largest to date to show these associations, Jeffery notes, and adds to research demonstrating that stress and poor health outcomes are often mediated by other factors, such as unhealthy eating habits.

13   Another new study—**lauded** as groundbreaking by many scientists—provides a possible biological explanation and working model for why

people may eat fattier foods when under chronic stress. The study, by neuroscientist Mary Dallman, PhD, of the University of California, San Francisco, and colleagues, also suggests why stress eaters may initially gain weight in the abdomen. The research, reported in the *Proceedings of the National Academy of Sciences* (Vol. 100, No. 20), compared rats placed under chronic stress by physical restraint or exposure to cold with rats under acute stress and those not stressed at all. Chronically stressed rats chose fattier, more sugary diets, gained weight in their bellies and became calmer as a result. It also paints to likely hormonal underpinnings of those behaviors—essentially, that chronic stress activates a particular negative hormonal feedback system in rats' brains that's aborted when the animals eat high-fat food and gain belly fat.

14   "The research strongly suggests that eating high-carbohydrate and high-fat diets increased abdominal fat in these rats," says Dallman. "That, in, turn, reduced the brain's drive to activate the chronic stress response system." The reason weight goes to the belly rather than elsewhere, Dallman posits, is that belly-fat cells host more steroid receptors than **subcutaneous** fat cells, allowing fat move to quickly to the liver and be converted to energy. "The belly is a wonderful depot, as long as you don't overdo it," Dallman says. "If you do overdo it, it gets you into all kinds of trouble—the kinds of problems doctors worry about when they see patients who have a 'gut,'" she notes.

The Gene Factor

15   Others are examining genetic reasons why some of us may be more prone to weight gain than others, given the same environmental influences. Neurobiologist Sarah Leibowitz, PhD, of Rockefeller University, has been studying strains of rats that are prone or resistant to obesity. Some of the rats are genetically engineered, or inbred, while others represent natural variation, called outbred. While she studies obesity-proneness in both strains, Leibowitz says she is "particularly eager to detect predictive markers in the outbred animals because they mimic the human population." About 30 percent show a strong **propensity** toward obesity, she says.

16   Obesity-prone rats of both types, she is finding, have different **endocrine** responses to eating than resistant rats. These responses are associated with disturbances in gene expression in the brain, she is finding, and also predict long-term weight gain. Over time, Leibowitz says, she'd like to define markers of gene expression in obesity-prone rats while they're still of normal weight, to help predict future weight gain and to design interventions accordingly. "The understanding of such markers could eventually help us target these kinds of systems in people at an early age," she explains.

17   Related to these findings, a November study reported in the new online journal *PLoS Biology* by French researcher Philippe Froguel and colleagues shows that obese people harbor a different form of a chromosome 10 gene, *GAD2*, than their non-obese relatives. The researchers hypothesize that having the gene variant may increase the amount of the neurotransmitter GABA—known to stimulate appetite—in the **hypothalamus** of the obese subjects. The two findings square with general scientific wisdom on the topic, which holds that genes may influence different people's susceptibility to obesity and overweight, says CDC's Dietz. Some studies, in fact, suggest that as much as 50 percent of the population may be so prone, he says.

What to Do?

18 Given the apparent difficulty of knocking weight off, especially for some of us, what's to be done? Individual and group interventions are one solution, and a number boast intriguing success. Other proposed fixes include wide-scale public health and policy interventions. State legislatures introduced about 150 bills last year related to the topic, and federal legislators are jumping on the bandwagon as well. In November, Rep. Rosa L. DeLauro (D-Conn.) and Sen. Tom Harkin (D-Iowa) introduced companion bills in the House and Senate that would extend nutrition labeling beyond packaged foods to include foods at fast-food and other chain restaurants. (Groups like the Center for Consumer Freedom are proposing **countervailing** legislation that would ban obesity-related lawsuits against restaurants.)

19   Brownell says such legislative hardball is a good solution: Food companies that create unhealthy food products and use aggressive or underhanded means to promote their products should be challenged, he says, much in the manner that the tobacco industry has been challenged. Likewise, he writes in *Food Fight,* political leaders should be encouraged to be innovative and to remove political barriers that prevent good national policy on the matter, he says.

20   Brownell acknowledges, however, that answers may end up coming not from the political arena, but from the grassroots. He cites recent moves by the cities of Los Angeles and New York to ban soft drink machines in schools as examples. He also believes in framing the argument around protecting children. "If we feel that children are victimized by this environment and that they are a group we need to protect, then many things will fall into place," he explains.

21   Hill is involved in an innovative public intervention that starts with a simple **premise**: energy in = energy out. Called "America on the Move," the program is based on calculations showing that the average

American—who has been gaining an extra pound or two a year—has to burn off about 100 extra calories a day to "break even" at the end of the year. Hill deliberately touts the program as one to help people prevent weight gain rather than lose weight—an aim he says is the product of 25 years of seeing how difficult permanent weight loss can be, especially for some. Using the energy-balance formula, "it doesn't matter what your genetic pattern is, you won't gain weight," he explains.

22   Eight states are currently signed up for the program and 20 more are interested, Hill says. It's being **disseminated** through a number of vehicles including a Web site (www.americanonthemove.org), organizations including the YMCA, AARP and American College of Sport Medicine, and soon, health-care professionals. Hill notes that while people can achieve the 100-calories-a-day goal by eating less or exercising more, he emphasizes physical activity because of how difficult it is to restrict eating. Among his simple suggestions is using a step counter to log an extra 2,000 steps a day—the distance, roughly a mile—that it takes to burn 100 calories.

23   He admits that given the complexity of the problem, it's a pretty basic plan. "It's a simple idea, and that's what we were worried about—that people would say, that's just too simple to work," he notes. "But, in fact, it's simple enough that it works." ◆

CONSIDERING THE ISSUES

1. What environmental factors often kept people from gaining too much weight in the past? Which of these environmental factors does society now lack? What has changed and why?

2. Consider the kinds of food you purchase. What do you buy? Do you buy fast food? How often? Are your choices driven by necessity—that is, do you pick foods that can be eaten on the go or are easy to prepare? Do you try to find "healthy" items, or is it difficult to tell what is good for you and what is not? Explain.

CRAFT AND CONTENT

1. DeAngelis uses subtitles throughout her essay. Do these subtitles help organize her main points and keep her article on target? Do they lead the reader to make certain conclusions regarding her content?

2. Outline this essay using the organizing techniques described in the introduction of this textbook. Remember to include thesis statement, subtitles, and primary and secondary points.

CRITICAL THINKING

1. The author refers to a cause-and-effect conundrum regarding television viewing and eating. In your opinion, does TV-viewing promote greater food intake or are children gaining weight watching television because they are being too sedentary?

2. As part of her conclusion, DeAngelis gives several suggestions to stop the rise of obesity. Evaluate her suggestions, and explain which ones you think are the most effective or appropriate for Americans to follow. Explain.

WRITING ABOUT THE ISSUES

1. Think about the food served in the cafeterias at your college. What variety of food is offered? Is the claim made by Yale University psychologist Kelly Brownell that "healthy foods are less accessible, less convenient, less tasty, not promoted and more expensive" true in your cafeteria? What responsibility, if any, do colleges and other institutions have to provide and promote healthy dietary options? Explain.

2. Write a cause-and-effect essay in which you show how factors such as "easy access to fast food and junk food, sedentary jobs and high stress rates" can lead to obesity, or why they do not.

You Want Fries with That?
Richard Daynard

Richard Daynard is a professor in the School of Law at Northeastern University. He is well-known for his work to establish the legal responsibility of the tobacco industry for tobacco-induced death, disease, and disability, and currently serves as chair of the Tobacco Products Liability Project and editor-in-chief of the *Tobacco Products Litigation Reporter.* This essay was published in the May 2003 issue of *Northeastern University Magazine.*

CONNECTING TO THE TOPIC

Many people have heard about the lawsuits against big tobacco companies for deceptive practices. One comment made during the height of the cigarette litigation was that if tobacco could be sued, fast food and other "non-healthy" products would soon follow. In 2002, two teenage girls did just that—they sued McDonald's for making them fat. While their case was thrown out, it opened the door for similar, more targeted lawsuits. In the next piece, law professor Richard Daynard discusses why he feels the fast-food industry is ripe for a lawsuit. Is the fast-food industry responsible for widespread obesity? Should they pay? Should they change?

WORDS IN CONTEXT

libertarian (2)   one who advocates maximizing individual rights and minimizing the role of the state (n.)

purveyor (2)   one that offers provisions, especially food (n.)

aesthetic (8)   concerning the appreciation of beauty (adj.)

inundation (12)   flood (n.)

hedonism (13)   pursuit of pleasure, especially the pleasures of the senses (n).

epidemiological (17)   concerning the branch of medicine that deals with the study of the causes, distribution, and control of disease in populations (adj.)

1   **W**hen I was organizing lawsuits against the tobacco industry in the 1980s and 1990s, the tobacco companies' favorite spin became like a mantra: "First, they go after cigarettes. Next, it'll be red meat and dairy products!"

2   Recently, a writer for a **libertarian** magazine caustically reminded me my response had always been "No way." Yet here I am, a decade or two later, urging litigation against **purveyors** of meat and dairy (and sugar) products—fast-food and packaged-food companies, in particular.

3   What gives? Well, I had a conversion. It began in April 2002, after New York University nutritionist Marion Nestle wrote a book entitled *Food Politics*, and I was asked to comment on whether her thesis opened the door to obesity litigation.

4   Nestle argues that Americans are getting dangerously fat because we're consuming more food than we did twenty years ago, largely because food companies maximize their profits by maximizing the amount of food their customers eat.

5   The companies accomplish this through a variety of misleading marketing ploys, and by buying off or manipulating those who are supposed to protect us—politicians, dietitians' organizations, and school boards, for instance.

6   I found Nestle's argument plausible and disturbing. What really shocked me was the scope and seriousness of the obesity crisis. In 1978, 15 percent of Americans were obese (meaning, more than thirty pounds above a healthy weight). This was a modest uptick from 13 percent twenty years earlier.

7   But by 2000, the obesity percentage had more than doubled, to 31 percent. An additional 34 percent of the population was overweight (ten to thirty pounds above a healthy weight). In other words, 65 percent of Americans were too heavy. The statistics for children, though lower than those for adults, were escalating even more dramatically.

8   And the problem isn't just an **aesthetic** one: Overweight and obese people are developing diabetes, heart disease, cancer, and other medical conditions in huge numbers. Indeed, in 2000, annual premature deaths related to obesity were estimated at roughly 300,000, approaching the figure for tobacco-related deaths. Perhaps most striking is the epidemic of type 2 diabetes among children and adolescents; until recently, this disease was known as adult-onset diabetes.

9   But questionable behavior that contributes to a public-health crisis doesn't by itself add up to a viable lawsuit. The obvious differences between Big Macs and Marlboros made me question whether my experience with tobacco litigation was applicable to the food industry.

10   There's no such thing as "moderate" smoking, for example. Even a little is bad for you (though a lot is obviously worse). Eating, on the other hand, is a biological requirement; too little food for a sustained period is as bad as too much.

11   And there are other important distinctions. People who eat too much get immediate feedback, in the form of an expanding waistline; smokers can harbor lung cancer or heart disease for years without symptoms. Nicotine is strongly addictive, which explains why people continue to smoke even when they know the dangers. Finally, though cigarettes can injure or kill nonsmokers, there's no such thing as "passive eating."

12   Nonetheless, the more I learned about the food industry's operations—the massive marketing budgets; the deceptive health and low-fat claims; the rush to supersize everything; the **inundation** of soft-drink promotions and machines in schools; the extra sugars and fats added to seemingly healthy potato, chicken, and fish dishes at fast-food restaurants—the more I became convinced that changing the industry's behavior is the key to stopping the obesity epidemic.

13   True, the food industry isn't responsible for many factors that contribute to obesity: "bad" genes, inactivity, conflicting advice from nutrition experts, **hedonism**, lack of willpower.

14   But these factors don't account for our bigger belt sizes. The genetic makeup of a population doesn't change much over a few decades. Weakness of will and hedonistic desires are pretty much what they've always been. Average physical activity may have declined since the late 1970s, but it wasn't very impressive then. What's making us fat has to do with changes in the way we're eating. And the food industry is obviously responsible for a lot of these changes.

15   But where does litigation fit in? Back in 1988, I wrote an article for the *Journal of the National Cancer Institute* in which I described five possible public-health benefits of tobacco-industry litigation.

16   First, that holding tobacco companies financially responsible for even a fraction of the cost of tobacco-related medical care and lost productivity—more than $100 billion annually—would force them to raise prices, thereby discouraging consumption, particularly among children and adolescents. This has in fact happened: Dramatic price increases prompted by the industry's settlement of lawsuits brought by the states were followed by equally dramatic reductions in smoking among minors.

17   Second, that lawsuits would have an important educational effect, translating **epidemiological** statistics into easily understood cases of real people. This too has happened. Even the industry's "personal responsibility" defense—anyone stupid enough to smoke shouldn't complain about getting lung cancer—helps discourage smoking by underlining a causal link the tobacco companies otherwise used to deny.

18   Third, that the ability of plaintiffs' lawyers to obtain and publicize internal industry records documenting misbehavior would serve to delegitimize the industry, making legislative and regulatory remedies politically practicable. More than thirty million pages of such documents are now available. The shocking behavior they reveal has made "tobacco executive" a term of opprobrium and tobacco money a dangerous commodity for politicians.

19   Fourth, that health insurers would be able to seek industry reimbursement for money spent caring for tobacco victims. To date, tens of billions of reimbursement dollars have been paid to the states.

20   And fifth, that if the tobacco industry responded like other industries confronted with product-liability claims, it would change its behavior: make its products less deadly, for example, or its marketing less deceptive. This alone has not happened, the tobacco industry having apparently concluded that its only future lies on the "dark side."

21   Similar benefits can be anticipated from food litigation, whether it takes the form of product-liability suits on behalf of obese citizens or, more likely, consumer-protection suits on behalf of classes of customers ripped off by unfair or deceptive marketing practices.

22   For instance, there's no reason why the cheapest foods should be the least nutritious. Foods made with added sugars and fats are especially "obesigenic." If, as a result of litigation costs, the most obesigenic foods carry a higher price tag than simpler, more nutritious foods—the kind your parents or grandparents used to cook at home—that would make a big difference to the American waistline.

23   Food litigation has already produced an explosion of media coverage, which has spotlighted the obesity epidemic. Food-industry trade groups

have responded—to the current suit against McDonald's, in particular—by insisting that everyone knows you shouldn't eat a steady diet of fast foods, despite the fact that most fast-food business comes from customers who do precisely that.

24   Unearthing documents that show how food companies manipulate and mislead consumers into buying their obesigenic products is likely to anger the public and complicate the benign image of food executives. And if health authorities can establish a causal connection between, for example, soft-drink concessions in schools, obesity, and the resulting health effects and costs, suits to recover these costs might be possible. Finally, if McDonald's has to pay for the harm caused by its Chicken McNuggets (which a court recently described as "Chicken McFrankenstein") or Filet-O-Fish, maybe it'll figure out how to formulate them without all the added fats and starches.

25   After all, food companies don't have to walk on the dark side. ◆

CONSIDERING THE ISSUES

1. Have you ever been on a diet? If so, what motivated you to go on one in the first place? Do you think the media influences how attractive we believe ourselves to be? If you have never considered your weight to be an issue, write about why it has not been a concern for you.

2. Consider the meaning behind Daynard's comment that the problem of obesity isn't simply an "aesthetic" one. Why does he use this word? What does it imply about obese and overweight individuals? Another way of looking at this question is to think about our common perceptions of beauty. What is a beautiful body? Is the obesity problem more connected to beauty or health? What do you think?

CRAFT AND CONTENT

1. Daynard cites five benefits of tobacco-industry litigation. What is the relevance of this list to his argument supporting lawsuits against the fast food industry? Explain.

2. Daynard has been teaching law since the 1960s. In what ways could this essay serve as a lecture? Identify areas of his argument that make it seem you are in a classroom listening to Daynard teaching. What questions would you ask him based on his lecture, and why?

3. In his conclusion, Daynard notes that a "court recently described" Chicken McNuggets as "Chicken McFrankenstein." What does this statement imply? Does it lead the reader to make a particular assumption about the opinion of the court?

The judge who made this comment also threw out the lawsuit against McDonald's. If you did not know this, would you think that the judge was in favor of a lawsuit against McDonald's? Explain.

CRITICAL THINKING

1. Daynard proposes in paragraph 22 that the price of nutritious food be made cheaper so that people with lower incomes can afford it. What does food cost? Consider the differences in price for "junk food" versus "healthy food." Do you think Daynard makes a good point? Explain.
2. Following Daynard's example, create a similar list of five reasons why suing fast-food companies is a good idea.

WRITING ABOUT THE ISSUES

1. Have the lawsuits filed in 2003 had any impact on fast-food menu items? Take a look at some menu offerings on the websites of several large fast-food chains such as McDonald's, Burger King, and Taco Bell. Do you think healthy additions to fast-food menus will help alleviate the obesity epidemic? Why or why not?
2. Track your calorie intake over a two- or three-day period, noting everything you eat. Don't change the way you normally eat so that the test can accurately measure your eating habits. Tabulate your total intake for each day and average the number. Note your serving sizes (for example, a "serving" of macaroni and cheese is about 260 calories, but a whole box is about 780 calories). Did you consume more or less than you thought you would? What about serving size—is a serving an accurate way to measure how much you should eat of a particular item? Write a short essay about your experience and what it indicates about your eating habits.

Time to Trim

In February of 2011, *Slate* magazine launched "Time to Trim" a crowdsourcing project that aimed to generate new ideas on the issue of childhood obesity. Over 350 ideas were sent in, and *Slate* readers voted for their favorites. Six were chosen as top reader picks, and six more were chosen by a panel of experts in nutrition and pediatrics. Posted here are the top picks from the judges and of *Slate* readers. All the results can be viewed at http://hive.slate. com/hive/time-to-trim.

CONNECTING WITH THE TOPIC

Crowdsourcing is the act of outsourcing tasks to a large group of people or community members through an open call. Can the childhood obesity problem be solved by a consensus of the minds? And is it even possible to implement the ideas expressed on *Slate*?

WORDS IN CONTEXT

multi-factorial (1) involving several factors (adj.)
subsidize (4) support financially, usually through government assistance (v.)
communicable (5) easily passed from one person to another, contagious (adj.)
prevalence (6) quality of being widespread (n.)
imploring (9) begging someone earnestly or desperately (v.)
intrinsic (9) belonging naturally; essential (adj.)
auspices (10) divine or prophetic signs (n.)
sanctity (10) sacredness
paradigm shift (11) a radical change in underlying beliefs or practices (n.)
engendering (11) to cause or give rise to, such as a feeling or situation (v.)
antithetical (12) directly opposed, mutually incompatible with (adj.)
caveat (13) warning or caution (n.)
audacious (15) bold, reckless, flying in the face of convention (adj.)

Stop Being Afraid of the Food Industry
Submitted by Maria

1   As a nutritionist who works mainly with low-income children and their parents, I see the problem of childhood obesity on a daily basis. The problem is obviously **multi-factorial**, so the solution needs to address the multitude of factors involved. I think one of the biggest problems in this

country has been the unwillingness to deal with the food industry head-on. As we saw with tobacco, the industry has to be forced to acknowledge its responsibility before real solutions can be implemented. Of course, the food industry is enormous, and employs powerful lobbyists in Washington, so the prospect of any policy restrictions on the food industry seem to be slim to none at this time.

2   However, I believe it is time to stop letting big corporations get away with enticing children to consume their high-calorie, high-fat and high-sugar products with billions of dollars in advertising, and then using the "personal responsibility" excuse to avoid all corporate responsibilities in this matter. Obesity and overweight are shaping up to be the most important public health problem for our society, and the time to act should be now.

3   Our children are suffering from a number of conditions that were only observed in adults decades ago. I regularly see children as young as 5 years old with high cholesterol, high triglycerides and elevated liver enzymes (indicating accumulation of fat in the liver). I have personally seen children as young as 12 already diagnosed with type 2 diabetes. What are we doing to our children? Why can't we be more courageous in taking the bull by the horns and solving this problem in an efficient way?

4   So this is what I propose: (1) Immediately ban all advertising of high-fat, high-sugar, high-sodium, low-fiber and highly processed foods and beverages to children of all ages. (2) Enact a tax on the above mentioned items to fund well-designed public health media campaigns and information campaigns, targeted to children of all age groups and their parents, to promote the intake of fruits, vegetables and whole grains, as well as physical activity, and to increase awareness of the dangers of high-fat, high-sugar and highly processed foods. (3) Speed the implementation of the recently passed federal law regarding school lunches. (4) Expand and **subsidize** research on the addictive quality of the above mentioned foods in order to establish scientific evidence and rationale for policy changes regarding food and advertisement issues. (5) Stop government subsidies of crops that contribute to the obesity problem, and implement a system of subsidies for highly nutritious fruits and vegetables. (6) Make physical education (P.E.) mandatory in all grade levels.

5   By implementing these and other possible solutions that tackle the problem directly, that is, that confront the source of the problem which is the food we eat, we may finally begin to see solutions that actually work. As long as we continue to bow down to the food industry and their lobbyists, obesity will continue to be a threat to our health and the future well-being of our children.

Push Play Instead of Push-Ups

Submitted by Matt Bowers

6   In 2008, the Centers for Disease Control and Prevention released its annual report on health trends in the United States. In it, the organization heralds the improvements that have been made in preventing and treating many chronic and **communicable** diseases, as well as increases in the average life-span. One of the few areas where little progress was noted, however, was in the realm of obesity and physical activity. As the report warns, "of concern for all Americans is the high **prevalence** of people with risk factors such as obesity and insufficient exercise, which are associated with chronic diseases such as heart disease, diabetes, and hypertension.

7   Obesity rates do not appear to be increasing as rapidly as they did in past decades, but remain at unacceptable levels. The percentage of adults . . . who engage in regular leisure-time physical activity and strength training [also] remains low." After over half a century of federal efforts to increase the physical fitness of America's populace, be it through the President's Council on Physical Fitness beginning in the 1950s and 1960s or more recent developments such as the CDC's Physical Activity for Everyone program, we find ourselves at a critical juncture in the evolution (or devolution) of our nation's health where we must be willing to ask if our fitness-based public health initiatives are producing the outcomes we had envisioned.

8   The answer, at least according to the data, is that they are not. In 2005–2006, only one-third of adults in our country participated in regular leisure-time physical activity and an equal number were considered to be obese. These figures are not reflective of well-functioning policy; in fact, I believe that these data suggest a fundamental disconnect between the programming and its people. While Let's Move represents a step in the right direction, for too long the federal government has poured funding into programs like Physical Activity for Everyone, which are designed to promote walking, jogging, strength training, and more solitary, exercise-based physical activity. I cannot help but wonder where the fun comes into play? For too long, the social psychology of fitness has been one predicated on discipline, hard work, and character-building—attributes which seem more aligned with a day at the office than leisure time. Consequently, the joy that can accompany physical activity has been systematically corroded from our national subconscious. Now, when people think about physical activity, they often find themselves immersed in imagery of treadmills, dumbbells, and push-ups.

9   While I cannot speak for all Americans, I can certainly speak for myself when I say that those images do little to make me want to leave the comfort of my couch. Instead of **imploring** people to exercise through guilt and implicit challenges to their moral fiber, I propose taking health promotion in a new direction: one that fosters lasting **intrinsic** motivation through a fun and playful community-based portfolio of sport programs.

10   While many of you are likely to point out that we already have community sport programs, I would respond that the scholastic, club, and recreational sport opportunities that presently exist in our communities are only pieces of a bigger puzzle that has yet to be assembled. What I mean by this is simply that, under the **auspices** of these current sport programs, there is a deceptively narrow range of potential sport experiences for children and adults. As a result, many non-participants view community sport, in its current form, as ostensibly about reinforcing the value of winning, becoming the best, and developing our elite youth athletes into collegiate stars. Although this type of sport outcome is undoubtedly appealing to many, it is time that we challenged the **sanctity** of what sport is supposed to be and took on an attitude of inclusion and humility such that we might development alternative sport opportunities for those who may not seek the glory of competition, but just want an opportunity to socialize and be active a few times a week.

11   Admittedly, the concept of retooling our top-down system of health promotion requires a **paradigm shift** by the leadership of our country's sport systems. But if our ultimate goal is to help more people become physically active in the hopes of reducing obesity rates and fighting chronic disease, we must be willing to acknowledge that a one-size-fits-all model of health promotion simply is not effective enough. Similarly, we need to also understand that sport alone is not the answer; it is merely a means through which we can reach people that is potentially capable of **engendering** more fun, meaningful physical activity than current exercise-based initiatives.

12   To begin, it is important to point out that I view this sport-based approach toward tackling obesity and lack of physical activity as a supplemental prong to complement the methods that are currently in place, namely fitness initiatives and current competitive sport systems. While this tack may seem **antithetical** to the philosophy I have espoused thus far, I understand that these health issues are complex and that just as a one-size-fits-all fitness-based model has failed to this point, the outcome would not necessarily change if we simply replaced fitness with sport. A fitness approach has worked for some people—just not enough; and competitive sports have helped many stay active, but there are many that feel alienated and unwanted in such a setting. If we coordinate the efforts of these different types of sport opportunities, however, we begin to see the broader appeal of a portfolio system.

13   With this **caveat** in mind, I propose developing a broad range of programming that encourages people to interact with those in their community in ways that benefit the spirit as much as the heart rate. Just because
Little Johnny may not possess the athletic ability and work ethic to be an
All-Star in Little League does not mean that he could not attain the same
social and health benefits by joining a peer-coached group. Or just because
Bill may be a paraplegic whose body will not allow him to participate
in traditional basketball leagues does not mean that he could not benefit
from a modified sport league that allows able-bodied and disabled athletes
to use each other's strengths to work together to achieve a goal. Or even
just because a parent and a child are a generation apart does not mean that
one must coach while the other plays. Why not develop sports experiences
where parents and children can work together on the same field, generating memories and health at the same time?

14   The point of these little **vignettes** is simply to demonstrate the trans-
formative power of sport that often remains untapped because of our
unwillingness to explore experiences outside of the traditional models.
In order to create a system capable of generating the types of sport experiences I just described, I have identified four critical steps that would
require implementation. First, as I've already alluded to, we must be willing to question our assumptions about sport and begin to design sport
experiences that require sport to conform to the participant, instead of the
participant to conform to the sport. A top-down, one-size-fits-all model
is not responsive enough to generate the type of pervasive sport adoption
I believe necessary to reverse the troubling physical activity and obesity
trends in our country. Second, we must encourage an open dialogue between the community members and the sport program administrators. If
we can foster this type of collaborative climate, the third step of actually
developing a supplemental portfolio of alternative programs based on this
dialogue becomes far more feasible. Finally, the fourth step would be to
implement the programs and provide grassroots feedback channels to continue the process of dialoguing and adapting, which then cycles back into
first step.

15   In this extremely difficult economic climate, I acknowledge that a program requesting further financial resources to support sport, one of the few
fields seemingly capable of withstanding the financial crisis, may seem
rather **audacious**. However, taking control of our nation's health requires
some audacity, and while the idea of funding sport initiatives might rub
some the wrong way in a time like this, the basic funding structure reveals
a much more conservative approach. I first ask that the government consider its current distribution of monetary support in the struggle to increase
physical activity. Perhaps there is a philosophical basis for redistributing
some of the funding that currently supports fitness-based initiatives into

other avenues as well. Our apologies to those organizations whom this might adversely affect, but after all, the ultimate goal remains the same: to help our children lead healthier lives for both their sake and the future of the healthcare system. In fact, I view this policy as an investment in the health of American children, and one that has a potential return-on-investment that would far outpace its cost.

16   So, as we come together today to chart a new course for the health of our nation's children, let us not be so consumed by the outputs of the system that we myopically neglect to also consider its inputs. If we can nurture an enduring love of physical activity through sport, as opposed to treating it as a moral imperative indicative of one's character and fortitude, we have the potential to transform physical activity into an intrinsically-rewarding experience in which people willingly participate. Perhaps if we remove the connotation of "work" from working out, and replace it with an experience that is both social and fun, we may finally begin to see our physical activity levels increase and obesity levels decline, instead of the other way around. As I have already suggested, if we design a new type of sport portfolio system that is grounded in meaningful, community-based, inclusive sport experiences, more people are likely to be physically active and the pressure that is currently placed on our healthcare system will begin to ease, thus facilitating a much more efficient system for all involved.

17   My recommendations are simple: redirect a portion of current public health initiative funding to help create an array of locally responsive sport opportunities that encourage fun, meaningful experiences for a broader spectrum of people. If we want people to be physically active, perhaps we must return them to their days as children playing with friends in the backyard. People work hard enough as it is; let's stop asking them to turn their leisure time into work as well. If we can do that, we might just find that individuals begin to actually enjoy physical activity in and of itself, with little thought given to the positive health benefits they are likely to accrue. Perhaps only in this state, when physical fitness becomes a by-product of enjoyable physical activity instead of pain and suffering, will people stop thinking about exercising and start playing.

CONSIDERING THE ISSUES

1. How did you learn about nutrition and healthy food choices? From your parents? At school? From books or on television or the Internet? What influenced your perception of healthy eating habits the most? Explain.
2. How important is physical education to students' overall fitness? Should it be required until grade 12? Why or why not?

CRAFT AND CONTENT

1. Consider how Maria frames her argument that the fast-food industry must assume some responsibility for rising childhood obesity rates. How compelling is her argument? What support does she give?
2. How does each writer establish credibility to their audience? Who are they writing to? Explain.
3. Both writers provide a summary of their proposed solutions. Evaluate each summary. Do they each provide enough evidence to support their recommendations? Explain.

CRITICAL THINKING

1. These two *Slate* readers propose very different solutions to address rising childhood obesity rates. Which solution seems more compelling to you, and why?
2. What response do you think Matt Bowers would give to Maria's fifth solution (make PE mandatory in schools to grade 12)?

WRITING ABOUT THE ISSUES

1. Go to *Slate*'s Hive site http://hive.slate.com/hive/time-to-trim and read the top answers selected by the judges and the top answers chosen by *Slate* readers. Which solution do you think deserves to be first place, and why?
2. Both writers note that money will be needed to advance their initiatives for successful outcomes. What challenges might each face in making a case for funding? Explain. What arguments might they make to encourage the financial support to initiate their solutions?

Blog Matters

A blog ("web log") is an online diary or commentary site that features regular entries that describe events, impressions, and viewpoints. Blogs may contain text, images, video, and often link to other websites, blogs, and online media. Most blogs allow readers to comment on the content of the post and respond to each other. As of September 2011, there were over 160 million public blogs in existence. While many blogs are maintained by individuals, some are run by journals, newspapers, and other media outlets. Remember that most blogs are not monitored for factual accuracy and often express the opinion and views of the "blogger" writing the content.

The commentary blog below is hosted by *AdBusters Magazine*, "a global network of artists, activists, writers, students, educators and entrepreneurs who wish to advance a social activist movement of the information age," maintained by Adbusters Media Foundation.

Bare Bones

Emily Wierenga
March 25, 2008

1   I have a friend named Carolyn who lives in the hospital. Carolyn is 12 years old. She prefers the white-walled rooms to her home, because there she doesn't have to go hungry.

2   At home, she doesn't let herself eat. Food is a sweet-talking demon that haunts her mind and threatens her life. Her stomach rumbles 24 hours a day, a comforting lullaby to her starved brain. She sees World Vision commercials and remarks, "Those children are so lucky. They don't have to eat."

3   How twisted have we become? Jealous over bloated African children who would do anything for a crust of bread, while we're regurgitating entire loaves? Something has to change.

4   *CosmoGIRL!*, *Teen Vogue*, *YM*, *Seventeen* . . . piles of wasted trees trashing up the perspectives of today's North American Children. Skinny models decorate the pages, bare bones jagged and useless, faces gaunt with disillusionment and hunger, ribs exposed for the world to count.

5   We've been suckered into a disgusting cycle: we pile on the pounds from chocolate bars and potato chips, drive through McDonald's for a greasy heart-stopper, and top it all off with a Slurpee from 7-Eleven. Later, we race the treadmill for an hour, chasing away our guilt, only to plop in front of the television to gorge on celebratory ice cream and commercials.

6   Then there are those who veer to the other side of the health-highway: organic fruits and vegetable, extra lean beef, lite cheese, no-fat yogurt, no-calorie sodas, anti-oxidant tomatoes, polyunsaturated margarines, green teas, flourless bread and high doses of Omega 3, topped off with some salty Styrofoam snacks known as Rice Cakes.

7   What are we teaching our children? To choose between one of two extremes? Whatever happened to good old-fashioned balance?

8   Cut the cable cord, spend the summer on a farm, and work up an appetite growing your own food. Fill your offspring with nutrients and values that will strengthen their bones and nurture their minds.

9   Then maybe instead of being jealous of starving children overseas, this generation will weep in compassion for the unnecessary wealth we regurgitate every day.

RESPOND TO THE BLOG:

What do you think? Are we caught up in a culture that is making kids fat and then making them feel bad about it? What can be done to fix the problem?

Body Mass Index
National Institutes of Health

CONNECTING TO THE TOPIC

Body mass index (BMI) is a measure of body fat based on height and weight that applies to both adult men and women. According to the National Institutes of Health, BMI is a reliable indicator of total body fat, which has been found to increase your risk of disease and death. While the score is usually valid, BMI isn't perfect. It may overestimate body fat in athletes and others who have a muscular build, and underestimate body fat in older persons and others who have lost muscle mass.

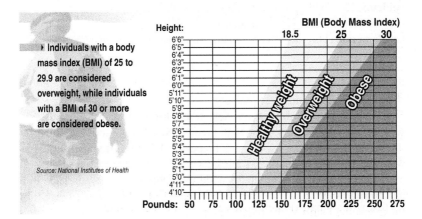

▶ Individuals with a body mass index (BMI) of 25 to 29.9 are considered overweight, while individuals with a BMI of 30 or more are considered obese.

Source: National Institutes of Health

Indiana Jones and the Kingdom of Fat Kids

Rahul K. Parikh, M.D.

Rahul K. Parikh, MD, a fellow of the American Academy of Pediatrics, is a pediatrician in the San Francisco Bay area. He has written for the *Chronicle*, the *Contra Costa Times,* and *New America Media* and is regularly published on Salon.com where he writes on medical issues. Parikh also serves as chief of patient education at Kaiser Permanente Medical Center in California.

CONNECTING TO THE TOPIC

One particularly lucrative merchandising technique is having fast-food restaurants place movie-related toys in their kids' meals. There movie tie-ins are extremely popular with children and promote both the movie and the fast-food restaurant; however, with childhood obesity at alarming rates, movie tie-ins to fast food are irresponsible, says this pediatrician. In this open letter to George Lucas and Steven Spielberg, posted on Salon.com on May 21, 2008, Dr. Parikh appeals to the famous directors to stop cutting deals with fast food companies and promoting unhealthy lifestyles to America's most impressionable population—its children.

WORDS IN CONTEXT

cardiovascular (5)   pertaining to the heart (adj.)
epidemic (5)   widespread, affecting many people or populations (n.)
correlated (9)   connected, associated (adj.)
conglomerate (11)   describing corporations made up of several companies (adj.)

1   **D**ear Mr. Lucas and Mr. Spielberg,
2   When I was a kid, your movies were a big part of my summers. So were all the goodies that came with them—"Star Wars" action figures, Indiana Jones trading cards, Reese's Pieces (E.T.'s favorite candy). Somewhere in my parents' house, I think I've still got a box of treasures with all of those memories. Among them are souvenirs I picked up at Taco Bell and Burger King, like a "Return of the Jedi" soda glass with a portrait of the menacing Darth Vader painted on it.
3   A generation later, I still eagerly anticipate your movies. My friends and I lined up hours in advance to see "The Phantom Menace" in 1999,

and I weaseled my way out of a family obligation with the in-laws so I could catch "Attack of the Clones" in 2002. A couple of weeks ago, I hopped online to check out the trailer for the new Indiana Jones movie, "Indiana Jones and the Kingdom of the Crystal Skull," and I'm looking forward to buying the first three films on DVD.

4   In the 30 years since you've started making movies, one thing that hasn't changed is a kid's (or in my case, a grown man's) imagination and wonder. And who sparks that better than you?

5   But a lot of other things about kids have changed. Their health is one of them. Today, almost one in four kids is obese, putting them at risk for, among other things, diabetes and **cardiovascular** disease. The **epidemic** of obesity is serious enough that we're predicting that this current generation won't live as long their parents and grandparents. That's incredible if you think about it.

6   Which brings me to why I wrote this letter. I'm a pediatrician, and every day I see overweight kids coming into my office. Getting families and kids to change how they eat is an uphill battle, and it doesn't get easier when big studios like yours wheel and deal with companies that peddle junk food and fast food.

7   You tied "Star Wars" to Pepsi and Frito-Lay, plastering Yoda and Obi-Wan over 2-liter bottles and Doritos bags. Recently I was watching

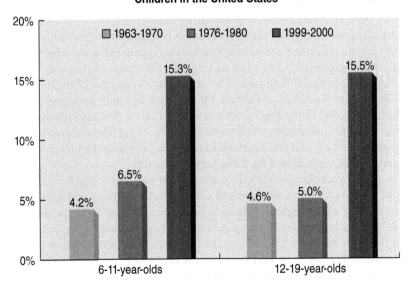

Proportion of Overweight Children in the United States

Source: Centers for Disease Control and Prevention, National Center for Health Statistics, Health, United States, 2003, Table 69.

CNBC and saw the chief marketing officer of Burger King unveil the Indy Whopper, a mammoth, juicy burger with pepper jack cheese and jalapeño sauce (to give it "adventure," the CMO pointed out), a tie-in to "Indiana Jones and the Kingdom of the Crystal Skull." I see you also got Mars to manufacture a Snicker's Adventure Bar with coconut and chai that has Dr. Jones' face on the wrapper.

8   Besides the fact that none of these foods is healthy, one has to ask if they're what your characters would eat. Would Lord Vader chug down a Pepsi before he wielded his light saber? (If he did, would he drink it with a straw or take off his entire mask?) Wouldn't Indy, now a senior citizen, have more than just a little bump in his cholesterol if he had scarfed down his namesake burger with fries and a soda? How could he be fit enough to chase down ancient relics while dodging boulders and outwitting Nazis?

9   You may think I'm playing the blame-the-media-and-Hollywood game. But an increasing body of medical evidence shows that child advertising and obesity are **correlated**. Take a look at a study by the Kaiser Family Foundation. According to the report, each week American kids spend a full-time job's worth of time in front of the TV, on the Web and playing video games. They will see about 40,000 ads per year, and two-thirds of those ads are for junk food and fast food. Studies show that what kids see on TV is what they tell their parents they want for supper. No doubt the Indy Double Whopper—with bacon!—will be flying off the greasy grill in short order.

10   It's not all the media's fault. Parents need to take charge of what foods they're buying and how they're preparing those foods. Many families, especially poor ones, get a whole lot for their hard-to-earn dollars when they buy cheap, processed and calorie-dense foods. Fresh fruits and vegetables are more expensive, don't last as long and take time to prepare—time that's hard to find if both parents work full time to pay the bills. This gap between the waistlines of the rich, middle class and poor is only going to get worse with rising food prices. It's also a crime that many hospitals, like shopping malls, now contain a McDonald's, where patients with Type 2 diabetes, cancer and other serious illnesses can gorge on fast food before and after they get treated for those very diseases.

11   So I'm asking you: Why do you still tie in your movies with junk food and fast food? I know that you and your corporate partners make millions from deals with **conglomerate** food companies and fast-food chains. But do you really need the extra cash at this point? Wouldn't it be better, in a corporate crusader kind of way, to change course? Stop these deals, or partner with somebody who thinks a little healthier?

12   I don't want to single out just movies. There's a ton of companies that use characters and celebrities to peddle junk food. Check out this summary from the Center for Science in the Public Interest. Being a sports fan,

my favorite is the one about Jason Giambi, who endorsed Pepsi by saying that drinking several a day really "lifts him up." (Actually, I think it's safe to say that it was more than Pepsi that lifted Jason's batting average during the 1990s.)

13   On the other hand, you are two of the most powerful and influential people in the media today. Mr. Lucas, you've even been called the forefather of the movie tie-in. So if you change, and do so publicly, others may well follow suit. About two years ago, Disney backed out of its long-term partnership with McDonald's in part because of the issue of childhood obesity. Would you both be willing to do the same?

14   If not, then perhaps a little truth in advertising, or in cinema, is in order. You should show us how your characters would look if they ate the food that you helped peddle. In that vein, you got Jabba the Hutt right. But Princess Leia in her skimpy steel bikini with cellulite? Indiana Jones having to hit the brakes during a car chase and find a glass of water so he can take his Lipitor? Now that I think about it, wouldn't Viagra have been the best tie-in for the new movie?

15   Humor aside, I ask you to consider the reality of childhood obesity. It's a serious problem; it needs serious solutions. Doing your part would help more than you might imagine.

16   Sincerely, Rahul K. Parikh, M.D. ◆

CONSIDERING THE ISSUES

1. In your opinion, who is responsible for addressing the issue of childhood obesity—parents, schools, the government, restaurants, the media, others? Explain.

2. Both as a child and as an adult, have you ever wanted or purchased a food product because it had a famous movie character or person on it? Was the food healthy or "junk food"? What made you want to purchase the product?

CRAFT AND CONTENT

1. This argument against movie tie-ins was written as an "open" letter to two famous movie directors. Why do you think that Dr. Parikh chose to write his argument this way, and what do you think was the reaction of Mr. Lucas and Mr. Spielberg upon learning of this "letter"?

2. Find the thesis statement to Dr. Parikh's argument (when the author states his purpose for writing the letter). Where is it located? What is he writing about before he gets to his thesis statement? Why do you think he chooses to begin his letter in this way?

CRITICAL THINKING

1. The author asks for "a little truth in advertising, or in cinema." If movie makers use tie-ins to products, should the movie then be compelled to portray its characters using these products in a realistic way? How would this affect the movie-going experience?
2. Parikh states, "Humor aside, I ask you to consider the reality of childhood obesity." In what ways is Parikh being humorous, and does Parikh's use of humor add to or detract from the effectiveness of his argument? Is using humor a good technique for persuasion? Explain.

WRITING ABOUT THE ISSUES

1. Craft a letter back to Dr. Rahul K. Parikh in which you pretend to be either Mr. George Lucas or Mr. Steven Spielberg. Think of how Lucas or Spielberg would realistically respond to Parikh's argument.
2. Dr. Parikh asks for Mr. Lucas and Mr. Spielberg to "Check out this summary from the Center for Science in the Public Interest." Go to the Center for Science in the Public Interest website at http://www.cspinet.org/new/200311101.html and view the CSPI report, which "identifies a plethora of ways that companies target kids in their homes, in their schools, on the web, and wherever else kids go." Then brainstorm a list of other ways that companies target children.

When America Relaxes, "Food Police" Should Keep Quiet
Paul King

Paul King is senior editor of *Nation's Restaurant News,* in which this article was first published in the August 25, 2003, issue.

CONNECTING TO THE TOPIC

Americans love fast food. But if we try to blame the fast-food industry for America's obesity problem, could we end up with "banned" foods? Could fast-food companies deem some foods just too high a liability? What could happen to our freedom of choice? Could the "food police" ruin fast food?

1   he Walt Kelly cartoon character Pogo once uttered the now-famous line. "We have met the enemy, and they is us!"

2   In the quickly heating debate over obesity in America, nowhere was the inescapable truth of Pogo's statement more evident for me than during my recent vacation in Pittsburgh.

3   The scene was on The Boardwalk, the collection of eateries found at a water park called Sandcastle. It was a great place for people-watching, especially if you wanted to view out-of-shape adults in ill-advised swimwear.

4   It was also the first place I actually had encountered the fried Twinkie. I had heard and read about the fat-laden, cream-filled sponge cake, but I never had seen one. There it was, on the menu at one of the snack stands, alongside the funnel cakes and—believe it or not—fried Oreos.

5   I just had to taste the fried Twinkie—for research only, of course— and so while my children took one more slide down the Tornado water ride, I got on line to place my order, two Twinkies for $2.50.

6   For the uninitiated, making a fried Twinkie is simple. You take a chilled Twinkie—you have to chill it so the cream filling doesn't liquefy in the fryer—dip it in funnel cake batter and then quickly deep-fry it. The chilling-and-frying method gives you a hot-cold combination when you bite into it.

7   "Do you get many orders for these?" I asked the blonde teenager behind the counter while I waited for my made-to-order treat.

8   "Yeah, we get some," the girl answered. "But more people order the Oreos."

9   "Do you like them?" I asked.

10   "Nope," she said. "I think they're nasty. I just eat the funnel cakes."

11   As I waited, I noticed the heavy-set couple directly to my right, who were waiting for their order, the Funnel Cake Supreme. Sandcastle, which operates its own foodservice, makes that colossally caloric confection by taking its already artery-clogging fried dough and topping it with a thick ribbon of vanilla or chocolate soft-serve ice cream. Then, to gild the lily, your server pours a generous helping of syrupy strawberries on the ice cream.

12   For $4 the dessert is a real bargain in that it easily could feed four people. But the couple had ordered one apiece. I stared, slack-jawed, as they walked away to the seating area. I was so mesmerized by the sight that I didn't immediately hear my order being called.

13   As my family gathered around the table to taste our dessert, I mentally recalled all the stories I'd been reading over the past few months about lawsuits being filed against fast-food chains and about activists railing against soda and chips being sold to our nation's school-children.

14   In all truthfulness I think that the "food police" have a very valid point: Most Americans, given several nutritional paths, will choose the

tastiest road. That way leads to madness, but many people gladly are willing to go crazy in that manner.

15   They also are right to be concerned about the message most food advertising sends to our young people and to try to counter that with nutrition education and some modicum of control over what foods our kids can buy while they are in the hands of our educators.

16   But do we really need crusading attorneys who blame the fast-food industry for the nation's obesity woes, and their ilk, to save us from ourselves? Does our already litigious society need to clog the courts with nutrition lawsuits faster than our eating habits can harden our blood vessels? I don't think so.

17   I'll never eat a Funnel Cake Supreme. But when I'm treating my family to a day out, whether at an amusement park or a sports event, I expect to have the opportunity to have that choice. The enemy may be us, but I'll accept that. It's sweeter than the alternative. ◆

CONSIDERING THE ISSUES

1. In his essay, King watches with great interest an obese couple eating an excessively caloric dessert. Do you notice what other people eat around you? Do you make judgments about those people based on what they eat and how they look? Do you consider your own menu choices when you know others may see what you are eating? Explain.

2. Could lawsuits influence what kinds of foods we are offered at fast food chains in the future? How have lawsuits already affected menu offerings? Do you think Big Macs and Whoppers could face extinction? Why or why not?

CRAFT AND CONTENT

1. What is the purpose of the Walt Kelly quote at the beginning of King's narrative? How does this quote connect to his essay? Explain.

2. How does King describe lawyers in paragraph 16? What does his word choice reveal about how King feels about fast food litigators?

CRITICAL THINKING

1. How does King feel about the large couple's choice of dessert? Does he feel that they should have ordered two Funnel Cake Supremes? Do you think he would have had the same opinion if the couple was more physically fit?

2. Who are the "food police"? What impact could they have on our fast food choices? Explain.

WRITING ABOUT THE ISSUES

1. Write a personal narrative mirroring King's experience. Go to a fast-food outlet and order something on the menu. Note the people around you, and what they are eating. Write about your impressions of the experience.

We Eat; Therefore, They Are
Rosie Mestel

Rosie Mestel is a medical writer at the *Los Angeles Times*. In addition to the *LA Times*, her articles have appeared in many publications, including *New Scientist*, *Health* magazine, and *Discover*.

CONNECTING TO THE TOPIC

While many people assume that board-certified physicians help develop and approve the government's dietary recommendations, few are aware of the intense political lobbying that goes on behind the scenes influencing these recommendations. Food is big business in the United States. Companies that sell foods that are high in fat or sugar have a great deal riding on what dietary recommendations the government officially supports. As this article published in the August 10, 2004, edition of the *LA Times* explains, official recommendations may not be free of political influence.

WORDS IN CONTEXT

regally (1) as if holding court; with a kingly air (adv.)
haggard (6) appearing worn or tired (adj.)
castigated (12) severely criticized (adj.)
tepid (22) lacking enthusiasm; literally, lukewarm (adj.)
ire (24) with anger; intense anger (n.)
strenuous (24) requiring great effort or energy (adj.)
blight (26) something that prevents or impairs growth; lacking in hope or ambition (n.)
rollicking (28) high-spirited and enthusiastic (adj.)

1   Inside a packed ballroom at the local Holiday Inn, 13 government-appointed scientists sat **regally** around a table, debating servings of fish.

2   "What do we want to recommend for children? Fish twice a week?" asked chairwoman Janet King.

3   "Small fish," another panel member said.

4   "Children are advised to eat smaller portions of fish than adults?"

5   "Can we defer a vote on that?" pleaded another.

6   The august panel of nutrition researchers had been talking this way for 45 minutes. The ballroom was filled with silent listeners scribbling away on notepads. Some of the listeners were looking a little **haggard**. They had already witnessed exhaustive discussions on protein, sugar, fat, grains, breakfast, exercise and a record-breaking 2 1/2-hour standoff on vitamin D. "Mind-numbing isn't the half of it," said a woman in line for the restroom. "I want to strangle them."

7   After a year's work, the Dietary Guidelines Advisory Committee is in the final stages of overhauling the Dietary Guidelines for Americans, which will be formally adopted next year. Since 1980, the guidelines—consisting of seven to 10 short statements and an accompanying booklet—have been issued every five years by the departments of Agriculture and Health and Human Services.

8   School menus must comply with the guidelines; so must the Women, Infants and Children program, which provides food to low-income mothers. The food pyramid, currently receiving its own overhaul, is also based on the guidelines. America now waits hungrily for the latest update.

9   Do these scholars think we should still "choose a variety of fruits and vegetables daily" as the guidelines currently decree? Should we continue to "choose and prepare food with less salt," and "aim for a healthy weight"? Would it remain wise to "choose beverages and foods to moderate your intake of sugars"?

10   To reach their conclusions, committee members—unpaid volunteers generally drawn from academia—have waded through thousands of pages of studies on fat, heart disease, television watching, obesity and the effect of fiber on stool weight. They have investigated the best way to wash broccoli and argued bitterly on the matter of sugar. They have been aided by testimony and letters from hundreds of groups and individuals, including the Sugar Association, the Grocery Manufacturers of America, the American Heart Association, People for the Ethical Treatment of Animals, the Bible-based Hallelujah Diet and scads of disciples of Dr. Joseph Mercola, author of "The No-Grain Diet."

11   The job is "enormous—probably one of the most difficult jobs I ever had," said Dr. Cutberto Garza, director of the division of nutritional sciences at Cornell University and chairman of the 2000 Dietary Guidelines Advisory Committee.

12   He didn't get paid, but he had some exciting times. Before the job was done, his committee sparked a lawsuit by an advocacy group claiming the panel had a pro-milk bias, was challenged by one senator for being too positive about alcohol and **castigated** by 30 other senators for being too negative about sugar.

13   Writing the dietary guidelines is honor, toil, aggravation and tedium— in unequal measure. The results of the group's work are bland and seemingly obvious bits of advice that most Americans have never read.

14   "It is interesting to see how they put it all together," whispers one audience member. "It is a little bit boring, of course." [. . .]

15   Complaints surfaced from the moment the committee was appointed last year. The Center for Science in the Public Interest pointed fingers at seven of the 13 selected committee members for having financial relationships with industry groups, including the Sugar Association, the Campbell Soup Company and the American Cocoa Research Institute.

16   How, asked the consumer group, could Americans be sure the scientists were unbiased?

17   Richard Hanneman, president of the Salt Institute, was pretty ticked too. He has peppered the committee with letters complaining about the unfair and unscientific treatment given to salt in the 2000 guidelines, which told Americans to "choose and prepare foods with less salt."

18   "We could not accept that," said Hanneman, who hasn't missed a dietary guideline meeting since 1990. "We don't think there's evidence that the public should consume less salt."

19   The Sugar Association and the Grocery Manufacturers of America both wrote to say that the guidelines don't focus enough on physical activity— just on what people eat. The grocery manufacturers have suggested that the name of the guidelines be changed to the Dietary and Physical Activity Guidelines.

20   Such intensity about eating advice did not exist a century ago when the government began issuing guidelines, said Marion Nestle, a professor of nutrition, food studies and public health at New York University and author of the 2002 book, *Food Politics: How the Food Industry Influences Nutrition and Health.*

21   In the early days, the Department of Agriculture advised people to eat widely and plentifully, in keeping with its role promoting American agriculture. The advice has changed through the years—there were five food groups in 1917, 12 in 1933, eight in 1942 and either seven or 11 in 1943, depending on which pamphlet you consulted.

22   The tips were at times on the **tepid** side: The 1979 "Hassle-Free Guide to a Better Diet" told readers that many scientists felt diet contributed to chronic disease, but others did not, "so the choice is yours."

23   The trouble began when the government started advising people to start eating less of certain foods, Nestle said. One flap erupted in 1977

after a Senate committee report suggested Americans cut back on saturated fats, sugar, cholesterol and salt. The cattle, dairy, egg and sugar industries protested—and the report was revised, easing up on salt and cholesterol and dumping the phrase "reduce consumption of meat" for a friendlier "choose meats, poultry and fish which will reduce saturated fat intake."

24   The food pyramid also drew **ire** upon its completion in 1991 because its pointed shape indicated that some foods should be eaten less than others. **Strenuous** objections from the National Cattlemen's Association and National Milk Producers Federation—both of whose products were nearer the top of the pyramid—caused a one-year delay in the pyramid's release.

25   Creating the guidelines is still "political—from start to finish," said Nestle, who was on the 1995 Dietary Guidelines Committee. "It's science politics. It's politics politics. It's corporate politics." She recalled tensely standing her ground to ensure that a phrase she hated—"there is no such thing as a good or bad food; all foods are part of a healthy diet"—was not included in the 1995 guidelines.

26   Nestle bemoaned the fact that even as Americans fatten up, no one is ever told to eat less of any specifically identified food—not even a candy bar or soft drinks. And she snorted at the guideline about sugar, which as far as she's concerned has been infected by a creeping **blight** of wishy-washiness.

27   In 1980, people were flatly told to "avoid too much sugar." By 2000, the committee was going to tell Americans to "choose beverages and foods to limit your intake of sugar"—but the word "limit" was tossed out at the last minute by the government (after industry protests) and replaced with the weaker word "moderate." This time, people are holding their breath to see if there will be a sugar guideline at all. [. . .]

28   [The May] meeting of the committee was supposed to be the last, but a **rollicking** debate about vitamin D threw everything off schedule. No one was certain when the meeting would end. "I'm figuring midnight," said a USDA employee, placidly stitching away on a patchwork quilt to pass the time. Fresh science, it seemed, had emerged since 2000, revealing that many people are deficient in the vitamin. But some committee members were nervous about recommending a big jump in intake.

29   Brisk progress was made on some subjects: Eight draft guidelines were crafted advising Americans to "keep food safe to eat," "monitor your body weight to achieve health," "choose and prepare foods with less salt" and "be physically active every day."

30   For the first time, the committee planned to recommend Americans slash their intake of trans fats, those hardened, partially hydrogenated vegetable oils found in stick margarines and many baked goods.

31   But sugar was a sticky mess. As the committee took up the issue again, an excited rustle went through the audience like so many candy bars being unwrapped. Dr. Carlos Camargo, assistant professor of medicine

and epidemiology at Harvard University, cited three recent studies reporting that kids drinking the greatest number of sugary soft drinks ended up plumper later on.

32   Nutrition researchers Teresa Nicklas, professor of pediatrics at Baylor College of Medicine, and Joanne Lupton, professor of nutrition at Texas A&M University, lobbed back other types of studies that didn't find that link.

33   Camargo, noting his position as president of the American College of Epidemiology, said that the other types of studies were inferior in design.

34   Well, Lupton said, if we're going to ignore them for sugar, we have to ignore those kinds of studies for other issues too.

35   "We're here to make a difference," Camargo said.

36   "I don't think we are here to make a difference," Lupton said. "I think we are here to evaluate the science."

37   The mood began to lighten when sugar was put off again and matters drifted on, past cholesterol and fish to a discussion of alcohol, in which nothing, as usual, was left unquestioned. The panel debated a recommendation that alcohol be avoided by children and those operating heavy machinery. One committee member asked for the pertinent data.

38   They forged ahead, moving on to fiber's impact on heart disease and bowel motion. Lupton explained that there had been more than 100 studies on the effect of fiber on stool weight and its consequent speedier passage through the bowel. "So there is a very strong . . . are you laughing at me for talking about this?" she said.

39   Some committee members were giggling.

40   "It is interesting where we, as a society, have placed our research efforts . . . 100 trials on stool," Camargo said. Lupton tried to explain that constipation is one of the most common disorders in Western countries, affecting up to 10% of children and maybe 20% of people aged 65 and older. A blond woman five rows back was laughing so hard she was crying.

41   Some people in the audience took advantage of the uproar and sneaked out for an evening snack.

CONNECTING TO THE TOPIC

1. Does the U.S. government, with its "official" food pyramid, have a responsibility for the overall public health? Why or why not?

2. Do you follow the Dietary Guidelines for Americans? For example, do you look at the nutritional information on the sides of food products? Does the information on the panel influence what you eat? Explain.

CRAFT AND CONTENT

1. In paragraph 27, Mestel describes how the very words used to caution Americans on sugar intake became a subject of great debate. The recommendation changed from "avoid" to "limit" to "moderate." What do these words mean to the average consumer? Would you be influenced to eat less sugar if you were told to "limit" your intake as opposed to "moderate" it? Explain.

2. In paragraph 36, in response to Dr. Carlos Camargo's charge that the committee was there "to make a difference," professor Joanne Lupton replied, "I don't think we are here to make a difference. I think we are here to evaluate the science." What does she mean? Do you agree with Camargo's position or Lupton's position, and why?

CRITICAL THINKING

1. Before reading this article, were you aware of how the Dietary Guidelines for Americans were determined? What assumptions regarding government recommendations did you have? After reading this article, are you more or less confident in the government's strategy for developing the new guidelines? Explain.

2. Marion Nestle expresses frustration that while Americans are obviously dealing with health problems related to expanding waistlines, "no one is ever told to eat less of any specifically identified food—not even a candy bar or soft drinks." Should certain foods carry warnings? Is it up to the individual to know which foods are healthy and which ones are not? Is it the government's responsibility to guide the public? Explain.

WRITING ABOUT THE ISSUES

1. Write an essay exploring your own eating habits as they are influenced—or not influenced—by the guidelines set forth by the government or on the sides of prepared-food packages. Include in your response the nutritional information cited online by fast-food companies such as McDonald's. Is this information helpful? Why or why not?

2. Mestel provides a glimpse into the inner workings of a government panel responsible for developing the Dietary Guidelines for Americans. Based on what you have read, explain how you feel about this panel and its effectiveness. If you wish, make recommendations of your own about how the Dietary Guidelines for Americans should be drafted.

VISUAL CONNECTIONS

Now What Do We Eat?

CONNECTING TO THE TOPIC

Over the last two decades, thousands of schoolchildren were taught the "food pyramid" approved by the United States Department of Agriculture. Many Americans believed that they understood what healthy eating habits included, even if they didn't actually have such habits themselves.

In 2001, Walter Willett, a physician and nutrition researcher from Harvard School of Public Health, created his own version of the food pyramid, which he published in his book *Eat, Drink and Be Healthy.* His pyramid was vastly different from the one that was promoted by the USDA at the time.

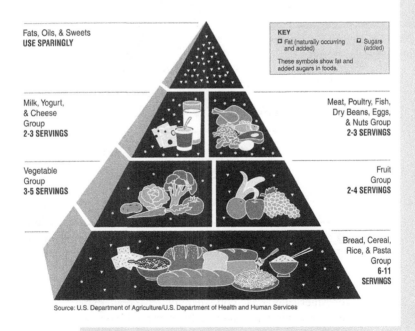

Food Guide Pyramid
A Guide to Daily Food Choices

Fats, Oils, & Sweets
USE SPARINGLY

KEY
◻ Fat (naturally occurring and added)   ◻ Sugars (added)
These symbols show fat and added sugars in foods.

Milk, Yogurt, & Cheese Group
2-3 SERVINGS

Meat, Poultry, Fish, Dry Beans, Eggs, & Nuts Group
2-3 SERVINGS

Vegetable Group
3-5 SERVINGS

Fruit Group
2-4 SERVINGS

Bread, Cereal, Rice, & Pasta Group
6-11 SERVINGS

Source: U.S. Department of Agriculture/U.S. Department of Health and Human Services

In response to growing concerns regarding the American obesity problem and issues raised by nutritionists and physicians like Dr. Willett, the USDA updated the food pyramid in 2005, renaming it "My Pyramid." The new pyramid aimed to encourage physical activity, moderation, and proportion based on a personalized dietary plan, and gradual improvement toward healthier lifestyles. But the new pyramid seemed to do nothing to help the problem, and in 2011, the USDA updated its guidelines yet again, replacing the "My Pyramid" with "My Plate."

Here, the graphic of the traditional food pyramid, familiar to most people from their days in health class, appears first, followed by Dr. Willett's revised version, which is based on the style of the original USDA version. His graphic is followed by the USDA's "My Pyramid," used in schools over the last five years. The final graphic is the new "My Plate" guideline released in 2011.

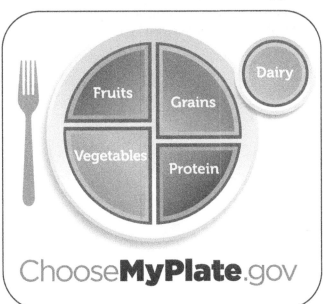

CONSIDERING THE ISSUES

1. Did you try to follow the recommendations of traditional USDA food pyramid or of "My Pyramid"? How much food, based on servings, do you think you would eat if you followed the traditional pyramid? Or "My Pyramid"? Or "My Plate"? Are you likely to follow any guidelines from the USDA or other expert? Why or why not?

2. What information do you need to know in order to understand what is happening in these graphics? Explain.

CRITICAL THINKING

1. Review the recommendations of each graphic carefully. How do your dietary habits compare to each graphic?

2. What pyramid seems more healthy, and why? How does your diet compare to the recommendations in each graph? Explain.

3. Which pyramid is easiest to understand? Critically evaluate how accessible each pyramid is. Based on the usability of each, how likely do you think it is that students and adults would follow a particular pyramid's recommendations? Explain.

4. Based on what you read in Mestel's article, what factors do you think influenced the creation of the "My Pyramid," and later, the "My Plate" guidelines created by the USDA?

TOPICAL CONNECTIONS

GROUP PROJECTS

1. Discuss in your group the following question: If you could be either very beautiful or very wealthy, what would you choose? Explain the motivation behind your choice. Based on your group's multiple responses, can you make any conclusions about the influence of body size, beauty, and social acceptance in today's society?

2. Together with your group, develop a lawsuit against a popular fast-food chain. Identify the reason behind the suit, the people on whose behalf you are suing, and the expected restitution. Refer to specific points made in the essays in this chapter.

WEB PROJECT

1. One of the issues explored in this chapter is whether the fast-food industry should assume some financial responsibility for health issues connected to obesity in this country. In Colorado, laws protect certain industries and workers, such as dude ranches and ski-lift operators, from "frivolous lawsuits." In January 2004, the Colorado legislature submitted a bill to protect fast-food industries against obesity lawsuits. Research this issue in greater depth on the Internet (try newspapers such as http://www.denverpost.com). Should states pass such bills? Are they a good idea? Why or why not?

FOR FURTHER INQUIRY

1. The obesity crisis is not just an adult problem—childhood obesity rates have tripled over the last 20 years. Disease conditions such as type 2 diabetes, more commonly called "adult onset" diabetes, and heart disease are striking children at an alarming rate. Research the issue of childhood obesity. Why are children getting heavier? What can be done to stop this disturbing trend? And what could happen if we don't? Visit the Kid Source website addressing childhood obesity at http://www.kidsource.com/kidsource/content2/obesity.html for more information.

9 | Will Our Economy Ever Bounce Back?

Today's college graduates face challenges many of their parents and grandparents did not. The United States remains in the throes of the first true economic recession in years. Tuition rates are at their highest and so are unemployment rates. The price of gasoline, in the wake of political unrest in the Middle East, hovers around $4 a gallon. The housing market, much to the dismay of homeowners and realtors alike, continues to decline, and bankruptcy and foreclosure rates remain unabated.

But it isn't all doom and gloom. Some optimists point out that Americans have stopped their frenzied spending on luxury items of little value. Others point out that housing prices had gotten ridiculous, and the bubble burst is just returning prices to more realistic levels. Americans tend to job hop less and are finding ways to enjoy life on a budget. While some people may long for the distant days when they could just run out and buy whatever they wanted, others note that there is some pleasure in saving for things—a sense of achievement. Savings accounts are now in style.

However one views the economy, things are different. This chapter explores some of the challenges many college students will face as they enter a changed economic landscape. What future will meet graduates once they receive their diplomas? How has our view of credit and saving changed? What steps can students take now to ensure a better economic future later? And what will the long-term impact be on our society as a whole?

CRITICAL THINKING

1. Who are the people in the cartoon and what is their relationship to each other?
2. What do you need to know to understand what is happening in this cartoon and the point the cartoonist is trying to make?
3. What "side" is the cartoonist on? How can you tell?
4. Could audiences of different generations interpret this cartoon in different ways? Explain.

September's Song

Natalie Southwick

Natalie Southwick is a 2010 graduate from the Medill School of Journalism at Northwestern University. This article first appeared in the *Lifestyle* section of *The Boston Globe* on September 20, 2010.

CONNECTING TO THE TOPIC

In this essay, a recent college graduate yearns for the innocence of her childhood—and the world she remembers before 9/11. What was your childhood like? What do you remember about the economy? Your lifestyle? How you envisioned the future? Do you still have similar dreams and aspirations, or has the economy changed your sights?

WORDS IN CONTEXT

nostalgia (1)   a bittersweet longing for things, persons, or situations of the past; the condition of being homesick (n.)
aughts (7)   zero (n.)
divisive (7)   creating disagreement or conflict (adj.)

1   If you've been paying attention to the music world or watching *The Daily Show* in the last month, you might have heard—or at least heard of—indie band Arcade Fire's sublime new album, "The Suburbs." And if you spend too much time online, you may have discovered the astounding interactive video for the band's song, "We Used to Wait," http://www. thewildernessdowntown.com that combines animation from director Chris Milk with footage of the viewer's childhood neighborhood taken from Google Maps. It's a heavy-handed tug at the heartstrings, but it works. Watching it, I felt pangs of **nostalgia** for my childhood—and I'm only 22 years old.

2   Nostalgia might seem premature in a recent college graduate, but I'm not the only one yearning for the days of my (earlier) youth. In the past few years, it's become hard to miss the number of movies, TV shows, and other entertainment catering to young adults who long to be irresponsible children again. *Toy Story 3* might have been disguised as a kids movie, but it was even more meaningful for those of us who grew up with those beloved characters. Just watching the gorgeous trailer for last year's film adaptation of Maurice Sendak' s classic children's book, *Where the Wild*

Things Are, brought tears to my eyes. The film itself was obviously—and successfully—marketed straight at my demographic: twenty-somethings who fell in love with the book as children and still identify with its bitter-sweet view of growing up.

3   In this economic climate, growing up seems less appealing to many of us, and in some ways, less possible than ever. Making that transition to adulthood is not so easy anymore, says Dr. Montana Miller, associate professor in the popular culture department at Bowling Green State University. Lots of people these days can't do it because of the economy. People get trapped in this phase of life where they don't feel independent yet, and it's hard to embrace and enjoy adulthood when you feel like you're being held back, so people are looking for things that remind them of their childhood.

4   It's definitely an important factor, but I don't think the economy is the only reason the so-called Millennial generation harbors a soft spot in our hearts for our childhood years. For us, the desire to return to childhood has far more to do with falling towers than falling stock prices.

5   My 13th birthday—already a landmark moment in a new teenager's life—fell on Sept. 13, 2001. It might be cliché, but that week was the first time I understood that there was a world beyond cafeteria pizza and dancing in my friend's room to the Spice Girls and that world wasn't necessarily friendly. Of course, everyone in the country has their own "where I was when I heard" story, but for those of us who were young teenagers or preteens, there is an additional layer to the discussion. To us, "Remember where you were?" also means, "Remember when you realized you couldn't really be a kid anymore?"

6   Of course, this isn't unique to today's young adults. Everyone, as the saying goes, has to grow up eventually. But I think it's safe to say that not since the JFK assassination has there been an event that so profoundly shattered our national sense of security and invincibility—and that feeling of vulnerability trickled right down to the middle schools. We may not have understood the international implications of what had happened, but we did realize that our parents couldn't protect us from everything anymore. At 12, that's a pretty staggering concept to absorb.

7   The 1990s were a great time to be a kid in America—the economy was booming, nobody was directly threatening us with nuclear obliteration, and Nickelodeon had maybe the best lineup in its history. This new-found nostalgia of the **aughts** seems less for an age than for an emotional state, when the most important decisions were about what flavor of Pop-Tarts to snack on, and the most **divisive** debate was over the superiority of the Backstreet Boys or N Sync, when troop surges and foreclosure were words we didn't understand because there was no need to know them. It's impossible to return to that era now, but for two hours in a darkened movie theater, it doesn't hurt to try. ◆

CONSIDERING THE ISSUES

1. Which movies, TV shows, and other entertainment have you noticed lately that is "catering to young adults who long to be irresponsible children again"?
2. Think about an event that changed your life forever. Consider how and why it changed you.

CRAFT AND CONTENT

1. Do you find it contradictory that the author claims her generation longs for its childhood and at the same time finds it too hard to grow up? Explain.
2. Southwick mentions that everyone has a "where I was when I heard" story about September 11, 2001. What is your story? How old were you on September 11, 2001, and how did the events that happened on that day influence your view of the world?

CRITICAL THINKING

1. Southwick's editorial reflects on the past. Consider your future. Where do you see yourself in 10 years, both professionally and financially?
2. Southwick observes, "We may not have understood the international implications of what had happened, but we did realize that our parents couldn't protect us from everything anymore. At 12, that's a pretty staggering concept to absorb." In your view, did the events of September 11 force you to grow up more quickly than you should have?
3. If you had come of age (graduated and gotten your first job perhaps) in 2000, do you think your professional and financial future would be better or worse than the future you face now? Explain.

WRITING ABOUT THE ISSUES

1. Watch Arcade Fire's music video "We Used to Wait" at www.thewildernessdowntown.com. After watching the video, write a letter to yourself in which you give advice to the younger you—for example, the three most valuable lessons you've learned since you left elementary school. What do you wish you could have known?
2. Locate the lyrics to Arcade Fire's song "We Used to Wait." Analyze the lyrics and then write an essay in which you interpret what the lyrics might mean both literally and figuratively.

How a New Jobless Era Will Transform America

Don Peck

Don Peck is a deputy managing editor of *The Atlantic*. In 2011, Liberty Media Corporation honored Peck with its second annual Media for Liberty Award. The award recognizes media contributions that examine the link between economic and political liberty. The following piece is an abridged article that appeared in the March 2010 issue of *The Atlantic*.

CONNECTING TO THE TOPIC

The great recession may be over, but this era of high joblessness is probably just beginning. Before it ends, it will likely change the life course and character of a generation of young adults. It will leave an indelible imprint on new graduates. How does the economy connect to our sense of achievement, self-image, and reaching true adulthood and self-sufficiency? Could the down economy warp our culture and change the character of our society?

WORDS IN CONTEXT

stagnant (1)   dull and sluggish, inactive (adj.)
chronic (4)   continuing for a long time (adj.)
noxious (4)   harmful, poisonous (adj.)
pervasive (5)   widespread, usually to ill effect (adj.)

1   How should we characterize the economic period we have now entered? After nearly two brutal years, the Great Recession appears to be over, at least technically. Yet a return to normalcy seems far off. By some measures, each recession since the 1980s has retreated more slowly than the one before it. In one sense, we never fully recovered from the last one, in 2001: the share of the civilian population with a job never returned to its previous peak before this downturn began, and incomes were **stagnant** throughout the decade. Still, the weakness that lingered through much of the 2000s shouldn't be confused with the trauma of the past two years, a trauma that will remain heavy for quite some time.

2   The unemployment rate hit 10 percent in October [2010] and there are good reasons to believe that by 2011, 2012, even 2014, it will have declined only a little. Late last year, the average duration of unemployment

surpassed six months, the first time that has happened since 1948, when the Bureau of Labor Statistics began tracking that number. As of this writing, for every open job in the U.S., six people are actively looking for work.

3   All of these figures understate the magnitude of the jobs crisis. The broadest measure of unemployment and underemployment (which includes people who want to work but have stopped actively searching for a job, along with those who want full-time jobs but can find only part-time work) reached 17.4 percent in October, which appears to be the highest figure since the 1930s. And for large swaths of society—young adults, men, minorities—that figure was much higher (among teenagers, for instance, even the narrowest measure of unemployment stood at roughly 27 percent). One recent survey showed that 44 percent of families had experienced a job loss, a reduction in hours, or a pay cut in the past year.

4   There is unemployment, a brief and relatively routine transitional state that results from the rise and fall of companies in any economy, and there is *unemployment*—**chronic**, all-consuming. The former is a necessary lubricant in any engine of economic growth. The latter is a pestilence that slowly eats away at people, families, and, if it spreads widely enough, the fabric of society. Indeed, history suggests that it is perhaps society's most **noxious** ill.

5   The worst effects of **pervasive** joblessness—on family, politics, society—take time to incubate, and they show themselves only slowly. But ultimately, they leave deep marks that endure long after boom times have returned. Some of these marks are just now becoming visible, and even if the economy magically and fully recovers tomorrow, new ones will continue to appear. The longer our economic slump lasts, the deeper they'll be.

The Recession and America's Youth

6 Over the past two generations, particularly among many college grads, the 20s have become a sort of netherworld between adolescence and adulthood. Job-switching is common, and with it, periods of voluntary, transitional unemployment. And as marriage and parenthood have receded farther into the future, the first years after college have become, arguably, more carefree. In this recession, the term *funemployment* has gained some currency among single 20-somethings, prompting a small raft of youth-culture stories in *The Los Angeles Times* and *San Francisco Weekly*, on Gawker, and in other venues.

7   Most of the people interviewed in these stories seem merely to be trying to stay positive and make the best of a bad situation. They note that it's a good time to reevaluate career choices; that since joblessness is now so common among their peers, it has lost much of its stigma; and that since they don't have mortgages or kids, they have flexibility, and in this

respect, they are lucky. All of this sounds sensible enough—it is intuitive to think that youth will be spared the worst of the recession's scars.

8   But in fact a whole generation of young adults is likely to see its life chances permanently diminished by this recession. Lisa Kahn, an economist at Yale, has studied the impact of recessions on the lifetime earnings of young workers. In one recent study, she followed the career paths of white men who graduated from college between 1979 and 1989. She found that, all else equal, for every one-percentage-point increase in the national unemployment rate, the starting income of new graduates fell by as much as 7 percent; the unluckiest graduates of the decade, who emerged into the teeth of the 1981–82 recession, made roughly 25 percent less in their first year than graduates who stepped into boom times.

9   But what's truly remarkable is the persistence of the earnings gap. Five, 10, 15 years after graduation, after untold promotions and career changes spanning booms and busts, the unlucky graduates never closed the gap. Seventeen years after graduation, those who had entered the workforce during inhospitable times were still earning 10 percent less on average than those who had emerged into a more bountiful climate. When you add up all the earnings losses over the years, Kahn says, it's as if the lucky graduates had been given a gift of about $100,000, adjusted for inflation, immediately upon graduation—or, alternatively, as if the unlucky ones had been saddled with a debt of the same size.

10   When Kahn looked more closely at the unlucky graduates at mid-career, she found some surprising characteristics. They were significantly less likely to work in professional occupations or other prestigious spheres. And they clung more tightly to their jobs: average job tenure was unusually long. People who entered the workforce during the recession "didn't switch jobs as much, and particularly for young workers, that's how you increase wages," Kahn told me. This behavior may have resulted from a lingering risk aversion, born of a tough start. But a lack of opportunities may have played a larger role, she said: when you're forced to start work in a particularly low-level job or unsexy career, it's easy for other employers to dismiss you as having low potential. Moving up, or moving on to something different and better, becomes more difficult.

11   "Graduates' first jobs have an inordinate impact on their career path and [lifetime earnings]," wrote Austan Goolsbee, now a member of President Obama's Council of Economic Advisers, in *The New York Times* in 2006. "People essentially cannot close the wage gap by working their way up the company hierarchy. While they may work their way up, the people who started above them do, too. They don't catch up." Recent research suggests that as much as two-thirds of real lifetime wage growth typically occurs in the first 10 years of a career. After that, as people start families and their career paths lengthen and solidify, jumping the tracks becomes harder.

12   Strong evidence suggests that people who don't find solid roots in the job market within a year or two have a particularly hard time righting themselves. In part, that's because many of them become different people. Krysia Mossakowski, a sociologist at the University of Miami, has found that in young adults, long bouts of unemployment provoke long-lasting changes in behavior and mental health. "Some people say, 'Oh, well, they're young, they're in and out of the workforce, so unemployment shouldn't matter much psychologically,'" Mossakowski told me. "But that isn't true."

13   Examining national longitudinal data, Mossakowski has found that people who were unemployed for long periods in their teens or early 20s are far more likely to develop a habit of heavy drinking (five or more drinks in one sitting) by the time they approach middle age. They are also more likely to develop depressive symptoms. Prior drinking behavior and psychological history do not explain these problems—they result from unemployment itself. And the problems are not limited to those who never find steady work; they show up quite strongly as well in people who are later working regularly.

14   Journalists and academics have thrown various labels at today's young adults, hoping one might stick—Generation Y, Generation Next, the Net Generation, the Millennials, the Echo Boomers. All of these efforts contain an element of folly; the diversity of character within a generation is always and infinitely larger than the gap between generations. Still, the cultural and economic environment in which each generation is incubated clearly matters. It is no coincidence that the members of Generation X—painted as cynical, apathetic slackers—first emerged into the workforce in the weak job market of the early-to-mid-1980s. Nor is it a coincidence that the early members of Generation Y—labeled as optimistic, rule-following achievers—came of age during the Internet boom of the late 1990s.

15   Many of today's young adults seem temperamentally unprepared for the circumstances in which they now find themselves. Jean Twenge, an associate professor of psychology at San Diego State University, has carefully compared the attitudes of today's young adults to those of previous generations when they were the same age. Using national survey data, she's found that to an unprecedented degree, people who graduated from high school in the 2000s dislike the idea of work for work's sake, and expect jobs and career to be tailored to their interests and lifestyle. Yet they also have much higher material expectations than previous generations, and believe financial success is extremely important. "There's this idea that, 'Yeah, I don't want to work, but I'm still going to get all the stuff I want,'" Twenge told me. "It's a generation in which every kid has been told, 'You can be anything you want. You're special.'"

16   In her 2006 book, *Generation Me*, Twenge notes that self-esteem in children began rising sharply around 1980, and hasn't stopped since. By 1999, according to one survey, 91 percent of teens described themselves

as responsible, 74 percent as physically attractive, and 79 percent as very intelligent. (More than 40 percent of teens also expected that they would be earning $75,000 a year or more by age 30; the median salary made by a 30-year-old was $27,000 that year.) Twenge attributes the shift to broad changes in parenting styles and teaching methods, in response to the growing belief that children should always feel good about themselves, no matter what. As the years have passed, efforts to boost self-esteem—and to decouple it from performance—have become widespread.

17   These efforts have succeeded in making today's youth more confident and individualistic. But that may not benefit them in adulthood, particularly in this economic environment. Twenge writes that "self-esteem without basis encourages laziness rather than hard work," and that "the ability to persevere and keep going" is "a much better predictor of life outcomes than self-esteem." She worries that many young people might be inclined to simply give up in this job market. "You'd think if people are more individualistic, they'd be more independent," she told me. "But it's not really true. There's an element of entitlement—they expect people to figure things out for them."

18   Some of these characteristics are worrisome, given a harsh economic environment that requires perseverance, adaptability, humility, and entrepreneurialism. Perhaps most worrisome, though, is [a sense of] fatalism and lack of agency in today's young adults. Trained throughout childhood to disconnect performance from reward, and told repeatedly that they are destined for great things, many are quick to place blame elsewhere when something goes wrong, and inclined to believe that bad situations will sort themselves out—or will be sorted out by parents or other helpers.

19   In his remarks at last year's commencement, in May, *The New York Times* reported, University of Connecticut President Michael Hogan addressed the phenomenon of students' turning down jobs, with no alternatives, because they didn't feel the jobs were good enough. "My first word of advice is this," he told the graduates. "Say yes. In fact, say yes as often as you can. Saying yes begins things. Saying yes is how things grow. Saying yes leads to new experiences, and new experiences will lead to knowledge and wisdom. *Yes* is for young people, and an attitude of yes is how you will be able to go forward in these uncertain times." ◆

CONSIDERING THE ISSUES

1. How has the economic down-turn changed our social view of unemployment?

2. What are your expectations for your life after college? Do you plan on living with your parents? Getting a permanent job? Living with a significant other? Starting a family? How do your plans connect to the economy?

CRAFT AND CONTENT

1. In paragraph 4, Peck provides two different definitions of the same word "unemployment." What distinctions does he make as he differentiates between two states? How does his reader understand that he is defining two different situations? Explain.
2. What support does Peck provide when he asserts that the longer college graduates go without finding a job, the more damaging it is to their long-term success? Evaluate his sources and determine if he provides enough evidence to support his alarming conclusion.

CRITICAL THINKING

1. What is "funemployment"? How have attitudes toward youth culture influenced the lifestyle choices of young adults? What influence, if any, has the current economy had on the lifestyle path of 20-somethings?
2. In what ways does the author believe that the self-esteem movement contributed to the challenges many college graduates and young adults face in today's job market? Do you agree with his viewpoint? Explain.

WRITING ABOUT THE ISSUES

1. Peck states that evidence suggests that graduates who don't find "solid roots" in the job market within two years have a particularly challenging time establishing their careers. What steps do you plan on taking following graduation to ensure that you set your career on the right track?
2. Write an essay in which you explore the long-term social implications of "delayed adulthood." How could extended adolescence impact the economy? Families? The job market? Education?
3. It seems that each generation believes that the generations that follow do not work hard enough or have poor work ethics. Speak to several people from different generations (20s, 40s, 60s) and ask them to recount their career track. What advice is useful today, and what do you think no longer applies, and why?

Blog Matters

A blog ("web log") is an online diary or commentary site that features regular entries that describe events, impressions, and viewpoints. Blogs may contain text, images, video, and often link to other websites, blogs, and online media. Most blogs allow readers to comment on the content of the post and respond to each other. As of September 2011, there were over 160 million public blogs in existence. While many blogs are maintained by individuals, some are run by journals, newspapers, and other media outlets. Remember that most blogs are not monitored for factual accuracy and often express the opinion and views of the "blogger" writing the content.

The blog below is by Kimberly Palmer, author of the new book *Generation Earn: The Young Professional's Guide to Spending, Investing, and Giving Back* (2010), who posted this entry on September 29, 2010. In this entry, she explains why some of the commonly held beliefs about recent college grads are simply not true.

5 Myths About Generation Debt

Kimberly Palmer
September 29, 2010

The term "generation debt" tends to get thrown around a lot when it comes to describing today's young professionals. Media pundits—especially older ones who have long paid off their own student loans—like to point out that we carry a lot of debt and spend more than our paychecks. But is that really true? Here are five myths—and truths—about our generation and money.

5. Myth: We're clueless about finances.

1   Truth: It turns out we know a lot—in some cases, more than our parents' generation. A survey by the online brokerage firm Scottrade found that the recession actually inspired 20-somethings to educate themselves about how the economy works as well as to learn more about their own personal financial situations.

2   In addition, a higher percentage of respondents said they're doing more research before investing relative to older groups. Scottrade reports that part of the reason we're excelling at managing our money is because we see it as fun, instead of a tedious obligation.

4. Myth: We're depressed about our financial future.

3   Truth: It's true, we've had it rough: We've experienced two recessions before we've even hit our career strides (first from the dot-com bust, then from the real estate implosion) and unemployment is highest among young adults—an astounding 37 percent of people between the ages of 18 to 29 are unemployed or out of the workforce.

4   But we still manage to stay upbeat about our futures, an essential skill if we're going to ride out these challenges. According to the Pew Research Center, only three in ten young people say they earn enough money to lead "the kind of life they want," while nine in ten say they believe they will be able to do so in the future. Only 76 percent of Gen Xers and 46 percent of Baby Boomers say the same thing.

3. Myth: We waste our money on frivolous purchases.

5   Truth: We care less, not more, about brand names and keeping up with the latest fashion compared to older generations. Surveys taken since the recession show that 20-somethings report caring less about following the latest trends and styles, preferring a newer, frugal mindset. A survey by TNS Retail Forward found that shoppers in their 20s and 30s were most likely to buy the least expensive versions of products. Part of that comes from the fact that we're savvy consumers—we grew up knowing how to use the Internet to find the best deal, and we don't hesitate to use it.

2. Myth: We earn less than our parents did at our age.

6   Truth: In many ways, we're the richest generation to have existed. Yes, we face a relatively high unemployment rate, but the jobs we do have come with record benefits—largely health insurance-related. Studies by the Federal Reserve Bank of Minneapolis show that after you adjust for inflation and benefits, median compensation rates have increased 28 percent since 1975.

7   That helps explain why a Pew survey—taken after the recession—found that 60 percent of respondents under the age of 40 say their standard of living is better than that of their parents at the same age. Just 15 percent said it was worse.

1. Myth: We deserve the name "generation debt" because we have so much of it.

8   Truth: Yes, many of us carry student loan debt. And some of us carry monster credit card debt. But we're not defined by it, because there's so much more on our minds. We want to own nice homes, feel financially successful, support our families, one day send our kids to college, and change the world at the same time. Although we may now have some money to invest, our goals involve far more than just becoming rich.

9   The financial crisis of 2008 dovetailed with a growing interest in sustainability, simplicity, and even frugality. Instead of living exclusively for our own pleasures, we have embraced a new level of social consciousness. We care about the environment, our cities, and social justice.

10   The bottom line? We don't need to resign ourselves to lives defined by debt. We can earn more, save more, and live more richly—largely because we've redefined what "rich" means.

RESPOND TO THE BLOG:

What do you think? Do you feel "defined" by your debt? Do you agree with Palmer that you just might be part of the richest generation? Why or why not?

Saving Yourself
Daniel Akst

Writer Daniel Akst is the author of several books including *We Have Met the Enemy* (2011) and *Wonder Boy* (1996). His essays have appeared in The *New York Times, Wall Street Journal, Los Angeles Times, Boston Globe, Slate* and other leading publications. This essay, abridged for space, can be read in its entirety in the summer 2009 issue of *Wilson Quarterly*.

CONNECTING WITH THE TOPIC ────────────

America's enduring love affair with big spending is fetching up against some unromantic realities. The spending of the Baby Boomers, coupled with the instant gratification demanded by Gen-Xers and Millennials, have created unheard of levels of personal debt. But a lifelong saver assures us that there are worse fates than socking it away for a rainy day. This generation of college graduates will be more frugal and live better, more thrifty lives. Writer Daniel Akst defines what it means to be thrifty and explains how thrift can be much sexier than the alternative—poverty. Has the time come to rethink our social perspective of thrift?

WORDS IN CONTEXT ────────────

connotations (1)   meanings (n.)
skinflint (1)   a miser, one who does not want to part with money (n.)
solvent (2)   financially stable (adj.)
temperance (3)   moderation (n.)
preternatural (3)   out of the ordinary (adj.)
arduous (4)   requiring a great deal of effort or strength (adj.)
unbridled (6)   unrestrained, uncontrolled (adj.)
catalyzed (6)   caused an action to begin (v.)
albeit (8)   although (conj.)
Karl Marx (9)   a philosopher who put forth the economic and sociopolitical view that capitalism creates class struggle and social unrest (n.)
inculcated (10)   taught a value, idea, or habit (v.)
repression (10)   held back, as in emotions, actions, or ideas (n.)
submergence (10)   suppression (n.)
primeval (10)   ancient (adj.)
utopianism (11)   belief in an impossibly ideal society (n.)
dubious (12)   suspicious, doubtful (adj.)
demotic (12)   common, everyday (adj.)
refusenik (15)   a person who refuses or declines something (n.)
consternation (16)   amazement or dismay that causes confusion (n.)

1   Thrift, supposedly, is back, implying, as the dictionary tells us, "using money and other resources carefully and not wastefully." Personally, I'm not certain that the resurrection of thrift—heralded on the covers of *Time* and *BusinessWeek,* among other places—is anything more than temporary. But as a lifelong cheapskate, I'm grateful that at least thrift no longer carries quite the musty and ungenerous **connotations** it once did. If we **skinflints** are the last ones to step out of the closet, it only means we can appreciate all the more heartily how nice it is to escape the smell of mothballs.

2   I'm talking here about real thrift, which for the most part involves *not spending money*. Real thrift, the skeptical, calculating kind that can make a difference between being **solvent** and not. The penny-pinching I'm talking about used to have a bad name indeed, in much the same way as "spinster" and "cardigan."

3   There was a time, of course, when thrift was in favor. It was practically a matter of life and death for the Puritans and a cornerstone of their work ethic, along with **temperance**, diligence, and piety. They excelled at deferring gratification, and it is one of the great ironies of American history that their **preternatural** self-discipline and industry launched us on the path to such unimaginable riches that thrift would be forgotten in the stampede to the mall. (On the other hand, if you have to be a victim of something, it might as well be your own success.)

4   Benjamin Franklin, who was hardly puritanical in any modern sense of the term, nonetheless embraced thrift and famously reminded us that "a penny saved is a penny earned" even before the advent of income taxes (which have made a penny saved worth *even more* than a penny earned). A relentless self-improver, Franklin as a young man "conceived the bold and **arduous** project of arriving at moral perfection," and as an aid in this venture developed a kind of moral spreadsheet, writing the days of the week across the top and listing 13 virtues along the side, so he could plot his failings by date and category in a grid. Frugality ("waste nothing") was number five on the list.

5   We have self-help gurus today, of course, and some of them even stress the connection between money and morals, but that's not why they are known or attended. We simply want the advantages of financial security and a higher standard of living. The reward for good financial management is a big house, a nice car—all the things that come from bad financial management, without the debt.

6   How did we get here? The transformation of thrift from a virtue into something verging on a social disorder occurred sometime between the 1880s and 1920s, when America transformed itself from a nation of want into one of, well, *wants*. **Unbridled** economic growth (fueled by decades of self-restraint and invested savings) undermined the Protestant ethos of self-denial and reticence, while the rising merchant class did its best to change the country's long-ingrained aversion to luxury. Consumer credit became more widely available, and religious denominations laid off the hellfire and brimstone in favor of a therapeutic approach to happiness in the present. Vast new big-city "department stores" leveled the full force of their merchandising grandeur at women, who understandably preferred to purchase items they had once laboriously made. **Catalyzed** by mass communications (which made possible the stimulation of mass desire through advertising) and the rise of an urbanized middle class, consumerism exploded.

7   The loud noise caught the attention of two important social theorists, one of them famous and the other largely forgotten. It's yet another irony in the saga of America's love/hate relationship with thrift that we live by the precepts of the thinker whose name hardly anyone remembers.

8   First, the one you may know about. Thorstein Veblen, the Norwegian-American economist (he died in 1929, shortly before the great crash that might have brought him grim satisfaction), is best known today for his theory of conspicuous consumption, which argued that a lot of spending is just a wasteful attempt to impress. In effect, Veblen explained consumerism in terms of status and display, bringing evolutionary ideas to bear on economics and consumer behavior to powerful effect. Reading Veblen is a little like reading Freud or Darwin, **albeit** on a smaller scale: Do so and you'll never look at the world in quite the same way again.

9   There was another voice heard back when thrift was in its death throes—that of Simon Patten (1852–1922), like Veblen a maladjusted economist who had strong ideas about spending. Patten can seem naive and even crass to us today, for he used his pulpit at the University of Pennsylvania's Wharton School to advocate the very thing that **Karl Marx** feared: that business and consumer spending should sweep away all the old arrangements and remake the world according to the doctrine of plenty. And he imagined a large role for economists in the running of it.

10   Unlike Veblen, Patten came on the scene not to praise thrift but to bury it. The old values that "**inculcated** a spirit of resignation" and "emphasized the **repression** of wants" must be abandoned, Patten argued, adding, "The principle of sacrifice continues to be exalted by moralists at the very time when the social structure is being changed by the slow **submergence** of the **primeval** world, and the appearance of a land of unmeasured resources with a hoard of mobilized wealth."

11   In important ways Patten and Veblen were both right about consumerism, but of the two Patten was the true radical. Beside his starry-eyed **utopianism** Veblen's sour conservatism is plain to see. As things turned out, it's Patten's world we live in, even if we use the language of Veblen to understand it.

12   Patten and Veblen both died in the 1920s, a decade when affluence, technology, and changing social mores joined forces to drive a stake through the heart of pecuniary restraint. Since then, modern America has effectively banished thrift by foisting on the world those four horsemen of the financial apocalypse: the automobile, the television, the credit card, and the shopping cart. Besides costing money to buy and operate, cars opened up the landscape so that more Americans could have bigger houses on bigger lots. To fill them up, people enjoyed the **dubious** guidance of television, which helped them figure out what they should want. Credit cards enabled us to conjure money on the spot to pay for stuff. And the shopping cart, unthinkable in traditional department stores but

indispensable in their **demotic** successors—Wal-Mart and Target—gave Americans a way to get all that booty out to the automobile, which they could use to drive it home.

13   After the hardships of the Great Depression and the rationing and other deprivations of World War II (during which Americans saved roughly a quarter of their income), nobody was too focused on thrift, and I can't say I blame them. Besides, spending stimulated the economy, which was something like a patriotic duty.

14   Unfortunately, for a people who love money, we've become very good at making it disappear, a task to which we've brought characteristic ingenuity and verve. Reckless overspending was until recently a course open to practically every American, just like reckless investing. And suddenly we were all Emma Bovary, bent on financial suicide. "It is because she feels that society is fettering her imagination, her body, her dreams, her appetites," Mario Vargas Llosa once wrote, "that Emma suffers, commits adultery, lies, steals, and in the end kills herself."

15   He might well have been describing America, circa 2007. Four-dollar coffee drinks? Fourteen-dollar cocktails? Bottled water from Fiji, priced higher than gasoline? You've got to be kidding. Now that it's safe to come clean, I will confess to having been a bit of a **refusenik** about all this for most of my, er, 39 years on this earth. Every stick of furniture in my house is secondhand, as are many of my family's clothes, computers, bicycles, books, pieces of art, and other items. We've mostly had used cars, and we still have the new ones we bought in a single mad burst in 2001. The funny thing is, it's amazing what a nice life you can have with a middle-class income and a frugal attitude about money.

16   More people are waking up to this particular old-time religion. Since early 2008 personal saving has crept back up a few percentage points above zero (much to the **consternation** of stimulus-minded economists), and some long-term trends are likely to reinforce today's renewed interest in controlling spending.

17   It helps that conspicuous consumption, like tobacco, has fallen into social disrepute, a change that removes some of the pressure felt by many families to keep up with the Joneses (who may well have been foreclosed by now). Veblen was right that much spending is meant to be conspicuous, and if the display incentives surrounding consumption have changed, so will consumption.

18   Rising environmental consciousness ought to be a further spur to thrift, for what could possibly be greener—or more demonstrative of piety—than eschewing wasteful consumption? Although cutting global greenhouse emissions by building new power plants and the like can be expensive, many of the ways individuals can make a difference will actually put money in your pocket: eating less red meat, driving a fuel-efficient car, and taking fewer planet-warming plane trips, to name a few.

The same goes for buying less stuff; making do with what you have or going secondhand uses fewer resources and of course reduces spending as well. A rising scavenger subculture threatens to erase the stigma that was associated with "garbage picking" when I was a kid, transforming shame into virtue. Like so many other things, this "freecycling" is assisted by Craigslist.

19   You'll need to consider garbage picking now and then because in the years ahead we'll have to pay not only for our individual and collective overspending in the boom years, but also for our gigantic national outlays during the ensuing crash to bail out banks, insurers, and automakers and stimulate the economy to stave off a depression. We've been paying for all this by borrowing, so expect to pay higher taxes to retire these debts. Speaking of retirement, have I mentioned Social Security and Medicare? Maybe I shouldn't.

20   Fortunately, thrift is far from the worst thing we can have thrust upon us. To be thrifty, after all, is to save, and to save is not only to keep but to rescue. Thrift is thus a way to redeem yourself not just from the unsexy bondage of indebtedness but also from subjugation to people and efforts that are meaningless to you, or worse. Debt means staying in a pointless job, failing to support needy people or worthwhile causes, accepting the strings that come with dependence, and gritting your teeth when your boss asks you to do something unethical (instead of saying "drop dead"). Ultimately, thrift delivers not just freedom but salvation. ◆

CONSIDERING THE ISSUES

1. In this essay, Daniel Akst describes "spenders" and "savers." Which are you and why? Would you like to be a better saver? Or do you think there is something stingy about saving?

2. What cultural influences drive our spending habits? How does where we live and with whom contribute to our ideas of thrift? Explain.

CRAFT AND CONTENT

1. What assumptions does Daniel Akst make about his readers? Would you consider yourself Akst's target audience? For example, what do you need to know in order to understand Akst's historical references? What about his vocabulary? Explain.

2. Akst uses many synonyms in his essay to define thrift and thrifty. Which other words does he use in its place? What words have more negative meanings, and which ones have a more positive meaning?

CRITICAL THINKING

1. What is thrift? What associations does the word have for you? Is it negative, positive, or neutral? Is being thrifty "un-American"? Why has it gained a negative connotation?
2. The author states that going green is equal to becoming thrifty. What are some examples he gives that prove his point? Besides the examples that Akst lists in his essay, which other ways can leaving a smaller carbon footprint actually put money in your pocket?
3. Do you agree with Akst's thesis: being thrifty is more honorable and intelligent than being a spendthrift? Is there a middle ground? Explain.

WRITING ABOUT THE ISSUES

1. According to Akst, you can have a "nice life" with a middle-class income and a thrifty attitude about money. Provide an outline of your definition of a "nice life." Based on your viewpoint, do you agree that a nice life can be had this way? Why or why not?
2. Akst recounts the role of thrift in his own life, as a middle-aged writer who admits he is a "skinflint." Write an essay in which you explore the concept of thrift from the perspective of a college student. What role, if any, does it play in your life and in the lives of your peers? It is as important today as it was 50 years ago? Does it run counter to the way you wish to live your life? Why or why not? If you are already thrifty, explain whether you are so because of respect for the idea, or because of necessity.

VISUAL CONNECTIONS

Students Making Skewed Judgments About College Costs

Student Poll is a collaboration between the College Board and Art & Science Group, LLC that administers and publishes the results from national surveys measuring the opinions, perceptions, and behavior of college-bound high school students and their parents. *Student Poll* shares this information with college and university senior leaders and enrollment officers to provide insights into the thinking of college-bound students.

CONNECTING WITH THE TOPIC

According to recent research by *Student Poll*, many students and their parents may be overestimating how much they are likely to receive in financial aid, particularly merit aid awarded on the basis of academic credentials or special talents. Other findings suggest that, to some degree, students and their families are engaged in a bit of wishful thinking when it comes to how they will finance a college education. For example, students' unrealistic expectations about paying for college are evident in the fact that across all SAT score ranges, a majority of students assume they will receive merit-based financial aid based on their academic abilities—even those with the lowest SAT scores. This wishful thinking also appears to be reflected in the fact that students generously estimate that grants and scholarships are likely to cover more than one-third of their college education when the national average is only around 15 percent of total college costs covered by grants and scholarships.

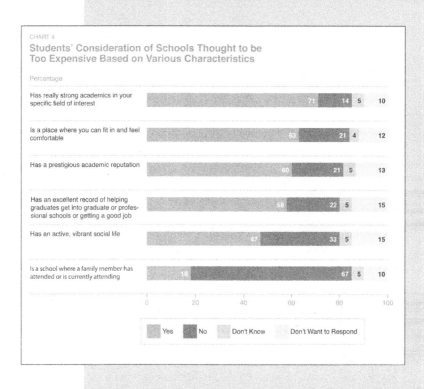

CHART 4

Students' Consideration of Schools Thought to be Too Expensive Based on Various Characteristics

Percentage

Has really strong academics in your specific field of interest — 71 | 14 | 5 | 10

Is a place where you can fit in and feel comfortable — 63 | 21 | 4 | 12

Has a prestigious academic reputation — 60 | 21 | 5 | 13

Has an excellent record of helping graduates get into graduate or professional schools or getting a good job — 58 | 22 | 5 | 15

Has an active, vibrant social life — 47 | 33 | 5 | 15

Is a school where a family member has attended or is currently attending — 18 | 67 | 5 | 10

0   20   40   60   80   100

Yes   No   Don't Know   Don't Want to Respond

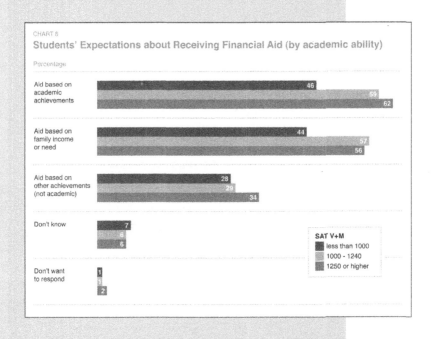

CHART 6

Students' Expectations about Receiving Financial Aid (by academic ability)

Percentage

Aid based on academic achievements
46
59
62

Aid based on family income or need
44
57
56

Aid based on other achievements (not academic)
28
29
34

Don't know
7
6
6

Don't want to respond
1
1
2

SAT V+M
less than 1000
1000 - 1240
1250 or higher

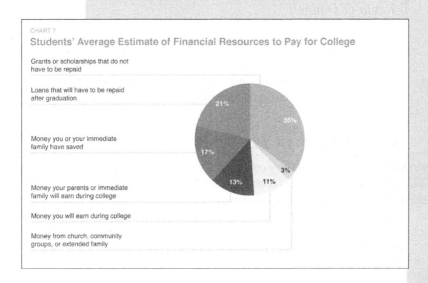

CHART 7

Students' Average Estimate of Financial Resources to Pay for College

Grants or scholarships that do not
have to be repaid

Loans that will have to be repaid
after graduation

Money you or your immediate
family have saved

Money your parents or immediate
family will earn during college

Money you will earn during college

Money from church, community
groups, or extended family

CRITICAL THINKING

1. What presumptions do many students make when planning how much college will cost them? What did you presume when making your own plans?
2. According to the survey, students overestimate how much aid they will receive and not need to pay back. Did you make similar predictions? If you are planning your college financial debt, are you banking on scholarships and grants? Explain.
3. Based on the information in these charts, and others you find online at the *Student Poll* website, what recommendations would you give high-school seniors planning for college?

Why Won't Anyone Give Me a Credit Card?

Kevin O'Donnell

Kevin O'Donnell is an assistant editor at *Rolling Stone* magazine, where he covers music, television, and pop culture. He also contributes regular reviews and features on books and pop music to *The Washington Post* and *The Village Voice*. This essay appeared in *Slate* on September 18, 2009.

CONNECTING WITH THE TOPIC

Many college students carry credit card debt. For many years, credit card companies were falling over themselves trying to entice college students to sign on the dotted line, much to the chagrin of credit counselors and parents alike. While carrying a lot of credit card debt is never a good idea, it turns out that college may be the best time to start building your credit profile. As 27-year-old Kevin O'Donnell explains, he doesn't have bad credit, but the companies keep turning him down. Why the change of heart?

WORDS IN CONTEXT

dubious (1)   suspicious, doubtful (adj.)
precipitously (3)   steeply (adv.)
paradoxical (5)   seemingly contradictory (adj.)
prudence (6)   caution, exercising restraint (n.)

1 **W**hile picking up a new shirt at J.Crew a few months ago, I asked about opening one of those store credit cards—you know, the ones that give you a discount on the first purchase. I filled out the paperwork, and the cashier phoned the lending bank and gave them my information. "You'll hear if you've been approved by mail in a few days," he said. A few weeks later, I got a letter from World Financial Network National Bank (how **dubious** does that sound?) saying they would not be able to extend me a line of credit.

2 The J.Crew card was the fourth one I'd applied for over the past year, and it was my third rejection. I am a 27-year-old professional with a full-time job, no mortgage, no children, and no student loans. With the exception of one outstanding dental bill, I have absolutely no debt. I pay my bills on time; I never miss rent. I should be an ideal candidate for a credit card, right? Not so.

3   With the economy in the dumps, it's harder than ever to get a card. The amount of credit card offers mailed to U.S. households has dropped **precipitously** in 2009, from an estimated 1.13 billion in the first fiscal quarter of 2008 to 372.4 million in the same period this year. Why the decline in junk mail? Last month, credit card default rates reached their highest point since the recession began. Bank of America claimed its rate hit 14.54 percent, while Citigroup (which issues MasterCard) saw its default rate go from 10.03 percent to 12.14 percent. American Express, however, reported a slight decrease—from 8.9 percent to 8.4 percent— in default rates. Perhaps that decline is related to AmEx offering certain customers a $300 bribe to *close* their accounts.

4   Well, that explains why my American Express application got rejected. But why, despite my decent financial record, am I a particularly bad candidate for a credit card? I've got no credit history. Typically, the best time to get your first credit card is in college, when banks litter campuses with offers. One study estimated that students receive 25 to 50 applications per semester. I was always wary of getting a credit card as an undergrad. I was living hand-to-mouth, and it was always easy enough to pick up a bar tab with a debit card. What I didn't realize was that I'd very soon need a credit card to live. If I'm doomed to a life without plastic, what am I going to do if I want to buy a house or lease a car? There are certain things you can't put on a debit card.

5   My quest for credit is a **paradoxical** one: How can I establish a credit history when banks won't let me create one in the first place? When my American Express, MasterCard, and Continental Chase Rewards applications were denied, I did what friends and relatives advised—try to take out a card with a department store, hence the J.Crew Card. It turns out they gave me bad advice—J.Crew, just like everybody else I had tried before, requires applicants to have a prior credit history. Gail Cunningham, the spokeswoman for the National Foundation for Credit Counseling, told me that, historically, gas cards and department store cards have been relatively easy to get because the companies' "risk is pretty small—how much can you charge at the filling station?" But in this time of economic decline, even those once-freewheeling retailers are cutting back on the number of applications they approve. Standard & Poor's recently reported that U.S. retail outlets that extend credit claimed losses of 12.2 percent in May, the highest since S&P started tracking such data in January 2000.

6   So what *should* I do to get a credit card? I could just keep filling out applications—and I'd probably have a better chance with smaller community banks, as they didn't suffer the financial blows that the larger institutions did. But sending in loads of applications will probably hurt me in the end. When lenders review applicants, they look at five factors: identification, account history, public records (bankruptcy filings, court records of

tax liens), consumer statements (challenges to the status of an account with a lender), and inquiries. That last item is the most crucial for those of us with no credit: It shows how many times lenders have requested to review an applicant's credit history. The more times that information has been reviewed (and rejected), the more suspicious you look as an applicant. Since I have no credit history, I basically don't exist to these lenders—and since I've only started applying for credit in earnest since the start of the credit crunch, I pose more of a gamble to these banks, who aren't willing to take risks on applicants who can't prove their fiscal **prudence**.

7   As a last resort, I went to a branch of Chase Bank, the place that happily accepts my twice-monthly direct deposits. "You don't have credit?" the customer service rep asked. "Well, it's going to be very hard to get [a card]." I had heard about secured credit cards, which require you to put up cash as collateral—think of it as a credit card with training wheels. When I asked the financial adviser about that option, she laughed— laughed!—and said Chase didn't offer those. It was like that scene in *Pee-wee's Big Adventure*, when Pee-wee asks to see the basement of the Alamo and gets heckled off the grounds by the tour guide.

8   My quest for credit does have a happy ending, however. Bank of America actually does offer one of those secured credit cards, the BankAmericard Visa Secured Card. Mine just arrived three weeks ago. First purchase? A hotel stay for a friend's wedding out of town. (My balance is almost maxed out for the month, alas.) It will take about a year before I've proven my worth and can get those ridiculous credit-card training wheels removed—my account will be evaluated periodically and, provided I'm in good standing, my credit score will increase. And you know what? If my mailbox suddenly becomes flooded with offers, I promise I won't complain. ◆

CONSIDERING THE ISSUES

1. Do you have a credit card? If so, did you get it through a campus offer? Through a department store? How old were you when you got your first card, and how well have you managed your credit profile?

2. O'Donnell complains that no one will offer him a credit card. Why might credit card companies be eager to offer college students cards while they are still in school, but reluctant once these students graduate?

CRAFT AND CONTENT

1. Evaluate O'Donnell's tone in this essay. Can you relate to his story and to him as a person? Why or why not?

2. O'Donnell notes that when he asks about a secured credit card at Chase Bank, he leaves feeling like Pee-Wee Herman. What do you need to know in order to understand this reference? Did you understand it? Can you understand his feelings if you don't know about this episode in *Pee-Wee's Big Adventure*?

CRITICAL THINKING

1. Some students are given credit cards by their parents "for emergencies." Do you think this is a good idea? If you have such an arrangement, have you ever used your card for something other than an emergency? What constituted an "emergency"?
2. O'Donnell is very eager to get a credit card. Why does he want one? Is it a marker of adult life? Simply a way of life? Can you survive in this world without credit cards and the debt that comes with them? Explain.

WRITING ABOUT THE ISSUES

1. O'Donnell notes that he avoided credit cards in college because he knew they would be too easy for him to abuse. Write about a time when you had to make a personal choice that involved getting into, or staying out of, debt. Describe the circumstances and your feelings about the incident.

Recession Generation

Rana Foroohar

Rana Foroohar is an assistant managing editor for *TIME* magazine. Previously, she served as the deputy editor in charge of international business and economics coverage for *Newsweek*. She has also worked as a general editor at *Newsweek*, a reporter for *Forbes* magazine, and as a writer and editor at various other national and international publications. This essay appeared in *Newsweek*, on January 9, 2010.

CONNECTING TO THE TOPIC

In a reversal of fortune, the next generation may start to behave more like their great grandparents who lived through the Great Depression—frugal and thrifty. Those entering the workforce now will likely make less and save more—not just in the short term but for the rest of their lives. But could this change in our spending habits end up being for the best? Or are we just trying to make the best of a bad situation?

WORDS IN CONTEXT

milieu (1)   an environment, setting, place (n.)
seismic (1)   earthshaking (adj.)
spate (2)   an outpouring, rush, flood (n.)
paradoxically (2)   seemingly contradictory but nonetheless true (adv.)
grapple (2)   to struggle with (v.)
skew (2)   to distort (v.)
zeitgeist (2)   the spirit of the time; the characteristic of a period or generation (n.)
psyches (3)   the spirit or soul; the center of thought (n.)
frugality (3)   the act of spending little; being thrifty (n.)
specter (4)   a haunting or disturbing image or prospect (n.)
vulnerable (7)   susceptible to physical or emotional injury; weak (adj.)
populist demagogues (7)   persons with political cunning and ruthless ambition (n.)
exacerbated (7)   aggravate; intensify (v.)
forestall (9)   to delay, hinder, or prevent (v.)
depreciated (10)   lessened the price or value of (v.)
subprime derivatives (11)   securities whose values are tied to exotic high interest loans (n.)

1   We all know the type of person who came of age in the Great Depression. They are the grandmothers and grandfathers who can't use a tea bag too many times, yet are enjoying comfortable retirements in warm climates. And we know what the children of the 1950s are all about. They are the optimistic boomers who embodied an age of continual upward mobility and possibility. They have often spent more than they earned, because for them it has been a truism that times can only get better. It's no accident that the psychology of entire generations is shaped by the **milieu** in which they grew up; economic research tells us that our lifelong behaviors are determined in large part by the **seismic** events—good or bad—of our youth. So, given that we have just experienced the worst economic period in 70 years, it's no surprise that people have begun to wonder what sort of consumers, investors, and citizens will be bred by the Great Recession. Will there be, in effect, a "Generation Recession" of young people whose behaviors will be permanently shaped by the downturn?

2   Some optimists—pointing to a recent **spate** of positive economic data, including increases in car sales, upticks in factory production, and a robust stock market, say no: the downturn simply hasn't been bad enough,

for long enough, to create the next Depression generation. Yet there is powerful evidence that belies this argument; a National Bureau of Economic Research (NBER) paper released this past September looking at data from 1972 to 2006 shows that even one really tough year experienced in early adulthood is enough to fundamentally change people's core values and behaviors. Meanwhile, there's an entire body of research to show that recession babies not only invest more conservatively, they tend to make less money, choose safer jobs, and believe in wealth redistribution and more government intervention. Yet **paradoxically**, they are also more cynical about public institutions and, arguably, about life, embracing the European notion that success is more about luck than effort. To the extent that they **grapple** with unemployment, they are more likely to be more depressed and disconnected from their communities. Politically, they can **skew** either left or right, depending on the cultural **zeitgeist** and the leaders who seize the moment. Economic downturns, after all, not only created the New Deal, but also the Third Reich.

3   We have now technically emerged from recession. But there's a broad feeling that Americans' **psyches** and behaviors will be somehow permanently altered by the crisis. There's now a booming cottage industry among consultants and investment managers to describe and capitalize on "the New Normal," which will likely be the opposite of the hypercapitalist market culture of the past 25 years. That moment was perhaps most eloquently captured by former Clinton labor secretary Robert Reich in his 2007 book, *Supercapitali*sm, and it's fitting that he is now working on a book title*d Aftersho*ck. "Every time we've had a major downturn, there have been predictions that Americans will permanently change their ways and embrace **frugality**," says Reich, now a professor at the University of California, Berkeley. "Since World War II, it hasn't happened." Yet Reich and many other respected academics, economists, and investors—from George Soros to Pimco's Bill Gross to Goldman Sachs's chief economist Jim O'Neill—say that it will happen this time, not only because of the megashock of the financial crisis, but also because the global landscape has simply shifted in such a way that the American consumer will no longer be the single dominant force in the world, even if the U.S. economy continues to recover. Rather, the key emerging markets (read: China, India, Brazil, and others) will continue to emerge and become more powerful; the dollar will continue to weaken; American labor will continue to face more and more competition from abroad; and, thanks to a new era of big government, reregulation, and (possibly) protectionism, money flows will stay tight. Throw in the probable rise in inflation and you've got an inevitably slower-growth future in which Americans will also have to come to grips with average unemployment levels that will likely stay much higher than they've been in decades.

4   Unemployment and the **specter** of instability it creates will really shape the behavior of Generation Recession. A weaker dollar will make all Americans feel poorer by raising the cost of goods, but the young generation graduating and going to work now may actually end up poorer in real terms. Unemployment among 20- to 24-year-olds in the U.S. is more than 15 percent, compared with the nationwide average of 10 percent, and statistics show that for every percentage point in higher unemployment, new graduates take a 6 percent pay cut—an effect that lasts for decades. Skills loss could be a huge issue, too, especially because the average duration of unemployment has increased. Although wages in the U.S. have been relatively flat since the 1970s, Generation Recession may be the first in 30 years to see theirs actually fall.

5   The behavioral shifts resulting from the New Normal have, of course, already begun. The personal savings rate has more than quadrupled from its 2008 low to the current rate of 4.5 percent. Research done by AlixPartners found that Americans don't want to stop there, but hope to save 15 percent of their income going forward (they won't be able to, but the desire itself speaks volumes about their sense of insecurity about the future—particularly since the number has continued to rise even as the economy has improved). Half of those surveyed by AlixPartners have stopped investing in the markets altogether, and the majority say they won't put money into stocks for another three years; 43 percent don't expect the economy to ever recover to pre-recession levels.

6   The disconnect between these sorts of poll results and the recently improving economic data underscores another megatrend that Generation Recession will have to deal with: the growing divide between the fortunes of big American firms and the average American worker. Markets may be up, yet unemployment, while slightly down, is still at its highest level in decades, and even the most bullish economists believe it will stay higher than average for years to come. Large U.S. firms are well into the black, in part because of the labor-cost savings they've enjoyed from IT improvements and offshoring to cut expensive U.S. jobs, yet the small- and medium-size firms that generate the majority of new jobs at home have been hurt most by the financial crisis as their lines of credit have dried up. "We are in a very unique period, in which we're seeing the biggest disconnection between financial capitalism and the real economy since modern economies began in the 19th century," says Nobel laureate and Columbia economics professor Edmund Phelps, who runs the university's Center on Capitalism and Society. "That's not to say that banks don't fund some useful projects like wind farms or whatever, but increasingly they're existing in a virtual sphere in which they are more interested in funding each other, and developing complex securities, than in funding real businesses."

7   This division between capital and labor and the permanently high unemployment that it seems to encourage not only depresses wages, it

depresses people; a large body of research shows they tend to withdraw from their communities and societies after being laid off (their spooked neighbors, encouraged to work ever harder, do too). Parental unemployment has huge negative consequences for children, making them more likely to fall behind in school, repeat grades, and exhibit anxiety disorders. During the Great Depression, such negative social consequences were partly buffered by a stronger civil society—attendance at churches, clubs, and community centers was greater than now. The worry today, say Reich, Soros, and political scientists such as Harvard's Robert Putnam, is that fearful, **vulnerable** people will become more easy prey for ugly class politics, being drawn, as Reich puts it, to "**populist demagogues** on either side of the political spectrum." Certainly during this recession there has been sniping at the usual targets of free trade and immigration. Many experts worry about the current trade and currency squabbles between the U.S. and China, which could easily spiral into the sort of protectionism that **exacerbated** the Great Depression. There could also be future political wars along demographic lines, as boomers worried about health care and Social Security fight for a shrinking slice of the public pie with younger people demanding more money for education and job training.

8   The situation could get even uglier if, as many predict, a depressed post-crisis landscape forces Americans to let go of the mythology of upward mobility. As Brookings fellows Isabel Sawhill and Ron Haskins point out in their new book, *Creating an Opportunity Society,* this myth hasn't been true for some time: by international standards, intergenerational social mobility in the U.S. has been falling since the 1970s, and is lower than in countries such as Britain, Sweden, and Denmark. As everyone from de Tocqueville to the producers of *MTV Cribs* has observed, Americans generally have a high tolerance for inequality. Yet that tolerance may wane as we enter a new age in which young graduates can't expect to do better than their parents—and one in which Wall Street is perceived as being able to continue business as usual while Main Street struggles. "Americans are OK with inequality," says Reich, who believes we are at a tipping point, "as long as they feel the system isn't rigged."

9   Unfortunately that feeling seems to be associated not only with this past year's massive bailouts and halfhearted efforts to regulate finance, but with recession itself. The NBER study examining the attitudes of people ages 18 to 25 who began their adulthood in economic downturns from 1972 onward found that they all tend to believe that success in life depends more on luck than on effort, and they have less trust in public institutions. This is an unfortunate attitude to breed in a generation that will undoubtedly have to live in an age of bigger governments working with more powerful international public institutions to **forestall** future financial and environmental disasters. It also has real-world economic implications. As Paola Giuliano, a professor at UCLA's Anderson School of

Management and one of the authors of the study, notes, "People who buy into the idea of luck over effort tend to work less hard, and that lowers productivity, which of course can lower economic growth." Indeed, this may go some way toward explaining the often mysterious growth edge that "can-do" Americans have long enjoyed over "yes, but" Europeans, who tend to mock such Type A behavior. Whether Americans will eventually follow them is an interesting question: the Conference Board recently released numbers showing that U.S. job satisfaction is at its lowest level in two decades.

10   All this said, there are some glimmers of hope in the New Normal. For starters, a weakening dollar and huge productivity gains made in the past year could end up being a salvation for U.S. manufacturing. McKinsey estimates the U.S. could create 1 million jobs if the dollar **depreciated** by just 10 percent. Indeed, Global Insight chief economist Nariman Behravesh believes that American exports will rise by 11 percent a year between 2010 and 2013, compared with just 7 percent in Germany. Smart investors like Warren Buffett have bought into the vision: his $26 billion bet on the Burlington Northern Santa Fe rail line is clearly a gamble that in the New Normal more American workers will be holding wrenches and loading cargo (from solar panels to bags of grain) onto trains, à la the post-Depression generation, rather than fiddling with BlackBerrys.

11   And, if the current trend lines continue, Generation Recession may mirror Generation Depression in more profound ways. For example, more talented graduates may choose public service over the private sector, not least because then, as now, that's where the jobs will be. Happiness research shows that fewer choices tend to be more satisfying than endless ones. Just as our tea-bag-saving grandparents seemed to do fine with less, so might the children of this downturn. A number of consultancies, like BCG, have released studies showing that post-crisis, consumers are putting a greater value on time spent with family and friends than on money (a good thing when there's little of the latter around). There's also a glimmer of possibility that hard times might make us nicer to each other. Kathleen Vohs, a consumer psychologist at the University of Minnesota, has shown that simply thinking about money made subjects less sensitive to pain, and less likely to help each other or want to connect with strangers. Perhaps rather than stepping over each other, 1980s style, on the climb to the top, we will stop to lend a hand. Certainly, we'll be more wary of falling down the ladder of life, and thus more empathetic, than our predecessors were. Generation Depression never stopped saving, and couldn't have conceived of buying into interest-only mortgages or flat-screen televisions on credit. It's likely that the generation coming of age today will also realize that things that seem too good to be true—from jobs that come with free lattes and signing bonuses to **subprime derivatives**—probably are. ◆

CONSIDERING THE ISSUES

1. Do you embrace the European idea that success is more about luck than effort? Explain your answer through specific personal examples.
2. If the economic climate is tough when you graduate, what is the most menial job that you would be willing to take to ensure that you are working? If times are stable, what would you consider as your dream job?

CRAFT AND CONTENT

1. Explain what the term "Generation Recession" means. How would you feel if your generation was referred to as "Generation Recession"?
2. Foroohar gives the reader "some glimmers of hope" about growing up in the "Recession Generation." According to the author, what are the positive aspects that may come out of living in a time of national financial instability?

CRITICAL THINKING

1. The author asserts that an economic downturn can create the New Deal, or on the other extreme, the Third Reich. Explain what the author means by this.
2. Would you consider yourself frugal? How difficult would it be for you to "embrace frugality"? Explain.
3. According to the National Bureau of Economic Research, having even one "really tough year" financially can change someone's "core values and behaviors." Have you or your parents or anyone you know ever had a really tough financial year, and if so, did you see any remarkable changes in core values or behaviors? Explain. If not, explain why not.

WRITING ABOUT THE ISSUES

1. Write an essay declaring if you are optimistic or pessimistic about your financial future, that is, if you have, or have not, given up on the "mythology of upward mobility." Use research and concrete examples to prove your reasoning.
2. Interview a parent, grandparent, guardian, campus staff member, or other adult about his or her own personal job satisfaction. Ask 10 questions on topics such as career-path chosen, favorite and least favorite jobs, job satisfaction or dissatisfaction over the years, and outlook on future employment. Record the answers in writing and write an essay exploring the idea that successful careers are the result of luck or hard work.

TOPICAL CONNECTIONS

GROUP PROJECTS

1. Research recent articles on the current financial crisis. Have things improved since the articles in this chapter were written? Based on your research and the information in this chapter, prepare a summary with your group in which you forecast what your classmate's economic future might look like over the next 5 to 10 years.

2. The term "generation debt" has been used to describe postmillennial youth. Is this an appropriate title for this generation? Discuss this phrase as a group and explain why it is or is not appropriate.

WEB PROJECTS

1. Learn more about the history of credit cards at www.PBS.org— *The Secret History of the Credit Card*. Based on what you learn from the Frontline documentary (you can watch the entire episode online), write an essay in which you explore the ethics of credit card marketing.

2. Several authors in this section refer to parents or grandparents who came of age during the Great Depression, using them as examples of a time when people lived more financially responsible lives. Research the social impact of the Great Depression. What are the merits, if any, of thrift? What role does it play in our social consciousness? As America once again faces the most challenging economic climate since the Great Depression, how might your generation measure up?

FOR FURTHER INQUIRY

1. Watch Danny Schechter's documentary *In Debt We Trust* (see http://www.indebtwetrust.org). Write a synopsis of the film and explain whether you agree or disagree with the following review and why: "Schechter's film is a compelling chronicle of how we got in over our heads . . . it should be required viewing for all high school and college students . . ."(Erica Freudenberger, *Wood Stock Times*, July 27, 2006).

2. Former United States Comptroller General David Walker recently compared the United States today to Rome before its fall. Research the fall of Rome. While the ancient world is very different from our modern one, what cultural similarities exist? What might we learn from history?

10 What Does It Mean to Be "Green"?

The issues of climate change and our impact on the environment are inspiring broad changes in our thinking and behaviors in the United States and abroad. From recycling programs in kindergarten classrooms to Fortune 500 companies constructing "green" buildings that meet rigorous environmental standards, it seems that everyone is aware of the importance of living more conscientiously.

Living green may require some sacrifices, but most people recognize the long-term benefits. Moreover, living green dovetails with the current economic climate as well. As noted by several writers in Chapter 9, thrift is in. Fewer people think that the "disposable" lifestyle is desirable. More than ever before, we are choosing consumer products that are kinder to the environment, from cleaning supplies to cars.

The experts warn that change is needed. Many scientists caution that if humans do not reduce greenhouse emissions, we could face catastrophic environmental consequences. This chapter explores some of the implications of what it means to be "green," and what could happen if we are not. How hard is it to embrace "green" choices and to live a "green" life? Are cows worse than cars for the environment? Is the idea of green living just a gimmick designed to make us feel good about ourselves? How much are we willing to change our daily lives to be green?

CRITICAL THINKING

1. What is happening in this cartoon? Who are the people in the cartoon? What do they represent?
2. Why is the woman asking the man about whether his company is environmentally friendly?
3. What is the cartoonist trying to say about "green" companies? About the environmental movement?
4. Are you more likely to want to do business with a "green" company than with one that does not highlight this as part of its general business practice? Does a company's "green" status influence your purchasing decisions? Why or why not?

How We Can Stop Being Eco-Hypocrites

Raina Kelley

Raina Kelley is a senior writer for *Newsweek*. This article appeared in the November 10, 2010, issue of *Newsweek*.

CONNECTING TO THE TOPIC

In the conversation about living "green," it is easy to confuse morality with science. "Green" awareness is sweeping the nation. As we learn more about our individual impact on the environment, we are often left in a quandary—how do we balance the ideals of being ecoconscious with the comforts and conveniences we have grown accustomed to? And is it really fair to look down our noses at those who fall short of the mark? In this next article, author Raina Kelley lays out some of the most important ways to be "green" and in the process sheds light on the hypocrisy of those who don't practice what they preach.

WORDS IN CONTEXT

heinous (1)   utterly despicable or wicked (adj.)
gallingly (1)   causing irritation or annoyance (adv.)
finite (6)   having bound or limits (adj.)

1   When it comes to my tree-hugging acquaintances and ecofriendly neighbors, I am considered an eco-dinosaur. Why? Because I do **heinous** things like eat meat, own a car, and, **gallingly**, refuse to feel guilty about them. I also don't tut-tut disapprovingly at "that co-worker" who prints out every e-mail. And I definitely don't burst into tears every time somebody pulls out plastic utensils or sips bottled water.

2   This is why some people think I heart BP, when the reality is that reality is somewhere in the middle. I take public transportation, recycle plastic bags, and use CFL bulbs. I do worry about polar bears and global warming, and toxic messes, but I don't use my concerns to push people into doing what's "right." The simple reason: I don't want to be an eco-hypocrite. If you think you don't know what that means, trust me, you do.

3   I'm talking about the type of people (I mean you, Laurie David) who never waste an opportunity to tell the rest of us how the world is going to hell thanks to inappropriately disposed batteries and energy-sucking

lightbulbs, while often breaking eco-rules themselves. They do that because it's impossible not to break the rules, given that some of the things that hurt the environment most are ones we all depend on. Don't believe me? Check out a few examples of things we—eco-hypocrites included—should do if we really want to help this planet.

Get Rid of Trash

4 Ridding a city of waste is not as farfetched as it sounds. San Francisco has already vowed to go waste-free by 2020, and has set up one of the most aggressive recycling programs in the nation. It may seem like a hippie pipe dream, but all properties are required to recycle and compost. That's right, the entire city does not throw away food scraps, soiled paper, or plants—more than 62,000 tons since the program began in 2009. Recology San Francisco, the city's waste-management department, will even pick up large items and clothes. For other places that could use some help going green, Greenercities.org offers a tool kit to help each community identify local priorities and develop a plan.

Stop Driving

5 I know, it sounds drastic, but so does destroying the earth. Americans and their cars emit more carbon dioxide than the entire economy of any other nation except China, and U.S. auto driving gobbles seven out of every 10 barrels of oil we consume. "The U.S. is the owner of the world's largest transportation system, and reducing emissions from this system is critical to an effective GHG reduction strategy," says Eileen Claussen, president of the Pew Center on Global Climate Change. Cities such as San Diego, New York, and Boston are already promoting a low-car diet. Instead of reflexively hopping into the car, people are encouraged to take buses or trolleys, get on a bike, or just walk. New York has built miles of new bike lanes, while San Diego and Boston are pushing people to give up their cars altogether and use Zipcar services when a car is necessary. Sure, we should continue to buy all the fancy reusable bags we want, but if we don't work on our transportation issues, we're just rearranging deck chairs on the *Titanic*.

Watch Your Water

6 This means more than turning off the sink when you're brushing your teeth. While water is (for the most part) plentiful in the U.S., that's not the case everywhere in the world. Unpolluted fresh water is a **finite** resource and is increasingly in demand as the human population grows. Right now, the world's supply is being drained faster than nature can

replenish it, and the U.N. predicts that demand will exceed supply by at least 30 percent in 2040. Along with the environment, this is already affecting food supplies. Want more information on what's being done and how you can help? Organizations like the World Water Council are a good place to start.

Push for Cleaner Skies

7 According to a recent *USA Today* article, on a flight from New York to Denver a commercial jet generates from "840 to 1,660 pounds of carbon dioxide per passenger. That's about what an SUV generates in a month." Should we all stop flying? Not necessarily. One solution that's been offered by the Union of Concerned Scientists, an organization dedicated to halting carbon emissions, is the use of bio jet fuel. "It's time to get this industry back on track by launching a program to produce the first billion gallons of clean, cellulosic biofuels," says Jeremy Martin, senior scientist with the UCS's Clean Vehicles Program. "Done right, cellulosic biofuels could curb America's oil dependence, reduce carbon pollution, and generate new economic opportunities across rural America." The Federal Aviation Administration sees some value in this and is working with the commercial airline industry to develop appropriate feed stocks that can be efficiently processed into jet fuel.

Buy Less

8 We have too much stuff. If you want numbers to prove it, here they are. According to the National Organization of Professional Organizers (yes, that's real), Americans spend more than a year of their lives looking for lost items buried in their piles of things. We also chuck about 25 percent of our groceries. As it is, the World Wildlife Federation's "Living Planet 2010" report states that "even with UN projections for modest population growth, consumption and climate change, by 2030 humanity will need the capacity of two Earths to absorb CO_2 waste and keep up with natural resource consumption." No one expects you to stop buying altogether, but start buying less. Depending on the country, you can participate in events like Buy Nothing Day. ◆

CONSIDERING THE ISSUES

1. Define what being a hypocrite means to you and then give some concrete examples of hypocrisy from your own experience.
2. According to this article, what steps has Raina Kelley personally taken to be ecofriendly? In your own life, what do you do that would be considered ecofriendly?

CRAFT AND CONTENT

1. What tone does Raina Kelley use in her article? Find at least three examples of textual evidence to support your point.
2. Kelley uses one analogy in her article. Which analogy does she use? Explain the analogy she is making, and state if you find it to be an effective one.

CRITICAL THINKING

1. Kelley asserts that she doesn't feel guilty about eating meat, owning a car, or being an "eco-dinosaur." Have you found yourself feeling guilty about not doing enough to help the environment? Explain.
2. In her article, the author blatantly calls Laurie David an eco-hypocrite. Who is Laurie David? Why does Kelley feel that she is a "eco-hypocrite"?

WRITING ABOUT THE ISSUES

1. In this article, author Raina Kelley mentions the steps that cities such as San Francisco, San Diego, New York, and Boston are doing to help save the planet. Do research on your hometown, or where you are living now, to see what initiatives have been done, are being looked into, or will be put in place regarding being environmentally friendly. Report on your findings.
2. This article really doesn't have a conclusion. Write an appropriate conclusion for this article, drawing from points made in the article and information you may find from other sources.

Living Without a Car: My New American Responsibility

Andrew Lam

Andrew Lam is a writer and the 1993 winner of the Outstanding Young Journalist Award from the Society of Professional Journalists. He is currently the web editor of New America Media and a regular contributor to National Public Radio's *All Things Considered*. Lam is the author of *Perfume Dreams: Reflections on the Vietnamese Diaspora* (2005). This article was first published on July 24, 2008, by New America Media.

CONNECTING WITH THE TOPIC ——————————————

What is your eco-threshold? Many people make an effort to recycle their bottles, cans, and old papers. Some go out of their way to use eco-friendly products, actively conserve resources, and adopt green practices, such as not using plastic and even installing solar panels. But would you give up owning a car? In this next essay, author Andrew Lam explains why he feels that "the covetous American way of life" has become unsustainable. Cars, he explains, are just not necessary for many of us living in cities and we should divest ourselves of them, even if it is a little inconvenient.

WORDS IN CONTEXT ——————————————

expediency (2)   speed; haste (n.)
intrinsically (5)   inherently; naturally (adv.)
downtrodden (8)   oppressed; poor (adj.)
sedentary (9)   remaining or living in one area; not moving (adj.)
ennui (11)   boredom (n.)
chimerically (11)   imaginatively; fancifully (adv.)
covetous (12)   extreme desire to possess or acquire (adj.)
complacency (13)   self-satisfaction; unaware of danger (n.)
acquisition (15)   something gained or acquired (n.)
unprecedented (15)   having no previous example (adj.)
repudiating (16)   rejecting; disowning (v.)

1   For the first time in nearly two decades, I am no longer a driver. A few months ago, facing spiking gas prices and much-needed repairs, I donated my car to an organization that takes care of foster kids.

2   It's an odd feeling to be on this side of being green. Without a car, my sense of time and space have been immediately altered. What was once a matter of **expediency** is now an effortful navigation.

3   "I'll be there in 15 minutes!" I used to tell a good friend who once lived nearby but who now resides, without a car, at an inconvenient distance. Going to my favorite Asian food market suddenly has turned into another arduous chore: Once a 30-minute event, it has become a two-hour ordeal, with bags in hands, and bus transfers.

4   Owning a car has always been a luxury in the Third World, something beyond the pale of the middle class. In countries like Vietnam, Peru and Bangladesh, just to name a few, only the very rich owned cars. When I came here from Vietnam with my family at the end of the war, I remember such delight when my older brother bought his first car. We were still sharing an apartment with my aunt and her children, but as we cruised the streets at night, it felt as if we were becoming Americans.

5   The automobile, after all, is **intrinsically** American, and owning one largely determines how we Americans arrange our daily lives—it is as essential to us as the train and metro are to Japanese or Europeans. Indeed, a car is the first thing a teenager of driving age desires; to drive away from home is an established American rite of passage. Even the working poor are drivers here.

6   For immigrants, the car is the first thing we buy before the house. Vietnamese in Vietnam marvel at the BMWs and Mercedez Benzes that their relatives drive in America, and no doubt the sleek photos sent home cause many to dream of a life of luxury in the United States.

7   It seems a natural progression that the housing crisis should quickly lend itself to a car crisis. Both were readily available at one time, with easy loans and cheap gas. But now, with skyrocketing gas prices and faltering mortgages, many have had to give up one in order to keep the other.

8   Not surprisingly, the car is often the last thing that **downtrodden** Americans let go. "I can see losing my house, but I can't imagine losing my van," one unemployed friend told me. "I can live in my van. But not being able to get where I need to go would be worse than not having a house."

9   Mobility defines us far more than **sedentary** life, thus the car is arguably more important than the house. Americans, despite accepting global warming as de facto, are still very much in love with the automobile. On average, we own 2.28 vehicles per household.

10   Our addiction to the automobile is as much a symptom of our nomadic culture as it is a matter of necessity: Urban sprawl, combined with little public transportation, makes the car essential. A job seems almost always to require it. The distance between here and there is daunting without a vehicle at one's command.

11   The car, culturally speaking, is mobility and individualism combined. It is sex, freedom and danger. Thelma and Louise escaped from urban **ennui** by hitting the freeway with the wind in their hair, the horizon shimmering **chimerically** ahead. They found romance on the road. Indeed, their final moment approaches the mythic, as the blue Thunderbird Convertible flies across the Grand Canyon, taking the notion of freedom beyond any open road.

12   Our civilization, too, is driving toward an abyss. The **covetous** American way of life—in the age of climate change and dwindling energy resources—has become unsustainable.

13   On TV recently, former Vice President turned eco-activist Al Gore called for a radical change in our collective behavior. He wants us to completely replace fossil fuel-generated electricity with carbon-free energy sources like solar, wind and geothermal by 2018. "The survival of the United States of America as we know it is at risk," he said. "The future of human civilization is at stake." We are now being called upon, the Nobel Prize winner told us, "to move quickly and boldly to shake off **complacency**, throw aside old habits and rise, clear-eyed and alert, to the necessity of big changes."

14   I wish he were exaggerating, but my gut tells me that the green guru is pointing us in the right direction. How and if we'll ever get there, how we'll find a collective will to act, I have no idea. But I do know this: Humanity has arrived at a historic juncture and it now seems that a drastic shift in the collective behavior is called for. If this means finding the will to be frugal and give up certain luxuries, then so be it.

15   America was built on the premise of progress and expansion. Yet our vision of a future of unimpeded opportunities and comfort is now in conflict with the health of the planet. The consumer culture requires continuous **acquisition**, and it is built on the concept of disposable goods. Our way of life—which is copied the world over—has created an **unprecedented** crisis on a planetary scale.

16   I can tell you from experience, however, that being on the right side of the green divide is not easy. As I trudged to work this morning, a 40-minute trek, I dearly missed my car. As I budget my time and memorize bus routes and timetables, it seems as if I am returning to my humble immigrant beginnings, **repudiating** some notion of being an American. But I'm not. Giving up the car is my new American responsibility. ◆

CONSIDERING THE ISSUES

1. Do you have any examples of "being green" in your own lifestyle or behavior? Explain.
2. Could you live without owning a car? If you don't own a car, can you imagine not having one after graduation? Explain.

CRAFT AND CONTENT

1. Explain how Lam uses a full-circle approach to his introduction and conclusion. Do you find this approach effective?
2. Paraphrase paragraph 15 and then explain what you think would have to happen in the world for all nations to finally take significant action toward saving the planet.

CRITICAL THINKING

1. Lam suggests that if Americans had to give up either their house or their vehicle, they would give up the house. Do you agree with this statement? Which would you give up and why?
2. Lam asserts, "Mobility defines us far more than sedentary life." Why might he say this? Have you moved around a lot during your lifetime? Explain.

WRITING ABOUT THE ISSUES

1. This article asserts that owning "a car is the first thing a teenager of driving age desires: to drive away from home is an established American rite of passage." Write a one-paragraph narrative essay in which you describe your first (or most important) automobile experience.

2. In his article, Andrew Lam uses the film *Thelma and Louise* as an example to explain the "sex, freedom, and danger" associated with owning a vehicle. Watch the film and then write a five-paragraph essay analyzing how the movie explores these issues of sex, freedom, and danger.

VISUAL CONNECTIONS

Going Green but Getting Nowhere
Gernot Wagner

CONNECTING TO THE TOPIC

Many people try to do the right thing and recycle and support "green" efforts such as reducing paper waste and reusing plastic and paper products. But economist Gernot Wagner says this is not enough. One person, or even a bunch of people, all doing the right thing will not slow down global warming and reduce carbon emissions. He argues that broad-scale governmental action is needed, and unfortunately it doesn't look like most of the world's governments are interested in the environment right now. This essay appeared in *The New York Times* on September 7, 2011.

You reduce, reuse and recycle. You turn down plastic and paper. You avoid out-of-season grapes. You do all the right things.

Good.

Just know that it won't save the tuna, protect the rain forest or stop global warming. The changes necessary are so large and profound that they are beyond the reach of individual action.

You refuse the plastic bag at the register, believing this one gesture somehow makes a difference, and then carry your takeout meal back to your car for a carbon-emitting trip home.

Say you're willing to make real sacrifices. Sell your car. Forsake your air-conditioner in the summer, turn down the heat in the winter. Try to become no-impact man. You would, in fact, have no impact on the planet. Americans would continue to emit an average of 20 tons of carbon dioxide a year; Europeans, about 10 tons.

What about going bigger? You are the pope with a billion followers, and let's say all of them take your advice to heart. If all Catholics decreased their emissions to zero overnight, the planet would surely notice, but pollution would still be rising. Of course, a billion people, whether they're Catholic or adherents of any other religion or creed, will do no such thing. Two weeks of silence in a Buddhist yoga retreat in the Himalayas with your BlackBerry checked at the door? Sure. An entire life voluntarily lived off the grid? No thanks.

And that focuses only on those who can decrease their emissions. When your average is 20 tons per year, going down to 18 tons is as easy as taking a staycation. But if you are among the four billion on the planet who each emit one ton a year, you have nowhere to go but up.

Leading scientific groups and most climate scientists say we need to decrease global annual greenhouse gas emissions by at least half of current levels by 2050 and much further by the end of the century. And that will still mean rising temperatures and sea levels for generations.

So why bother recycling or riding your bike to the store? Because we all want to do something, anything. Call it "action bias." But, sadly, individual action does not work. It distracts us from the need for collective action, and it doesn't add up to enough. Self-interest, not self-sacrifice, is what induces noticeable change. Only the right economic policies will enable us as individuals to be guided by self-interest and still do the right thing for the planet.

Every ton of carbon dioxide pollution causes around $20 of damage to economies, ecosystems and human health. That sum times 20 implies $400 worth of damage per American per year. That's not damage you're going to do in the distant future; that's damage each of us is doing right now. Who pays for it?

We pay as a society. My cross-country flight adds fractions of a penny to everyone else's cost. That knowledge leads some of us to voluntarily chip in a few bucks to "offset" our emissions. But none of these payments motivate anyone to fly less. It doesn't lead airlines to switch to more fuel-efficient planes or routes. If anything, airlines by now use voluntary offsets as a marketing ploy to make green-conscious passengers feel better. The result is planetary socialism at its worst: we all pay the price because individuals don't.

It won't change until a regulatory system compels us to pay our fair share to limit pollution accordingly. Limit, of course, is code for "cap and trade," the system that helped phase out lead in gasoline in the 1980s, slashed acid rain pollution in the 1990s and is now bringing entire fisheries back from the brink. "Cap and trade" for carbon is beginning to decrease carbon pollution in Europe, and similar models are slated to do the same from California to China.

Alas, this approach has been declared dead in Washington, ironically by self-styled free-marketers. Another solution, a carbon tax, is also off the table because, well, it's a tax.

Never mind that markets are truly free only when everyone pays the full price for his or her actions. Anything else is socialism. The reality is that we cannot overcome the global threats posed by greenhouse gases without speaking the ultimate inconvenient truth: getting people excited about making individual environmental sacrifices is doomed to fail.

High school science tells us that global warming is real. And economics teaches us that humanity must have the right incentives if it is to stop this terrible trend.

Don't stop recycling. Don't stop buying local. But add mastering some basic economics to your to-do list. Our future will be largely determined by our ability to admit the need to end planetary socialism. That's the most fundamental of economics lessons and one any serious environmentalist ought to heed.

CRITICAL THINKING

1. Why does Wagner believe that individual efforts to reuse, reduce, and recycle are not sufficient to improve the planet? Explain.
2. What solution to the problem does Wagner offer? How much hope does he give readers that his solution may be adopted?
3. How does the cartoon accompanying the article complement the editorial?
4. What is happening in the cartoon? In what ways is it ironic?
5. How do you feel after reading the editorial and viewing the cartoon? Explain.

The Only Way to Have a Cow
Bill McKibben

Bill McKibben is an American environmentalist and author who has written extensively on the impact of global warming. He is currently a scholar in residence at Middlebury College. He is a founder of the grassroots climate campaign 350.org, which has coordinated 15,000 rallies in 189 countries since 2009. His articles have appeared in *The New York Times*, *The Atlantic Monthly*, *Mother Jones,* and *National Geographic* among others. He is the author of many books on the environment, most recently *Eaarth: Making a Life on a Tough New Planet* (2010), which recounts the rapid onset of climate change. This article was published in the March/April 2010 issue of *Orion* magazine.

CONNECTING TO THE TOPIC

Most of us know that carbon emissions from cars and factories are doing nothing to help the environment. But what about eating meat? How does meat production really impact the environment? And are there any solutions? In this next essay, environmentalist Bill McKibben explains the harm of industrialized meat production and how we might turn the problem around. But are his solutions throwing a teaspoon of water on a forest fire? Can they really be implemented? And more importantly, do we care enough to change?

WORDS IN CONTEXT

abstainer (1)   one who does not partake in a particular activity or food item, such as alcohol (n.)

fracas (2)   a noisy disturbance or quarrel (n.)

emissions (2)   production and discharge of something, especially gas or radiation (n.)

emanates (2)   issue or spread out from (v.)

arable (3)   suitable for growing crops (adj.)

eructate (3)   belching or burping gas from the digestive tract through the mouth (v.)

ungulates (4)   a hoofed mammal (n.)

uncouth (4)   lacking good manners or refinement (adj.)

stationary (5)   not moving or not intended to be moved (adj.)

sequestered (6)   isolated or hidden away (adj.)

1   **M**ay I say—somewhat defensively—that I haven't cooked red meat in many years? That I haven't visited a McDonald's since college? That if you asked me how I like my steak, I'd say I don't really remember? I'm not a moral **abstainer**—I'll eat meat when poor people in distant places offer it to me, especially when they're proud to do so and I'd be an ass to say no. But in everyday life, for a series of reasons that began with the dietary scruples of the woman I chose to marry, hamburgers just don't come into play.

2   I begin this way because I plan to wade into one of the most impassioned **fracases** now underway on the planet—to meat or not to meat—and I want to establish that I Do Not Have a Cow in this Fight. In recent years vegetarians and vegans have upped their attack on the consumption of animal flesh, pointing out not only that it's disgusting (read Jonathan Safran Foer's new book) but also a major cause of climate change. The numbers range from 18 percent of the world's greenhouse gas **emissions** to—in one recent study that was quickly discredited—51 percent. Whatever the exact figure, suffice it to say it's high: there's the carbon that comes from cutting down the forest to start the farm, and from the fertilizer and diesel fuel it takes to grow the corn, there's the truck exhaust from shipping cows hither and yon, and most of all the methane that **emanates** from the cows themselves (95 percent of it from the front end, not the hind, and these millions of feedlot cows would prefer if you used the word eructate in place of belch). This news has led to an almost endless series of statistical calculations: going vegan is 50 percent more effective in reducing greenhouse gas emissions than switching to a hybrid car, according to a University of Chicago study; the UN Food and Agriculture Organization finds that a half pound of ground beef has the same effect on climate change as driving an SUV ten miles. It has led to a lot of political statements: the British health secretary last fall called on Englishmen to cut their beefeating by dropping at least a sausage a week from their diets, and Paul McCartney has declared that "the biggest change anyone could make in their own lifestyle to help the environment would be to become vegetarian." It has even led to the marketing of a men's flip-flop called the Stop Global Warming Toepeeka that's made along entirely vegan lines.

3   Industrial livestock production is essentially indefensible—ethically, ecologically, and otherwise. We now use an enormous percentage of our **arable** land to grow corn that we feed to cows who stand in feedlots and **eructate** until they are slaughtered in a variety of gross ways and lodge in our ever-larger abdomens. And the fact that the product of this exercise "tastes good" sounds pretty lame as an excuse. There are technofixes—engineering the corn feed so it produces less methane, or giving the cows shots so they eructate less violently.

But this type of tailpipe fix only works around the edges, and with the planet warming fast that's not enough. We should simply stop eating factory-farmed meat, and the effects on climate change would be but one of the many benefits.

4   Still, even once you've made that commitment, there's a nagging ecological question that's just now being raised. It goes like this: long before humans had figured out the whole cow thing, nature had its own herds of hoofed **ungulates**. Big herds of big animals—perhaps 60 million bison ranging across North America, and maybe 100 million antelope. That's considerably more than the number of cows now resident in these United States. These were noble creatures, but **uncouth**—eructate hadn't been coined yet. They really did just belch. So why weren't they filling the atmosphere with methane? Why wasn't their manure giving off great quantities of atmosphere-altering gas?

5   The answer, so far as we can tell, is both interesting and potentially radical in its implications. These old-school ungulates weren't all that different in their plumbing—they were methane factories with legs too. But they used those legs for something. They didn't stand still in feed-lots waiting for corn, and they didn't stand still in big western federal allotments overgrazing the same tender grass. They didn't stand still at all. Maybe they would have enjoyed **stationary** life, but like teenagers in a small town, they were continually moved along by their own version of the police: wolves. And big cats. And eventually Indians. By predators.

6   As they moved, they kept eating grass and dropping manure. Or, as soil scientists would put it, they grazed the same perennials once or twice a year to "convert aboveground biomass to dung and urine." Then dung beetles buried the results in the soil, nurturing the grass to grow back. These grasslands covered places that don't get much rain—the Southwest and the Plains, Australia, Africa, much of Asia. And all that grass-land **sequestered** stupendous amounts of carbon and methane from out of the atmosphere—recent preliminary research indicates that methane-loving bacteria in healthy soils will sequester more of the gas in a day than cows supported by the same area will emit in a year. We're flat out of predators in most parts of the world, and it's hard to imagine, in the short time that we have to deal with climate change, ending the eating of meat and returning the herds of buffalo and packs of wolves to all the necessary spots. It's marginally easier to imagine mimicking those systems with cows. The key technology here is the single-strand electric fence—you move your herd or your flock once or twice a day from one small pasture to the next, forcing them to eat everything that's growing there but moving them along before they graze all the good stuff down to bare ground. Now their manure isn't a problem that fills a cesspool, but a key part of making the system work. Done right, some studies suggest, this method

of raising cattle could put much of the atmosphere's oversupply of green-house gases back in the soil inside half a century. That means shifting from feedlot farming to rotational grazing is one of the few changes we could make that's on the same scale as the problem of global warming. It won't do away with the need for radically cutting emissions, but it could help get the car exhaust you emitted back in high school out of the atmosphere.

7   Oh, and grass-fed beef is apparently much better for you—full of omega-3s, like sardines that moo. Better yet, it's going to be more expensive, because you can't automate the process the same way you can feedlot agriculture. You need the guy to move the fence every afternoon. (That's why about a billion of our fellow humans currently make their livings as herders of one kind or another—some of them use slingshots, or dogs, or shepherd's crooks, or horses instead of electric fence, but the principle is the same.) More expensive, in this case, as in many others, is good; we'd end up eating meat the way most of the world does— as a condiment, a flavor, an ingredient, not an entrée.

8   I doubt McDonald's will be in favor. I doubt Paul McCartney will be in favor. It doesn't get rid of the essential dilemma of killing something and then putting it in your mouth. But it's possible that the atmosphere would be in favor, and that's worth putting down your fork and thinking about. ◆

CONSIDERING THE ISSUES

1. McKibben says that he is married to someone whose "dietary scruples" preclude her from eating meat, and thus he rarely eats meat himself. If you are a vegetarian or vegan, explain why you made this choice or why someone else might benefit by following your example. If you are not a vegetarian, try skipping meat for a week and write about your experience.

2. In your opinion, is it better to adopt a vegetarian lifestyle or to give up your car? What seems worse to you—cars or cows?

CRAFT AND CONTENT

1. McKibben begins his essay by telling us that he does not usually eat meat. Why do you think he choses to begin his argument this way? How might you receive his argument if you knew that he did, for example, eat at McDonald's?

2. Why does McKibben make an effort to establish that he "does not have a cow in this fight"? What does he mean?

CRITICAL THINKING

1. What evidence does McKibben use to prove that industrial live-stock production is "essentially indefensible"? How well does he support his position? Do you agree or disagree with his argument?
2. Why does McKibben think that both McDonald's and Paul McCarthy wouldn't agree with his solutions? What position do both have on meat? Explain.

WRITING ABOUT THE ISSUES

1. What factors are contributing to CO_2 levels? What do we need to do to reduce them? Visit 350.org, Bill McKibben's environmental organization, and learn more about what the number 350 means for the environment. What impact would McKibben's solutions have on reducing CO_2 levels?
2. Explore the reasons why meat has become an integral part of the American diet. What cultural influences do we have to eat meat? Who drives these influences? Give your own personal examples of mealtimes in childhood as well as exploring the concept of the American meal.

My Carbon Footprint: A Documentary, a Daughter, and All That Is Dear

Jennifer Davidson

Jennifer Davidson is a writer living in northern California, where she is a regular contributor to the *Sacramento News & Review*, in which this essay appeared on March 8, 2007.

CONNECTING TO THE TOPIC

Columnist Jennifer Davidson thought of herself as a "moderate environmentalist" as she engaged in Earth-friendly practices to ensure a better environmental future for her daughter. After watching the 2006 movie, *An Inconvenient Truth*, however, Davidson finds herself in a fit of despair. The movie, which features Al Gore, "offers a passionate and inspirational look at [Gore's] fervent crusade to halt global warming's deadly progress in its tracks by exposing the myths and misconceptions that surround it." In this editorial,

Davidson wonders what sort of world her daughter will live in if climate change continues unchecked.

WORDS IN CONTEXT

Ichabod Crane (2)   Ichabod Crane is a fictional character in Washington Irving's short story *The Legend of Sleepy Hollow* who is chased by the headless horseman.
niche (12)   a specialized area or unique space (n.)

1   I've always felt like a modest environmentalist. I use canvas grocery bags (OK, sometimes). I primarily buy cruelty free products, recycle at work and contribute a small stipend each month to purchase a portion of my energy from green sources. My daughter and I are protectors of snails in danger of being squashed on sidewalks, and we let no six-pack plastic ring go uncut. We care. Somehow I convinced myself that was enough.

2   Recently I had the opportunity to watch Al Gore's *An Inconvenient Truth*, documenting the state of Earth's global-warming condition due to greenhouse gases. Educated as a scientist, I appreciated the wealth of hard data Gore had compiled, but what brought me to weep, as if I had lost someone I loved, was the manner in which he gave meaning to the data. Under the layers of percentages, charts and graphs, the exposed bloody heart of his message beat as loud as **Ichabod Crane's**. Everything I love, everything that is dear to me, is at stake.

3   Everything I do is for my daughter. And for the first time I realized that none of it will matter if her ability to live on Earth is not sustained, or if I leave her a planet where the fresh water supply for millions is gone, where she'll face unbearably hot summers, an Arctic with no ice, and, in turn, warmer oceans, a teetering marine ecosystem and higher sea levels that will swallow coastal communities worldwide in one gulp. And will she walk upon a barren Earth, void of the rich species we have today? If these are the legacies I leave to my daughter, I will have realized my greatest failure as a parent.

4   Global warming is the result of a worldwide dependency on fossil fuels. However, America contributes slightly more than 30 percent of the problem. Here's what happens in bustling American homes much like my own. Unnecessary lights are left on, a few notches on the thermostat are chosen over a heavier sweater, the TV is alive, the radio hums, the dishwasher and dryer are rumbling at peak hours, and, "Shoot! I need to run to the store in my high-performance vehicle for the cat food I forgot earlier."

5   In the simplest terms, Gore explains what the emissions from the energy and gasoline we gorge ourselves on each day do to our atmospheric layer—the thin, fragile shell that stabilizes the Earth's temperature. As we

send more and more carbon emissions into our atmosphere, the very composition of this layer changes and thickens, trapping the sun's heat and unnaturally warming the planet.

6   Without perspective, a few degrees warmer doesn't really sound that bad. But as temperatures slowly continue to rise, the change in climate begins to unravel the fabric upon which the natural world is built, upon which human civilization depends. Gore took this fairly ambiguous concept and gave it life in tangible measures of potential destruction, suffering and extinction.

7   Our Arctic is melting. As the ice dwindles, more of the sun's rays are absorbed by the ocean rather than reflected by the ice that has disappeared. This warms Arctic waters and fuels destruction of the remaining ice.

8   Warmer temperatures have slurped-up ice shelves in Antarctica as well. Twenty to 25 miles of the Larsen B 700-foot tall ice shelf, the largest in the world, was expected to be stable for more than 100 years, explained Gore. But within 35 days it disappeared in March of 2002.

9   Reruns of what Gore referred to as "massive rushing torrents" in the middle of Greenland's ice sheet play over and over in my head. You see it and instinctively know something is very wrong. It was eerie and I felt vulnerable, as if the only thing protecting me from the rushing torrents was the thin layer of glass in my television. Freaky.

10   As silly as it sounds, it may not be far-fetched. Scientists from the National Center for Atmospheric Research, U.S. Geological Survey and several universities completed their research last year, funded by the National Science Foundation, on melting polar ice sheets due to temperature increases. The findings anticipate worldwide sea levels to rise more than 20 feet by the end of this century.

11   Gore paints a simpler picture. The San Francisco Bay? Underwater. Southern Florida? Gone. The World Trade Center Memorial in New York City? Swallowed. How about the Netherlands, Beijing, Shanghai, Calcutta? More than one-hundred-million people will be displaced. Where will they go? How will we handle a catastrophe of this magnitude with immeasurable social, economical and environmental consequences? I have so many questions. Warmer oceans also threaten our ocean currents, weather patterns and the health of marine ecosystems. In the Arctic, polar bears are drowning from hypothermia and exhaustion as they attempt to swim increasing distances between fewer and fewer floating chunks of sea ice. Their diminishing habitat prompted the U.S. Fish and Wildlife Service to propose listing the bear as threatened under the Endangered Species Act in December of 2006.

12   Some species can respond to rising temperatures by rapidly migrating to an ecological **niche** with cooler temperatures. But this has significant consequences in the natural world. As new species invade, competition for resources, such as food, shelter and territory, can threaten or extinguish the

weaker species. New strains of diseases can be introduced, which can wipe out a healthy population. Prey that was once controlled by predators can go unchecked and wreak havoc on the environment. In essence, we've triggered the Earth to wage war against itself. And we know what war looks like.

13   Gore wove a very personal side of his life into the documentary. He took us back in time when he was a small boy and he and his sister, Nancy, helped his father, a tobacco farmer, grow and harvest the plant. He talked about the death of his sister years later, when she succumbed to lung cancer from smoking since she was 14. "The idea that we were a part of this was so painful on so many levels. Whatever explanation that made sense in the past didn't cut it anymore. The day of reckoning comes, and you wish you had connected the dots more quickly."

14   I understand now. I've connected the dots, and it is my turn, as Gore says, to decide how I will react. ◆

CONSIDERING THE ISSUES

1. What do parents—indeed, all adults—owe, if anything, to the next generation? If you are a parent, describe how being a parent has made you more (or less) aware of the greater world you live in.

2. Davidson points out some changes that could happen if the Earth's climate continues to get warmer. How concerned are you about the environment. Is it an abstract issue, as it was for Davidson before she watched Gore's movie, or a pressing concern that you are actively involved in? Explain.

CRAFT AND CONTENT

1. In what ways does this essay appeal to the emotions? How does it appeal to the intellect?

2. How compelling is Davidson's argument? Does the fact that she has a science background influence your opinion of her points? Does her background as a parent make her more compelling or credible? Explain.

CRITICAL THINKING

1. What strikes Davidson about the way Gore's movie describes climate change? Why does it "bring her to weep"? Explain.

2. Davidson describes herself as a "moderate environmentalist." What does she mean by this? What do you think she will do as a result of watching Gore's movie?

WRITING ABOUT THE ISSUES

1. Watch the movie *An Inconvenient Truth* and write a review of the film. What are the movie's strengths and weaknesses? What struck you as compelling? Questionable? Is the movie balanced? Biased? Slanted? Fair? Does it offer solutions? What is your personal reaction to the film?

2. Write about a time when the weather or climate had a significant impact on your own life. It could be a memory of a blizzard when you were a child or a personal experience with a recent catastrophe, such as Hurricane Katrina.

Blog Matters

A blog ("web log") is an online diary or commentary site that features regular entries that describe events, impressions, and viewpoints. Blogs may contain text, images, video, and often link to other websites, blogs, and online media. Most blogs allow readers to comment on the content of the post and respond to each other. As of September 2011, there were over 160 million public blogs in existence. While many blogs are maintained by individuals, some are run by journals, newspapers, and other media outlets. Remember that most blogs are not monitored for factual accuracy and often express the opinion and views of the "blogger" writing the content.

The Greenwashing Blog examines examples of companies or individuals misleading consumers on their environmental impact. "Greenwashing" is a term used to describe inaccurate claims made about a company's environmental friendliness. As corporations become more mindful of the social shift to a more environmentally conscious world, many are trying to take advantage by rebranding themselves as "green" or "eco-friendly."

Greenwashing: Nestle Plastic Water Bottle

Cyrus Patton
March 27, 2009

1   The ad for the Nestle Pure Life water bottle notes that it has an "Eco-Shape" (notice the trademark there). With this fashionably thinner bottle that has 15% less plastic we can all make a difference. Notice the asterisk* next to the "15% less plastic."

2   I've looked into it and on the Nestle website it says the bottles now have 30–40% less plastic which might be nice. The note for the asterisk was very hard to find; it was covered by other text and itself was not text, it was a text-turned-image so I couldn't copy and paste, also the color made it hard to read. It's the grey text here:

3   The part I can read says, "… .5L bottles across twelve cities. Over 130 different .5L bottles were weighed across the water, soda, juice and tea categories. On average, the Eco-Shape bottle was found to be the lightest .5L bottle on the market containing 30% less plastic when compared to the average of other .5L bottles." It's actually really hard for me even to determine what this means. Are they saying they have less plastic when you compare it to the weight of other bottles? Does that mean that they aren't actually looking at the exact numbers and statistics of how much plastic goes into their product compared to others, they are just measuring it solely by the weight of other same-sized bottles? Does anyone have a better idea at what this means?

Nestle Pure Life Water

4   It does seem like they are using less plastic than they use to, even if their measurement standards are a bit unreliable. But I'm not sure that I want to buy their product simply because their bottle has a little less plastic. Let's be honest here, plastic is never really that great of a thing. If it doesn't get recycled it lasts a super long time and it's not actually "easier to live with" as the Nestle website claims. I've become increasingly wary of the plastic packaging that is wrapped around every little thing, like breath mints, fruit at Trader Joes (that's another story), and water. We are told we can just throw it away, as if throwing it away is going to make it disappear forever….

RESPOND TO THE BLOG:

What do you think? Are companies "greenwashing" their products? Can you think of other products that clearly "greenwash" to appeal to more eco-conscious consumers? Cite some examples from your own personal experience.

Green Living Takes Root But Old Habits Die Hard

Patrick O'Driscoll and Elizabeth Weise

Patrick O'Driscoll is a former reporter for *USA Today* now working as a public affairs specialist with the National Park Service. Elizabeth Weise covers science for *USA Today* addressing a variety of topics including but not limited to biotechnology, agriculture, food safety, stem cells, and cloning. Weise began her journalism career as a reporter for KUOW, Seattle's National Public Radio affiliate. *USA Today* first published this article on April 4, 2007.

CONNECTING WITH THE TOPIC

Most Americans believe that dramatic steps are needed to conserve energy and reduce the threat of global warming. But Americans get more uncomfortable with the idea of going green if it means limiting their choices in daily life. Many people are finding out that doing the right thing isn't easy, even for those who want to. How much would you sacrifice to help the planet? And how much are you influenced by the sacrifices (or unchanged behaviors) of others?

WORDS IN CONTEXT

barrage (5)   an overwhelming quantity or explosion. (n)
fabricate (15)   to construct or create (v)

1   Most Americans believe that dramatic steps are needed to conserve energy and reduce the threat of global warming, but they are willing to go only so far in changing their lifestyles to "go green."

2   A *USA TODAY*/Gallup Poll finds that more Americans than ever— 60%, up from 48% a decade ago—believe that global warming has begun

to affect the climate. A slightly larger percentage think it will cause major or extreme changes in climate and weather during the next 50 years.

3   And in a reflection of the impact the environmental movement has had on Americans' attitudes in the nearly four decades since the first Earth Day celebration, most people now believe that they should take more steps as individuals—such as riding mass transit and making their homes more energy efficient—to help reduce carbon dioxide and other greenhouse gases that trap heat in the atmosphere.

4   Even so, most people are wary of any government effort to protect the environment by imposing restrictions on how they live, work or get around. A majority of those surveyed in the poll, conducted March 23–25, said they wouldn't want a surcharge added to their utility bill if their homes exceeded certain energy-use levels. And most Americans would oppose any laws requiring cars sold in the USA to dramatically improve their gas mileage or restrictions on development to try to limit suburban sprawl.

5   Taken together, the poll responses indicate that Americans are going green on their own terms, depending on their interests and their wallets. The survey comes as a **barrage** of warnings about global warming—most recently in March, from a United Nations science panel—has transformed the climate-change debate. Going green has moved past politics to become a fashion statement, and big business.

6   It's a shift reflected not just in the Academy Award for *An Inconvenient Truth*, the film on former vice president Al Gore's global-warming lecture. It's also evident in magazines from *Vanity Fair* to *Fortune*, whose recent "green" issues included hints about how to get green—or invest in companies that are.

7   America's move toward going green also can be seen in the ad campaigns and store aisles of the nation's largest retailers. Wal-Mart, the world's largest buyer of organic cotton, aims this year to sell 100 million compact fluorescent bulbs, which last longer and use far less energy than regular bulbs. The fluorescent bulbs typically cost five to seven times more.

8   In the *USA TODAY* poll, Americans showed a willingness to spend more money to help the environment.

9   More than two-thirds of those responding said they should use only fluorescent bulbs in their homes. And 62% said they should buy a gas-saving hybrid car such as the popular Toyota Prius. Gas-electric hybrids typically cost thousands of dollars more than cars with gas-only engines, and buyers usually have to keep the cars for several years to break even financially.

10   Meanwhile, more than eight in 10 said a company's environmental record should be an important factor in deciding whether to buy its products. And 78% thought spending several thousand dollars to make their homes more energy-efficient is a good idea.

11   But like Ari Adler of East Lansing, Mich., most Americans get more uncomfortable with the idea of going green if it were to mean limiting choices in daily life. Adler says his 2003 Jeep Wrangler "has the aerodynamics of a brick, but I enjoy the vehicle I have." As his old lightbulbs burn out, "I'll replace them with fluorescents. But I'll resist the idea that we should be required to do that." Adler, 39, who works in public relations, says he is "one of those people (who) tries to do the right thing for the environment and knows there is more I should be doing, but don't necessarily do."

12   Indeed, only about half of those polled thought they do a good job personally of protecting the environment. Less than 10% rate their efforts as "excellent."

13   Andy McDonald of South Bend, Ind., says he used to recycle his household trash—until the city made it mandatory and doubled his garbage bill to pay for it. "I was doing it anyway," McDonald says. "They were trying to force me to do it. I don't like that." McDonald, 29, who services motor-home diesel engines, says he often sees contradictions in his customers' commitment to going green. "In the shop, people drive in with $500,000, $600,000, $700,000 motor homes with 500-horsepower engines that get, at best, 6 mpg on the highway," he says. "And yet they tow a hybrid around to drive when they get there. It's better than driving a regular vehicle, but maybe not driving the motor home could be a greater impact."

14   Products that help people use less energy—or leave a smaller "environmental footprint," as green advocates say—often are more costly than their alternatives, causing some to argue that going green is only for those who can afford it. Those in older homes have to pay several thousands of dollars to replace windows with energy-saving, double-paned glass. Organic food, grown without chemicals potentially harmful to land, water, wildlife and people, costs more. So do hybrid vehicles and electricity generated by wind turbines or solar panels.

15   In a CBS News/*New York Times* poll last year, fewer than half of the respondents said they had bought a costlier, "eco-friendly" product during the past year. "The fact is, most of these products sold as 'green' cost more than the alternative," says Myron Ebell of the Competitive Enterprise Institute, a Washington think tank that dismisses climate-change warnings as scare tactics not based on sound science. "You're already pricing people at the lower end out." He cites a study by an automotive research group, CNW Marketing Research in Bandon, Ore., that calculated total energy use for several car models. Ebell says the overall energy outlay for the Prius—from design to the junkyard—is costlier "than for an SUV like my Chevy TrailBlazer. It takes a huge amount of energy just to **fabricate** those batteries."

16   Matt Golden heads a San Francisco firm that does home-energy audits to examine power use and heat loss and recommends ways residents

can save. "We don't have to live like cave people," Golden says. "You don't have to give things up. You just have to get smarter" about what it takes to run high-tech gadgets and appliances. When Golden examined the home of Cliff and Monica Knudson in San Jose, Calif., he found that their plasma TV, with a digital video recorder and DVD player, drew 100 watts of power when turned off—the equivalent of burning a 100-watt light bulb 24 hours a day. Golden's solution: Plug everything into a power strip that can be turned off when the TV is not in use.

17   Several websites such as alittlegreener.com have popped up to offer advice to consumers about how to save energy, recycle and green up their lives—without being fanatic about it. "It needs to be easy. It needs to be OK to start small," says Meredith Thomas of San Francisco, who launched alittlegreener.com last year as a guide for the not-so-eco-savvy consumer.

18   Astrid Usong of Redwood City, Calif., went to Thomas' site to find places to recycle building materials from a house she is remodeling with her husband, Patrick Weston. What she found there "touches every facet of your life: food, baby, family, work, vacation," says Usong, 29, a designer for a financial website.

19   Some analysts say the green movement is overhyped. "Despite how ubiquitous this whole green message is, a lot of people still don't know what the hell this is about," says energy marketing consultant Suzanne Shelton of Knoxville, Tenn. A survey by her firm last year found 58% of Americans could not identify a source of "green, renewable or sustainable energy," such as solar or wind. Shelton adds that 10% to 20% of those questioned say they participate in "green power" programs to pay a little extra for electricity generated by wind turbines or solar arrays. She says data from power companies show that no more than 4% actually participate. "Their answers aren't consistent with reality," Shelton says. She says she isn't certain if the responses stem from social pressure to say the right thing or if "they're misunderstanding the terminology."

20   The *USA TODAY*/Gallup Poll shows wide differences over what the government should do about global warming. About two-thirds favor spending many billions more on research into new sources of energy. But just one-third are comfortable with land-use restrictions to curb suburban sprawl, which necessitates more car trips. Only about a third favor imposing tough restrictions on U.S. industries and utilities.

21   For some, going green isn't about the environment as much as saving on home energy bills. Austin stockbroker Andrew Ma replaced more than 130 lightbulbs with compact fluorescents in his 5,800-square-foot house after "doing the math." "It makes a lot of sense," says Ma, 34. But he says he won't give up his "gas hogs"—a Yukon Denali SUV and

a Mercedes-Benz SL600 convertible—"that carry us in style and comfort. I'm not going to get a Prius. The fun factor is not there yet," he adds. "I do treasure the environment. But I'm not one of the tree huggers." ◆

CONSIDERING THE ISSUES

1. At the end of this article, Andrew Ma notes that he is "not one of the tree-huggers." What is a "tree hugger"? What reputation do they have? Is it a derogatory term or merely one that identifies certain behaviors and choices regarding the environment? Explain.
2. What factors influence your "green" decisions? Explain.

CRAFT AND CONTENT

1. How does this article use information from surveys and polls? What factors can influence the data gathered from polls? Can you identify any data that might be questionable? Explain.
2. This article uses many quotations. Does this improve or detract from the article and your impression of it? Explain.

CRITICAL THINKING

1. What happens when eco-friendly practices are "pushed" upon people? Would you be less likely to want to participate in recycling projects if you were told you had to do it, or would you just simply do it? Explain.
2. The article notes "some analysts say the green movement is overhyped." Do you agree? In what ways is the green movement overhyped? Or is it not forceful enough? Explain.
3. Energy marketing consultant Suzanne Shelton observes, "a lot of people still don't know what the hell this [the green movement] is about." Summarize the green movement in your own words. How would you explain it to someone who does not understand it?

WRITING ABOUT THE ISSUES

1. Conduct your own poll on this issue. Using this article as a guide, and perhaps referencing the actual polls from *USA Today*, interview 20–30 students on campus and compare their responses to those of the people mentioned in the article. Are students more or less conscious of eco-friendly practices? Are they more likely to adopt green choices? Explain.

2. Using the information from this essay as a guide, how might an environmental specialist responsible for developing a program for a small city design a plan that is most likely to be adopted by citizens?

TOPICAL CONNECTIONS

GROUP PROJECTS

1. Review surveys online at the Pew Research Center website. How concerned are Americans about enviormental issues? Do you think age is a factor in how people respond to these concerns? Does political affiliation have any influence on the responses of college students? Does your survey reveal any strong disparities between groups? Explain.

2. You are part of a group of urban planners who have been given the task of planning a carbon friendly city. Using the information gathered in this chapter as well as outside resources, design your perfect city. If you wish, you may want to rent the SimCity Societies game that encourages you to build eco-friendly cities. Try using some of your ideas with the program and evaluate the results.

WEB PROJECT

1. Visit the Woods Hole Oceanographic Institution website and read its position on the environment at http://www.whoi.edu/institutes/occi. Select a recent WHOI Feature Story (posted on the website under the "Related Topics" heading) and prepare a summary of the article for class discussion.

FOR FURTHER INQUIRY

1. The United States is one of the few nations that did not ratify the Kyoto Protocol. Go online to look up the details on the Kyoto Protocol. After learning more about it, write a one-page response expressing whether you believe the United States should or should not ratify it. In addition to the treaty itself, you may reference the reasons other nations have cited for ratifying (or not ratifying, as in the case of Australia) the treaty. Share your response as part of an in-class debate on whether the United States should have ratified the Kyoto Protocol.

2. Research the issue of greenwashing and how companies are deceiving consumers. With a critical eye, review current ads both online and in print and try to spot incidents of "greenwashing." What could the long-term ramifications of greenwashing be on the American public? Explain.

Credits

Image Credits

Page 16: "FRESH STEP® is a registered trademark of The Clorox Pet Products Company. Used with permission."; 19: Mike Luckovich Editorial Cartoon used with permission by Mike Luckovich and Creators Syndicate. All rights reserved; 23: Cardow, The Ottawa Citizen; 51: Patrick Coorigan/Toronto Star; 65: Chris Slane/Privacy Cartoons; 88: USPS; 93: REUTERS/Joshua Lott; 101: Steve Greenberg; 135: The Advertising Archives; 136: Image Courtesy of the Advertising Archives; 137: The Advertising Archives; 138: The Advertising Archives; 139: Image Courtesy of the Advertising Archives; 140: Courtesy of Adbusters.org; 149: Lisa Benson Editorial Cartoon used with the permission of Lisa Benson, the Washington Post Writers Group and the Cartoonist Group. All rights reserved; 172: ZITS PARTNERSHIP, KING FEATURES SYNDICATE; 179: Frank Micelotta Photography; 189: Clangnuts.com; 207: Photo by Kyle Fasanella; 225: Mike Luckovich Editorial Cartoon used with permission by Mike Luckovich and Creators Syndicate. All rights reserved; 248: By: Daryl Cagle, www.politicalcartoons.com; 249: By: John Cole, www.politicalcartoons.com; 259: By: Andy Singer, www.politicalcartoons.com; 267: Bureau of Labor Statistics/USDL; 284: Justin Lubin/NBC/NBCU Photo Bank via AP Images; 289: Randy Glasbergen; 311: National Institutes of Health; 313: Centers for Disease Control and Prevention, National Center for Health Statistics, Health, United States, 2003, Table 69; 325: U.S. Department of Agriculture/U.S. Department of Health and Human Services; 326: From EAT, DRINK, AND BE HEALTHY by Walter C. Willett, M.D. Copyright © 2001 by the Presidents and Fellows of Harvard College. Reprinted by permission of the Free Press, a division of Simon & Schuster, Inc.; 327; USDA (U.S. Department of Agriculture); 327: USDA (U.S. Department of Agriculture); 331: By: Jeff Parker, www.politicalcartoons.com; 351: Permission to use StudentPOLL graphs granted by Art & Science Group. Art & Science co-publishes StudentPOLL with The College Board; 352: Permission to use StudentPOLL graphs granted by Art & Science Group. Art & Science co-publishes StudentPOLL with The College Board; 353: Permission to use StudentPOLL graphs granted by Art & Science Group. Art & Science co-publishes StudentPOLL with The College Board; 367: Cathy Wilcox/The Sydney Morning Herald; 376: Leif Parsons.

Text Credits

Daniel Akst, "Saving Yourself." *The Wilson Quarterly,* Summer 2009. Reprinted with permission.

American Civil Liberties Union, "National ID Cards: 5 Reasons Why They Should Be Rejected." www.aclu.org. Reprinted by permission.

Benjamin Barber, "Black Friday . . . Gray Thursday." Huffingtonpost.com, November 26, 2007. Reprinted by permission.

Kate Beals, "Faceless on Facebook." Reprinted with permission of the author.

Alex Beam, "Why Stop at Huck Finn?" *The Boston Globe,* January 11, 2011. Reprinted by permission.

Judy Blume, "Is Harry Potter Evil?" *The New York Times,* October 22, 1999. Reprinted by permission.

Myrna Blyth, "The Female Fear Factor." *Spin Sisters: How the Women of the Media Sell Unhappiness—and Liberalism—to the Women of America* by Myrna Blyth. Copyright © 2004 by the author and reprinted by permission of St. Martin's Press, LLC.

danah boyd, "growing up in a culture of fear: from Columbine to banning of MySpace." www.zephoria.org, November 2, 2005. Reprinted by permission of the author.

Margaret Carlson, "The Case for a National ID Card." *TIME,* January 14, 2002. Copyright © 2002 TIME, Inc. Reprinted by permission.

Damien Cave, "On Sale at Old Navy: Cool Clothes for Identical Zombies!" *Salon,* November 22, 2000. Reprinted by permission.

Andy Coghlan, "Consumerism is 'eating the future.'" *New Scientist,* August 7, 2009. Reprinted by permission.

Andrew Curry, "Why We Work." *U.S. News & World Report,* February 24, 2003. Copyright © 2003 U.S. News & World Report, LP. Reprinted by permission.

Daily Mail, "America's Bizarre Secret to Happiness: More Work." http://www.dailymail.co.uk/news, April 19, 2011.

Jennifer Davidson, "My Carbon Footprint" A Documentary, a Daughter, and All that is Dear." *Sacramento News & Review*, March 8, 2007. Reprinted by permission.

Richard Daynard, "You Want Fries with That?" *Northeastern University Magazine,* May 2003. Reprinted by permission of the author.

Tori DeAngelis, "What's to blame for the surge in super-size Americans?" *Monitor on Psychology,* January 2004. Copyright © 2004 by the American Psychological Association. Reprinted with permission. The official

Michael Kinsley, "Kidding Ourselves About Immigration." *TIME* magazine December 6, 2007. Reprinted by permission.

Paul King, "When America Relaxes, 'Food Police' Should Keep Quiet." *Nation's Restaurant News,* August 25, 2003. Reprinted by permission.

Andrew Lam, "Living Without a Car: My New American Responsibility." *New America Media,* July 23, 2008. Reprinted by permission.

John Leo, "Free Inquiry? Not On Campus." *City Journal,* Winter 2007. Reprinted by permission.

Dafna Linzer, "The Problem With Question 36." *Slate,* February 23, 2011, http://www.slate.com/id/2286258/pagenum/all/#p2. Reprinted with permission.

Renée Loth, "Measuring Success." The *Boston Globe Magazine,* June 1, 1997. Reprinted by permission.

William Lutz, "With These Words I Can Sell You Anything." *Doublespeak,* HarperCollins, 1989. Reprinted by permission of the author.

Bill McKibben, "The Only Way to Have a Cow." *Orion Magazine*, March/April, 2010. Reprinted by permission.

Rosie Mestel, "We Eat; Therefore, They Are." *Los Angeles Times,* August 10, 2004. Reprinted by permission.

Jason Lee Miller, "Yahoo Says Americans Work Too Much." *WebProNews,* April 6, 2007. Reprinted by permission.

David Mitchel, "Branding in Pop Culture: How Brands Avoid Negative Associations." *DuetsBlog,* March 16, 2010. Reprinted with permission of the author.

Kevin O'Donnell, "Why Won't Anyone Give Me a Credit Card?" *Slate,* September 18, 2009. Reprinted with permission.

Patrick O'Driscoll and Elizabeth Weise. "Green Living Takes Root but Old Habits Die Hard." *USA Today*, April 19, 2007. Reprinted with permission of the publisher.

Peggy Orenstein, "I Tweet, Therefore I Am." *The New York Times,* July 30, 2010. Reprinted by permission.

Kimberly Palmer, "Myths About Generation Debt" (originally titles "5 Myths About Generation Debt"). *Us News & World Report,* Money Blogs. September 29, 2010. Reprinted by permission.

Rahul K. Parikh, MD. "Indiana Jones and the Kingdom of Fat Kids." Salon.com, May 21, 2008. Reprinted with permission.

Don Peck, "How a New Jobless Era Will Transform America." *The Atlantic,* March 2010. Reprinted by permission.

David Plotz, "Privacy is Overrated," as David Plotz revised it, August 26, 2004. Reprinted by permission of the author.

Index of Authors and Titles